D0500167

PHILIP COLLINS

WHEN THEY GO LOW, WE GO HIGH

SPEECHES THAT SHAPE THE WORLD AND WHY WE NEED THEM

The Overlook Press
New York, NY

To the memory of Jennifer Anne Taylor (1942–2014)
and Frederick John Collins (1940–2015)

This edition first published in the United States in 2018
by The Overlook Press, Peter Mayer Publishers, Inc.

141 Wooster Street
New York, NY 10012
www.overlookpress.com

For bulk and special orders, please contact sales@overlookny.com,
or write us at the above address.

Cataloging-in-Publication Data is available from the Library of Congress

Manufactured in the United States of America

33614080686495   ISBN: 978-1-4683-1616-2

2 4 6 8 10 9 7 5 3 1

WHEN THEY GO LOW, WE GO HIGH

CONTENTS

ACKNOWLEDGEMENTS

I have been privileged to write speeches in one great institution and about them in another. In 10 Downing Street I had the pleasure of writing for Tony Blair, which changed the course of my career, if such a word is appropriate for my random array of jobs. *The Times* then took me in and my thanks are due to Daniel Finkelstein for suggesting that move in the first place. Then also to successive editors, James Harding and John Witherow, for commissioning the speech analysis format which I have followed in this book.

For the way the format stretched into an ambitious thesis, I salute Claire Conrad, my agent, and Helen Garnons-Williams, my editor, whose diplomatic skill in making a major rewrite sound like a tweak was exemplary. I think I minded more, not less, because she was always right. Thanks to Siobhan Reynolds for reading things so that I didn't have to and to the team at 4th Estate for doing such a professional job, so quickly. I hope I did the same.

Finally, an enormous yes to Geeta Guru-murthy and the two perfect perishers, my chief critics, Hari and Mani Collins. If any errors have eluded their searching questions the fault for that will be mine. That's their story, anyway. My story is in the pages that follow.

SPEECHES

PROLOGUE

THE PERILS OF INDIFFERENCE

The Birth of Rhetoric

The beautiful ideas of rhetoric and democracy were born in the same moment, in the winter of 431 BC in Athens, when the statesman Pericles stood to deliver his Funeral Oration. It might seem grimly appropriate, as democracy struggles through yet another of its crises, that its birth should have been marked by a funeral oration. There are plenty of predictions that another doleful eulogy will be required soon. Democracy is going through a troubled time and rhetoric is in the dock beside it. The chapters that follow have been written in the conviction that no funeral oration is needed for either.

In his speech, Pericles commemorated the sons of Athens lost in the Peloponnesian War, but he also applauded the glory of the city and made a sparkling case for government with the consent of the people. The currency of persuasion in a democracy, he argued, is not force or authority. It is speech. The moment that fiat is replaced by consent is the moment that oratory begins to count. Rhetoric and democracy are twinned; their histories run together. In this book I shall tell these parallel stories and mount a vigorous defence of the practice of politics in a time when cynicism has become the norm.

The politics of ancient Athens and Rome are distant and unfamiliar to us today except for a single unchanged element. The spectacle of a single person walking to a podium to persuade an audience remains now exactly as it was then. Very few disciplines survive twenty centuries. Nothing of the science of the period is of much more than curiosity value. The drama is still performed, but most of its stylistic conventions are anachronisms. Disciplines tend to date, positions are superseded, ideas fall into disuse, new frontiers are discovered. None of that is true of rhetoric. Reputations in the ancient republics were won and burnished by theatrical performance, and in politics today, they still are. Whether they know it or not, public speakers of all the succeeding ages owe a debt to Aristotle's *The Art of Rhetoric* and Cicero's *De oratore*.

Cicero gives us a portrait of the ideal orator. There was no separation, for him, between rhetoric and politics, so the orator needed to be steeped in political wisdom, to display a command of language and psychological insight into the audience, to be witty, shrewd and funny. In an age in which speeches were delivered by heart, the orator needed perfect recall. They also needed a resonant voice, although not all of them have had it. Demosthenes practised with pebbles in his mouth with the aim of improving his timbre. Abraham Lincoln was barely audible at Gettysburg, Winston Churchill sought medical help over his lisp, and John F. Kennedy's voice was often said to be too reedy for his grand words.

The central point of *De oratore*, what Cicero calls the Topic, should be engraved over the desk of every speechwriter: make sure you know your central point. This is advice that has worked for all speakers, in every nation and every time, and will always work. The central point of this book is that liberal democracies are the best imaginable places to live and that this claim needs to be compressed poetically into a clear message of hope. As I write, democracy is once again coming under threat from populists, and rhetoric is, like nostalgia, one of those things that are always said not to be as good as they used to be. The threat to democracy is linked to the attack on rhetoric. If we want to attend to the good health of our democracy, and we really must, then we need to attend to the integrity of the way we speak about politics.

The Sophisticated Speechwriter

For many years it was my job to write the words that carry public arguments. As the chief speechwriter to Prime Minister Tony Blair I tried to draft words that did justice to the hopes and passions of politics while at the same time respecting the limitations involved. It was a fascinating and privileged vantage point on the politics of Britain and its chief allies. If Blair's speeches feature prominently in the chapters that follow it is because of that personal insight rather than necessarily a claim that the words bear comparison with the finest rhetoric in history.

During my time as Blair's speechwriter I regularly fielded the accusation that rhetoric had declined and that the duplicity of crafted words was contributing to the low repute of politics. These are dangerous illusions that need to be countered. Rhetoric is not crafted deception and it is not worse than it was. There is a serious prospect that, in our time, we are losing faith in politics. The words of politicians float by, practised and polished, but profligate. The respect, veneration and hope first expressed by Pericles, has gone missing. It is the grand purpose of this book to help to call it back.

The accusation that rhetoric is simply duplicity has a long pedigree, and speechwriters have always come in for opprobrium as purveyors of fine falsehoods. In the sixth and fifth centuries BC, Greece was making the transition from aristocracy to democracy. Social class was no longer enough to support a political career, as every free male citizen enjoyed the right to speak in the assembly. This created a novel demand for tuition in the art of rhetoric. A band of itinerant writers and teachers of oratory met that demand, for high fees. They were known as the Sophists and they came in straight away for vilification. Taking money for instruction was thought to be ignoble and the Sophists were immigrants who imported new and unwelcome ideas, such as the notion that truth was not transcendent but emerged from the clash of arguments.

In 423 BC, in *The Clouds*, Aristophanes was the first to note that rhetorical genius can be turned to ill effect or can conceal dubious motives: *It's just rhetoric*, we say. Aristophanes satirises Socrates' rhetorical fluency and his ability, in the boast of the Sophist

Protagoras, to 'make the weaker case appear the stronger'. In *The Clouds* Aristophanes has Socrates teach a boy how to argue that a son should beat his parents. They take revenge by burning down Socrates' 'Thinking Shop'. Plato, who lived in Athens in the generation following the arrival of the Sophists, shared Aristophanes' distrust and wrote the classic statement of suspicion about rhetoric. In his dialogue *Gorgias*, he condemned rhetoric as a 'knack of flattering with words' which led not to truth but to mere persuasion. Plato regarded rhetoric as a low art form of no great import, like cookery, in particular pastry cookery. The writer might be an enchanter, thought Plato, but his work touched the surface alone and never penetrated to the deeper truths.

Plato's villain, the superficial malignant, was the Sophist speechwriter rather than the speaker himself. Tacitus echoed the complaint at the beginning of the second century AD. When the emperor Nero gave a speech praising his predecessor Claudius, Tacitus criticised Nero for reading words written by his tutor, Seneca. It is often said that political leaders would be more authentic if they wrote their own material. Many of them, in fact, have. Cicero was a student and a theorist of oratory as well as a practitioner. Benjamin Franklin, Thomas Jefferson and Abraham Lincoln all composed their own words. Franklin D. Roosevelt wrote his famous Inaugural Address of March 1933. Winston Churchill never stopped reading and writing his own speeches. Even now, the most senior politicians write more of their own words than is commonly supposed. Barack Obama was heavily involved in his major speeches. I can attest that Tony Blair often took his fountain pen and scribbled his own words in a spider hand.

But why should a politician not seek help for a task as central to democracy as making a case? George Washington got help for his Farewell Address from Alexander Hamilton and James Madison, though neither took the title of speechwriter. Judson Welliver, the man credited with coining the phrase 'the Founding Fathers', was known as a 'literary clerk' when he wrote for Warren Harding and Calvin Coolidge between 1921 and 1925. Herbert Hoover always denied that French Strother wrote his words. Franklin D. Roosevelt had a group of advisers that he called his Brains Trust, to help with his speeches.

The first man to be given the title of speechwriter in the White House was Emmet J. Hughes, who wrote for President Dwight D. Eisenhower. The turning point, when the speechwriter becomes a shadowy figure of national importance, is often said to be President Kennedy's relationship with his amanuensis Ted Sorensen, though it was actually Richard Nixon who was the first president to establish a Writing and Research Department in the White House. The supposed promotion to a department of their own concealed a change that would have puzzled and irritated Cicero. Before they were separated into a distinct craft, writers took part in policy deliberation. In Nixon's new dispensation they became wordsmiths. The industrial term describes the demotion from profession to trade, from statecraft to prettifying decisions made somewhere else.

The speechwriting office, once established, never closed, and every president employed a host of writers, sometimes as many as six. There is a cultural difference here between the common practice of America and that of Britain. British speechwriters tend to be cats who prowl alone, like Joe Haines who wrote for Harold Wilson and Ronald Millar who wrote some of Margaret Thatcher's best speeches. Though the British speechwriter writes solo, he or she has to contend with the attention of a multitude. Part of the job is to be editor-in-chief, fielding the reams of unsolicited passages sent in by academics and pet projects pushed by ministers. It is a curiosity of the job that people seem to believe that if they send in a few lines with no context then the speech can be assembled from all these bits, like flat-pack furniture comprised of the parts from different chairs. In Britain it can be a lonely task, whereas counterparts in the White House are collectively crafting clap lines in pairs or, for big speeches such as the State of the Union, in numbers even greater.

However they do it, their words really count. Robert Schlesinger, the author of *White House Ghosts*, a history of presidential speechwriters (one of them was his father Arthur, who wrote for Kennedy), has suggested that there may be cause and not just correlation in the fact that the one-term presidents – Ford, Carter, George H. W. Bush – were poor speakers while the charmers – Reagan, Clinton, Obama – talked themselves into second terms. No politician ever fares better with phrases ragged and unformed. Their words would, to use an old speechwriting joke, be read long after Milton and Shakespeare are forgotten – but not until then. For all the fine speakers who make it for the consideration of posterity there are countless would-be orators whose dreary platitudes would have benefited from the attention of a writer with an ear for rhythm.

The Temple of Concord

The enemy of good writing is not the good speechwriter. It is bad politics. When a politician is timid they will avoid all controversial topics. They will then have nothing to say. The cause of the distance that opens up between the people and politics is empty talk. Then, into the vacuum, there is always the danger that something unpleasant can insert itself. That is where we will find ourselves heading again, if we fail to attend to the quality of political speech. The suggestion of manipulation by fiendish speechwriters is the first denigration. The second accusation is that rhetoric is now boring. The travails of democracy are attributed to the poor quality of contemporary speech. The truth is closer to the opposite. If speeches are duller today than they once were, that is largely on account of the manifold successes of the liberal democracies.

This charge is also perennial. Every change brings an accusation of decline; every age is written off as a dying fall. Abraham Lincoln revolutionised rhetoric on the field at Gettysburg and attracted criticism for the plainness of his novel style. Robert Peel, whose maiden speech in Parliament in 1810 was judged to be one of the finest ever given, was mocked when he replaced the ornate Thucydides-inspired curlicues of Chatham, Burke and Fox with a flatter, demotic vocabulary. Roosevelt and Churchill adapted their rhetorical style to the new technology of the wireless, which demanded a quieter, more intimate tone than a podium calls for. They too incurred the claim that rhetoric was in decline. This is more than a lament about language. As rhetoric and democracy run together, any allegation about the decline of rhetoric is always a coded way of claiming the concomitant decline of politics itself. We need to be clear that both claims are nonsense. Rhetoric is thriving and so is democracy. They have simply changed together.

The extension of the franchise meant that oratory had to become more demotic. The electorate of the late eighteenth century in England would have been classically educated, and all to the same extent. The Great Reform Act 1832 added the merchant class to the electorate, and further extensions to the franchise in 1867, 1884, 1918 and 1928 brought the whole adult nation into the conversation. The pivotal change was not that politicians became more stupid or less literary but that the audience grew. Classical and biblical references and quotations from Shakespeare and Dickens were once commonplace because a speaker could be sure that the audience would share them. With a larger audience, the common denominator is lower and political language becomes less courtly, more colloquial. The decline of the grand oratorical style is thus the same process as the extension of the franchise. To lament the consequence without recognising the cause is a form of historical snobbery.

Less florid rhetoric is not necessarily worse rhetoric. There is a tendency, even today, for poor writers to come on like a pastiche of Robin Williams in *Dead Poets Society* because they think of that style as somehow properly *rhetorical*. But purple prose does not sound black and white when it is spoken. When he was criticised by William Faulkner for his limited vocabulary, Ernest Hemingway gave a reply that was not intended as advice for speechwriters but works as such anyway: 'Poor Faulkner. Does he really think big emotions come from big words? He thinks I don't know the ten-dollar words. I know them all right. But there are older and simpler and better words and those are the ones I use.'

Soon after the audience started to grow, the world started to shrink. Radio, television and the internet have vastly extended the reach of a political speech. Before mass media connected leaders to their public, rhetoric was an elite game. The political class talked *about* the people but largely *to* each other. The real setting of the great speech is no longer the Temple of Concord, Freedom Hall or the steps of the Capitol, even though the words may be spoken there. The speech exists in the lines cut into soundbites on social media, edited to seven seconds on the evening news or published in next day's newspaper. Even that had ceased until I revived the format in *The Times*, which now carries analyses of all the major political speeches. The format devised there appears in this book, for the select band of speeches that have endured among the mass that have been given.

The test of time proves too much for most rhetoric, plenty of which falls victim to the sheer pace of modern politics. There are two types of modern politician, the quick and the dead. No one can afford to be silent for long, and the outcome is that politicians today speak far too often. Gladstone and Disraeli would deliver polished speeches three times a year. Their speeches would be deeply researched and considered rather than knocked out in the heat of a passing crisis. Most political speeches today are unnecessary: press releases stretched far beyond their natural span. They also have to stretch further than they did. Government has grown broader in scope, and more complex. Speeches get made about such unpromising subjects as environmental directives and the gradient of welfare benefit tapers.

The great causes, at least in the rich, fortunate democracies, have gone. If there are fewer uplifting speeches today than there once were, then the chief cause is a heartening one. Momentous speeches are always given in answer to a signal injustice or crisis – think of Abraham Lincoln, Martin Luther King, Nelson Mandela. The success of the developed democracies means injustice is less acute than it once was. The great questions – the entitlement to vote, material and gender equality, freedom of association and speech, war and peace – are not entirely resolved, but the first decades of the twenty-first century show progress that would have been unimaginable two centuries before.

The line towards freedom is crooked, as we shall see. Nevertheless, the issues are smaller, the injustices largely less raw. The conflict between capitalism and communism pitted two sets of utopian aspirations against each other, with liberals and socialists everywhere painting the war of ideas in vivid colours. The victory of capitalism over socialist planning changed politics even in countries that had never been run by the communists. It meant that the left-of-centre parties largely accepted the writ of the market. The argument continued about where the lines of regulation should be drawn, but the dispute was now in the details, not the principles. At much the same time, the political Left won a cultural victory over the respect that was due to people of all creeds and colours. Each side, by and large, accepted the lesson it had been taught by the other, and the upshot was the creation of a new, benign, largely liberal consensus.

This means that public speech that truly sings is harder to pull off. Rhetoric, like all drama, needs a dispute. Agreement writes white, as Montherlant said about happiness. Politics, though, has to go on and this explains the rather exaggerated, overwrought nature of rhetoric today. No politician ever gets into office by volubly agreeing with his opponents. The political dispute therefore carries on regardless, as if there were no consensus. Public speech is easily reduced to an exercise in caricature, confected and boring, with the volume set too high. Amid this vast ado about nothing, it is little wonder that a decline in the standard of rhetoric is declared. But it is an illusion, and if public speech is boring the proper response is to be thankful. There are plenty of examples of shining speech in this book given during times when politics was far from boring and some of it was terrifying.

There is, though, still a reasonable complaint here. Language in the public square today does not always rise to the occasion. Too little of what is said in politics is memorable. It needs to be. Politics is the best idea about government that anybody ever had, or ever will have. Words need to inspire because disenchantment with politics fosters the illusion that there is an alternative. It is certainly still possible to write well rather than badly. The Obamas, Barack and Michelle, have shown that it is still possible to go high when everyone else is going low. It is still possible, as Mark Twain put it, to apply 'a minimum of sound to a maximum of sense'. The aim of good public speaking is to borrow the rhythms of everyday speech but at the same time to heighten its effects. The objective is to write high-octane ordinary speech, as if an eloquent person were speaking naturally at their best, fluent and uninterrupted, with all the connecting threads edited away.

The greatest speeches are essays in simple language, easily comprehensible to a democratic audience, but works of beauty and profundity all the same. As a collection, the finest public speeches tell the story of the unfolding of human accomplishment through politics. This book is not a story of human progress in the manner of the old Whig theory, in which history moves serenely from darkness towards the light. There have been too many desperate times. But to the extent that there has been progress in the material conditions of life, as unquestionably there has, that progress is owed to political argument that began with the Funeral Oration of Pericles and continues to this day.

That is the spirit, and the thesis, of this book, which defines five political virtues and applauds the greatest words that have been spoken in their defence. The first political virtue is that through politics the voice of the people is heard. The second is that politics commits us to persuasion rather than force. The third virtue is that through politics the demand for recognition can be heard. Fourth, the equal consideration of all citizens in free societies is the means by which the material condition of the population is improved. Then, fifth, perhaps the most profound point of all: it is only when politics prevails that the worst of human instincts can be tamed. All of these virtues require poetic political speech.

The Quarrel with Ourselves

William Butler Yeats once said that poetry was made out of a quarrel with ourselves whereas rhetoric derived from the quarrel with others. It can, alas, be more than a quarrel. We now face new threats to the liberal democratic order, from both without and within. In the wealthy democracies today an insidious lack of confidence has set in. Conspiracy theories have flourished and people are tempted towards fringe candidates. This lack of confidence in democracy is misplaced and dangerous. Cynicism with politics is everywhere and it is everywhere nihilistic.

The history of fine speech is proof against cynicism of this kind. Public speech can be elevated and it can still be uplifting. It needs to be because it is in the spoken word that the defence of politics has to be conducted. The final speech in this book tells the most heartbreaking story of the modern age. 'Not far from Goethe's beloved Weimar, in a place of eternal infamy called Buchenwald', says Elie Wiesel, the worst of instincts was let loose. Politics is the human achievement that prevents a repetition of terrors such as this. The title of Elie Wiesel's great speech is a reminder to us all of *the perils of indifference*. We can compose a funeral oration for politics if we choose. Or we can fight back.

This book exhibits the examples that we can choose to follow. By explaining what the great speakers meant and how they said it, I hope to elucidate the principles through which good politics can be conducted. All we have at our disposal are beautiful words, but what a weapon to hold. Stirring words in a skilled arrangement are all the power we need. The question for us now, when confidence in politics and democratic process is low, is not whether good things are still being said. Good things *are* still being said. The question is whether we are still listening.

1

DEMOCRACY: THROUGH POLITICS THE PEOPLE ARE HEARD

The Best State of the Commonwealth

Good politics is founded on extraordinary hope. Political imagination is the fancy that the world can get better and that the actions of men and women can together make it so. That act of utopian imagination is a description of democratic politics at its best. It is heard to great effect in the words of Marcus Tullius Cicero, Thomas Jefferson, Abraham Lincoln, John F. Kennedy and Barack Obama. This is where we hear the idea of popular power expressed in language lifted to move the people. It is politics enchanted once again.

One of the flaws of liberal democracies is that, when they succeed, they start to sound boring. Over time, power has a tendency to corrupt language, though not because politicians are venal. It is because success turns a politician from a campaigner into a technocrat. Their speeches — and I plead guilty to writing some of them — become one half braggadocio about achievements to date and one half technical exposition on policy detail. The enchantment goes missing and so does utopian hope.

Half a millennium ago, in 1516, Thomas More published a strange and remarkable volume called *Utopia*. Oddly, for a man with a deserved reputation for severity, a lifelong wearer of a hair shirt, More was fond of jokes, and the title of his most famous book is a tease. Does he mean *eutopia*, the good place, or does he mean *outopia*, no place at all? He adds to the sense of play by giving his narrator the name of Raphael Hythloday, which translates from Greek as 'speaker of nonsense'. More's text causes us to ponder whether *Utopia* is his version of the perfect society or a kind of Tudor cabaret act.

The clue to the riddle is also the link between Cicero and the rhetoric of the American republic, and it is found in More's subtitle *Optimus status republicae*: 'The Best State of the Commonwealth'. Or to put it in a current idiom, the perfect state of the union. More sends his narrator Hythloday on a journey to Utopia where he discovers, ready-made in the ocean, a society that dramatises Cicero's argument for the Roman republic. That argument, which More revives and which Jefferson, Lincoln, Kennedy and Obama all articulate, is how the people are to be heard. More's answer to that question is politics. The noble life, he argues, is one that is dedicated to public service in the name of the people. This marks a change from the Greek tradition in which it was thought that a citizen had to be of noble birth. Cicero's argument is that virtue, rather than inherited wealth, should have its reward. It is in the finest speeches about popular power that this idea is expressed.

But it is not just the beauty of the idea that makes these speeches fine. The beauty of the diction counts too. Fixing problems is the purpose of democratic politics but saying so is never enough. As La Rochefoucauld said, 'the passions are the only orators that convince'. Democratic politics still needs the elevation of Cicero's case for the Roman republic, Thomas Jefferson's praise of the blessing of equal liberty for all, Abraham Lincoln's ability to summarise the promise of democracy in a single phrase, John F. Kennedy's call for an active citizen body and Barack Obama's extraordinary, audacious hope. All these speakers express in unforgettable cadences the political virtue of granting power to the people.

But, in our time, an alternative utopia to liberal democratic politics has risen again in the form of populism. If politics is to turn away from this phoney appeal to the people, it can only do so in words that once again resound to the times. If politics has become dry then it needs to be reinvigorated by the precious democratic gift represented by the principle of hope.

Popular politics cannot work without utopian spirit. We need to draw from More's *Utopia* its sense of possibility, because the spirit of utopia is a desire for progress. It is a way of thinking that reminds us that the world might be different. This hope needs to be expressed in

words that take wing. Rhetoric is the art of public persuasion, and if
the ideas of liberal democracy are to retain their hold over the imagination of the people, they need to be argued with clarity and elevation. In the speeches that follow, they are.

MARCUS TULLIUS CICERO

First Philippic against Mark Antony

The Senate, the Temple of Concord, Rome

2 September 44 BC

Marcus Tullius Cicero (106–43 BC) was the first man to claim that rhetoric can save the state. Cicero was a philosopher, politician, lawyer and writer. He was the first among equals of the rhetoricians, both as a speaker himself and as the man who made the subject a systematic field of study. Cicero's *De oratore* is still the best rhetorical instruction manual. He is headmaster of the school of oratory.

Cicero's five canons of rhetoric still work; they will always work. *Invention*, he says, is the drafting of good arguments; *disposition* is the arrangement of those arguments for best effect; *style* is giving the argument shape in language; *memory* is recall in an age before autocue; *pronunciation* is delivery on the day. Cicero also identified three styles. The plain style should be used to teach, the ornate middle style to please, and the grand style to arouse the emotions. But *De oratore* was more than a book of instructions on how to talk. It was a book of statecraft as well: the subjects were for Cicero indivisible. If rhetoric and democracy were born together with Pericles, then rhetoric and statecraft were united by Cicero.

After a spell as a slum landlord, Cicero devoted his life to the theory and practice of oratory. He learned his trade in Rome under the tutelage of Crassus, the leading orator of his day. Cicero was debarred from a career in politics due to his ignoble plebeian ancestry. He grew up in the provincial town of Arpinum, the son of a fuller, a cloth-maker who soaked wool in urine for cleansing purposes. Cicero instead built a reputation as a lawyer of great integrity and gained public recognition when he acted in the impeachment of the corrupt governor Gaius Verres in 70 BC. Low birth notwithstanding, he did then make it into politics. In 63 BC he exposed a plot by Lucius Sergius Catiline to launch a coup against the Roman republic. The Orations against Catiline are the most ferocious tirades against a rival in the history of speech. The story is told, fictionalised to dramatic effect, in Robert Harris's trilogy of historical novels about Cicero.

When Cicero said of Catiline in the Temple of Jupiter: 'Among us you can dwell no longer', he ended Catiline's career. But he also damaged himself. Cicero was granted the title of *Pater Patriae*, Father of the Fatherland, but he was exiled from the republic for having, in the aftermath of triumph, executed a Roman citizen without trial. The law of the republic made no exceptions, even for its saviour.

It is to the curatorial brilliance of Cicero's devoted secretary Tiro that we owe the fifty-eight Cicero speeches, of the eighty-eight we know he gave, that we have today. We also know Cicero from his letters to Atticus, which were discovered by Petrarch in 1345 and which are the source of the influence that Cicero was to have on the European Renaissance. In the decade of his retreat after fleeing Rome in 55 BC, Cicero composed a series of works that have among their debtors the significant names of Hobbes, Locke, Voltaire, Montesquieu, Burke, Adam Smith and Rousseau.

The speech that follows was delivered in the wake of the slaughter of Julius Caesar on 15 March 44 BC. Cicero had been no supporter of Caesar's tyranny but, mindful that the republic was bigger than any ruler, he had negotiated a settlement in which Caesar's late decrees would be honoured. The consul Mark Antony confirmed that he would consent, but then, at Caesar's funeral, seemed to renege on the commitment by inflaming public opinion against the conspirators. Cicero fled the city, disillusioned at the decline of the republic, but returned, to be greeted by multitudes in the streets. The next day, rather than turn up at the Senate to hear Mark Antony, he pleaded fatigue. The Senate met again a day later, when Cicero delivered this speech.

We know it now as the first in a series of fourteen venomous speeches directed at Mark Antony. In a knowing reference to Demosthenes, who, between 351 and 341 BC, tried to rouse the Athenians against the threat of domination by King Philip II of

Macedon, Cicero referred to these speeches as 'Philippics'. Lest this be thought too much invective to be spent solely on Mark Antony, remember that Cicero's true purpose was to save the republic. In the Second Philippic, published as a pamphlet rather than spoken, Cicero compares Mark Antony with Catiline. The series then leads towards the explicit conclusion of the Fourteenth Philippic that Mark Antony was the enemy of the people and a threat to the republic. When politics fails, the only option, Cicero warns, is discord. The Philippics are the high point of Cicero's career. In his fledgling years he had been full of ingenious phrases searching for an appropriate cause. Twenty years before, the Catiline conspiracy had given him his first great moment. The Philippics are his glorious second act. All at once his verbal fluency rhymed with the times.

> *Before, O conscript fathers, I say those things concerning the republic which I think myself bound to say at the present time, I will explain to you briefly the cause of my departure from, and of my return to the city. When I hoped that the republic was at last recalled to a proper respect for your wisdom and for your authority, I thought that it became me to remain in a sort of sentinelship, which was imposed upon me by my position as a senator and a man of consular rank. Nor did I depart anywhere, nor did I ever take my eyes off the republic …*

The opening of a speech, like the first still in a film, should contain the address in miniature. Cicero here defines his Topic: the future of the republic. He gets to the main point quickly, as all speakers ought. The point is the defence of the republic and the liberty of the people against those, the tyrants Caesar and Mark Antony, who would violate its principles. This is rhetoric about crisis which increases the crisis with each utterance. Note how Cicero establishes his credentials as sentinel, senator and consul, which give him standing in the republic. He does this to justify his intervention in a dispute from which he has been absent.

The stakes are high, hence Cicero's dramatic language. The conspirators against Caesar knew, and Cicero himself knew, that his voice in the Temple of Concord could be decisive. Defeat would probably mean death. There is also a personal frailty on display. Cicero had at first struggled to break into politics because his family were plebeian rather than patrician. If he sounds more than a little defensive, ostentatiously reading out his curriculum vitae, this is why. He also has a material reason for defending his calling. The republic thrives on argument; dictatorship would banish his skill. Cicero's standing as a man of repute rests on the credentials he begins with and the mastery of argument that he commands.

> *I declare my opinion that the acts of Caesar ought to be maintained; not that I approve of them (for who indeed can do that?) but because I think that we ought above all things to have regard to peace and tranquillity. I wish that Antonius himself were present, provided that he had no advocates with him. But I suppose he may be allowed to feel unwell, a privilege he refused to grant me yesterday. He would then explain to me, or rather to you, O conscript fathers, to what extent he would defend the acts of Caesar. Are all the acts of Caesar that may exist in the bits of notebooks, and memoranda, and loose papers, produced on his single authority, and indeed not even produced, but only recited, to be ratified? And shall the acts he caused to be engraved on brass, in which he declared that the edicts and laws passed by the people were valid for ever, be considered as of no power? I think, indeed, that there is nothing so well entitled to be called the acts of Caesar as Caesar's laws.*

This speech registers Cicero's deep disapproval of the way in which Mark Antony is squandering Caesar's legacy. Cicero dismisses Mark Antony with bitterly feigned generosity about the privilege of being deemed unwell. Later passages in this Philippic make it clear that Cicero's absence the previous day had been as pointed as Antony's is today. Cicero therefore hardly deserves the high moral ground on which he stands to make his central accusation that Antony is betraying the legacy of Caesar. Framed as a battery of rhetorical questions – always a tactic to sound reasonable while delivering a vicious blow – Cicero here fatally undermines Antony's claim to be the guardian of Caesar's legacy. Later in the speech Cicero bluntly accuses Mark Antony of 'branding the name of the dead Caesar with everlasting ignominy, and it was your doing – yours I say'.

The vivid passage about the notebooks shows how a good image adorns an argument. An audience gets only one hearing, and pictures dwell longer in the mind than abstract arguments. As Cicero describes them, we can see the contents of Caesar's office. This is the only time Caesar is depicted as a person rather than a representative of the lost republic. The image has a brutal purpose. Cicero is insinuating that Antony is abusing his access to Caesar's private papers, entrusted to his care by Caesar's widow. Cicero requests that Mark Antony supply an explanation, not to himself but to the fathers of the republic. That act of transference identifies his own status and perspective with that of the wider republic itself.

> *And yet, concerning those laws that were proposed, we have, at all events, the power of complaining; but concerning those that are actually passed we have not even had that privilege. For they, without any proposal of them to the people, were passed before they were framed. Men ask, what is the reason why I, or why any one of you, O conscript fathers, should be afraid of bad laws while we have virtuous tribunes of the people? ... The forum will be surrounded, every entrance of it blocked up; armed men placed in garrison, as it were, at many points. What then? — whatever is accomplished by those means will be law. And you will order, I suppose, all those regularly passed decrees to be engraved on brazen tablets. 'The consuls consulted the people in regular form' — (is this the way of consulting the people that we have received from our ancestors?) — 'and the people voted it with due regularity.' What people? That which was excluded from the forum? Under what law did they do so? Under that which has been wholly abrogated by violence and arms? But I am saying all this with reference to the future, because it is the part of a friend to point out the evils that may be avoided; and if they never ensue, that will be the best reflection of my speech. I am speaking of laws that have been proposed, concerning which you have still full power to decide either way. I am pointing out the defects; away with them! I am denouncing violence and arms; away with them, too!*

There are direct and deliberate echoes of the Philippics of Demosthenes throughout Cicero's speeches against Mark Antony. Rhetoric, even at this early stage, is already a tradition. We can see this first at the level of style. Cicero's interest in Demosthenes was a reaction to a movement of orators in Rome known as the Neo-Attics, who criticised the elder statesmen, of whom Cicero was the sovereign example, of being stylistically weighed down by decoration. The criticism, that Cicero was, to use the contemporary term, an "Asiatic" orator, was always unfair; Cicero never set much store by purple prose. He insisted that a sentence needed rhythm rather than the 'embroidery' he found in some Greek examples, notably the work of Gorgias. The Philippics are, though, plainer in style than Cicero's previous work.

Not having a style is, of course, a style of its own. 'I am no orator, as Brutus is, but as you know me all, a plain, blunt man, that love my friend,' says Antony in *Julius Caesar*, which is about as rhetorically effective as it gets. The Philippics do not, by the standards of the day, set off many fireworks. They are exact and precise, perhaps to a fault, and they are rather light on memorable imagery. The picture of Antony's wife Fulvia, in the Second Philippic, with the blood of innocent soldiers splashed on her clothes, is exceptional. For the greater part, the series is forensically argued.

There are also echoes of Demosthenes in Cicero's argument. Both profess that liberty is in peril, threatened by a dominant individual whose seizure of arbitrary power must be resisted. This is a threat to peace because, as Cicero argues later, peace follows liberty. Both Cicero and Demosthenes before him were seeking to persuade a divided and hesitant audience to take action. There is a choice for both between self-government and tyranny, between true peace and illusory peace, between liberty and slavery.

What I am more afraid of is lest, being ignorant of the true path to glory, you should think it glorious for you to have more power by yourself than all the rest of the people put together, and lest you should prefer being feared by your fellow citizens to being loved by them. And if you do think so, you are ignorant of the road to glory. For a citizen to be dear to his fellow citizens, to deserve well of the republic, to be praised, to be respected, to be loved, is

glorious; but to be feared and to be an object of hatred, is
odious, detestable; and moreover, pregnant with weakness and
decay.

This short section is a clear definition of the philosophical tradition of the Roman republic. This is the argument that was passed
down from the classical world to the European Renaissance. The
esteem in which Cicero is held is satirised by Erasmus in his 1528
treatise *Ciceronianus*, written in the form of a dialogue, which
contains a character who has emptied his library of all books except
those by Cicero.

The idea of the Roman republic begins with the fact that the
central goal of the city was peace. The greatest danger to peace, says
Cicero, is discord. The setting for this speech is the Temple of Concord,
but how is concord to be attained? Concord requires justice for all,
and that can only be achieved if all the citizens live in liberty. There
can be no freedom except in a republic, and the citizen of the free
republic is the engaged man, the political man. This is an echo of an
argument Cicero uses in *De re publica*, where he suggests that political participation can overcome the constant dangers of complacency,
'the blandishments of pleasure and repose'.

The law of the republic is a vital institution, but Cicero argues
that the actions of those who will defend the republic, even to the
extent of murder, are legitimate all the same because they uphold
the honour of the republic. The story goes that when Caesar was
murdered on the Ides of March in 44 BC by a group of senators who
called themselves the *liberatores*, one of their number lifted his
bloodstained dagger and cried out the name of Cicero, imploring him
to 'restore the republic!' Cicero's primary objective in the speech was
therefore the restoration of the *res publica libera* — the free
republic.

And, indeed, you have both of you had many judgements delivered
respecting you by the Roman people, by which I am greatly
concerned that you are not sufficiently influenced. For what was the
meaning of the shouts of the innumerable crowd of citizens
collected at the gladiatorial games or of the verses made by the
people? Or of the extraordinary applause at the sight of the statue

of Pompeius? And at that sight of the two tribunes of the people who are opposed to you? Are these things a feeble indication of the incredible unanimity of the entire Roman people? What more? Did the applause at the games of Apollo, or, I should rather say, testimony and judgement there given by the Roman people, appear to you of small importance? Oh! Happy are those men who, though they themselves were unable to be present on account of the violence of arms, still were present in spirit, and had a place in the breasts and hearts of the Roman people.

It is evident from this first Philippic that Cicero is vying to be the leader of the political opposition. Look at how brazenly he enlists the audience in his cause. In mocking Mark Antony's deafness to popular opinion, Cicero casts himself as the tribune of the people. It is a reminder that the verdict on a public speech in a democracy is settled by the audience. This is an indispensable lesson for every speaker, at every level. It's not, in the end, you who decides whether a passage works. The audience will decide for you.

Mark Antony reacted with fury to the accusation that he disdained his audience, and seventeen days later delivered a withering attack on Cicero's career in the Senate. Cicero did not attend because his safety could not be guaranteed. Fearful for his life, he published the Second Philippic as a pamphlet and issued instructions through his friend Atticus for it to be circulated carefully and narrowly. The Second Philippic is written as though it were a speech, with plentiful references to the setting, the occasion, to Antony's dandy dress sense, and it contains a direct request for a fair hearing. But it was never actually delivered. In his *Tenth Satire*, Juvenal says that the Second Philippic is Cicero's masterpiece, the eloquent testament that cost him his life. Antony ordered that Cicero's right hand, the one which had written the Philippics, be amputated. For good measure the head which had devised and spoken them was cut off. That severed head and hand were nailed to the Rostra on the Forum to discourage imitation. Legend has it that Antony's wife Fulvia stabbed her hairpins through the dead man's tongue, which gives chilling meaning to the cliché *dangerous rhetoric*. Cicero left behind a lament for this and for all times: '*O tempora, O mores*' – 'Oh, the times! Oh, the manners!'

Cicero once said that 'the real quality of an orator can only be deduced from the practical results his speech-making obtains'. By that strict measure the Philippics must count as a failure. Any speaker who ends up with his head and hand nailed to the Rostra is obliged to conclude that the speech might have gone better. Mark Antony went on, with Marcus Lepidus and Caesar's nephew Octavian, to form a dictatorship known as the Second Triumvirate. The group fell apart, not furthered in its harmony by Mark Antony, who married Octavian's sister, beginning his affair with Cleopatra. Civil war broke out in 31 BC. Antony and Cleopatra fled to Egypt, where they committed suicide together.

The republic did not end well, but Cicero left a legacy unrivalled in the field. Time and again the speeches of the American republic invoke the spirit of Cicero. It is there in Benjamin Franklin's defence of the constitution, with all its faults. It is there in Thomas Jefferson's appeal for exact and equal liberty for all. It is there in Abraham Lincoln's tribute to popular power and in Barack Obama's quest for the perfect state of the union. John Quincy Adams said that American democracy had been 'spoken into existence'. Cicero was one of the scriptwriters.

THOMAS JEFFERSON

Equal and Exact Justice to All Men

First Inaugural Address, Washington DC

4 March 1801

Thomas Jefferson (1743–1826) was a Founding Father and the third president of the United States, serving two terms from 1801 to 1809. As the principal author of the Declaration of Independence, Jefferson stood, against Alexander Hamilton, for a version of the American republic in which the power of the federal government would be limited.

Born and educated in Virginia, where he trained as a lawyer, Thomas Jefferson was asked, in 1776, to draft a statement describing to the world America's break with Britain. The resulting Declaration of Independence, which 'affirmed the natural rights of humanity to protect itself from arbitrary and autocratic forms of government', was adopted by the Second Continental Congress in 1776.

For the rest of the American Revolution, Jefferson served as a governor of Virginia, in which position he remains rightly renowned for his Statute on Religious Freedom. He then succeeded Benjamin Franklin as America's minister to France and, during five years spent in Paris, witnessed the start of the French Revolution, which he regarded – wrongly as it turned out – as an extension of the example lately offered by America. Upon his return, Jefferson accepted President George Washington's request that he serve as the nation's first secretary of state.

Jefferson in Cabinet participated in the most creative tension in democratic history. His own preference for a weak constitution that gave the greater power to the states ran into the objections of Alexander Hamilton, secretary of the Treasury, who wanted a stronger mandate for the federal government. The conflict was managed, rather than resolved, with the formation of the young republic's first opposition party, Jefferson's Republicans.

This speech is how Jefferson chose to inaugurate his first presidency, with a statement of his mission in politics. As president after 1801 Jefferson set about reducing government, cutting the budgets of the army and navy and closing diplomatic missions. He was elected for a second term and in 1807 signed the Act Prohibiting Importation of Slaves – this despite being himself a slave owner and fathering a child with one of his slaves.

Jefferson retired in 1809, aged sixty-five, but went on to found the University of Virginia. He died on 4 July 1826, the fiftieth anniversary of the adoption of his Declaration of Independence.

> *Friends and fellow citizens, called upon to undertake the duties of the first executive office of our country, I avail myself of the presence of that portion of my fellow-citizens which is here assembled to express my grateful thanks for the favour with which they have been pleased to look toward me, to declare a sincere consciousness that the task is above my talents, and that I approach it with those anxious and awful presentiments which the greatness of the charge and the weakness of my powers so justly inspire … Utterly, indeed, should I despair did not the presence of many whom I here see remind me that in the other high authorities provided by our Constitution I shall find resources of wisdom, of virtue, and of zeal on which to rely under all difficulties.*

Jefferson's modesty would be excessively false were it not for his political purpose. His intention is not so much to diminish himself, but rather – like Cicero in the Temple of Concord – to venerate the republic, beside which any individual must appear small. Jefferson, in fact, had named Cicero as an influence on his drafting of the Declaration of Independence.

We know, from the three handwritten texts that survive in Jefferson's papers at the Library of Congress, that he amended his script to make it more overtly republican with each iteration. His first sentence originally read 'executive magistrate'. The final version instead lauds 'the executive office', which transfers the honour from himself, the president, to the office, the presidency.

Jefferson sought to embody this humility in the spartan festivities of the day. Even though he had done so much to bring the city of Washington DC into being, Jefferson eschewed the splendid parades that had inaugurated George Washington and John Adams. In the Senate Room, the only completed room in the new Capitol, he dressed in the habit of a plain citizen without any badge of office or ceremonial sword. There was no festive ball afterwards either. Legend has it that after his lecture he walked back to his boarding house, where he stood in line for dinner to be served as usual.

The absence of flourish in the speech was taken to excess in the manner of delivery. Jefferson's tone was so low that, apart from those at the front, most of the audience had to read what he said in the Washington papers the following morning. Before electronic amplification, to be audible to a sizeable audience was no easy task. Early presidents scattered emissaries around the crowd, whispering the text as the principal spoke.

During the contest of opinion through which we have passed the animation of discussions and of exertions has sometimes worn an aspect which might impose on strangers unused to think freely and to speak and to write what they think; but this being now decided by the voice of the nation, announced according to the rules of the Constitution, all will, of course, arrange themselves under the will of the law, and unite in common efforts for the common good. All, too, will bear in mind this sacred principle, that though the will of the majority is in all cases to prevail, that will to be rightful must be reasonable; that the minority possess their equal rights, which equal law must protect, and to violate would be oppression. Let us, then, fellow-citizens, unite with one heart and one mind. Let us restore to social intercourse that harmony and affection without which liberty and even life itself are but dreary things. And let us reflect that, having banished from our land that religious intolerance under which mankind so long bled and suffered, we have yet gained little if we countenance a political intolerance as despotic, as wicked, and capable of as bitter and bloody persecutions.

This call for unity sounds routine today. Kennedy said it; Obama said it; every president says it. But Jefferson *needs* to say it. Technology has quickened politics but it hasn't coarsened it much and the election of 1800 remains one of the nastiest in American history. Under the pretext of articulating differing destinies for the republic, the two candidates, John Adams, the New England lawyer from a modest background, and Jefferson, the lofty Virginia intellectual, conducted an acrimonious campaign. Jefferson accused Adams of being pro-English, quite an accusation to level at a Founding Father of the republic, and Adams countered by mocking Jefferson's association with the violence of revolutionary France and by revealing that Jefferson had fathered a child with Sally Hemings, one of his slaves. When Jefferson won, Adams churlishly left Washington DC before the new president spoke. Hence, if the emollient tone is laid on thick that's because a lot of mollifying was required.

Jefferson worked hard on this pivotal section, balancing minority rights against the will of the majority. The tactic worked. The Federalists of the time praised Jefferson's caution and wisdom. James Monroe wrote that the speech conciliated the opposing party. Note how this is done by avoiding specific positions, on which a speaker can be pinned down. Instead, Jefferson elevates his language into the floridly abstract. This is a more flowery section than the rest, which is usually the tip-off that a writer has less to say.

But every difference of opinion is not a difference of principle. We have called by different names brethren of the same principle. We are all Republicans, we are all Federalists. If there be any among us who would wish to dissolve this Union or to change its republican form, let them stand undisturbed as monuments of the safety with which error of opinion may be tolerated where reason is left free to combat it. I know, indeed, that some honest men fear that a republican government cannot be strong, that this Government is not strong enough; but would the honest patriot, in the full tide of successful experiment, abandon a government which has so far kept us free and firm on the theoretic and visionary fear that this Government, the world's best hope, may by possibility want energy to preserve itself? I trust not. I believe this, on the contrary, the strongest Government on earth. I believe it the only one where every man, at the call of the law, would fly to the standard of the law, and would meet invasions of the public order as his own personal concern. Sometimes it is said that man cannot be trusted with the government of himself. Can he, then, be trusted with the government of others? Or have we found angels in the forms of kings to govern him? Let history answer this question.

This passage is the fault line of the American republic, the substance of the dispute between Jefferson and Hamilton about where power should lie. It is the great political cleavage that persists in our time: Democrats for a little more government, Republicans for a little less. There is no easy philosophical reconciliation, so Jefferson does what good rhetoric often does. He slides over the difference with a well-balanced, high-minded, euphonious sentence – 'We are all Republicans, we are all Federalists' – and evokes the virtues of the nation which belong to Americans of any persuasion. All presidents do this. Barack Obama said there were no blue states or red states, there was just the United States. Jefferson had more call to do it than most, as he was nursing an infant democracy that was prone to tantrum.

Note how unequivocal and confident Jefferson is in declaring the United States to have the strongest form of government on earth. Then, cleverly, at the end of this section he brings the people to his side, drawing the implicit contrast that I, the Republican, trust the people, whereas you, the Federalist, arrogate power to the state. He concludes with a vivid rhetorical question about whether we have found angels in the form of kings to govern men, then adds the redundant answer that history will be the judge. Or to put the effect more bluntly but less poetically: No, we haven't and we never will. This is why we need to curtail power; it is why we need democratic institutions. Because men are not angels.

Let us, then, with courage and confidence pursue our own Federal and Republican principles, our attachment to union and representative government. Kindly separated by nature and a wide ocean from the exterminating havoc of one quarter of the globe; too high-minded to endure the degradations of the others; possessing a chosen country, with room enough for our descendants to the

*thousandth and thousandth generation; entertaining a due sense of
our equal right to the use of our own faculties, to the acquisitions of
our own industry, to honour and confidence from our fellow-
citizens, resulting not from birth, but from our actions and their
sense of them; enlightened by a benign religion, professed, indeed,
and practiced in various forms, yet all of them inculcating honesty,
truth, temperance, gratitude, and the love of man; acknowledging
and adoring an overruling Providence, which by all its
dispensations proves that it delights in the happiness of man here
and his greater happiness hereafter – with all these blessings, what
more is necessary to make us a happy and a prosperous people?
Still one thing more, fellow-citizens – a wise and frugal
Government, which shall restrain men from injuring one another,
shall leave them otherwise free to regulate their own pursuits of
industry and improvement, and shall not take from the mouth
of labour the bread it has earned. This is the sum of good
government, and this is necessary to close the circle of our
felicities.*

To us, wearied by repetition at a time when democracy can feel
old and worn, a claim to American superiority sounds arrogant. But
in early American speeches this was a claim of hopeful naivety and
youthful excitement in an era when democracy was a novel experiment at home and a rarity anywhere else. So look past that claim
towards the really suggestive words here, which are 'to close the circle
of our felicities'. As well as begging the listener to pay attention, the
phrase concludes a profound point: wise government is defined more
by what it prevents than either what it does or what it permits. This
passage could be read as the origin of the American suspicion of the
encroachment of the federal government, and it is that too, but the
point runs deeper. Perhaps the greatest achievement of democratic
politics is that public authority is limited to create the space for
private autonomy. It closes the circle of our felicities.

The circle closes here, though, over a dark question. It is inconceivable surely, as he drafted the speech in the two weeks before the
Inauguration, that Jefferson did not reflect on his slaves. Not for them
the bread they have earned. The fellow-feeling and empathy of the
rest of this passage hardly seems consistent with such a blind spot,

although we can also hear a vocabulary of politics that seems lost to us now. It would be a brave politician today who would wish for happiness and blessings, but it was an idiom that came easily to Jefferson and his peers. Political conversations are drier than they were and Jefferson has something to teach us. Blessings and happiness should find their way back into our rhetoric.

About to enter, fellow-citizens, on the exercise of duties which comprehend everything dear and valuable to you, it is proper you should understand what I deem the essential principles of our Government, and consequently those which ought to shape its Administration. I will compress them within the narrowest compass they will bear, stating the general principle, but not all its limitations. Equal and exact justice to all men, of whatever state or persuasion, religious or political; peace, commerce, and honest friendship with all nations, entangling alliances with none; the support of the State governments in all their rights, as the most competent administrations for our domestic concerns and the surest bulwarks against anti-republican tendencies; the preservation of the General Government in its whole constitutional vigour, as the sheet anchor of our peace at home and safety abroad; a jealous care of the right of election by the people – a mild and safe corrective of abuses which are lopped by the sword of revolution where peaceable remedies are unprovided; absolute acquiescence in the decisions of the majority, the vital principle of republics, from which is no appeal but to force, the vital principle and immediate parent of despotism; a well-disciplined militia, our best reliance in peace and for the first moments of war till regulars may relieve them; the supremacy of the civil over the military authority; economy in the public expense, that labour may be lightly burdened; the honest payment of our debts and sacred preservation of the public faith; encouragement of agriculture, and of commerce as its handmaid; the diffusion of information and arraignment of all abuses at the bar of the public reason; freedom of religion; freedom of the press, and freedom of person under the protection of the habeas corpus, and trial by juries impartially selected. These principles form the bright constellation which has gone before us and guided our steps through an age of revolution and reformation. The wisdom of our sages and blood of our heroes have been devoted to their attainment. They should be the creed of our political faith, the text of civic instruction, the touchstone by which to try the services of those we trust; and should we wander from them in moments of error or of alarm, let us hasten to retrace our steps and to regain the road which alone leads to peace, liberty, and safety.

This passage is the last word on democratic liberties. Try editing it. Try cutting. It is all but impossible to take out a single phrase without doing grievous harm to the whole. Jefferson provides the most comprehensive spoken list since Pericles of the attributes of democracy. This is democracy's evergreen. It is a checklist of institutions and a standard against which to measure how close a nation approximates to the ideal of popular power. The most resonant phrase in the speech – 'equal and exact justice for all men' – is almost a direct quotation from the Funeral Oration of Pericles. The quotation is almost lost in the litany of virtues, but this is a supreme definition of minority rights which shines in the text today as much as it did then. Of course, it wasn't exactly true. Not every person in America was a bearer of rights. But that does not mean this passage should be thought of as hypocritical. It's not; it's a statement of an ideal, a foundation myth and a utopian aspiration. As he did in the Declaration of Independence, when he simply asserted that all men were created equal and were entitled to life, liberty and the pursuit of happiness, Jefferson is setting a standard. America didn't meet it then; no nation does now. But the claim that liberal democracy represents the terminus of political philosophy rests on the list of popular freedoms contained in this passage. The political battle to instantiate them in existing societies goes on but, philosophically, this is the last word.

I repair, then, fellow-citizens, to the post you have assigned me. With experience enough in subordinate offices to have seen the difficulties of this the greatest of all, I have learnt to expect that it will rarely fall to the lot of imperfect man to retire from this station with the reputation and the favour which bring him into it ... I shall often go wrong through defect of judgment. When right, I shall often be thought wrong by those whose positions will not

command a view of the whole ground. I ask your indulgence for
my own errors, which will never be intentional, and your support
against the errors of others, who may condemn what they would
not if seen in all its parts ... Relying, then, on the patronage of
your good will, I advance with obedience to the work, ready to
retire from it whenever you become sensible how much better
choice it is in your power to make. And may that Infinite Power
which rules the destinies of the universe lead our councils to what is
best, and give them a favourable issue for your peace and
prosperity.

There is a crucial wisdom about politics as a career here which is also captured in Enoch Powell's less accurate axiom that all political careers end in failure. Some careers do pass through success but no success is ever final; politics must go on. The point Jefferson is making here is that the political capital of a leader is at its highest at the beginning of his tenure, when experience is least, and statecraft at its least developed. The statesman's learning and his popularity run counter to each other. As wisdom gathers, popularity declines. See Tony Blair's *A Journey* for a dramatic recent example of the process. Barack Obama is an example of a swell of general hope giving way to specific disappointment. Donald Trump will be subject to the same law of political inflation and deflation.

Jefferson makes a plea that sounds today all too contemporary. He asks forgiveness for his mistakes, and appeals to those who may not be able to see the whole picture to forbear from judgement. Perhaps the most corrosive aspect of modern political culture is the rush to judge on the assumption that every error must be self-serving. Elegantly, Jefferson asks here for a lost art of democratic politics: patience and understanding. It is a lesson we would do well to heed, though we have forgotten how to do so.

ABRAHAM LINCOLN

Government of the People, by the People, for the People

The Gettysburg Address
19 November 1863

Abraham Lincoln said simply in a sentence something it can take whole books to complicate. If there were a manifesto for democratic politics, Lincoln's most famous line might be too long to be the title, but it would certainly offer the subtitle. Given that he could cram so much into ten words, it is a wonder he needed all of 272 for the whole speech.

Abraham Lincoln was not, however, the man who really delivered the Gettysburg Address. That honour goes to the forgotten orator Edward Everett, who was top of the bill on the Pennsylvania battlefield in November 1963, to speak the funeral eulogy after the poets Longfellow, Whittier and Bryant turned the invitation down. Lincoln's task was to come on afterwards and do what were, by comparison with Everett's lavish address, parish notices. It is the greatest example of stealing the show in all the arts.

Abraham Lincoln (1809–65) served as the sixteenth president of the United States of America from March 1861 until his assassination by a resentful Confederate-supporting actor, John Wilkes Booth, in Ford's Theatre in Washington on 14 April 1865. He is one of the icons of American democracy, famously immortalised at the Lincoln Memorial in Washington. His is the name most often summoned in the speeches of the presidents who followed him. He is the re-founding father of the American constitution.

Lincoln was born in Hardin County, Kentucky, the son of a frontiersman. It was, according to Lincoln himself, 'a wild region, with many bears and other wild animals still in the woods'. It was not a literate childhood, and in later life he thought himself lucky to be able to 'read, write and cipher'. Political opponents would later patronise him by wondering how a man of such unpromising literary beginnings could command the language as he did. The answer is bound to be a mystery, especially as he was a self-effacing man. In the words of the writer and diplomat John Bigelow: 'He [Lincoln] was so modest by nature that he was perfectly content to walk behind any man who wished to walk before him.'

Lincoln's political career began when he joined the Illinois state legislature in 1834 and, self-taught in the law, was admitted to the Bar in 1837. 'His ambition', said his law partner, 'was a little engine that knew no rest.' This led Lincoln to a term in the House of Representatives between 1847 and 1849. His political zeal was awakened by the Kansas–Nebraska Act, which allowed states and territories to decide for themselves whether to allow slavery.

A reputation as an eloquent opponent of slavery helped Lincoln secure the Republican Party's nomination for president in 1860. It is also the source of his indelible reputation as one of the great presidents of the American republic. Lincoln's moral stature on slavery infused his leadership throughout the Civil War and helped to preserve the Union during a spell of potentially terminal peril. As if all that were not enough, there is something else to reinforce the abiding myth of Abraham Lincoln in American life. He is the frontiersman who made it to the White House. He is the incarnate American dream. The man who showed that virtue derives from public service rather than noble birth.

> *Fourscore and seven years ago our fathers brought forth on this continent a new nation, conceived in liberty, and dedicated to the proposition that all men are created equal.*

The first thing you notice about the Gettysburg Address is its length; just 272 words compressed into ten sentences. It challenges every other writer to cut. The famous final words encapsulate the whole in just ten words. Of the 272 words, 204 are of a single syllable, mostly of Anglo-Saxon or Norman derivation, like ordinary speech. High political rhetoric until Lincoln had tended to look to Rome or

Greece, for both structure and vocabulary. The phrase 'conceived in liberty' is an echo of Cicero's argument that the only constitution in which a citizen can flourish is a republic. But stylistically, Lincoln here exemplifies the link between successful oratory and plain speech. Great rhetorical prose is not complex. It is ordinary speech elevated to the heights.

The entire text can be read out in under two minutes, and the concision is all the more marked by the fact that the audience had waited so long for it. The procession that had escorted Lincoln to the field had been greatly delayed. Everett, the day's main orator, then took his time getting to the platform. Before he spoke there was a lengthy prayer and some music, and then he spoke for all of two hours. By the time Lincoln rose to the lectern, the audience had been on its feet for close to four hours.

It was worth the wait. The opening words are a date spoken in a musical cadence, but also more than that. 'Fourscore and seven years' takes the listener back from 1863 to 1776, the moment of the Declaration of Independence, rather than to 1791, the signing of the Constitution. Lincoln is making a critical point: he is saying that the ideals of the revolution have been violated in the Civil War. If the war is to honour the dead it must be fought for a purpose higher merely than preserving the Union. It must hark back to the founding idea that 'all men are created equal'. Without once mentioning the word, Lincoln is talking about slavery. In January of 1863 Lincoln had issued the Emancipation Proclamation. Slavery is nowhere in his text but it is everywhere.

> *Now we are engaged in a great civil war, testing whether that nation, or any nation so conceived and so dedicated, can long endure.*

The repetition of the word 'nation', which recurs five times, shows what, and how much, Lincoln believes to be at stake. The words 'nation' and 'birth' share a common root and often come back together at moments of heightened rhetoric. As early as the second sentence, Lincoln upsets the equilibrium he has established in the first. The nation, defined in the respect for the equal moral worth of all, is placed in peril in a single crisp sentence.

To say so much so quickly requires complete control, which raises the question of how a text so learned could be composed by a man of such jejune education. Writers are often asked where their ideas come from. The best answer may be Larkin's: 'pure genius'. Fitzgerald perhaps came closer to the truth when he wrote, in a letter to his daughter which described exactly what he never did himself, that a good style forms through good reading. Lincoln is known to have read Aesop's *Fables*. Robert Burns was his favourite poet and he knew both the Bible and Shakespeare. There is, though, some magical property in verbal composition that can make a novelty out of a reading list, and Lincoln had that mesmerising quality.

We know that the words are Lincoln's own because we have the testimony of his private secretary, John G. Nicolay, who saw the text, written in ink, in Lincoln's hand. Nicolay also points to an important truth when he says that Lincoln wrote half the speech the day before he left Washington and the other half when he arrived in Gettysburg. Political speech has a short half-life. It goes stale fast and should therefore be composed as close to the deadline as possible. Bad writers are apt to think they will get better by taking longer, but taking pains can simply add to the agony.

This is quite different from the myth, which first appeared in a 1906 book by Mary Raymond Shipman Andrews called *The Perfect Tribute*, that Lincoln was so slapdash that he composed the speech, literally, on the back of an envelope. The Gettysburg Address attracts myths. Harriet Beecher Stowe also claimed that Lincoln had written the speech in a few moments, and Andrew Carnegie insisted that Lincoln had used his pen. Don't believe a word of it. It is clear from the finished version, let alone from the surviving manuscripts, that, though the craft cut close to the deadline, Lincoln himself worked on it until he had the desired effect.

> *We are met on a great battle-field of that war. We have come to dedicate a portion of that field, as a final resting-place for those who here gave their lives that that nation might live. It is altogether fitting and proper that we should do this.*

Lincoln is taking a risk with this speech. He is speaking at the dedication of the Soldiers' National Cemetery in Gettysburg, Pennsylvania, four months after the Confederacy forces were defeated there by the Union armies in the only battle in the war to be fought on Northern soil. More than 40,000 men had been wounded and 5,000 had perished. Most had been hastily buried in shallow graves just where they had fallen. The citizens of Gettysburg, led by Judge David Wills, had purchased seventeen acres of ground on Cemetery Hill. The graves were arranged in a semicircle and a speaking platform erected to face away from the buried dead so that the gathered would not defile their memory by trampling on the graves.

The setting could scarcely have been more sombre, yet Lincoln's references to the gravity of the day are rapid and perfunctory. He does not, as Everett had before him, recite a roll-call in remembrance of the American dead. No sooner has he read this parish notice than he changes the subject, in a shift reminiscent of the Funeral Oration of Pericles, from the individual to the nation. The speech is sprinkled with the imagery of birth, life, and death in reference to a nation 'brought forth', 'conceived', and a system of government that shall not 'perish'. The dead of the battle have become the nation incarnate.

> *But, in a larger sense, we cannot dedicate – we cannot consecrate – we cannot hallow – this ground. The brave men, living and dead, who struggled here, have consecrated it far above our poor power to add or detract. The world will little note nor long remember what we say here, but it can never forget what they did here. It is for us, the living, rather, to be dedicated here to the unfinished work which they who fought here have thus far so nobly advanced.*

This is as clever a transition as you will find in all public speech. The triple formulation 'we cannot dedicate, we cannot consecrate, we cannot hallow' is a routine rhetorical device. The language is resonant but the cliché is really transformed by what Lincoln does next. He picks up the word 'consecrate' to note that the combatants on this ground have done more in deed than he can ever do with words. Then, even better, he repeats the idea of dedication but alters its meaning. The first instance refers to the dedication of sacred ground;

the second implores the people of the United States to complete the revolution. A smooth transition is one of a speech's technical problems and Lincoln here packs it into a single word. Surreptitiously, with a disguised repetition, he slides from the dedication of a memory to the dedication to a cause. With subtle brilliance that no listener will notice, Lincoln has moved from the past to the future, the direction of every good speech.

> *It is rather for us to be here dedicated to the great task remaining before us – that from these honoured dead we take increased devotion to that cause for which they gave the last full measure of devotion; that we here highly resolve that these dead shall not have died in vain; that this nation, under God, shall have a new birth of freedom; and that government of the people, by the people, for the people, shall not perish from the earth.*

Lincoln shows that the only rule in writing is that there is no rule that cannot be broken if the speaker retains control of the words. This single sentence is set up and paid off with four succeeding clauses, all referring back to the beginning. In the hands of a poor writer it would be too long, but the broken rhythm enhances the effect when the flourish comes. Speeches should accelerate, intellectually and audibly, as they come to their end. The repetition of 'dedication' enlists the dead in Lincoln's cause as he states, much as we shall see Pericles doing, that they died for the purpose he is applauding. Whether they did or not is really a moot point.

The only extempore addition to the script was the phrase 'under God'. It was an uncharacteristically spontaneous revision for Lincoln, but he kept the change in all three copies of the address he prepared later. The phrase *under God* became controversial again in 2013 when, in a recording he made of the Gettysburg Address, Barack Obama omitted the improvised phrase. This loosed a volley of criticism that Obama was censoring and secularising Lincoln's words. In fact he did nothing of the sort. There are five extant versions of the Gettysburg Address, only three of which contain the phrase 'under God'. Obama was reading from Nicolay's draft, the first draft, which does not include it, because it was prepared before delivery.

At the end, Lincoln elevates the pitch even further. The question is now not just the ending of slavery but the very survival of democratic representation. Government of, for and by the people: the whole subject in one memorable phrase. It probably wasn't Lincoln's coinage, though. The prologue to John Wycliffe's first English edition of the Bible in 1384 includes the phrase: 'This Bible is for the government of the people, for the people and by the people', which seems too close not to be the source.

Lincoln's language may seem biblically dramatic to us now, yet it is considered to be a turning point in the nature of public speech. Before Gettysburg, orators tended to speak like Edward Everett, who said, among many purple passages, 'standing beneath this serene sky, overlooking these broad fields now reposing from the labours of the waning year, the mighty Alleghenies dimly towering before us, the graves of our brethren beneath our feet, it is with hesitation that I raise my poor voice to break the eloquent silence of God and Nature'. There were 13,000 words in that vein. Here is the ancient battle between the Attic and the Asiatic styles, brought forward twenty centuries onto a battlefield in Pennsylvania. Oratory changed that day and Lincoln, in a speech far plainer than Everett's grand-style classicism, changed it.

Not that the speech was wonderfully received. Lincoln was heard in silence. Not many listeners realised they were in the presence of a speech that would be one of the first in every anthology. It took time for the verdict to settle that Lincoln had delivered a lapidary masterpiece. Its brevity, which had caused consternation on the day in Gettysburg, has since come to be seen as poetic concision rather than short-changing the audience. Lincoln gave meaning to the terrible sacrifice of battle. He defined again the purpose of the United States of America. He gave voice to democracy and equality, the foundations of the nation which he had laid once again.

JOHN F. KENNEDY

Ask Not What Your Country Can Do for You

Washington DC

20 January 1961

John F. Kennedy (1917–63) feeds the American desire for myth. In life he was American modernity incarnate, an image that death petrified and preserved. His assassination in 1963 produced the first tumult of conspiracy theories which, half a century later, threaten to overwhelm the quest for truth. More Americans believe that Kennedy's death was the result of a conspiracy than disbelieve it.

In 1960, at the age of forty-three, Kennedy had become the first child of the twentieth century to become president, the second-youngest man to take that office after the 42-year-old Theodore Roosevelt. Kennedy remains the only Roman Catholic to have been president and the only president to have won a Pulitzer Prize, for *Profiles in Courage*.

Kennedy was one of nine children born into a Massachusetts family of Irish lineage that had gone into state politics. In 1938, he came to London with his father, who had been appointed as Franklin D. Roosevelt's ambassador to the Court of St James's. He was in London on 1 September 1939, the fateful day that Germany invaded Poland, and attended the debates in the House of Commons in which war was announced. His Harvard thesis, about the British role in the Munich agreement, became a best-seller under the title *Why England Slept*.

The war changed Kennedy's life. His first attempt to enter military service was scuppered when he was disqualified for service due to chronic lower-back pain. It was only after months of exercise to strengthen the muscles that he joined the US Naval Reserve in

September 1941. War service gave him a stature that cannot be earned any other way. In August 1943, Kennedy's navy patrol boat was cut in half by a Japanese destroyer near New Georgia in the Solomon Islands. The crew abandoned the boat and swam to a small island three miles away. Kennedy injured his back in the collision but still towed one of his men, who was badly burned, through the water with a life-jacket strap clenched between his teeth. Kennedy was awarded the Navy and Marine Corps Medal and the Purple Heart Medal. On 1 March 1945 he was honourably discharged from the Navy Reserve with the full rank of lieutenant.

The war changed Kennedy's life in another way too. The mantle of future president had always been laid on his oldest brother, but the death of Joe Kennedy in 1944, killed on a mission over the English Channel at the age of twenty-nine, meant that his father's hopes for high office were transferred to Jack. Kennedy's first job after the war, arranged by his father, who knew the proprietor William Randolph Hearst, was as a special correspondent for Hearst newspapers. In that position he was in Berlin, the scene of his own later triumph with a speech (see chapter 2), to cover the Potsdam Conference.

Kennedy returned to America and set out on his political course. He represented Massachusetts in the House of Representatives from 1947 to 1953 and in the Senate from 1953 until 1960, in which year he became the Democrat nominee for president. In the general election of 1960, Kennedy won a tight victory over his Republican rival, Richard Nixon. The young president came to power bearing vast domestic hopes. He had plans for ending privation and poverty, for action in the cause of equal civil rights, federal funding for education, medical care for the elderly and a programme of economic stimulus, most of which would fall to his successor, Lyndon B. Johnson. The 1964 Civil Rights Act passed in part because Johnson invoked the memory of his slain predecessor.

Kennedy's short time in office was dominated, as the tenure of most presidents is, by foreign affairs. His first error was to overreact to a Cold War speech by the Soviet premier Nikita Khrushchev in early 1961 which poisoned the atmosphere of the Vienna Summit that year. Kennedy announced in Vienna that any treaty between Moscow and East Berlin which affected American access rights in West Berlin would be regarded as an act of war. The Russians proceeded nevertheless, and the prelude to war, with the threat of nuclear confrontation, began.

The next site of the struggle with communism was Cuba. Following Fidel Castro's victory against the US-backed dictator Fulgencio Batista in January 1959, Kennedy approved a plan he had inherited from President Eisenhower and ordered the invasion of the island using CIA-trained Cuban exiles. The landing at the Bay of Pigs on the night of 16/17 April 1961 ended in humiliation when the invaders were killed or captured. What took the world to the brink, though, were the events of the following October 1962, when the CIA took pictures of ballistic missile sites being built by the Soviet Union in Cuba. Against the advice of some hawks on the National Security Council, Kennedy settled on a naval quarantine. The world trembled on the cusp of nuclear war, but after a perilous period the Russians backed down and removed the weapons.

The next domino to fall was Vietnam. Kennedy vastly increased American involvement in Vietnam, but found no lasting solution and handed on an unresolved problem to his successor. It is still disputed, and will never be settled, whether America's entanglement in Vietnam would have happened had Kennedy lived longer.

Everyone remembers where they were on the day that C. S. Lewis and Aldous Huxley died. It was 22 November 1963, the day that John F. Kennedy was assassinated in Dallas, shot by Lee Harvey Oswald from the sixth-floor window of the Texas School Book Depository. After just two years and ten months in office, he became the youngest president to die. Perhaps because of that early death, Kennedy remains an icon of American politics.

The light has flooded in on his private life since his death. News has spread about his alleged infidelities, such as spending a week at Bing Crosby's house with Marilyn Monroe, and his illnesses, which were at times critical. Perhaps Kennedy's brief presidency would not have been possible in this more prurient age. There are plenty of commentators on American politics – Gore Vidal and Arthur J. Schlesinger, for example – who date the decline in trust in the political establishment to the death of John F. Kennedy.

None of the revelations appear to have besmirched his reputation. The Kennedy White House exists in a sepia reality in which hope is forever young. The culture and the politics never seemed so well aligned. Kennedy's approval rating remains the highest of any American president. It is now impossible to read the speech that follows without a retrospective sense of foreboding. This was Kennedy's only inaugural address, and it cannot be read now, as is also the case with Lincoln and the Gettysburg Address, free from the shadow of what is about to befall him. On his grave at Arlington Cemetery in Washington DC there is a plaque on which many of the lines from this speech are engraved.

> *We observe today not a victory of party but a celebration of freedom – symbolizing an end as well as a beginning – signifying renewal as well as change. For I have sworn before you and Almighty God the same solemn oath our forebears prescribed nearly a century and three-quarters ago.*

Before he began writing, Kennedy insisted that his speechwriter Ted Sorensen read all the previous inaugural addresses. Sorensen concluded that the best speech of all was Lincoln's Gettysburg Address, and resolved to keep his drafting simple, or at least to prune the finished text of ornamentation. A lot of hard work goes into making a speech sound simple. Sorensen has said that 'no Kennedy speech ever underwent so many drafts. Each paragraph was reworded, reworked and reduced'. This opening sentence began as: 'We celebrate today not a victory of party but the sacrament of democracy' and was then changed to: 'We celebrate today not a victory of party but a convention of freedom'. The final completed version has a better balance and does the required thing – required for Kennedy as it had been for Jefferson – which is to bring the nation back together. The 1960 election had been one of the closest of recent times. The difference in votes between the two candidates was tiny, although Kennedy emerged with a majority in the electoral college. America was, as it usually is, split between two competing visions of how it should be governed. Kennedy thus signals at once the function of the inaugural address, which is to heal fresh wounds.

The campaign had contained a famous incident that shows us that rhetoric is visual as well as oral. Kennedy and Nixon had taken part in the first televised presidential debates. The verdict of the radio audience was that the debate had been a draw. If pressed, that audience would probably have awarded the debate to Nixon. The television audience took a clear and differing view. Nixon looked tense and ill at ease, perspiring under a heavy five o'clock shadow. The professionally made up Kennedy was by contrast a picture of relaxation. This marks the moment television began to play a big part in American politics, although the impact of presidential debates on the outcome is exaggerated. It is not likely that many since 1960 have made much difference.

Kennedy, in fact, did give an inaugural speech that would fit neatly into the television schedule. He was determined to keep it short. 'It's more effective that way,' he said, 'and I don't want people to think I'm a windbag.' At under 2,000 words, 1961's was the shortest inaugural speech since 1905. It worked: as Harry S. Truman said afterwards, 'it was short, to the point, and in language anyone can understand ... Even I could understand it, and therefore, the people can.'

> *The world is very different now. For man holds in his mortal hands the power to abolish all forms of human poverty and all forms of human life. And yet the same revolutionary beliefs for which our forebears fought are still at issue around the globe – the belief that the rights of man come not from the generosity of the state but from the hand of God. We dare not forget today that we are the heirs of that first revolution. Let the word go forth from this time and place, to friend and foe alike, that the torch has been passed to a new generation of Americans – born in this century, tempered by war, disciplined by a hard and bitter peace, proud of our ancient heritage – and unwilling to witness or permit the slow undoing of those human rights to which this nation has always been committed, and to which we are committed today at home and around the world.*

The central theme of the speech is time passing: a new generation has arrived. This rather empty chronological point was given substance by the fact that Kennedy sat next to his predecessor, the seventy-year-old Dwight Eisenhower, once the Supreme Commander of Allied Forces in Europe while Kennedy had been a navy lieutenant in the Pacific. The young men Kennedy proposed to bring into his administration were visible behind the new president as he spoke.

The final text had not only undergone many mutations in the drafting. It had also had a number of previous airings on the campaign trail. Repetition of this sort would be assailed as plagiarism or lack of imagination now. In his acceptance speech in Los Angeles, for example, Kennedy had said 'man ... has taken into his mortal hands the power to exterminate the entire species some seven times over', which is a less polished version of what we have here. The line 'it is time, in short, for a new generation of Americans' has here acquired the light of a metaphorical torch.

This opening signals something unusual for a presidential Inaugural. Kennedy has ordered this speech to be exclusively about foreign policy. Domestic questions, which were plentiful and problematic – a third recession in seven years, the highest unemployment for two decades and the oppression of black Americans – were weeded out. This is the origin of the flat phrase 'today at home and around the world', which has the air of not being at all crafted. It was in fact inserted by Kennedy at the last moment because he suddenly took fright at the realisation that, as a speech devoted to foreign affairs, his Inaugural might read like an evasion on civil rights at home. The effect of seeking to have it both ways is that it doesn't work. Trying to patch the omission makes the absence of domestic topics glaring. It would have been better to leave out the reference, as his speechwriter had, because then the audience appreciates that the omission was a choice. A perfunctory inclusion makes the audience feel that it must have been an error.

Let every nation know, whether it wishes us well or ill, that we shall pay any price, bear any burden, meet any hardship, support any friend, oppose any foe to assure the survival and the success of liberty. This much we pledge – and more. To those old allies whose cultural and spiritual origins we share, we pledge the loyalty of faithful friends. United there is little we cannot do in a host of cooperative ventures. Divided there is little we can do – for we dare not meet a powerful challenge at odds and split asunder. To those new states whom we welcome to the ranks of the free, we pledge our word that one form of colonial control shall not have passed away

> *merely to be replaced by a far more iron tyranny. We shall not always expect to find them supporting our view. But we shall always hope to find them strongly supporting their own freedom – and to remember that, in the past, those who foolishly sought power by riding the back of the tiger ended up inside.*

The survival of liberty is, as a subject for a speech, 'nobly conceived', as John Steinbeck put it at the time. But words are close to deeds for a president, and Kennedy has, ever since then, faced the accusation that he locked himself into the stance of the cold warrior in the short time he governed with the pledge to 'pay any price, bear any burden' in the defence of liberty. Critics have drawn a straight line that runs through the fiasco of the Bay of Pigs invasion and the peril of the Cuban Missile Crisis to Vietnam and beyond.

Kennedy's rhetoric has both a lineage and a legacy. The lineage runs in the commitment to liberating the oppressed around the globe, which is an echo of Woodrow Wilson's internationalism. The legacy ensues in the echoes from 1963 that are audible in the first inaugural addresses of both Ronald Reagan and Bill Clinton, and in George W. Bush's rhetoric against tyranny in his second Inaugural, after 9/11. 'When you stand for your liberty, we will stand with you.' That could have been Kennedy; in fact it was Bush.

Bear in mind, though, that the calculation changes over time, and the same words in defence of liberty have one charge in 1961 and quite another forty years later. For Kennedy the threat to American liberty was real and domestic, as nuclear annihilation would respect no boundaries. By the time Clinton and Bush come to make speeches in the name of the liberal international order the demands are different. The question has become solely whether America should be out in the world helping to police liberty. But here Sorensen's writing is as sonorous as anywhere, and we see one of the dangers of rhetoric, which is that it can run away with the speaker. The words have a grandeur which, in the hindsight of the troubles to come, is skirting closer to hubris than Kennedy might have meant. Indeed, a famous later speech, at the American University in Washington in 1963, treated a similar topic in a much more emollient fashion.

Finally, to those nations who would make themselves our adversary, we offer not a pledge but a request: that both sides begin anew the quest for peace, before the dark powers of destruction unleashed by science engulf all humanity in planned or accidental self-destruction. We dare not tempt them with weakness. For only when our arms are sufficient beyond doubt can we be certain beyond doubt that they will never be employed. But neither can two great and powerful groups of nations take comfort from our present course – both sides overburdened by the cost of modern weapons, both rightly alarmed by the steady spread of the deadly atom, yet both racing to alter that uncertain balance of terror that stays the hand of mankind's final war. So let us begin anew – remembering on both sides that civility is not a sign of weakness, and sincerity is always subject to proof. Let us never negotiate out of fear. But let us never fear to negotiate. Let both sides explore what problems unite us instead of belabouring those problems which divide us. Let both sides, for the first time, formulate serious and precise proposals for the inspection and control of arms – and bring the absolute power to destroy other nations under the absolute control of all nations. Let both sides seek to invoke the wonders of science instead of its terrors. Together let us explore the stars, conquer the deserts, eradicate disease, tap the ocean depths and encourage the arts and commerce. Let both sides unite to heed in all corners of the earth the command of Isaiah – to 'undo the heavy burdens ... [and] let the oppressed go free'. And if a beachhead of cooperation may push back the jungle of suspicion, let both sides join in creating a new endeavour, not a new balance of power, but a new world of law, where the strong are just and the weak secure and the peace preserved. All this will not be finished in the first one hundred days. Nor will it be finished in the first one thousand days, nor in the life of this Administration, nor even perhaps in our lifetime on this planet. But let us begin.

That opening 'finally' must make the speechwriter cringe: we're only halfway through. It is the final part of its own section but it still sounds the only false note in the writing, which is otherwise perfectly controlled. The credit for that is due to Sorensen, who acted as editor-in-chief of the many contributions that Kennedy commissioned.

Solicited suggestions came in from the columnists Walter Lippmann and Joseph Kraft, civil rights advisers Harris Wofford and Louis Martin, and the economist John Kenneth Galbraith, along with a pile of unsolicited material. Secretary of State Dean Rusk added phrases. Billy Graham sent a list of possible biblical quotations, as did the leader of Washington's Jewish Community Council, Isaac Franck. Sorensen held the pen, though, and Galbraith, in particular, was disappointed that so few of his resounding phrases made the final cut. Years later he rather forlornly claimed that among the surviving words of his contribution was the simple refrain: 'Let us ...'

This is the passage in which Kennedy moves the argument on from rigid Cold War binary opposition. The speech does contain plenty of counterpoints to his deliberate show of strength – 'civility is not a sign of weakness'; the United Nations is 'our last best hope'; and the need for 'a grand global alliance' against 'the common enemies of man: tyranny, poverty, disease and war itself'. It would therefore be wrong to read this speech as nothing other than a resilient text of a cold warrior, although that is the essential context. In 1957 the Soviet Union had launched the first space capsule to orbit the earth. West Berlin had been threatened by a Soviet ultimatum. South Vietnam had been menaced by a guerrilla campaign from the communist regime in Hanoi. America felt ill-equipped for the challenge and wanted a strong response. That speech about the peril is in there certainly, but so too are the caveats and the entreaties. Kennedy's message to Khrushchev is clear. He will stand against armed encroachments, but he wants to lower the temperature with negotiations and cooperation.

In your hands, my fellow citizens, more than mine, will rest the final success or failure of our course. Since this country was founded, each generation of Americans has been summoned to give testimony to its national loyalty. The graves of young Americans who answered the call to service surround the globe. Now the trumpet summons us again – not as a call to bear arms, though arms we need – not as a call to battle, though embattled we are – but a call to bear the burden of a long twilight struggle, year in and year out, 'rejoicing in hope, patient in tribulation' – a struggle against the common enemies of man: tyranny, poverty, disease and war itself. Can we forge against these enemies a grand and global alliance, North and South, East and West, that can assure a more fruitful life for all mankind? Will you join in that historic effort?

With the claim that the future rests in your hands rather than mine, Kennedy drops the first hint of the line that will forever after be the title of this speech. It is notable that citizen action has not featured thus far. Suddenly the speech switches focus, from the world to America, from the president to the citizen body. This was a regular Kennedy theme. The president was irritated by his party's comfort-zone tendency to argue that government will fix social problems. He thought the Democrats were too ready to reach for the state. The speech he had given at the Democratic Convention, which became known as his 'New Frontier' speech, was notable for this reason. 'The New Frontier of which I speak', he said on that occasion, 'is not a set of promises – it is a set of challenges. It sums up not what I intend to offer the American people, but what I intend to ask of them.'

Kennedy dramatises this switch, and this focus, in the writing. He made a conscious decision during the drafting to strike out all uses of the word 'I'. He also eschews one obvious course, which is to make himself the embodiment of the new generation. Instead, new times will be defined by a compact between the governor and the governed. This is the irony in the existence of the prestigious John F. Kennedy School of Government at Harvard: an academy devoted to the craft of using state power is named after the president who is famous for wanting to devolve his power to the people. This evocation of 'we' over 'I' leads perfectly to the theme of his peroration, which is that power is dispersed. Power resides with the people. This is a way of asking for popular support and a reminder of the central virtue that democracy exhibits over other forms of government. It is only in a democracy that the people would be asked to contribute. In other forms of polity they would be told.

This was also a way of diverting attention from Kennedy's relative youth and inexperience, which had been a problem for him during the presidential campaign. The era of Eisenhower, De Gaulle and Adenauer was fresh in the memory. By making a speech of such gravity, and by drafting the people as partners, Kennedy is, in effect, saying that he is ready to serve in dangerous times.

In the long history of the world, only a few generations have been
granted the role of defending freedom in its hour of maximum
danger. I do not shrink from this responsibility – I welcome it. I do
not believe that any of us would exchange places with any other
people or any other generation. The energy, the faith, the devotion
which we bring to this endeavour will light our country and all
who serve it and the glow from that fire can truly light the world.
And so, my fellow Americans: ask not what your country can do for
you, ask what you can do for your country. My fellow citizens of
the world: ask not what America will do for you, but what together
we can do for the freedom of man.

The famous chiasmus comes at the end of the speech. In this formulation the words will last, but this was by no means their first airing. This was another line that had been tested on the road. In a televised campaign address in September 1960 Kennedy had said: 'We do not campaign stressing what our country is going to do for us as a people. We stress what we can do for the country, all of us.' By the time of the Inaugural, Kennedy has polished the words for effect. He told Sorensen that he was worried that the ending sounded very much like the one he had given in a recent speech in the Massachusetts legislature. Three other campaign speeches, in Anchorage, Detroit and Washington, had all included a variant of the same idiom.

The famous line – 'ask not …' – was an echo of Jefferson's belief, which he took from the ancient governments, that taking part is an important aspect of American citizenship. The words were an instant inspiration as soon as it was uttered. Numberless Americans joined the effort to fight poverty in America's inner cities. The Peace Corps took many volunteers overseas. By the end of Kennedy's presidency, more than 7,000 mostly young Americans were working in underdeveloped countries around the world.

For all that it is a wonderfully poetic sentence and a fine sentiment, and at the risk of heresy, it is a slightly odd conclusion to a foreign policy speech. What can any individual really do, in the context in which this advice is offered? This would have been a more comprehensible counsel in a speech about domestic policy, where active citizen engagement is part of the solution. Quite how the individual was to affect the conduct of the Cold War was less obvious.

However, it didn't feel like that at the time. The 1961 Inaugural shows how occasion matters to the verdict of greatness. This speech is not as important, historically, as the televised address from October 1962 in which the president revealed to the world the secret presence of Soviet intermediate-range nuclear missiles on Cuba. It is, though, the speech that is best remembered. The line it is remembered for is this one. It is the naming of popular power that makes it memorable. Kennedy gets into a magnificent rhetorical phrase one of the great insights into democratic politics, which is that it needs an active citizen body. It is the conclusion to a different speech, if we want to be fastidious about the structure. It is a brilliant conclusion nonetheless.

BARACK OBAMA

I Have Never Been More Hopeful about America

Grant Park, Chicago
7 November 2012

No matter what he achieved in office, Barack Obama changed the world simply by who he was. The forty-fourth president of the United States was the first black leader of a nation no more than a generation after it had been segregated by race. The shock proved too much for some opponents who confected a conspiracy that Obama was not actually American, a nonsense ended by the production of his birth certificate. More than any American leader since John F. Kennedy, Obama embodied, and spoke about, the idea of hope. Even more than Kennedy he owed his elevation in politics to the pitch and power of his rhetoric. In an age when oratory was deemed to have collapsed into stock phrases, Obama rescued the trade.

Barack Obama was born on 4 August 1961, in Honolulu, Hawaii, to a Kenyan intellectual and a white teenager from Kansas. After briefly living in Indonesia, he was raised by his grandparents in Hawaii. He studied law at Columbia and Harvard and worked as a civil rights lawyer in Chicago. Obama's political break came in 1996 with a seat in the Illinois state senate, followed by a US Senate seat in 2004. His book *The Audacity of Hope*, which prefigures many of the themes expressed in his speeches, became a best-seller. Political aficionados had spotted his rhetorical brilliance, but it was still somehow from nowhere that he ran, in 2008, a flawless campaign to beat Hillary Clinton to the Democratic presidential nomination. In a nod to the classical origins of the American Republic, Obama accepted the Democratic nomination in front of a reconstruction of a Roman forum.

It is as yet early to assess Obama's legacy as president, especially on foreign affairs, on which he was elected to pull America back from engagement. On this basis he was awarded a premature Nobel Peace Prize in 2009. As most presidents do, he found the world came to him even if he had not invited it in. Obama's domestic record may stand the scrutiny of time. The American economy recovered on his watch from the financial crisis of 2008, but his claim to political memory is the Affordable Health Care Act. Every Democrat president has promised universal health care for America. Every one before Barack Obama failed to put anything into statute; Obama did. If even a cover version of his legislation survives its assault by his successor, Obama will be remembered as the Democrat who succeeded.

Tonight, more than two hundred years after a former colony won the right to determine its own destiny, the task of perfecting our union moves forward. It moves forward because of you. It moves forward because you reaffirmed the spirit that has triumphed over war and depression, the spirit that has lifted this country from the depths of despair to the great heights of hope, the belief that while each of us will pursue our own individual dreams, we are an American family and we rise or fall together as one nation and as one people. Tonight, in this election, you, the American people, reminded us that while our road has been hard, while our journey has been long, we have picked ourselves up, we have fought our way back, and we know in our hearts that for the United States of America the best is yet to come.

The first task in the instant aftermath of every election victory is to bind the nation. Obama does this by placing himself within the history of the republic and attaching it to the entire present nation. Election campaigns are, by their nature, divisive. The criticism that politics divides people is always wrong. People are divided. It is the nature of human beings to disagree. Politics is the means by which that division is recognised, negotiated and settled.

That is Obama's opening and defining purpose in a speech that is a paean to politics itself. That central argument makes sense of the idea of perfecting the union. Obama, like Jefferson has before him, makes it clear that the process towards perfection will never end. It is, after all, only the pursuit of happiness that the constitution protects, not its accomplishment. The road is hard, the journey long, and success is never assured. The best resource that the public have in the eternal pursuit is to be as one, a single family brought together after the electoral verdict has been entered, as a single political community. The night of a general election realises and thwarts ambitions in an instant. The moment opens the crack. The task of the president is to let the light flood back in. That allows him to conclude that the best is yet to come.

I know that political campaigns can sometimes seem small, even silly. And that provides plenty of fodder for the cynics that tell us that politics is nothing more than a contest of egos or the domain of special interests. But if you ever get the chance to talk to folks who turned out at our rallies and crowded along a rope line in a high school gym, or saw folks working late in a campaign office in some tiny county far away from home, you'll discover something else. You'll hear the determination in the voice of a young field organiser who's working his way through college and wants to make sure every child has that same opportunity. You'll hear the pride in the voice of a volunteer who's going door to door because her brother was finally hired when the local auto plant added another shift. You'll hear the deep patriotism in the voice of a military spouse who's working the phones late at night to make sure that no one who fights for this country ever has to fight for a job or a roof over their head when they come home. That's why we do this. That's what politics can be. That's why elections matter. It's not small, it's big. It's important. Democracy in a nation of 300 million can be noisy and messy and complicated. We have our own opinions. Each of us has deeply held beliefs. And when we go through tough times, when we make big decisions as a country, it necessarily stirs passions, stirs up controversy. That won't change after tonight, and it shouldn't. These arguments we have are a mark of our liberty. We can never forget that as we speak, people in distant nations are risking their lives right now just for a chance to argue about the issues that matter, the chance to cast their ballots like we did today.

In its way one of the most quietly moving passages Obama has ever uttered. This is not the most dramatic speech he ever gave, nor the one that most directly stirs the emotions. Obama's speech about race in 2008 and his victory speech the same year in Grant Park may be greater. His decision to sing 'Amazing Grace' after the murder of the Reverend Pinckney in Charleston in 2015 is one of the most affecting moments of public speech there is. Obama often sounds like he is singing; on that occasion he actually was.

But here, in this prosaic passage, Obama sets out a manifesto for politics and the hope it carries for progress. For someone viewed as a lyrical speaker, you might be surprised to find that, like Molière's bourgeois gentleman, Obama has been speaking prose all his life. Mario Cuomo's line that politicians campaign in poetry and govern in prose is quoted too often, not least because it's wrong. Obama shows that politicians campaign in prose too, but that if the prose is good enough then the effect can be poetic.

More than any other speaker, with the exception of Martin Luther King, with whom he shares a vocal style, Obama needs to be heard rather than read. The way he slides down the consonants, dwelling on a word so that the stress imparts unmined meaning. The way he pauses, in complete control; his silences better than most people's words. The way his voice contains the music and the rhythm in a vocal pattern that is closer to singing than to speaking and which is the secular transfer of an idiom that can be heard in the black churches.

The comparison with King is irresistible but it will stretch only so far. King's language is biblical and showy: Attic in the ancient currency. Obama's is Asiatic; simple and plain. Read a speech by Dr King out for yourself and you can electrify the air. It's not as easy to do with a text by Obama. You can't say it like he does. The case he is making – about the liberty of a nation under democratic government – contains a quiet beauty, but it takes Barack Obama to really make it sing.

But despite all our differences, most of us share certain hopes for America's future. We want our kids to grow up in a country where they have access to the best schools and the best teachers. A country that lives up to its legacy as the global leader in technology and

discovery and innovation, with all the good jobs and new businesses
that follow. We want our children to live in an America that isn't
burdened by debt, that isn't weakened by inequality, that isn't
threatened by the destructive power of a warming planet. We want
to pass on a country that's safe and respected and admired around
the world, a nation that is defended by the strongest military on
earth and the best troops this world has ever known. But also a
country that moves with confidence beyond this time of war, to
shape a peace that is built on the promise of freedom and dignity
for every human being. We believe in a generous America, in a
compassionate America, in a tolerant America, open to the dreams
of an immigrant's daughter who studies in our schools and pledges
to our flag. To the young boy on the south side of Chicago who sees
a life beyond the nearest street corner. To the furniture worker's
child in North Carolina who wants to become a doctor or a
scientist, an engineer or an entrepreneur, a diplomat or even a
president — that's the future we hope for. That's the vision we share.
That's where we need to go — forward. That's where we need to go.
Now, we will disagree, sometimes fiercely, about how to get there.
As it has for more than two centuries, progress will come in fits and
starts. It's not always a straight line. It's not always a smooth path.
By itself, the recognition that we have common hopes and dreams
won't end all the gridlock or solve all our problems or substitute for
the painstaking work of building consensus and making the
difficult compromises needed to move this country forward. But
that common bond is where we must begin.

Politics is difficult. Change is ground out slowly. It is often boring to do, let alone to watch. Slow, incremental improvement – the vital currency of democratic politics – is hard to turn to rhetorical gold. It takes great skill to turn 'Let us proceed slowly and cautiously' into a rallying cry, but this is what Obama does here. He is borrowing the form of the uplifting call-to-arms to play down expectations. Obama is a master of the glorious compromise, the beautiful consensus, the slow change that lifts the heart.

Obama restates America's meritocratic idea of itself – a compliment America pays itself quite wrongly, its rates of social mobility being lower than most comparable democracies – in a reminder that the path to the ideal of the republic is never easy. It is an important dream. The idea that individual enterprise will gain its due reward is America's foundation myth. It's never been as true as it should be but it would be even less true than it is if there were no myth expressed at all. Obama, though, cleverly lays it on thin. Rhetoric is too easily an art that exaggerates, and Obama has more gifts in the art than most. Here, he is deliberately reining himself in, to make an important point about the application of power.

Our economy is recovering. A decade of war is ending. A long campaign is now over. And whether I earned your vote or not, I have listened to you, I have learned from you, and you've made me a better president. And with your stories and your struggles, I return to the White House more determined and more inspired than ever about the work there is to do and the future that lies ahead. Tonight you voted for action, not politics as usual. You elected us to focus on your jobs, not ours. And in the coming weeks and months, I am looking forward to reaching out and working with leaders of both parties to meet the challenges we can only solve together. Reducing our deficit. Reforming our tax code. Fixing our immigration system. Freeing ourselves from foreign oil. We've got more work to do. But that doesn't mean your work is done. The role of citizen in our democracy does not end with your vote. America's never been about what can be done for us. It's about what can be done by us together through the hard and frustrating, but necessary work of self-government. That's the principle we were founded on. This country has more wealth than any nation, but that's not what makes us rich. We have the most powerful military in history, but that's not what makes us strong. Our university, our culture are all the envy of the world, but that's not what keeps the world coming to our shores. What makes America exceptional are the bonds that hold together the most diverse nation on earth. The belief that our destiny is shared; that this country only works when we accept certain obligations to one another and to future generations. The freedom which so many Americans have fought for and died for comes with responsibilities as well as rights. And among those are love and charity and duty and patriotism. That's what makes America great.

The list of the items in the White House in-tray continues the theme of sober administration. It won't be every anthology that immortalises the line 'reforming the tax code'. I have a dream ... of reforming the tax code. Still, this is what good politics does. It is also crucial for Obama, the high priest of vague hope, to make a claim to practical achievement. This is his recognition that expressions of hope not anchored in the world are frivolous.

Then Obama reverses the burden of proof, much as Kennedy had done with 'ask not what your country can do for you but what you can do for your country' in his 1961 Inaugural. Presidential speeches, at least until Donald Trump, make up a single story, the story of American democracy. Presidents are conscious of each other, and no other country's leaders quote their predecessors more than the Americans do. They are not citing heroes or sainted icons, as a Labour Party figure would with Clement Attlee or Aneurin Bevan. They are invoking the prestige of the office. Obama's riff about what can be done by us rather than for us is more or less a direct lift from Kennedy, who was himself echoing Lincoln.

This is an elegant reminder of the limitations of politics and the narrow range of the state. Just as the law is upheld by voluntary compliance rather than by enforcement, so government makes demands of its citizens. Democracy is a culture and a pattern of behaviour. The early days of President Trump have shown us that this point applies to the president himself. The American constitution makes a fetish of its documents but it works in practice through the tacit understanding of the people who make it work. The president has to understand that if he pushes the executive order too far he is upsetting the balance. The formal mechanism of the court will strike back, but the very act of constitutional defiance is damaging. The checks and the balances are two separate things. The balance in the classical tradition is observed by the participants who are checked if they refuse to comply. Obama here defines the bond of America, the glory of the republic, as duty. The language is less ornate but, intellectually, this is classical. The ideas of the Roman republic are still intact.

I am hopeful tonight because I've seen the spirit at work in America. I've seen it in the family business whose owners would rather cut their own pay than lay off their neighbours, and in the workers who would rather cut back their hours than see a friend lose a job. I've seen it in the soldiers who re-enlist after losing a limb and in those SEALs who charged up the stairs into darkness and danger because they knew there was a buddy behind them watching their back. I've seen it on the shores of New Jersey and New York, where leaders from every party and level of government have swept aside their differences to help a community rebuild from the wreckage of a terrible storm. And I saw just the other day, in Mentor, Ohio, where a father told the story of his eight-year-old daughter, whose long battle with leukaemia nearly cost their family everything had it not been for healthcare reform passing just a few months before the insurance company was about to stop paying for her care. I had an opportunity to not just talk to the father, but meet this incredible daughter of his. And when he spoke to the crowd listening to that father's story, every parent in that room had tears in their eyes, because we knew that little girl could be our own. And I know that every American wants her future to be just as bright. That's who we are. That's the country I'm so proud to lead as your president.

The skilled speaker needs watching. This speech has been given with the aim of healing, and the first part of this passage is generously ecumenical. Vital categories are ticked off in a list of commendations: small-town American entrepreneurs, soldiers in the field, the US Navy. Note, in passing, how not saying something says it so effectively. The audience would all be aware that Obama is referring to the killing by Navy SEALs of Osama bin Laden, public enemy number one. The president doesn't need to spell it out. The success of the mission is evoked the better for being modestly done. Nothing establishes standing as a national leader like defeating an enemy – this is Cicero and Mark Antony revisited – and Obama uses it politically to make a point in his own favour.

He slides from this triumph to praise for the cross-party response to a hurricane in New Jersey, and from there into a story about health care. The craft of a wide-ranging speech is to find a theme that strings together its disparate parts. There is always a risk of contrivance; there really is nothing to link Osama bin Laden, the wrecked New Jersey shore and the Obama government's healthcare legislation. Obama therefore makes an emotional link, stringing the speech together with mood music.

In the thick of the pathos he sneaks in a trick. Healthcare was and is a great divide in American politics. Should it be a state or an individual responsibility? Only a moment before this, Obama had been advocating individual duty. With skilful manipulation of the mood and ordering of the topics, he swaps sides, clinching the case with a harrowing and irresistible story about the tears shed for a young girl's salvaged future. With the audience now involved emotionally, Obama then leaps to cite the young girl as the definition of America. A partisan policy has become, in a few deft sentences: 'That's who we are. That's the country I'm so proud to lead as your president'. Rhetorical skill like that is brilliant but we need to be on the alert.

And tonight, despite all the hardship we've been through, despite all the frustrations of Washington, I've never been more hopeful about our future. I have never been more hopeful about America. And I ask you to sustain that hope. I'm not talking about blind optimism, the kind of hope that just ignores the enormity of the tasks ahead or the roadblocks that stand in our path. I'm not talking about the wishful idealism that allows us to just sit on the sidelines or shirk from a fight. I have always believed that hope is that stubborn thing inside us that insists, despite all the evidence to the contrary, that something better awaits us so long as we have the courage to keep reaching, to keep working, to keep fighting. America, I believe we can build on the progress we've made and continue to fight for new jobs and new opportunity and new security for the middle class. I believe we can keep the promise of our founders, the idea that if you're willing to work hard, it doesn't matter who you are or where you come from or what you look like or where you love. It doesn't matter whether you're black or white or Hispanic or Asian or Native American or young or old or rich or poor, able, disabled, gay or straight, you can make it here in America if you're willing to try. I believe we can seize this future

> *together because we are not as divided as our politics suggests. We're not as cynical as the pundits believe. We are greater than the sum of our individual ambitions, and we remain more than a collection of red states and blue states. We are and forever will be the United States of America. And together with your help and God's grace we will continue our journey forward and remind the world just why it is that we live in the greatest nation on Earth. Thank you, America. God bless you. God bless these United States.*

Ever since Barack Obama was lifted to the presidency of the United States on a high tide of language, politicians have wanted to be like him. They should pause and consider the ways in which they are not like Barack Obama. There is, in fact, almost no end to the ways in which they are not like Barack Obama. First, they are not president of the United States. Second, they do not have his gift for language. Third, they do not have his voice. Fourth and most important, they are not a black president in a nation still scarred by slavery, the silent subject of the Gettysburg Address. Obama touches on that question in the meritocratic section of this passage, and it is granted the greater force because he is saying it. A black man becoming the president of the United States of America is one of the greatest stories ever told in all the annals of politics.

Martin Luther King's vision has not yet been achieved in full, but it would take a hard heart to suggest that Obama's presidency is not one act in the drama of his dream. This is the context when Obama speaks and it lends historic weight to his every word. None of this would apply if your task is to present the strategic objectives to the sales team or if you are on in the just-after-lunch slot discussing council tax at the annual conference of the *Local Government Chronicle*. Important a topic as that is (and it is), it has a register of its own which is not the same as that of a victorious president in the world's most powerful democracy. The lesson here is: respect your occasion. If you pretend you are speaking on the steps of the Lincoln Memorial and have the ear of the world cocked for your words, you do not elevate your subject; you diminish it. Obama can do this because of who he is and the context he speaks in. If the ending reads on the page as slightly boilerplate Obama, it works in the hearing. Hope is not always an audacious emotion to evoke. It can sound vacuous if it is not attached to the power to realise it in the world. Without pragmatic politics, hope is a wish-list. Which makes the defining point. The finest political hopes are those of an elected president of a free country.

THE GETTYSBURG ADDRESSES

On the centenary celebration of the Gettysburg Address on 19 November 1963, the sitting president of the United States was indisposed. He was required to fly down to Texas to appear in Dallas with Vice-President Lyndon Johnson. Instead of speaking at Gettysburg, as he had been requested to do, President John F. Kennedy sent a message that read: 'On this solemn occasion let us all rededicate ourselves to the perpetuation of those ideals of which Lincoln spoke so luminously. As Americans, we can do no less.'

Kennedy's place at Gettysburg was taken by a famous resident. Dwight D. Eisenhower had been stationed in Gettysburg during the First World War as the commander of the US Army Tank Corps Training Center. After the Second World War he had bought a 189-acre farm on the site where, in 1952, he held a picnic to open his campaign for the presidency. During his time in the White House, Eisenhower would often spend the weekend in Gettysburg, shooting skeet and inspecting his herd of Angus show cattle. It was here, in the farm that became known as the 'Temporary White House', that he recuperated from his heart attack in 1955 and here that he received the world's dignitaries.

In 1961, General and Mrs Eisenhower retired to Gettysburg, where the ex-president began work on his memoirs. He was called upon to perform this one last major service, though, to stand in for his successor President Kennedy. President Eisenhower used his centenary address to summon the noble destiny and unity which had inspired Lincoln. Though Lincoln's words retain their power to move, said Eisenhower, 'the unfinished work of which he spoke in 1863 is still unfinished; because of human frailty it always will be'. The task was to pass on, as best we could, the legacy bequeathed by Lincoln: 'a nation free, with liberty, dignity and justice for all'.

Despite the solemnity of the occasion and the gravity of his words, President Eisenhower's speech has been lost to posterity because three days later the man who should have made the speech at Gettysburg, John F. Kennedy, was assassinated. The bullets in Dallas completed a gruesome symmetry around the most famous speech in the political canon. Both the man who was never meant to make the Gettysburg Address, Abraham Lincoln, and the man who was but didn't, John F. Kennedy, were assassinated, almost a century apart.

Ever since Abraham Lincoln consecrated the spot in 1863, American presidents have repaired to the battlefield at Gettysburg, Pennsylvania, to pay homage to the American Republic that Lincoln's 272 words were designed to save. In 1878, Rutherford B. Hayes hoped that contemplation of the National Cemetery would allow Americans to appreciate those who 'gave their lives for the Union, liberty, and for a stable, constitutional government'. Beating even Lincoln for brevity, Hayes spoke just 253 words, forty-four of which were in quoting Lincoln's last sentence. In 1904, in a lesson about applying the disciplines of war to win the liberty of peace, Theodore Roosevelt commended the soldiers who had made their countrymen forever their debtors. On the fiftieth anniversary of Lincoln's address in 1913, Woodrow Wilson celebrated reconciliation and offered a paean to a nation 'undivided in interest'. On Memorial Day, 30 May 1928, Calvin Coolidge observed the usual pieties, dwelling on America's interest in maintaining global peace and depicting the American economy, just prior to the Wall Street crash of 1929, as prosperously content.

Two years later, in a Gettysburg Address abut the common good, Herbert Hoover issued a warning against demagoguery and said that 'the weaving of freedom is and always will be a struggle of law against lawlessness, of individual liberty against domination, of unity against sectionalism, of truth and honesty against demagoguery and misleading, of peace against fear and conflict.' In 1938, Franklin D. Roosevelt came to Gettysburg to sound a warning, which has extraordinary contemporary resonance, to those who seek to 'build political advantage by the distortion of facts; those who, by declining to follow the rules of the game, seek to gain an unfair advantage over those who are willing to live up to the rules of the game'. Roosevelt articulated better than most presidents the idea they all took from Lincoln of an America that forswears prejudice and seeks unity in the common welfare.

Perhaps the finest of the second-order Gettysburg Addresses was given six months before Eisenhower took Kennedy's place on the rostrum. Vice-President Lyndon B. Johnson used Memorial Day to make a significant speech about civil rights. Johnson spoke as the grandson of a Confederate soldier and responded to Martin Luther King's *Letter from a Birmingham Jail* by offering the black people of America a promissory note. 'Our nation found its soul in honour on these fields of Gettysburg a hundred years ago,' he said. To ask for patience now would be to court dishonour and impair that soul. 'In this hour', the vice-president went on, 'it is not our respective races which are at stake — it is our nation … The Negro says, "Now." Others say, "Never." The voice of responsible Americans — the voice of those who died here and the great man who spoke here — their voices say, "Together." There is no other way.'

Johnson does to a high standard what all American presidents do at Gettysburg, which is to sing a hymn to the Republic. All speakers, taking their cue from Lincoln's line about America being an experiment, reflect on the fragility of democracy, and they all say that, as long as the citizens remain committed to vigorous work, then a government of the people, by the people, and for the people could yet propel the nation towards greatness. That was, at least, the tradition. Then, on 22 October 2016, Donald Trump, at the time a candidate to be president of the United States, delivered his own Gettysburg Address and did none of this.

Instead, Trump gave a speech whose chief subject was not the American Republic but himself. It was both daring and egregious. After opening in the traditional fashion, by invoking and associating himself with Lincoln's battle against division ('hallowed ground … amazing place'), Mr Trump then proceeded to take the Address somewhere both unprecedented and unpresidential. Trump's scattergun hit Washington and Wall Street for rigging the game against 'everyday Americans'. He called his political opponent, Hillary Clinton, a criminal, claimed massive voter fraud without a shred of evidence, denounced unspecified corruption and fulminated against his enemies, home and abroad, real and perceived. He complained bitterly about named media outlets who he claimed were biased against him and which he alleged deliberately fabricated stories to discredit him. He labelled as liars the women who had made claims of sexual assault against him. It was a broadside against all the estates of the realm.

The worst of the speech is that Trump chose the site of the greatest-ever speech about the virtues of the Republic, to ask citizens not to trust the machinery of their own government. 'The rigging of the system', he said, 'is designed for one reason, to keep the corrupt establishment and special interests in power at your expense, at everybody's expense.' Throughout, Trump portrays himself as the only man who can fix the problem of the system that has been broken by the elite: 'I have no special interests but you, the American voter.' The speech divides government from people and proceeds to widen the gap with every barb. There is a sort of secular blasphemy in the nastiness of Trump's drearily inevitable conclusion: 'We will drain the swamp in Washington DC and replace it with a new government of, by and for the people. Believe me.' This is government of, by and for the populist.

Democracy in Crisis

Anti-politics is the most potent political idea of our time. The finest speeches in the popular tradition have always lent enchantment to politics, and it is salutary to be reminded of their magic. It would be naive, though, to ignore the worrying fact that the glamour has gone. We have mislaid the excitement of Cicero's battle with Mark Antony, the struggle of Thomas Jefferson to create the new republic, Abraham Lincoln's heroic attempt to salvage it, and John F. Kennedy's sense of renewal. There may be little trace left of Barack Obama once President Trump has tweeted his way through a term of office. The land made in broad daylight, in Alexis de Tocqueville's famous phrase about America, appears to be fading into the twilight. There is a dangerous claimant to the idea of popular power. An enticing new utopia is advertising its virtues. It is insurgent, protean and elusive and it goes by the misleading name of populism.

Democracy is in the midst of a crisis, but then it always is. As a system founded on the absorption and the negotiation of dissent, democracy invites sceptical voices. David Runciman, in *The Confidence Trap*, has pointed out that an excessive sensitivity to crisis, along with the ability to adapt their way out of the mess, are the twin characteristics of successful democracies. However, just because democracies have adapted their way out of messes before does not mean they will necessarily do so again. Just because politicians have hit upon the words in the past does not mean that they will do so in the future. The developed democracies face in strident chorus a threefold crisis of prosperity, of fear, and of confidence.

The crisis of prosperity is an anxiety about a future that the West appears to be losing. The fractious American and European politics of our time is in part explained by imminent economic decline. The West now has a potent rival in China. President Trump's electoral slogan, 'Make America Great Again', conceded the point. Larry Summers, the former US treasury secretary, has noted that, when America was growing at its fastest, living standards were doubling every thirty years. China has doubled its living standards three times in the last thirty years. But the threat is greater than the sheer numbers, and China is more than an economic rival. It is an affront to the very modus operandi of Western capitalism. Max Weber was the first serious thinker to note that capitalism thrived best under the conditions created by liberal democracy. The leaders of the Chinese Communist Party, by contrast, attribute their economic success to the tight control possible in a regime with no need to fret about the whims of the people. It seems to be working. The 2013 Pew Survey of Global Attitudes showed that 85 per cent of Chinese were 'very satisfied' with their country's direction. The number in the United States was just 31 per cent.

The growth of China threatens to break the monopoly that the democracies have enjoyed over capitalist prosperity. Just as this lesson was sinking in, developed capitalism suffered a self-inflicted crisis of its own. Financial hubris, which allowed the complexity of financial products to run ahead of the human capacity to regulate their effects, created a generational bust. For two decades in the USA and one in

Britain, real wages have stagnated. In the USA, median net worth for every group except the wealthiest 10 per cent fell between 1998 and 2013. Working-class Americans experienced a decline in their net worth over that time of a staggering 53 per cent. Meanwhile, the richest 10 per cent of people got 75 per cent richer. The republican bargain, in which hard work receives its merited reward, seemed to have been breached. It is not surprising that the idea took hold that capitalism and liberal democracy were loaded in favour of the privileged. It is not surprising that only one in four voters in the bottom two social classes in Britain believe democracy addresses their concerns well.

The crisis of shared prosperity has created a climate of cynicism. At the same time, an even more basic threat has thrown the efficacy of liberal democracies into question. There is no more important task that the state takes on in the name of the people than to ensure safety. The apparent incapacity of liberal democracies in the face of external threat is creating a serious crisis of fear. The experience of the wars in Afghanistan and Iraq was intensely damaging. Two invasions ostensibly designed to replace a tyrant with the will of the people collapsed into military disaster. The Left now regards the Iraq invasion as proof that democracy is a code for American imperialism. The Right concluded that even dictatorial stability is preferable to the chaos of change.

The struggle to conclude a successful military adventure in the name of the people was one more apparent indication that the writ of the West would no longer run. The institutions created out of the ruins of the Second World War – the United Nations, the European Union and the Bretton Woods financial institutions, the World Bank and the International Monetary Fund – appear bereft of power and irrelevant to the crises engulfing the world. Successive problems, in Ukraine and in Syria, appear to have passed power from the hands of democrats to eager tyrants. Russia and China are devising their own rules for the world diplomatic order.

Most potent of all, people in the liberal democracies have been subject to the fear of terror. In *The Secret Agent* Joseph Conrad described the invisible but palpable fear that governs a society under the threat of terrorist attack. The threat is all the more potent for being essentially invisible. The prospect of terrorism comes from no state, although states may turn a blind eye to its perpetrators or even sponsor them. It is a threat that can be activated by radicalised zealots, many of whom are reared in the comfort of free liberal democracies. Although one of the virtues of these democracies is that they tend not to rush towards a threat by negating the liberties that make them targets in the first place, there are always two temptations, to which some of their number may be yielding. The first is to blame a set of outsiders, usually these days the whole community of Muslims. The second is to repudiate some of the freedoms of the open society in the quest for a gilded cage of better security.

The crises of prosperity and fear make common cause to produce a crisis of confidence. After a century of progress, democracy appears to be in retreat. The fledgling democracies are struggling. Since the introduction of democracy in 1994, South Africa has been ruled by one party, the African National Congress, which has become progressively more self-serving. Turkey, which once seemed to combine moderate Islam with prosperity and democracy, is lapsing into corruption and autocracy under a leader, Recep Tayyip Erdoğan, who has begun to tear up the secular liberalism on which his nation's constitution was founded. In Bangladesh, Thailand and Cambodia, opposition parties have boycotted recent elections or refused to accept their results.

In some democracies disenchantment threatens to tip into authoritarian rule. In Hungary Viktor Orbán openly declares that national needs trump liberal values such as freedom. In France, Marine Le Pen and her nativist Front National denounce a political establishment that she blames for betraying the white people of France. Similar tunes are played by the Danish People's Party, the Swedish Democrats, the People's Party of Switzerland and the notoriously Islamophobic Geert Wilders in Holland. In Poland, the Law and Justice Party stands accused of trampling on the country's constitution to establish an 'illiberal democracy' of its own. But the most conspicuous setback for democracy has taken place in Russia. When the Berlin Wall fell in 1989 there were high hopes for a democratic order in the old Soviet Union, but these hopes faded in 1999 when Vladimir Putin replaced Boris Yeltsin. Putin, a former KGB operative, has since been both prime minister and president twice. He has muzzled the press, imprisoned opponents and presided over the murder of radical journalists, even as the display of democracy has been preserved.

The crisis of confidence is fuelled by impatience. Democracy has everywhere been a long time taking root, and it is unreasonable to expect that the transition will be either quick or smooth. The failure of Egypt to emerge as a functioning democracy when Hosni Mubarak's government fell to popular protest in 2011 was a setback to the hope that democracy might spread across the Middle East. Despair set in when the ensuing elections were won by Muhammad Morsi's Muslim Brotherhood Morsi promptly granted himself almost unlimited powers and created an upper house with a permanent Islamic majority. In July 2013 the army stepped in, Egypt's first democratically elected president was arrested and leading members of the Brotherhood imprisoned.

Syria and Libya too have seen incipient democratic revolutions run into the sand. Viewed in the right light, the Arab Spring that began in Tunisia in December 2010 was a series of popular uprisings of oppressed people desirous of the same liberties they witnessed in the developed world. That was certainly the hope and the initial interpretation. Yet it was naive to suppose that democracy was there ready to take wing, like the butterfly in the chrysalis. By the same token, to pretend that no impulse for popular sovereignty was part of the uprising in the first place is simply untrue. The demand for recognition was there; it has just not been met.

Quite remarkably, given their manifold advantage over other forms of government, the established democracies are losing confidence in their own goodness. Astonishingly, the 2011 World Values Survey found that 34 per cent of Americans approved of 'having a strong leader who doesn't have to bother with Congress or elections'. They might have been more careful what they wished for. A third of voters are at least prepared to say they would like to drop the inconvenient panoply of democracy. The young have been steeped in complacency. When Americans born before the Second World War were asked to say how essential it was to live in a democracy, on a decimal scale, 72 per cent rated it as maximally important. Only 30 per cent of the millennial generation did the same.

The same spectre stalks Britain. Sixty-four per cent of British people recently told YouGov they thought conventional politics was failing and 38 per cent had at least some sympathy with the statement that 'Democracy isn't always the best way to run a country'. Against this sentiment, we need to retort, without hesitation, that it most certainly is. The noble arguments of Cicero, Jefferson, Lincoln, Kennedy and Obama are not just random fancies. They are making the case for a system of government that is emphatically superior to other forms. If we are ever hapless enough to be cursed with any of the alternatives we will learn to regret our complacency.

The Populist Utopia

When people cease to believe in democratic politics they will not find it replaced with better politics. They will find it replaced by populism which, rather than representing the power of the people, arrogates power in their name. Populism is utopia's dark shadow.

The term *populist* derives from the 1890s, when the Populist movement in America set the rural Democrats against the more urban Republicans. The already elastic term then stretched further, across political movements of the fascist Right and the communist Left in Europe, the hearings of Senator McCarthy's House UnAmerican Activities Committee and the Peronistas in Argentina. Contemporary movements that include Syriza in Greece, Podemos in Spain, the less scrupulous advocates of departure from the European Union and those backing the election of President Trump in late 2016 have a range of natures. They are connected by their claim to be the envoys of the people in adopting the use of the term *populist*. This is the fraud that utopia can smuggle in along with its promise. It is crucial to comprehend the populist utopia the better to counteract it.

The populist utopia has no place for politics. In William Morris's *News from Nowhere* the House of Commons has been transformed into a storehouse for manure. The literary utopia erases all conflicts, which means that politics, the arbitration system, is redundant. In utopia, all desires have been satisfied and all the virtues miraculously consort in infinite combination in a land of no scarcity and abundant happiness. Individual rights can be revoked as unnecessary. The utopian takes all the complex questions of politics and promises, as if by magic, that they can be solved.

The idea that all good things can be had at once is a fantasy. The pursuit of a society that can satisfy everyone is a fool's errand. Robert Nozick put this point colourfully in *Anarchy, State, and Utopia* when he suggested that no single society can be imagined in which Hugh Hefner, the Buddha and Ludwig Wittgenstein would all be equally happy. The clever statesman is always trying to build a coalition across ideological lines. Cicero is seeking to win the approval of the Senate. Jefferson needs to heal the nation after a bruising election. Lincoln wants the country to unite after civil strife. Kennedy summons the citizen spirit of the American people. Obama makes a direct appeal to people who did not support him. All of them are speaking to the best in the circumstances, not to some absolute best.

The populist pretends that politics is easy. The only reason that the obvious solutions have not been arrived at is that the prevailing elite is venally self-regarding. This is why the defining trait of the populist is an anti-political division of the nation into rival tribes; the elite cast against the people. The only factor that unites populist movements of the nativist right and the socialist left is hostility to the governing elite. The 2016 campaign for Britain to leave the European Union was populated by advocates, some of them, bizarrely, government ministers, who agreed on nothing except hostility to views they caricatured as those of the establishment. The American historian Richard Hofstadter called populism 'the paranoid style of politics' because it is always based on a supposed betrayal. If only the elite weren't in it for themselves, the people would have been served.

In a notable speech in October 2016 Donald Trump hit all the discordant populist notes. 'This', he said portentously, 'is a crossroads in the history of our civilisation that will determine whether or not We The People reclaim control over our government.' There has rarely been a clearer exposition of the paranoid style than this. All those warnings about the fragility of democracy that were aired at Gettysburg sounded prophetic, and so did the alarms about the demagogue when Trump said: 'this election will determine whether we are a free nation, or whether we have only the illusion of Democracy but are in fact controlled by a small handful of global special interests rigging the system. This is not just conspiracy but reality, and you and I know it.'

The agents of this treachery, in the mind of the paranoid populist, are usually the media, and so it was in this case. 'The most powerful weapon deployed by the Clintons is the corporate media' – which, he went on to say, is now part of the conspiracy. The suspicion of the free press that is common to all populists is exactly the paranoia that Plato exhibits when he banishes the poets from his utopia in *The Republic.* We hear this argument in the social media echo-chamber today. According to this critique, the ideological prejudice of the media lackeys, who are themselves puppets of unscrupulous proprietors, enters unfiltered into the empty heads of the people. The minds of the people are so many *tabula rasa* on which the fiendish thoughts of the elite speaker will be imprinted. Conspiracy theories are always based on a credulous people and the populist is a full-bore conspiracist. 'This is a conspiracy against you, the American people,' said Trump. Utopia has always been just around the corner if only the corrupt elite had cared to venture there. 'We will rise above' said the candidate Trump, 'the lies, the smears, and the ludicrous slanders from ludicrous reporters.'

This is why the utopian's account is so fatuously inadequate about how change will come about. In More's *Utopia* a traveller, a speaker of nonsense, finds the perfect society in full working order in the ocean. The title of H. G. Wells's utopia accurately captures the lack of seriousness of the genre: *When the Sleeper Wakes.* These books are nothing more than grown-up fairytales. In the place where an account of change should be, the utopian populist substitutes the supreme leader. The paradox of populism is that it has a rhetoric of a movement but the practice of a cult. Camus once said that democracy is the system for people who know that they don't know everything. The populist utopian has all the answers. The omniscient figures are, variously, the priests, the philosophers, the intellectuals, the scientists, the process of history or the party. Plato believed in the rule of the sages, the Stoics in the power of reason, the seventeenth-century rationalists in metaphysical insight and the eighteenth-century empiricists in science.

The populist in government has the same status. No sooner has he ejected the hated elite than the populist's entourage become the elite themselves. He glosses the shift by posing as the tribune of the people. No need for a manifesto: he simply intuits the general will.

Populism is a movement with no ideological content beyond its resentment of an elite. It therefore requires a charismatic leader – lately a Trump, a Chávez, an Erdoğan – to glue it together. The movement gathers around the leader as if around a maypole. Its name proclaims allegiance to the people, but in fact populism requires the people to swear allegiance to the leader. The bargain rests on the populist knowing everything, but, of course, the truth is that he knows almost nothing. The populist has a utopian account of political change, which is to say no account at all.

It is no accident that populists such as Hugo Chávez in Venezuela and Alexis Tsiprias in Greece have proved to be so hopeless in office. The failure is baked into their arrogance about how easy it will be. President Trump believes that politics is usefully analogous to his dreary and ghostwritten business manual *The Art of the Deal*. This is not an analogy; it is a fantasy. The populist, devoid of politics, impatient with gathering allies, is bound to fail the test of administrative competence. Gratifyingly for him, the populist can invoke an easy escape clause. He can write off his failure as the conspiracy of the elite class which gave him his energy in the first place. The fact that he can offer no evidence for this absurd proposition only goes to show how clever a conspiracy it really is. Truth is always a casualty of populism.

It is not, alas, the only casualty. The foundation myth of populism – that the true way has been corrupted – means that the populist has to find a scapegoat. In the utopian literature, the leader is constantly marching backwards into battle. The safest refuge from the corrupt present is the blessed past. The promise to turn back the clock is a recurrent motif in utopia. In the Garden of Eden, in Hesiod's golden age before the decline, the bliss in Atlantis or Virgil's Kingdom of Saturn, in which all things are good, utopia is sadly discovered to be a paradise lost. The populist has nothing interesting to say about the future. He sets himself against progress and so is projected headlong into the past. Populism is a promise to return to popular wisdom before it was corroded by the Enemy.

This is not 'the people' as it is invoked by Lincoln. It is a *Gemeinschaft*, the binding of a community against outsiders, in a return to a bygone golden age. The outsiders in question are, in every instance of populism, the elite, but they are also often the immigrant.

These days, specifically, the Muslim or the Jew, but also sometimes the non-national. The words of Jefferson, Lincoln, Kennedy and Obama are all designed to bind a nation together. Populist politics, by contrast, needs to construct internal enemies as detached from the people. President Trump has proposed the deportation of undocumented immigrants and wants a wall to keep out the Mexicans. In Holland Geert Wilders wants to repeal hate-speech legislation. In Poland, Jarosław Kaczyński sought to make the use of the term 'Polish death camps' illegal.

As the incarnation of truth, the populist is a stranger to the doubts and humility that find expression in the speeches in this chapter. His utopia has none of the pluralism of a liberal democracy. The truth is no longer the upshot of open exchanges among free people; facts are what the populist leader says they are. Karl Popper has cited the Funeral Oration of Pericles as the moment that men began to glimpse the possibilities of an open society. The populist dismisses all that discussion as a waste of time and energy. Better to get things done with his prowess at embodying the popular will.

To live in utopia is to be amidst perfection already achieved. Nothing develops and nobody can change their mind. The populist stands at the top of this chain of certainty, a position, as William Blake said, 'like standing water, and breeds reptiles of the mind'. Disenchantment is inevitable, and when it sets in it can be vicious. Zamyatin's *We*, Huxley's *Brave New World* and Orwell's *Nineteen Eighty-Four* are images of how fatally the vigorous energy can turn to vice. It is never long before the leader tires of the constraints that are built into the constitutional apparatus. It was, after all, the paraphernalia of politics that he believes he was chosen to change. The tiresome mechanisms that we see Jefferson applauding are merely impediments to the populist. He is therefore bound to attack the free press, minority rights and judicial oversight as institutions that are seeking to defy the will of the people.

The era of populism sets the political leaders against their own constitutions. The purpose of political arrangements, most evidently the American constitution, is to curtail power. Politics is the wisest solution to the fact that men cannot always be trusted. It is founded on realism about fallen humans rather than utopian optimism. The balance between elements of the constitution, which Cicero set out and which were borrowed for the drafting of America's, are designed to hold populist power in check.

Most of the time the constitution holds. Silvio Berlusconi in Italy and the Kaczyńskis in Poland have tried largely in vain to undermine other sources of power. It is probable that President Trump will be frustrated by the absence of executive power that, following the liberal principles of Locke and Montesquieu, was deliberately built into his office. Yet we cannot always be so sanguine. Orbán in Hungary, Chávez in Venezuela and Erdoğan in Turkey have rewritten their constitutions to erase the inheritance from liberal democracy. Since the failed coup against Erdoğan in 2016, broadcasters, newspapers and magazines have been shut down and journalists detained. The public realm is now severely censored. In Russia, Vladimir Putin has done as he pleases regardless of constitutional propriety. Institutions that demand neutrality, such as judicial appointments, have been made partisan. The writ of law has been invaded by ideological correctness. The media has been silenced. It is dangerous, and sometimes fatal, for Russian journalists to pry too closely into sensitive subjects such as corruption and organised crime.

Populism begins with recriminations about the governing elite and, to use Donald Trump's extraordinary allegation, their 'criminal enterprise'. It ends with recriminations about the constitution. All the while it claims to have special knowledge of the will of the people. It is a fraud from start to finish. Plato hated democracy because he thought it led to populist rulers. There is a risk, if we do not find the words to advertise the virtues of conventional politics, that Plato's anguished prediction will be proved right. The task for the responsible democrat is therefore to describe what has gone awry and find words for a better future, like the wonderful writing in Jefferson's 1801 Inaugural Address and the compressed poetic expression of Lincoln's address at Gettysburg. The solution to disenchanted politics cannot be populism. It has to be better, more enchanted politics.

The Principle of Hope

Enchantment in politics does not mean a sweet lyric coating applied to toxic words. The case for popular power has to be rooted in the capacity of liberal democracies to respond to the three concurrent crises of prosperity, fear and confidence.

The first emotion that needs to be summoned is defiance. Democracy is the great philosophical success story of modern times. There were no democracies anywhere in 1799. Throughout the nineteenth century more than a third of the world's population lived in countries ruled by imperial powers and almost everyone else lived in countries governed by despots, not many of them enlightened. The first wave of democracy was crushed, in the midst of economic failure, by the malignant populists of the 1930s. The second half of the twentieth century saw the great flourishing. Empires, notably the vast terrain of the Soviet Union, ran out of time. The share of the world's population that lived under democracy grew quickly. In 1989 41 per cent of the nations on earth were *soi-disant* democracies. In 2015 it was 64 per cent. Now more than every second person lives in a democracy.

The reason for this is that politics can offer valid answers to the crises of prosperity, fear and confidence. We will see in chapters to come that the liberal democracies have a vastly superior performance in generating prosperity to any of their rivals. We shall see that democracies are very much the safest regimes in which to live. Voltaire said that heaven has given us two things – hope and sleep – to make up for the many miseries of life. We sleep more soundly in our beds if we know that our politics will keep us safe. Liberal democracies rely on fine articulations of the principle of hope, and we must rediscover our confidence in and our patience with the idea that politics will gradually improve the condition of the people. The short cut signalled by the populist is an illusion.

Liberal democracy is a series of failures, each one slightly better than the last. It can be hard to make that sound as dramatic as the populist's utopian insistence that we can make it to a perfect island in the ocean in a single leap. If the passion appears to be spent, if the extraordinary hopes that were once embodied in democratic politics now seem to be fraying, this is the moment to recall that liberal democracy was born as an insurgent idea. It was the utopia of its day, and the case in its favour, expressed in some of the finest words ever spoken, embodied the hope that tomorrow would exceed today.

We need to make the case again that Cicero inaugurates, for liberty and justice in the republic as a superior state to the rule of the demagogue. We need the uplifting words of Thomas Jefferson to maintain that the beauty of politics is its capacity to restrain men from injuring one another and that this is the only way to protect the rights of minorities. We need the retort to the populist that Abraham Lincoln supplies. There is no pithier expression of a fine idea in the archive of speech than Lincoln's imperishable formula of government of the people, for the people and by the people. We need to take heed of John F. Kennedy's warning that good government is done *with* the people rather than *to* the people. And we have Barack Obama's reminder, from not so long ago, that when hope connects to power it is still possible to be hopeful about America, and, by extension, about democracies the world over. Cicero, Jefferson, Lincoln, Kennedy, Obama – all, in their way, speak on behalf of representing the popular will through democratic institutions. They describe a utopia that is the best possible in the circumstances and they do so in words that yield to none in clarity, lucidity or beauty.

The utopia of the people that is described in democratic rhetoric is not a state of final perfection. It is an endless process rather than a truth out of Pandora's box. It is, as Richard Rorty writes in *Contingency, Irony and Solidarity*, 'the hope that life will eventually be freer, less cruel, more leisured, richer in goods and experiences, not just for our descendants but for everyone's descendants'. The conversation will never end, as the solution to one problem begets another. The purpose of democratic government is forever to adjudicate between rival expressions of reasonable desire. The calls for unity made by Jefferson, Lincoln, Kennedy and Obama are far more than political platitudes. They are the deepest wisdom of political thought.

These speeches communicate a spirit too. They are not dry political theories. They are words written to cajole, persuade and inspire, words that articulate the principle of hope which was described by Ernst Bloch in the book of that name as follows: 'Hope, superior to

fear, is neither passive like the latter, nor locked into nothingness.'
Populism, which trades on – relies upon – fear, is locked into nothingness. Camus's brilliant observation bears repeating. The democrat
is the one who knows he does not know everything. Only the populist
utopian thinks he has all the answers. He promises an odyssey to
utopia but he is going nowhere.

> *Being set on the idea*
> *Of getting to Atlantis,*
> *You have discovered of course*
> *Only the Ship of Fools is*
> *Making the voyage this year.*

Auden is right. We must not embark on the ship of fools.

2

WAR:
THROUGH POLITICS
PEACE WILL PREVAIL

So Little Masonry

In its final version it is one of the imperishable rhetorical classics, made all the more memorable for its echo of Shakespeare's line from *Henry V*: 'We few, we happy few, we band of brothers'. But it has a less distinguished history. In a by-election campaign in Oldham in 1899 the 24-year-old Liberal candidate, who was fighting the first political campaign of his career, had said, in all gravity: 'Never before were there so many people in England, and never before have they had so much to eat.' Nine years later the colonial under-secretary gave a speech on a projected irrigation scheme in Africa in which he said: 'Nowhere else in the world could so enormous a mass of water be held up by so little masonry.'

The name of the writer and speaker of these words in Oldham and in Africa was Winston Churchill, and neither of these were his finest hour. But then, suddenly, in August 1940, in a panegyric to the Battle of Britain fighter pilots who truly had stood between the nation and the barbarians, Churchill declared: 'Never in the field of human conflict was so much owed, by so many, to so few.' In its ultimate, eternal permutation it has a classic simplicity and an effortless flow that seem inevitable. Even at this distance in time it is still moving to say it out loud. For Churchill, the moment finally ascended to the height of the words and the effect is mesmeric.

Rhetoric cannot work when the phrases are too lavish for their topic. But there is no more important subject for the democratic politician than the coming or the conduct of war. The preservation of order is the first responsibility of the state, and so to launch a nation into war is the gravest thing a leader will ever do. There is no greater burden of office and, correspondingly, in the elevated words of Pericles, David Lloyd George, Woodrow Wilson, Winston Churchill and Ronald Reagan we hear some of the finest rhetoric in the canon. When the threat is as grave as war, the words must measure up to the task.

This is where the tradition of rhetoric began – with a eulogy to the lost sons of Athens. In the Funeral Oration, Pericles tried to console the bereaved with the argument that voluntary sacrifice in battle is the highest form of civic duty. We have seen that Lincoln used the same argument at Gettysburg in 1863 in his eulogy to those slain in the American Civil War: 'from these honoured dead we take increased devotion to that cause for which they gave the last full measure of devotion'.

We will see too that in a democracy war needs a purpose beyond the cessation of hostility. The speeches in this chapter are also about the purpose to which peace must be turned. Pericles offers a eulogy to democracy as much as to the departed. Lloyd George defines the land fit for heroes. Wilson imagines a global alliance of democratic nations. Churchill offers blood, sweat, toil and tears to see off the tyrant and Reagan stands to speak on the right side of the Berlin Wall which marks off the free world. In all instances, the war is being fought for a noble purpose, not merely to keep the enemy at bay, but to deepen the commitment to a free nation.

The original *casus belli* – that the nation was in peril – is never enough. The war has to be fought for better politics. The social legislation of the Labour Attlee government between 1945 and 1951 acquired its moral force from the aftermath of war. The conflict itself and its immediately succeeding years should be seen as a single event. The rhetorical work for what comes later begins during the war itself. War has always been, strangely enough, one of the ways in which democracies wield the resources to progress. Rhetoric that defends the idea of the people is the way that democracies heal their internal rifts. Rhetoric that commends the idea of the people against predators is the democratic response to threat. At a moment of peril the speech, the means by which the leader inspires the nation to withstand assault and live to fight another day, is vital. There is no other time when so much rests on so few words.

PERICLES

Funeral Oration

Athens
Winter, *c.*431 BC

Pericles (494–429 BC) stands at the front, if not necessarily at the top, of the history of rhetoric. Thucydides, who bequeaths us our knowledge of Pericles, rated him the finest speaker of his time, one of the few men in whose hands democracy, an otherwise dangerous creed, was safe. The Funeral Oration is the source of Pericles' reputation as, in a phrase from Thucydides, 'the first man among the Athenians'.

A general, an orator and a patron of the arts, Pericles was the guiding spirit of Athens from *c.*460 to 429 BC, the period in which the city was rebuilt after the destruction of war with Persia. The Parthenon was built on the Acropolis and Athens was established as the artistic and cultural centre of the Hellenic world. Pericles was a reformer. His introduction of payment for public service permitted many more members of the Athenian *demos* to take part in public affairs. But the judgement of Thucydides describes the paradox of Pericles as a democrat. Pericles is not the kind of democrat who would be so defined according to a modern sensibility. His very pre-eminence has a monarchical aspect in tension with the spirit of democratic politics. So does his support for Athenian imperialism and his proposal that citizenship should be limited only to those who could show that both parents had been citizens. We also need to be careful not to make a fetish of the word *democracy*. Citizenship in ancient Greece was denied to women and slaves, and not all free men had a vote in the assembly. When Pericles invokes the idea of the people he does not mean to include them all, or even half of them.

It is to Thucydides that we owe the text of the Funeral Oration. It is all but certain that this extract from the *History of the Peloponnesian War* differs from the words Pericles actually spoke. Quite how much the two diverge we cannot know, despite healthy scholarly disputes about the issue. It is likely that Thucydides was a witness to the speech, but he casts doubt on his own fidelity to the original when he writes: 'I have found it difficult to remember the precise words used in the speeches which I listened to myself ... so my method has been, while keeping as closely as possible to the general sense of the words that were actually used, to make the speakers say what, in my opinion, was called for by each situation.' What we have is Thucydides remembering, no doubt improvising, perhaps improving, Pericles.

We can be more certain that the oration was given at the end of the first year of the Peloponnesian War (*c.*431 BC) to honour the fallen, as part of the annual public funeral for the state's war dead. Rather like Donald Trump today, Thucydides makes much of the size of the audience, perhaps to stress the vital importance of the occasion. It is also recorded that Pericles delivered the speech on a rostrum built high, so that his declamation could carry. It was to be his final testament as an orator: not long after the Funeral Oration a plague swept the city and took Pericles with it. His words, though, have lived on, and as we have seen, their echoes ring in the speeches of American presidents in a new republic more than two millennia later.

> *Most of those who have spoken here before me have commended the lawgiver who added this oration to our other funeral customs. It seemed to them a worthy thing that such an honour should be given at their burial to the dead who have fallen on the field of battle. But I should have preferred that, when men's deeds have been brave, they should be honoured in deed only, and with such an honour as this public funeral, which you are now witnessing. Then the reputation of many would not have been imperilled on the eloquence or want of eloquence of one, and their virtues believed or not as he spoke well or ill. For it is difficult to say neither too little nor too much; and even moderation is apt not to give the impression of truthfulness. The friend of the dead who knows the facts is likely to think that the words of the speaker fall short of his knowledge*

> *and of his wishes; another who is not so well informed, when he hears of anything that surpasses his own powers, will be envious and will suspect exaggeration. Mankind are tolerant of the praises of others so long as each hearer thinks that he can do as well or nearly as well himself, but, when the speaker rises above him, jealousy is aroused and he begins to be incredulous. However, since our ancestors have set the seal of their approval upon the practice, I must obey, and to the utmost of my power shall endeavour to satisfy the wishes and beliefs of all who hear me.*

Pericles begins with a lament about the need for rhetoric. It would be preferable, he says, convincing nobody, if the dead could be honoured without the requirement for high-sounding testimony. It would, of course, be better if the dead could speak for themselves. In their absence Pericles, will do his best to rise to the occasion which is imperilled, he says, by the reliance on a single orator.

The funeral oration had become a familiar ritual in Greece by the late fifth century. The remains of the dead were left out for three days in a tent where offerings could be made. A funeral procession followed, with ten cypress coffins carrying the remains, one for each of the nine Athenian tribes and one for the remains of the unidentified. Any citizen was free to join the procession. A public sepulchre in the city's most beautiful suburb was reserved for those who fell in war. At the graveside, an orator, described by Thucydides as 'of approved wisdom and eminent reputation', delivered the eulogy.

The ritual created a civic unity which it was the task of the orator to express. A speech is always a ritual that enacts a moment, even before a word is spoken. In an era in which reports from the battlefield were distant and unreliable, the funeral oration created a single experience of the war for the assembled citizens. It became the sanctioned memory of the war. Pericles is writing history up on the rostrum even before Thucydides adds his second draft.

He does so with a form that has grown familiar. This is a variation on the theme of 'Words cannot express ...' But words have to express. That's all the orator is there for. Thus, Pericles is to be taken seriously but not literally. Like Mark Antony in *Julius Caesar*, he is feigning an inability to find words that have the weight to capture the moment. It's a conceit, of course. If Pericles really thought he couldn't meet the moment he wouldn't — he shouldn't — have taken the gig. But he did; he couldn't resist.

I will speak first of our ancestors, for it is right and seemly that now, when we are lamenting the dead, a tribute should be paid to their memory. There has never been a time when they did not inhabit this land, which by their valour they will have handed down from generation to generation, and we have received from them a free state. But if they were worthy of praise, still more were our fathers, who added to their inheritance, and after many a struggle transmitted to us their sons this great empire. And we ourselves assembled here today, who are still most of us in the vigour of life, have carried the work of improvement further, and have richly endowed our city with all things, so that she is sufficient for herself both in peace and war. Of the military exploits by which our various possessions were acquired, or of the energy with which we or our fathers drove back the tide of war, Hellenic or barbarian, I will not speak; for the tale would be long and is familiar to you. But before I praise the dead, I should like to point out by what principles of action we rose to power, and under what institutions and through what manner of life our empire became great. For I conceive that such thoughts are not unsuited to the occasion, and that this numerous assembly of citizens and strangers may profitably listen to them.

Having merely gestured towards the habitual routine of a funeral oration, Pericles then affronts convention. He does pay perfunctory tribute to the ancestral heritage of contemporary Athenians and to the acquisition of empire, but then he changes course. Military valour, the usual subject of such an occasion, he dismisses as a theme too familiar to dwell upon. There is more than a little political calculation in this manoeuvre. The war is not going well. The early results are disappointing, and Pericles is using the speech to see off his enemies.

The privilege of speaking uninterrupted at the commemoration of the war dead is an opportunity too good for a politician of his stature to miss. Pericles had promised that the war would bring glory, and glory so far had been conspicuously absent. This explains why he dares instead to shift the focus to the form of government that the city enjoys.

This is a signal moment. Rhetoric and democracy fuse in this argument. The fact that Pericles needs an argument at all is a much more critical point than it might on first hearing sound. The priest, the king, the tyrant, simply act. In a democracy, the judgement of words replaces the asserted wisdom of the tyrannical fiat. Democracy anoints the argument rather than the individual. For this reason, the public speech is essential to democracy. It is also the principal innovation of the new form of politics. Pericles insists that he is going to talk about Athens itself, reinterpreting the deaths of the citizens for the glory of its name. He is going to establish the *polis* as so splendid that death in war is a glorious, almost a desirable, contribution to the national story.

> *Our form of government does not enter into rivalry with the institutions of others. Our government does not copy our neighbours', but is an example to them. It is true that we are called a democracy, for the administration is in the hands of the many and not of the few. But while there exists equal justice to all and alike in their private disputes, the claim of excellence is also recognised; and when a citizen is in any way distinguished, he is preferred to the public service, not as a matter of privilege, but as the reward of merit. Neither is poverty an obstacle, but a man may benefit his country whatever the obscurity of his condition. There is no exclusiveness in our public life, and in our private business we are not suspicious of one another, nor angry with our neighbour if he does what he likes; we do not put on sour looks at him which, though harmless, are not pleasant. While we are thus unconstrained in our private business, a spirit of reverence pervades our public acts; we are prevented from doing wrong by respect for the authorities and for the laws, having a particular regard to those which are ordained for the protection of the injured as well as those unwritten laws which bring upon the transgressor of them the reprobation of the general sentiment.*

This speech contains democratic multitudes. Here is the first usage of the cliché that some might have thought a New Labour coinage: the many not the few. Here is 'equal justice to all', which later becomes the subject of a speech by Thomas Jefferson. Here is equality before the law, modern meritocracy, the private liberty of the citizen, respect for the public interest, protection of the vulnerable, the dignity of the institutions of state, and here is the court of public opinion. In this passage Pericles is inventing the democratic idiom, fashioning the phrases that come to define government by the people.

This is the first great address in praise of the idea of the citizen body. It is for this collection of democratic virtues, says Pericles in an audacious move, that the dead lived and died. The tombs of the dead metaphorically fade from view as the speech shifts from the particular to the general, from people to an idea.

Only an advocate of the idea of democracy would license such a switch, which explains why the Funeral Oration fell for many an age out of favour until its ideas came back into vogue. Democracy disappeared with the demise of the classical world until it was revived in the nineteenth century. Pericles thus reads better today than he did during most of later history. We bring to his words our anachronistic desire to defend our own practice, and find it described with startling contemporary exactitude in this passage. The survival of the Funeral Oration, and the loss of most of Athenian rhetoric, is not really, as Thucydides tries to persuade us, owed to the intrinsically finer quality of what Pericles says, or the way he says it. Its longevity, and its appeal today, is owed more to the fact that Pericles sounds rather like Thomas Jefferson, who in turn sounds somewhat like us. This section therefore heralds the moment when a tradition is founded.

> To sum up: I say that Athens is the school of Hellas, and that the individual Athenian in his own person seems to have the power of adapting himself to the most varied forms of action with the utmost versatility and grace. This is no passing and idle word, but truth and fact; and the assertion is verified by the position to which these qualities have raised the state. For in the hour of trial Athens alone among her contemporaries is superior to the report of her. No

enemy who comes against her is indignant at the reverses which he sustains at the hands of such a city; no subject complains that his masters are unworthy of him. And we shall assuredly not be without witnesses; there are mighty monuments of our power which will make us the wonder of this and of succeeding ages; we shall not need the praises of Homer or of any other panegyrist whose poetry may please for the moment, although his representation of the facts will not bear the light of day. For we have compelled every land and every sea to open a path for our valour, and have everywhere planted eternal memorials of our friendship and of our enmity. Such is the city for whose sake these men nobly fought and died; they could not bear the thought that she might be taken from them; and every one of us who survive should gladly toil on her behalf. I have dwelt upon the greatness of Athens because I want to show you that we are contending for a higher prize than those who enjoy none of these privileges, and to establish by manifest proof the merit of these men whom I am now commemorating. Their loftiest praise has been already spoken. For in magnifying the city I have magnified them, and men like them whose virtues made her glorious.

Pericles now declares that the democratic spirit that carries his praise also extends glory to the city in its foreign pursuits. There is, again, a highly contemporary resonance to this passage. In recent years it has been common to argue that the provinces of domestic and foreign policy have merged. Here Pericles does exactly that, claiming that the virtues at home in Athens equip the city for its greater good abroad. Under the pressure of war, he suggests, the ethics that Athens follows at home will sustain the glory of the city.

Pericles makes a major claim here about the superiority of democracy over rival forms of constitution. In one of the best-crafted phrases in the speech he says that only Athens is superior to the report of her. This intriguing phrase has the implication that democracies will, probably from envy, suffer unfair criticism from outside, from states that cannot believe that the advertised virtues of a democracy are real. He is also implying that democracy, by its very nature, will always be subject to critique from within, and there will be spells when the populace loses faith and is tempted by simpler solutions.

Pericles goes on to elucidate that democratic superiority will be measured by the kindness that a democratic state shows, both to its enemies and to its own subjects. Democracies hold themselves to higher standards of ethical behaviour than autocracies, and so they should. This point is later central to Tocqueville's *Democracy in America* – that some of the virtues of democracy are hidden in plain sight yet they prove their worth in the end. Pericles then dismisses the accounts of Homer as if he were swatting away disobliging reports in a hostile press. The test of democracy is time. Its superiority will become clear in the verdict in of the historians. Though there is no reason to suppose that Thucydides is speaking for himself here, it is important to bear in mind that this is his account of Pericles. It would be no great surprise if this were the moment the historian chose to turn up the volume.

The sacrifice which they collectively made was individually repaid to them; for they received again each one for himself a praise which grows not old, and the noblest of all tombs, I speak not of that in which their remains are laid, but of that in which their glory survives, and is proclaimed always and on every fitting occasion both in word and deed. For the whole earth is the tomb of famous men; not only are they commemorated by columns and inscriptions in their own country, but in foreign lands there dwells also an unwritten memorial of them, graven not on stone but in the hearts of men. Make them your examples, and, esteeming courage to be freedom and freedom to be happiness, do not weigh too nicely the perils of war ... Wherefore I do not now pity the parents of the dead who stand here; I would rather comfort them. You know that your dead have passed away amid manifold vicissitudes; and that they may be deemed fortunate who have gained their utmost honour, whether an honourable death like theirs, or an honourable sorrow like yours, and whose share of happiness has been so ordered that the term of their happiness is likewise the term of their life. I know how hard it is to make you feel this, when the good fortune of others will too often remind you of the gladness which once lightened your hearts. And sorrow is felt at the want of those blessings, not which a man never knew, but which were a part of his life before they were taken from him. Some of you are of an age at which they may hope to have other children, and they ought to bear their sorrow better; not only will the children who may hereafter be born make them forget their own lost ones, but the city will be doubly a gainer. She will not be left desolate, and she will be safer. For a man's counsel cannot have equal weight or worth, when he alone has no children to risk in the general danger. To those of you who have passed their prime, I say: 'Congratulate yourselves that you have been happy during the greater part of your days; remember that your life of sorrow will not last long, and be comforted by the glory of those who are gone. For the love of honour alone is ever young, and not riches, as some say, but honour is the delight of men when they are old and useless.

'The whole earth is the tomb of famous men.' Their memorial will be graven on the hearts of men rather than on stone. Pericles lays it on thick for the war dead, deploying the full scale of rhetorical flattery to disguise the fact that this is a truly brutal passage which, stripped of its eloquent veneer, more or less says: 'Try not to worry about your dead sons because you will be dead yourself soon.' This is the one moment in the speech when the greater glory of the city sounds a rather callous objective.

But Pericles is trying to inspire his listeners to summon their courage. That is why he goes as far as to say that there can be no greater demonstration of moral virtue, of *arete*, than willing death in battle. There is more than a hint of rhetorical duplicity here. Is it actually true, in fact, that the dead lost their lives for the glory of Athens? Does Pericles have privileged access to the thoughts of the valiant men as they went to their deaths? No, this is rhetorical projection. He is conjuring glory from demise, glory for the greater good of the city.

Speaking at a moment of crisis, Pericles is trying to head off the criticism that democracy stifles individual excellence. The usual way to do this would be to list the achievements of the war to date. It would be the first instance of a speech that will become a political staple – the 'a lot done, a lot still to do' speech. But Pericles has no achievements to offer to his audience. He therefore has to return to the higher principle for which valour has been spent, namely the love of honour. Athens was a society that held to a code of honour, and so

Pericles is saying that the men of Athens who died have nevertheless graduated with honours. The supreme standard of honour was martial valour, so those whose lives had been given in the service of the city deserved the renown that Pericles is here bestowing.

This is an awkward passage in which the gap between the requirement of a funeral oration and the political desire to heap laurels on the city opens to its widest. It is evident too how sensibilities have changed. Few would now venture to argue that not having children made someone care less about the future of the state. Indeed, when, in 2016, Andrea Leadsom implied just that of her rival for the Conservative Party leadership, Theresa May, Ms Leadsom was forced to resign from the process. It probably would not have rescued her, but she might have presented Pericles as a witness in her defence.

> *I have paid the required tribute, in obedience to the law, making use of such fitting words as I had. The tribute of deeds has been paid in part; for the dead have them in deeds, and it remains only that their children should be maintained at the public charge until they are grown up: this is the solid prize with which, as with a garland, Athens crowns her sons living and dead, after a struggle like theirs. For where the rewards of virtue are greatest, there the noblest citizens are enlisted in the service of the state. And now, when you have duly lamented, everyone his own dead, you may depart.*

Although it lay in cold storage for a long time during the wilderness years between the end of the classical era and nineteenth-century Europe, the Funeral Oration has been, since then, regarded as a classic, and Pericles has turned up in many guises. He was quoted in advertisements designed to boost morale during the First World War, and after the conflict his words appeared on war memorials. At Gettysburg, Lincoln begins, as Pericles does, with a reference to the city fathers. In the immediate aftermath of 9/11, Congressman Major Robert Owens declared: 'Defiant orations of Pericles must now rise out of the ashes.'

The state that Pericles describes has little in common with the faction-ridden, highly political atmosphere of Athens, but this is a eulogy and a little exaggeration is in order. That is not to say, however, that this is really a conventional funeral oration, because Pericles is doing the opposite of posting an obituary. He is defining an ideal state for the future. He has come not so much to bury the dead as to praise a living democracy. You can hear that in the opening to this passage: 'I have paid the required tribute'. He could hardly be more perfunctory. His enthusiasm only fires when he gets to the reason for the sacrifice. Real people died in the war, says Pericles, for the idea of the people in the abstract.

This is a gloriously expressed cold comfort, which is echoed, in its purpose, centuries later by David Lloyd George, Woodrow Wilson and Winston Churchill, all of whom make speeches seeking simultaneously to raise the morale of their audience and define the war for the higher cause of democracy. The Funeral Oration is an unusual, unexpected speech which is more a paean to politics than it is a panegyric to the war dead. The words of Pericles echo to us down the ages as we struggle to recall that this gift, the idea of democracy, is so precious an inheritance.

DAVID LLOYD GEORGE

The Great Pinnacle of Sacrifice

Queen's Hall, London
19 September 1914

The most famous Welshman to be born in Manchester, David Lloyd
George (1863–1945) was the unrivalled rhetorical genius of the first
years of twentieth-century British politics. His admirers, who were
many, called him the Welsh Wizard, and he was known as the Goat
to those, just as many, who did not trust him. In his years in office
Lloyd George was known as the Big Beast, and from the beginning
he was the self-styled Man from the Outside, a solicitor from
Porthmadog in Wales with no university education. This attitude
explains the sharp edges to his rhetoric and the alliances he struck up
with others whom he viewed as coming from without the established
fold.

Lloyd George was a contradictory man. He was, as A. J. P. Taylor
has written, the champion of the poor who fell in with the rich; the
scourge of Ireland who offered it the Free State. Some part of the
suspicion Lloyd George incurred was due to his oratorical gifts. The
famous address in Limehouse, east London, in defence of his tax-rais-
ing budget of 1909 was seen by opponents as an effort to stir up class
warfare. 'Limehousing' became a byword for rabble-rousing and
demagoguery.

David Lloyd George was brought up in a dissenting, Welsh-
speaking household in North Wales. For the first decade of his political career as a Liberal MP, he confined himself to Welsh issues, but
he later gained a reputation as a radical opponent of the Boer War.
His first Cabinet post was as president of the Board of Trade, in 1905.
After the Liberal landslide of 1906 – the victory, as George Dangerfield

famously said, from which the Liberals never recovered — Lloyd George served as chancellor of the exchequer. During these years he introduced reforms which, in retrospect, began the process of creating a national welfare state from the scattered voluntary provision of the time. With the start of war, he became, successively, Herbert Asquith's minister of munitions and minister of war, before the 1916 coup in which he took the top job himself. He remained prime minister until October 1922, when he and the rest of the coalition ministry were toppled by a backbench Conservative revolt, commemorated to this day in the collective name the Tory backbenchers give to themselves: the 1922 Committee.

In the speech that follows we see Lloyd George as chancellor of the exchequer charged with making the case that, on the brink of war, national honour demands that the country stand and fight. He did it so well that he talked himself into the role he had always coveted, as prime minister. His response was in striking contrast with Asquith's, who seemed too weak a leader to carry a nation through war. Asquith was never able to articulate the case for conscription with the poetic splendour that Lloyd George mustered in 1915 and 1916, and he never began to match the passion exhibited here.

I have come here this afternoon to talk to my fellow countrymen about this Great War and the part we ought to take in it. I feel my task is easier after we have been listening to the greatest battle-song in the world. There is no man in this room who has always regarded the prospects of engaging in a great war with greater reluctance, with greater repugnance, than I have done throughout the whole of my political life. There is no man, either inside or outside of this room, more convinced that we could not have avoided it without national dishonour. I am fully alive to the fact that whenever a nation has been engaged in any war she has always invoked the sacred name of honour. Many a crime has been committed in its name; there are some crimes being committed now. But, all the same, national honour is a reality, and any nation that disregards it is doomed.

Even after the stirring sound of 'Men of Harlech', which the audience had sung before he spoke, Lloyd George begins with a note that comes close to apology. Of all the people to make the case for war, he is in one sense the least likely. His early reputation as a politician had been forged in his opposition to the Boer War. He had only joined the war Cabinet after a great deal of anguished deliberation. When he did relent, he steered a middle way at first between those who had favoured intervention even before the demise of Belgium and those who opposed any intervention at all. He took a long time to acknowledge the threat of German aggression.

Not that you get any sense of doubt from this speech. Lloyd George commits himself to his case with characteristic gusto, using his previous scepticism to cast himself as the radical who came in from the cold. The case really needed the advocacy that Lloyd George offers. The standard picture of August 1914, with men rushing to join up, has been amended by more recent historical scholarship. Many men entertained the same doubts as Lloyd George. Here the zealous convert launches the task of persuading the reluctant that the cause is just.

Why is our honour as a country involved in this war? Because, in the first place, we are bound in an honourable obligation to defend the independence, the liberty, the integrity of a small neighbour that has lived peaceably, but she could not have compelled us, because she was weak. The man who declines to discharge his debt because his creditor is too poor to enforce it is a blackguard. We entered into this treaty, a solemn treaty, a full treaty, to defend Belgium and her integrity. Our signatures are attached to the document. Our signatures do not stand alone there. This was not the only country to defend the integrity of Belgium. Russia, France, Austria, and Prussia – they are all there. Why did they not perform the obligation? It is suggested that if we quote this treaty it is purely an excuse on our part. It is our low craft and cunning, just to cloak our jealousy of a superior civilisation we are attempting to destroy.

This is a very Welsh speech. Lloyd George took his rhetorical lessons from his uncle, a Welsh preacher, who had brought him up. Throughout his long career as a speaker, Lloyd George retained an evangelical, nonconformist air. The audience was made up of three thousand of the Welsh community in London, and Lloyd George was, at the time, in the thick of a battle to persuade Kitchener, the war secretary, to allow the creation of a specifically Welsh army corps. Repeated references to Wales assert the speaker's credentials by associating him with the nation, and the speech is thus constructed around the appeal to the honour of a small country, of which Wales is a resonant example.

This allows Lloyd George to hit his main motif, which is that the pike is about to consume the minnow. Wales, in effect, merges in the speech with Belgium, Serbia and the fraternity of small nations. Lloyd George's description of Belgium as 'peaceable, industrious, thrifty, hard-working, giving offence to no one' is a description of the virtues the Welsh audience would itself have claimed. Defence of the little nations was a regular refrain in Lloyd George's liberalism. The small nations must stand as one against this use of power. Britain gave an undertaking to Belgium to defend its honour, and that is the same, in effect, as our own honour, the honour of our own beloved small nation, Wales.

> That Treaty Bond was this: we called upon the belligerent Powers to respect that treaty. We called upon France; we called upon Germany ... It is now the interest of Prussia to break the treaty, and she has done it. Well, why? She avowed it with cynical contempt for every principle of justice. She says treaties only bind you when it is to your interest to keep them. 'What is a treaty?' says the German Chancellor. 'A scrap of paper.' Have you any five-pound notes about you? I am not calling for them. Have you any of those neat little Treasury pound notes? If you have, burn them; they are only 'scraps of paper'. What are they made of? Rags. What are they worth? The whole credit of the British Empire. 'Scraps of paper' ... Treaties are the currency of international statesmanship ... This doctrine of the scrap of paper ... that treaties only bind a nation as long as it is to its interest, goes to the root of public law. It is the straight road to barbarism and the

*whole machinery of civilisation will break down if this doctrine
wins in this war. We are fighting against barbarism. But there is
only one way of putting it right. If there are nations that say they
will only respect treaties when it is to their interest to do so, we
must make it to their interest to do so for the future.*

Two characteristics of Lloyd George mingle here in a brilliantly
minted passage. It is funny and it is devastatingly direct. The two
attributes create a sort of profundity. Lloyd George was influenced
by the music hall and was by no means averse to its tricks. There was
laughter in the Queen's Hall when Lloyd George asked the audience
if anyone had any money on them. A joke in a speech needs to pass
two tests. It must, of course, be funny but there is another requirement. The joke should be relevant and, like screenwriters concealing
a plot point with a gag, should contribute to the argument of the text.
Here the joke passes both tests. The laughter is genuine at the thought
that the chancellor might like to borrow a fiver, but the passage also
propounds an important metaphor.

Lloyd George came into this speech highly praised for his recent
action in stabilising the monetary system. The currency, an interna-
tional treaty; what are they but scraps of paper? The treaty is, says
Lloyd George, a promissory note of a nation's honour. France and
Prussia had both pledged to protect the integrity of Belgium. The
Prussians were now breaking the bond. See how much weight Lloyd
George places on the memorable phrase 'this doctrine of the scrap of
paper'.

He makes a profound point about the nature of the rule of law,
which is that it can only function if its subjects comply. Enforcement
of the law is costly and difficult and demands sacrifice. Germany is
violating this defining norm of compliance, and that justifies Lloyd
George's stringent verdict: this is barbarism and it has to be countered. Look how far he has travelled in this section. From a joke about
money, to the tokens of commerce, to the sacred obligation of honour-
ing a treaty, the breach of which is barbarism which has to be turned
back, even if the cost is war. By the conclusion, no one is left
laughing.

Belgium has been treated brutally, how brutally we shall not yet know. We know already too much. What has she done? Did she send an ultimatum to Germany? Did she challenge Germany? Was she preparing to make war on Germany? Had she ever inflicted any wrongs upon Germany which the Kaiser was bound to redress? She was one of the most unoffending little countries in Europe. She was peaceable, industrious, thrifty, hard-working, giving offence to no one ... What is their crime? Their crime was that they trusted to the word of a Prussian King. I don't know what the Kaiser hopes to achieve by this war. I have a shrewd idea of what he will get, but one thing is made certain, that no nation in future will ever commit that crime again. I am not going to enter into these tales. Many of them are untrue; war is a grim, ghastly business at best, and I am not going to say that all that has been said in the way of tales of outrage is true. I will go beyond that, and say that if you turn two millions of men forced, conscripted, and compelled and driven into the field, you will certainly get among them a certain number of men who will do things that the nation itself will be ashamed of. I am not depending on them. It is enough for me to have the story which the Germans themselves avow, admit, defend, proclaim. The burning and massacring, the shooting down of harmless people – why? Because, according to the Germans, they fired on German soldiers. What business had German soldiers there at all? Belgium was acting in pursuance of a most sacred right, the right to defend your own home.

In a war speech, home is not the only front. Lloyd George is determined to convey resolution to his adversary. There is no concession, no implicit negotiation here. Lloyd George's task of persuasion is the one that will confront Churchill, his friend and rival in rhetorical fireworks, twenty-six years later. For the moment, Lloyd George is the master. Contemporary accounts record the spell in which he held his audience bound. His voice was rich and resonant where Churchill's was reedy. The notion that Churchill had a stutter is a myth, but he certainly had a lisp, which meant that he struggled with sibilant sounds. Churchill, though, had one big advantage: his wartime speeches enjoy world renown, while Lloyd George's are largely lost to posterity. No one can outdo Churchill as a war speaker.

Lloyd George at his best stands second-best, but we have no record-ings of what he said. As Kenneth Morgan has put it: 'Churchill spoke to history; Lloyd George spoke only to his listeners.' The speech was covered in newspapers and distributed as a pamphlet. Far more people would have read than heard it, but the fact remains that Churchill had the wireless and Lloyd George didn't.

There is one more parallel between the two, which concerns the question of truth. Lloyd George judiciously refuses to swallow every story about the depravity of German soldiers. By acknowledging the likelihood of propaganda, he positions himself on higher moral ground. Yet the perilous circumstances of wartime mean there is something in the accusation that rhetoric skirts close to untruth. As Churchill will do in the House of Commons in 1940, Lloyd George is not giving a merely factual account of the status of the war effort. That would be too pessimistic for his purpose, which is to inspire confidence in ultimate victory. It is not untrue; but nor is it altogether true.

Russia has a special regard for Serbia. She has a special interest in Serbia. Russians have shed their blood for Serbian independence many a time. Serbia is a member of her family, and she cannot see Serbia maltreated. Austria knew that. Germany knew that, and Germany turned round to Russia and said: 'Here, I insist that you shall stand by with your arms folded whilst Austria is strangling to death your little brother. So lay your hands on that little fellow, and I will tear your ramshackle Empire limb from limb.' And he is doing it! That is the story of the little nations. The world owes much to little nations – and to little men. This theory of bigness – you must have a big empire and a big nation, and a big man – well, long legs have their advantage in a retreat. Frederick the Great chose his warriors for their height, and that tradition has become a policy in Germany. Germany applies that ideal to nations; she will only allow six-feet-two nations to stand in the ranks. But all the world owes much to the little five feet high nations. The greatest art of the world was the work of little nations. The most enduring literature of the world came from little nations. The greatest literature of England came from her when she was a nation of the size of Belgium fighting a great Empire. The heroic

*deeds that thrill humanity through generations were the deeds of
little nations fighting for their freedom!*

Transcripts record the huge number of occasions on which this
speech was interrupted by hisses, laughter, cheers, applause and
shouts of hear, hear. Audiences then were more demonstrative than
they would be now, and Lloyd George turns parts of the address into
call and response. Standing alone to speak can be a lonely event; it is
comforting to hear periodic appreciation. Applause also creates an
atmosphere. The end of this section is a classic 'clap line', signalled
even in Lloyd George's script with an exclamation mark. Poor speakers try to rouse the audience with only a rising intonation and an
increased volume at the end of a line, but the applause will only ever
be resounding when the vocal trickery is deployed for an important,
completed thought.

Lloyd George's mastery of technique is displayed by the way he
conjures grave days in demotic vocabulary and strikingly familiar
imagery. A vast body of research attests to the capacity of humans to
recall mind-pictures much quicker than abstract arguments. A
congruent image allows us to recall the argument for which it stands.
Russia as a brother standing, with his arms folded, while his brother
was attacked, will allow the audience to recall why passive quiescence
is not possible. The diminutive Lloyd George — himself notoriously
less than five feet tall — then goes into a comic riff that verges on the
absurd, describing big countries as the 'six foot two' nations and the
smaller nations as 'the five feet high' nations. It leads him to a paean
to the great literary achievements of Britain and a convenient omission of the fact that, though Britain may have been a small nation in
the days of Shakespeare, she did go on, within living memory of most
people in the audience, to became the world's biggest empire.

*Have you read the Kaiser's speeches? If you have not a copy, I
advise you to buy it; they will soon be out of print, and you won't
have any more of the same sort again. They are full of the clatter
and bluster of German militarists — the mailed fist, the shining
armour. Poor old mailed fist — its knuckles are getting a little
bruised. Poor shining armour — the shine is being knocked out of it.
But there is the same swagger and boastfulness running through*

the whole of the speeches ... I do not believe he meant all these speeches. It was simply the martial straddle which he had acquired; but there were men around him who meant every word of it ... You know the type of motorist, the terror of the roads, with a 60-h.p. car. He thinks the roads are made for him, and anybody who impedes the action of his car by a single mile is knocked down. The Prussian junker is the road-hog of Europe. Small nationalities in his way hurled to the roadside, bleeding and broken; women and children crushed under the wheels of his cruel car. Britain ordered out of his road. All I can say is this: if the old British spirit is alive in British hearts, that bully will be torn from his seat. Were he to win it would be the greatest catastrophe that has befallen democracy since the days of the Holy Alliance and its ascendancy. They think we cannot beat them. It will not be easy. It will be a long job. It will be a terrible war. But in the end we shall march through terror to triumph.

It is a mark of how seriously Lloyd George is taking the enemy that he opts for mockery. The clatter and the bluster, the mailed fist with bruised knuckles. He can get away with this because the speech is tightly argued, rich with historical examples. However, this is an example of how even a skilled writer can get carried away. Suggesting that the Prussians are the road-hog of Europe sounds quaint to us now. In fact, this reference was the height of modernity at the time. The motor car was a recent introduction to the streets of European cities. Mr Toad had been born in 1908, in *The Wind in the Willows*. Five years before Lloyd George gave his speech a poster had greeted travellers into London with a lament for the loss of employment and a claim that the newfangled motors would kill 'your children, dogs and chickens' and 'spoil your clothes with dust'. It was posted by the horse-and-cart lobby trying to stop the march of change. Lloyd George is therefore conjuring a fear of modernity, the idea that the Prussians are perverting the advance of science, using knowledge to illicit ends. It is, in other words, rather like Wagner's music: less bad than it sounds.

However, with that defence entered, it's all too stretched. By the time Lloyd George imagines turfing the Prussian bully out of the seat of the car, we feel that it is running away from him, to adopt his own metaphor. It also fails to set the mood for what follows, which is the necessary chorus of any war speech – the regular reminder that we, the forces of good, will prevail. A driver being taken off the road does not prepare us for the greatest catastrophe faced by democracy since the days of the Holy Alliance.

> *Those who have fallen have consecrated deaths. They have taken their part in the making of a new Europe, a new world. I can see signs of its coming in the glare of the battlefield. The people will gain more by this struggle in all lands than they comprehend at the present moment. It is true they will be rid of the menace to their freedom. But that is not all. There is something infinitely greater and more enduring which is emerging already out of this great conflict; a new patriotism, richer, nobler, more exalted than the old. I see a new recognition amongst all classes, high and low, shedding themselves of selfishness; a new recognition that the honour of a country does not depend merely on the maintenance of its glory in the stricken field, but in protecting its homes from distress as well. It is a new patriotism, it is bringing a new outlook for all classes. A great flood of luxury and of sloth which had submerged the land is receding, and a new Britain is appearing. We can see for the first time the fundamental things that matter in life and that have been obscured from our vision by the tropical growth of prosperity.*

The speaker at a time of war has two tasks: first to justify the war in the present; second to define the future it will be fought for. This is what Lloyd George does here. Because he is moving to his climax his terms are broad and imprecise. He could have drawn on his own record as a reforming chancellor of the exchequer: the nationalisation of the British welfare state began in 1911 with the work of Lloyd George in legislating for a state pension provision. He could have chosen to specify the land fit for heroes, as it was to become known, by drawing on his own reputation as a social reformer. It would risked bathos, though, to descend from the heights of war against a dangerous madman into the details of welfare benefits. Lloyd George instead trades on the assumed knowledge that his audience will know what he means. We see here the advantage of speaking to an audience whose level of political acquaintance is high.

The passage is like the historic war speech in miniature. The trajectory of war rhetoric, from Pericles onwards, is all there. War costs lives, and the only way to honour the war dead, to make a just cause from their sacrifice, is to remake the world. Military victory is never alone enough. Democracies turn war into a war for the improvement of democracy, and not just its survival.

> *May I tell you, in a simple parable, what I think this war is doing for us? I know a valley in North Wales, between the mountains and the sea – a beautiful valley, snug, comfortable, sheltered by the mountains from all the bitter blasts. It was very enervating, and I remember how the boys were in the habit of climbing the hills above the village to have a glimpse of the great mountains in the distance, and to be stimulated and freshened by the breezes which, came from the hilltops, and by the great spectacle of that great valley. We have been living in a sheltered valley for generations. We have been too comfortable, too indulgent, many, perhaps, too selfish. And the stern hand of fate has scourged us to an elevation where we can see the great everlasting things that matter for a nation; the great peaks of honour we had forgotten – duty and patriotism clad in glittering white: the great pinnacle of sacrifice pointing like a rugged finger to Heaven. We shall descend into the valleys again, but as long as the men and women of this generation last they will carry in their hearts the image of these great mountain peaks, whose foundations are unshaken though Europe rock and sway in the convulsions of a great war.*

This euphonious, flowing ending is what gains this speech a place in the anthologies. That and the fact that it is describing a country on the threshold of war. The anthologies of great speeches are records of what was said on great occasions rather than necessarily the finest words ever spoken. Occasionally, the writing climbs to the moment. But even when it doesn't, war speeches still matter. The poetry, as Wilfred Owen said, is in the pity. The gravity of the event warrants a certain elevation of style.

Reading Lloyd George's words a century after they were written sparks the thought that no politician would ever speak like this now. If anyone today referred to the 'great pinnacle of sacrifice pointing like a rugged finger to Heaven' they would be mocked for posting an application to be Poet Laureate. Yet at the time, Lloyd George was reproved for being too colloquial. Democratic politicians of recent years have responded to the universal franchise by speaking in less ornate fashion. Literary references are rare now, as the politician fears losing the audience by coming on too lofty. They should be braver; the audience may be able to bear a little more literature. 'People are always surprising a hunger in themselves to be more serious,' said Philip Larkin. Politicians should go high-brow. That is what Lloyd George does here, to great effect.

Note the argument that comes from Cicero – that in a democracy comfort can slide into dangerous complacency – and the invigorating call to arms to make it good. These words are hardy perennials; the conflict between complacency and politics is ubiquitous. Here, conflict is, alas, not a metaphor.

WOODROW WILSON

Making the World Safe for Democracy

Joint Session of the Two Houses of Congress
2 April 1917

Like his contemporaries Lloyd George and Churchill, Woodrow Wilson (1856–1924) was a student of oratory as well as a practitioner. Wilson's ascent to high office owed more than that of any president until Ronald Reagan to his capacity for beautiful public speech, good humour and easy charm. His career stands, in retrospect, as an example of both the power of fine rhetoric and its obvious limits.

Wilson is an internationalist exception in a country of natural isolationist bent. He took America into the Great War and devoted his career to the formation of the League of Nations. In this respect, his hopes were to be dashed, but his legacy thrives all the same. Wilson brought America to the world. The Fourteen Points he enunciated, that would make the world safe for democracy, were the basis of a deal that allowed the new German chancellor, Prince Maximilian of Baden, to end the war.

Woodrow Wilson was born in Virginia in 1856, the first son and third child of a Presbyterian minister of Scottish heritage. The young Woodrow saw the end of the Civil War as a boy and retained his allegiance as a Southerner all his life. He taught history at the College of New Jersey, now known as Princeton, and in 1902 produced his five-volume *History of the American People*, to some acclaim. Later that year he became the president of Princeton. His early politics were conservative but he trimmed that aspect of his character to make himself a more appealing prospect to the Democrats. Having won the endorsement of the party leaders in his home patch of New

Jersey, he charted a reforming course, under the slogan of New Freedom, to a presidential victory in November 1912.

As president, Wilson does have a domestic legacy. The Federal Reserve System and the Federal Trade Commission were created on his watch. Farm loan reform and child labour laws were enacted. He was however – and here weighs his heritage in the South – slow to support the right of women to vote. He also failed to advance the rights of the black population, allowing racial segregation to continue in federal offices.

But above all, Wilson was consumed by foreign policy. When war broke out in Europe in 1914, he was unready for it; he was still mourning the death of his beloved wife. His first announcement was that the United States would stay neutral, a stance that lasted two and a half years until Germany made it clear that no merchant ship servicing Britain and continental Europe would be safe from U-boat attack. At that point, Wilson concluded that America had to enter the war. His words in the speech that follows fell into an America happy to follow a lone path in the world. He was speaking before a joint session of Congress with the express purpose of seeking a declaration of war against Germany. Four days later, Congress did indeed vote, 82 to 6, for war. The House of Representatives concurred on 6 April by a vote of 373 to 50.

Gentlemen of the Congress, I have called the Congress into extraordinary session because there are serious, very serious, choices of policy to be made, and made immediately, which it was neither right nor constitutionally permissible that I should assume the responsibility of making. On the third of February last I officially laid before you the extraordinary announcement of the Imperial German Government that on and after the first day of February it was its purpose to put aside all restraints of law or of humanity and use its submarines to sink every vessel that sought to approach either the ports of Great Britain and Ireland or the western coasts of Europe or any of the ports controlled by the enemies of Germany within the Mediterranean ... The new policy has swept every restriction aside. Vessels of every kind, whatever their flag, their character, their cargo, their destination, their errand, have been ruthlessly sent to the bottom: without warning and without thought of help or mercy for those on board, the vessels of friendly neutrals along with those of belligerents. Even hospital ships and ships carrying relief to the sorely bereaved and stricken people of Belgium, though the latter were provided with safe conduct through the proscribed areas by the German Government itself and were distinguished by unmistakable marks of identity, have been sunk with the same reckless lack of compassion or of principle.

This is about as plain as speaking gets. There is no adornment to the opening. Wilson begins with his main point. If the audience had paid attention merely for a few seconds they would know something serious was afoot. Of course the consequence of opening in so grave a fashion is that it sets a tone it is hard to depart from. This helps to explain why this is a simple speech, sombre in its beauty.

The war speech almost always does what Churchill later does so well, which is to exude total confidence in eventual victory. Wilson's tone is much more professorial and scholarly. Tinged with doubt, he is clear that humanitarian principles demand American participation and victory but he does not seek to inspire his audience with the confidence that victory is inevitable. Wilson felt the responsibility for America's participation in the war very keenly, and though he clearly needs to be persuasive he does not want to gild his language too much. Too great a flourish would not be appropriate to the violence that he knows he is unleashing on those who will embark to Europe to fight the war. Too much optimism, given the carnage in foreign fields, would have rung very hollow.

That said, the grave nature of his speech's material and the controversy of his position does at least mean that Wilson did not have to strain for effect. Like David Lloyd George in Britain before him, Wilson was the anti-war radical who changed his mind. He was also a skilled writer and speaker, and contemporary accounts testify to his command. The speech was punctuated by applause and cheering. In this compressed opening Wilson summarises his theme. The reckless hostility of the Germans, their lack of compassion, their failure to adhere to any principle of restraint, lead to the inevitable conclusion that this must mean war.

I was for a little while unable to believe that such things would in fact be done by any government that had hitherto subscribed to the humane practices of civilized nations. International law had its origin in the attempt to set up some law which would be respected and observed upon the seas, where no nation had right of dominion and where lay the free highways of the world ... This minimum of right the German Government has swept aside under the plea of retaliation and necessity and because it had no weapons which it could use at sea except these which it is impossible to employ as it is employing them without throwing to the winds all scruples of humanity or of respect for the understandings that were supposed to underlie the intercourse of the world. I am not now thinking of the loss of property involved, immense and serious as that is, but only of the wanton and wholesale destruction of the lives of non-combatants, men, women, and children, engaged in pursuits which have always, even in the darkest periods of modern history, been deemed innocent and legitimate. Property can be paid for; the lives of peaceful and innocent people cannot be ... There has been no discrimination. The challenge is to all mankind. Each nation must decide for itself how it will meet it. The choice we make for ourselves must be made with a moderation of counsel and a temperateness of judgement befitting our character and our motives as a nation. We must put excited feeling away. Our motive will not be revenge or the victorious assertion of the physical might of the nation, but only the vindication of right, of human right, of which we are only a single champion.

Having posed the immediate threat, Wilson universalises it. He cites the heritage of international law whose fledgling achievements, he says, are threatened by German aggression. This speech is constructed around a simple binary opposition: the rest of the humane world against the Germans who have no respect for the norms and standards of international law. Theirs is therefore a war against all nations and a challenge to all mankind.

This is a vital strategy for the purpose of the speech in which Wilson is about to perform a major volte-face. Wilson had been inaugurated as president for a second term less than a month before he spoke, and at least some part of his popularity stemmed from his keeping America out of the European war; he had issued a declaration of neutrality in a speech in August 1914. Wilson's 1916 election slogan had been 'He kept us out of the war'. He calculates, therefore, that mere self-defence will not be sufficient. He has to gain a more Olympian height, as he is about to change a basic tenet of American foreign policy which has till now been based on calculations of narrow interest.

The speech now begins to unfold into a series of universal reasons for action, all of which have America at their centre and all of which depict Germany as in serious breach not just of international law as it stands, but of humanitarian principles that hold for all time.

> *There is one choice we cannot make, we are incapable of making: we will not choose the path of submission and suffer the most sacred rights of our Nation and our people to be ignored or violated. The wrongs against which we now array ourselves are no common wrongs; they cut to the very roots of human life. With a profound sense of the solemn and even tragical character of the step I am taking and of the grave responsibilities which it involves, but in unhesitating obedience to what I deem my constitutional duty, I advise that the Congress declare the recent course of the Imperial German Government to be in fact nothing less than war against the government and people of the United States; that it formally accept the status of belligerent which has thus been thrust upon it, and that it take immediate steps not only to put the country in a more thorough state of defence but also to exert all its power and employ all its resources to bring the Government of the German Empire to terms and end the war.*

After building the case of Germany as an aggressor against all civilised nations, Wilson gets to his point, which is to ask Congress to acknowledge that Germany has, in effect, declared a state of war. In 1915 a German U-boat torpedoed the RMS *Lusitania*, killing 128 Americans. Wilson had threatened action at the time which had come to naught. Now, his decision to seek permission to go to war was aided by a missive sent by the German foreign minister, Arthur

Zimmermann, to Germany's Mexican ambassador promising to help Mexico reclaim US land in exchange for support in the war.

But the claims Wilson makes that he did not want to fight are more than rhetorical play. He really was reluctant. Wilson had barely mentioned the outbreak of war in Europe. In 1914 he gave a 4th of July address little more than a week after the assassination of Franz Ferdinand at Sarajevo that did not even mention it.

Accounts of the preparation of this speech, which was all Wilson's own work, describe his fingers trembling as he turned the pages, seized as he was with the magnitude of what the words he had written foretold. Edward M. House, Wilson's closest aide, told Henri Bergson, the visiting French philosopher, that when Wilson declared war, he felt that 'God would hold him accountable for every American soldier killed'. Even if God would not, Congress would.

Neutrality is no longer feasible or desirable where the peace of the world is involved and the freedom of its peoples, and the menace to that peace and freedom lies in the existence of autocratic governments backed by organized force which is controlled wholly by their will, not by the will of their people. We have seen the last of neutrality in such circumstances. We are at the beginning of an age in which it will be insisted that the same standards of conduct and of responsibility for wrong done shall be observed among nations and their governments that are observed among the individual citizens of civilized states. We have no quarrel with the German people. We have no feeling towards them but one of sympathy and friendship. It was not upon their impulse that their government acted in entering this war. It was not with their previous knowledge or approval. It was a war determined upon as wars used to be determined upon in the old, unhappy days when peoples were nowhere consulted by their rulers and wars were provoked and waged in the interest of dynasties or of little groups of ambitious men who were accustomed to use their fellow men as pawns and tools.

After a long section setting out what it will mean for America to join the war, Wilson returns to the central principle. It seems odd, in the middle of the speech, to return to the binary opposition, like a popular song with a chorus but no verses. This time Wilson describes it as the battle between autocracy and freedom, between barbarism and civilisation. La Rochefoucauld once said that some forgotten notable was like a popular song that we only sing for a short time. Wilson's intention in his repetition is the opposite. His return to barbarism/civilisation or autocracy/freedom is because he knows this is operatic in scale. He needs to convince Congress to commit to war, and no such warrant will be granted unless the cause is large enough.

Wilson therefore co-opts the German people to his cause. The Germans are, in his account, victims of their autocratic government no less than are the citizens of invaded nations. This narrows the target further. It is not even Germany against the world, but the German elite against a world that includes the German people. 'Germany' in this speech is therefore retrospectively personalised. If the word 'Kaiser' were substituted for most of the references to Germany, the speech would not lose much in the way of sense. Recall that, in his earthier way, Lloyd George had done the same. An enemy with a human face is more frighteningly immediate than an abstraction, especially a deranged leader who commands military might. This separation of Germany from the Germans is a sleight of hand at which good orators specialise. The trick is smuggled in under cover of generosity about the German people with whom nobody has any quarrel.

A steadfast concert for peace can never be maintained except by a partnership of democratic nations. No autocratic government could be trusted to keep faith within it or observe its covenants. It must be a league of honour, a partnership of opinion. Intrigue would eat its vitals away; the plottings of inner circles who could plan what they would and render account to no one would be a corruption seated at its very heart. Only free peoples can hold their purpose and their honour steady to a common end and prefer the interests of mankind to any narrow interest of their own. Does not every American feel that assurance has been added to our hope for the future peace of the world by the wonderful and heartening things that have been happening within the last few weeks in Russia? Russia was known by those who knew it best to have been always in fact democratic at heart, in all the vital habits of her thought, in all

the intimate relationships of her people that spoke their natural
instinct, their habitual attitude towards life. The autocracy that
crowned the summit of her political structure, long as it had stood
and terrible as was the reality of its power, was not in fact Russian
in origin, character, or purpose; and now it has been shaken off and
the great, generous Russian people have been added in all their
naive majesty and might to the forces that are fighting for freedom
in the world, for justice, and for peace. Here is a fit partner for a
League of Honour.

How history can mock our hopes, let alone our prophecies. This
speech was delivered two months after the February revolution in
Russia that brought Alexander Kerensky to power and opened, for a
fleeting moment, the prospect of a social democratic future. Six
months later the October Revolution had shattered this hope. Briefly,
Wilson can dream. Indeed this whole section now reads like a dream
sequence, and it is hard to recapture the hope that was vested in it as
he spoke.

Wilson was to devote the latter part of his career to the idea of
the League of Nations that was formed in 1919 at the Paris Peace
Conference but folded in 1946. The United States never saw fit to
involve itself, despite the constant lobbying of this former president
who conducted a speaking tour to convince America of its virtues.
Wilson covered almost 10,000 miles and spoke in twenty nine cities.
The effort cost what remained of his depleted strength, and he
collapsed in Pueblo, Colorado, on 25 September 1919 and then the
following month at the White House. Not long after that he suffered
a serious stroke that left him half-paralysed and entirely secluded for
the rest of his presidency.

In January 1918 Wilson had returned to Congress to set out, in
the Fourteen Points, his war aims. The final one was to establish 'a
general association of nations ... affording mutual guarantees of
independence'. He later presented to the Senate the Versailles Treaty
which contained the Covenant of the League of Nations, and asked:
'Dare we reject it and break the heart of the world?' The election of
1918 had shifted the balance of Congress towards the Republicans,
however, and the answer, by seven Senate votes, was that they did
dare.

We are accepting this challenge of hostile purpose because we know that in such a Government, following such methods, we can never have a friend; and that in the presence of its organised power, always lying in wait to accomplish we know not what purpose, there can be no assured security for the democratic Governments of the world. We are now about to accept gauge of battle with this natural foe to liberty and shall, if necessary, spend the whole force of the nation to check and nullify its pretensions and its power. We are glad, now that we see the facts with no veil of false pretence about them to fight thus for the ultimate peace of the world and for the liberation of its peoples, the German peoples included: for the rights of nations great and small and the privilege of men everywhere to choose their way of life and of obedience. The world must be made safe for democracy. Its peace must be planted upon the tested foundations of political liberty. We have no selfish ends to serve. We desire no conquest, no dominion. We seek no indemnities for ourselves, no material compensation for the sacrifices we shall freely make. We are but one of the champions of the rights of mankind.

Wilson sings the chorus again, now to a rising inflection, so that it feels as if this must be the ending. The composer of a speech always faces a question about where to locate the best line. Should it come, like their finest hour, at the end? Should it open the speech? Or should it be – like 'the world must be made safe for democracy' – buried in the text? It does feel lost here. This is the formula that contains the two promises of all democratic societies – security and liberty – and he might have done better to leave with it, or maybe conclude with it. The effect of the repeated chorus structure is to amplify the point with each refrain, and after a section on the eternal contest between liberty and tyranny, it is hard to see where to go next.

Yet Wilson misses the full reach of his best phrase. It is not just that the world needs to be made safe so that democracy can flourish. The establishment of a democracy will itself be the guarantor of that safety. Democracy is not the system required once stability has been restored. It is itself the underwriter of international security.

The oversight probably stems from Wilson's reluctance to push Congress too far. Although Jefferson had used his first Inaugural

Address to proclaim America the 'world's best hope', and Lincoln had made similar high-sounding noises, these had been the vaguest of aspirations. No one had meant it like Wilson. Many presidents since have echoed Wilson's idealism, notably George W. Bush, who declared in his second Inaugural Address 'the ultimate goal of ending tyranny in our world'. Wilson's question here seems contemporary to us because it has always been the conundrum of American foreign policy: to withdraw or to engage.

> *It is a distressing and oppressive duty, Gentlemen of the Congress, which I have performed in thus addressing you. There are, it may be, many months of fiery trial and sacrifice ahead of us. It is a fearful thing to lead this great peaceful people into war, into the most terrible and disastrous of all wars, civilisation itself seeming to be in the balance. But the right is more precious than peace, and we shall fight for the things which we have always carried nearest our hearts, for democracy, for the right of those who submit to authority to have a voice in their own Governments, for the rights and liberties of small nations, for a universal dominion of right by such a concert of free peoples as shall bring peace and safety to all nations and make the world itself at last free. To such a task we can dedicate our lives and our fortunes, everything that we are and everything that we have, with the pride of those who know that the day has come when America is privileged to spend her blood and her might for the principles that gave her birth and happiness and the peace which she has treasured. God helping her, she can do no other.*

Wilson ends by singing the chorus in the most resonant way he can find, by invoking the nativity of America. We have had appeals to humanity, mankind, free peoples of the world and a 'League of Honour'. Now Wilson really gets up with the gods by appealing to America. This is the American answer to what ranks higher than a battle for civilisation – the American constitution. Wilson's stirring conclusion is clinched by locating the demand for action within the folds of American history. A nation such as this can do no other while remaining true to itself. It is the ultimate appeal to character. This is not just what we should do – it is who we are.

You might wonder why Wilson does not begin with the appeal to America and work out from his strongest point. The answer is that he needs the preceding argument in order to establish it because the point was exceptional. The standard American attitude before then had been, in the words of John Quincy Adams, that America 'goes not abroad in search of monsters to destroy'. The Monroe Doctrine of 1823 had committed America not to interfere in Europe, as well as vice versa. Wilson's demand that America take part in the spread of liberty was as much a rift in the argument then as it is now.

At the immediate conclusion of the speech there was a moment of silence which gave way to a great explosion of applause. Wilson then drove back to the White House past crowds of cheering people. 'My message today was a message of death for our young men. How strange it seems to applaud that,' he is recorded as having said on the way home. He was, of course, tragically right. Even by this time, the war had become one of the most murderous conflicts in human history. In his final words Wilson acknowledges this impending sacrifice by borrowing Martin Luther's words from the Diet of Worms: 'I cannot and will not recant anything, for to go against conscience is neither right nor safe. Here I stand. I can do no other, so help me God.'

WINSTON CHURCHILL

Their Finest Hour

House of Commons
18 June 1940

Winston Churchill (1874–1965) was, as David Cannadine said, a master and a slave of the English language. No figure in politics since Cicero has made a closer study of public speaking. Never before or since did any speaker lavish so much high-octane rhetoric on so few subjects to warrant it. Yet, as that parody suggests, nobody changed the future with words quite like Winston Churchill. For all his faults, and they were many, Churchill is a titan of the story of rhetoric. In *De oratore*, Cicero creates the template for the finest orator of all. Churchill has a claim on that title. This speech, with the nation on the verge of disaster, is his finest hour.

Winston Spencer Churchill was born on 30 November 1874, in Blenheim Palace, Oxfordshire. Ungifted scholastically, he joined the Royal Cavalry in 1895. As a soldier and a journalist he travelled widely. During his time as a subaltern in the Indian Army, he wrote a short pamphlet called *The Scaffolding of Rhetoric*. Churchill was himself a long time taking the scaffolding down. Almost as soon as he was elected as the Conservative MP for Oldham in 1900 he acquired a reputation for lavish verbosity. Disraeli's famous insult of Gladstone – 'a sophistical rhetorician inebriated with the exuberance of his own verbosity' – suits Churchill more neatly. An abundance of flourish applied to a dearth of subject matter made him the butt of satire from his peers. As he said himself: 'I have had to eat my words many times and I have found it a very nourishing diet.'

He didn't help himself by his erratic politics. Churchill defected to the Liberal Party in 1904, serving as first lord of the Admiralty, in which job he oversaw the disastrous Gallipoli campaign in the Great War. On resigning from the government, he travelled to fight on the Western Front. When he returned to domestic politics he crossed the floor back to the Conservatives, serving as Baldwin's chancellor of the exchequer from 1924. His next disaster, in a spiralling pattern, was his choice for Britain to rejoin the Gold Standard.

Churchill lost his seat in 1929 and spent much of the next decade writing and making speeches. On Indian independence he was a lonely and misguided voice, and at times a harmful one, which has left a stain on his reputation in India to this day. On the appeasement of Nazi Germany, however, he was triumphantly, and courageously, correct. When Neville Chamberlain resigned in 1940, Churchill succeeded him as prime minister and minister of defence, a position he created for himself, in an all-party coalition government.

Suddenly Churchill had a subject. Britain faced an adversary, in Hitler's Germany, that had, in Martin Amis's vivid phrase, found the core of the reptile brain and was building an autobahn that went there. In the summer of 1940, with the threat of imminent invasion and with the prospect of a hazardous air battle to come, civilisation hung in the balance. Churchill famously said, in his first great address of that summer, that he offered nothing but blood, sweat, toil and tears. He forgot to add words, which he called up for the war effort. Churchill spoke for the virtue of conversation over conflict, bombast rather than the bomb.

Proof that there is no gratitude in politics, though, came with the Labour victory in the 1945 general election, in which the demobbed soldiers voted for the promise of welfare-state security. Churchill disgraced himself in his old fashion with the stupid accusation that the Labour Party, his trusted coalition partner, would introduce a kind of native Gestapo. The defeat of the war hero in 1945 may seem surprising but, in retrospect, Churchill had played his part in an acceleration of history that had left him behind.

It is forgivable that he should have neglected the prospects for Britain after the war. As Churchill prepared his speeches in the summer of 1940 it didn't seem that his country had any prospects. But, despite the constant promptings of his deputy prime minister, the Labour leader Clement Attlee, Churchill showed little interest beyond the immediate conflict. In this respect he compares unfavourably with David Lloyd George, whose inspirational war rhetoric was always turned towards the future. But perhaps no present has ever been as dire as the present was for Churchill. It seemed, at times, to hold no future at all.

I spoke the other day of the colossal military disaster which occurred when the French High Command failed to withdraw the northern Armies from Belgium at the moment when they knew that the French front was decisively broken at Sedan and on the Meuse. This delay entailed the loss of fifteen or sixteen French divisions and threw out of action for the critical period the whole of the British Expeditionary Force. Our Army and 120,000 French troops were indeed rescued by the British Navy from Dunkirk but only with the loss of their cannon, vehicles and modern equipment. This loss inevitably took some weeks to repair, and in the first two of those weeks the battle in France has been lost. When we consider the heroic resistance made by the French Army against heavy odds in this battle, the enormous losses inflicted upon the enemy and the evident exhaustion of the enemy, it may well be the thought that these 25 divisions of the best-trained and best-equipped troops might have turned the scale. However, General Weygand had to fight without them. Only three British divisions or their equivalent were able to stand in the line with their French comrades. They have suffered severely, but they have fought well. We sent every man we could to France as fast as we could re-equip and transport their formations.

Churchill stood to speak to Parliament, on the 125th anniversary of the Battle of Waterloo, at a moment of present danger; four days after the fall of France and a fortnight after the evacuation of Dunkirk. The Germans had hit France, Luxembourg, Belgium and the Netherlands from the air while German forces advanced through the Netherlands, northern Belgium and Luxembourg into the Ardennes Forest; their next stop was France. The Dutch had surrendered after a brutal attack by the Luftwaffe on Rotterdam and the Allied attempts to defend Belgium were a fiasco, their forces squeezed between two German lines of advance. This pushed the British Expeditionary Force (BEF) back to the coast near the French port of Dunkirk. The evacuation, Operation Dynamo, took a week to accomplish and brought back more than 300,000 men across the English Channel in 800 civilian and military vessels, under a hail of bombs from the Luftwaffe. In all the history of retreats it is the most heroic, but it left France exposed. By 12 June German tanks had broken through the Maginot Line and on 14 June they entered Paris. Churchill had encouraged France to resist but had refused to commit more military resources.

The end came sooner than he had hoped. Four days after this speech France signed an armistice with Germany which, on Hitler's insistence, took place in the same railway car in which Germany had surrendered to France in 1918. The fear was that Britain was next. It seemed inevitable that Hitler would turn to Operation Sea Lion, his code name for his plans to cross the Channel. British intelligence had intercepted German radio transmissions that seemed to make invasion imminent.

This at once posed the problem, for Churchill, of tone of voice. He needed to be both realistic and optimistic, and the two tones clash. But if anyone could cope, then Churchill could. He remains the keenest student of rhetoric ever to have held high office. He had studied Cicero and Aristotle and he decided, to use the latter's term, to be forensic in the military detail he offered. Large sections of this speech are the work of an expressive war reporter.

We know from the transcript now held at Churchill College, Cambridge, that he sweated over this text, as he did with all his speeches. Churchill was a Stakhanovite labourer, whose methods of composition were eccentric. For weeks he would try out phrases at dinner, interrupting conversations to sound out the rhythm of a new witticism. He would write while on the telephone, circling the Great Hall at Chequers, propped up in bed or looking at maps of the conflict. But perhaps Churchill's favourite location for writing was his bath. He was inordinately proud of being able to control the taps with his feet as he dictated. Pity the poor typist, because Churchill never bothered to learn how to type; he dictated everything. The creative process absorbed him so completely that he became oblivious to the world. On one occasion he was so lost in his words that he did not notice that his cigar ash had ignited his bed jacket. A private secretary helpfully told him: 'You're on fire, sir. May I put you out?' Without pausing, Churchill replied: 'Yes, please do' and completed the sentence.

*I am not reciting these facts for the purpose of recrimination. That
I judge to be utterly futile and even harmful. We cannot afford it. I
recite them in order to explain why it was we did not have, as we
could have had, between twelve and fourteen British divisions
fighting in the line in this great battle instead of only three. Now I
put all this aside. I put it on the shelf, from which the historians,
when they have time, will select their documents to tell their stories.
We have to think of the future and not of the past. This also applies
in a small way to our own affairs at home. There are many who
would hold an inquest in the House of Commons on the conduct of
the Governments — and of Parliaments, for they are in it, too
— during the years which led up to this catastrophe. They seek to
indict those who were responsible for the guidance of our affairs.
This also would be a foolish and pernicious process. There are too
many in it. Let each man search his conscience and search his
speeches. I frequently search mine. Of this I am quite sure, that if
we open a quarrel between the past and the present, we shall find
that we have lost the future. Therefore, I cannot accept the drawing
of any distinctions between Members of the present Government. It
was formed at a moment of crisis in order to unite all the Parties
and all sections of opinion. It has received the almost unanimous
support of both Houses of Parliament. Its Members are going to
stand together, and, subject to the authority of the House of
Commons, we are going to govern the country and fight the war.*

Churchill then makes a call for unity. He has been prime minister for little more than a month and already the trials of war are closing in. The first task is to head off the claim that Britain should have sent more military help to France in its attempt to stem the German advance. Churchill and the generals had concluded that, callous as it seemed, they were better off husbanding their resources for the battles to come.

Then he confronts a domestic political issue. The search for scapegoats took the form of demands that the chief appeasers, Halifax and Chamberlain, should no longer be in the government. Churchill was himself the lucky general who had succeeded to the premiership despite being the man who oversaw the disastrous Norway campaign that had sealed the fate of Chamberlain. So it is perhaps with a touch of self-interest that Churchill asks, in the name of national unity, the press and political packs to back off.

He does so with the first display of sophisticated rhetorical technique in the speech. The stakes are already set high, and Churchill uses them to sound the warning. But how elegantly: a quarrel between past and present means that we lose the future. It's not quite true that public criticism of Lord Halifax would really undermine the war effort, but the dispute was a futile distraction and it irritated Churchill if people did not focus on the sole objective: to govern the country and fight the war. The felicity of the phrasing should not disguise the severity of the stricture. Instantly, anyone engaged in such a quarrel is made to feel frivolous at best and injurious to the nation at worst.

> *Those are the regular, well-tested, well-proved arguments on which we have relied during many years in peace and war. But the question is whether there are any new methods by which those solid assurances can be circumvented. Odd as it may seem, some attention has been given to this by the Admiralty, whose prime duty and responsibility is to destroy any large sea-borne expedition before it reaches, or at the moment when it reaches, these shores. It would not be a good thing for me to go into details of this. It might suggest ideas to other people which they have not thought of, and they would not be likely to give us any of their ideas in exchange. All I will say is that untiring vigilance and mind-searching must be devoted to the subject, because the enemy is crafty and cunning and full of novel treacheries and stratagems. The House may be assured that the utmost ingenuity is being displayed and imagination is being evoked from large numbers of competent officers, well-trained in tactics and thoroughly up to date, to measure and counterwork novel possibilities. Untiring vigilance and untiring searching of the mind is being, and must be, devoted to the subject, because, remember, the enemy is crafty and there is no dirty trick he will not do.*

In November 1941 Churchill observed in the House of Commons: 'Ministers, and indeed all other public men, when they make speeches at the present time have always to bear in mind three audiences: one our own fellow countrymen, secondly, our friends abroad, and thirdly, the enemy. This naturally makes the task of public speaking very difficult.' Most speeches have to speak to more than one audience, still more so in these days of instant communication, but the problem is never more acute than in wartime. Churchill is simultaneously addressing political friends and foes in Parliament, the nation at large (which he reached in a broadcast of the text verbatim at 9 p.m), the listening powers-that-were in the United States, neutral states who are attending carefully to his words as an index of the state of British strength, and of course the enemy, to whom he must betray no weakening of resolve. This has to be military report, popular inspiration and global diplomacy intertwined.

You get a glimpse here of Churchill's sense of humour when he says, with deliberate bathos, that the enemy is unlikely to offer any ideas in exchange. Any dictionary of quotations will show that Churchill is, without question, the wittiest senior politician there has been. War is not exactly the best material for comedy, though, for Churchill as it was for Lloyd George, mockery is an effective war weapon. The famous instance is his insistence on pronouncing 'Nazi' as 'Narzees'. Churchill had a problem with sibilant sounds which he practised by insistently rehearsing phrases like 'The Spanish ships I cannot see for they are not in sight', but 'Narzees' is taking the rise and the British public loved it.

His wit was a major part of how Churchill became, through his words, the embodiment of the British people during the war. Churchill did not really speak to the nation, as Roosevelt had done to America in the 1930s. Because at a time of war there really is only one issue, he spoke for them. Churchill had always idealised what, confusing his categories, he tended to call 'the British race'. The Britain of his imagination was populated with fearless and gallant yeomen whose sense of honour and decency was invincible. The people were a more important part of the Second World War than of the First. The Great War had pitted soldiers against their adversaries. As he was to say in August, in the speech known as 'The Few', in the Second World War the air war meant that the morale of the home population was a vital part of the effort.

Though, as Churchill said himself, 'rhetoric was no guarantee of survival', he revelled in the excitement. Not even Wellington, who really was a soldier, had worn uniform in office, as Churchill did. In the light blue livery of an honorary RAF commodore he even looked like the war. The cigar, the stovepipe hat, his fondness for red meat and wine for breakfast; the nation's secret wish list. He even recorded the broadcast of this speech while smoking a cigar. The effect was to make him sound drunk, but 60 per cent of the nation heard it and it clearly worked. A Gallup poll conducted in July gave Churchill an approval rating of 88 per cent.

This brings me, naturally, to the great question of invasion from the air, and of the impending struggle between the British and German Air Forces. It seems quite clear that no invasion on a scale beyond the capacity of our land forces to crush speedily is likely to take place from the air until our Air Force has been definitely overpowered. In the meantime, there may be raids by parachute troops and attempted descents of airborne soldiers. We should be able to give those gentry a warm reception both in the air and on the ground, if they reach it in any condition to continue the dispute. But the great question is: Can we break Hitler's air weapon? Now, of course, it is a very great pity that we have not got an Air Force at least equal to that of the most powerful enemy within striking distance of these shores. But we have a very powerful Air Force which has proved itself far superior in quality, both in men and in many types of machine, to what we have met so far in the numerous and fierce air battles which have been fought with the Germans. In France, where we were at a considerable disadvantage and lost many machines on the ground when they were standing round the aerodromes, we were accustomed to inflict in the air losses of as much as two and two-and-a-half to one. In the fighting over Dunkirk, which was a sort of no-man's-land, we undoubtedly beat the German Air Force, and gained the mastery of the local air, inflicting here a loss of three or four to one day after day ... There remains, of course, the danger of bombing attacks, which will certainly be made very soon upon us by the bomber forces of the enemy. It is true that the German bomber force is superior in numbers to ours; but we have a very large bomber force also, which we shall use to strike at military targets in Germany without intermission. I do not at all underrate the severity of the ordeal which lies before us; but I believe our countrymen will show themselves capable of standing up to it, like the brave men of Barcelona, and will be able to stand up to it, and carry on in spite of it, at least as well as any other people in the world. Much will depend upon this; every man and every woman will have the chance to show the finest qualities of their race, and render the highest service to their cause. For all of us, at this time, whatever our sphere, our station, our occupation or our duties, it will be a help to remember the famous lines: He nothing common did or mean, Upon that memorable scene. I have thought it right upon this occasion to give the House and the country some indication of the solid, practical grounds upon which we base our inflexible resolve to continue the war. There are a good many people who say, 'Never mind. Win or lose, sink or swim, better die than submit to tyranny — and such a tyranny'. And I do not dissociate myself from them. But I can assure them that our professional advisers of the three Services unitedly advise that we should carry on the war, and that there are good and reasonable hopes of final victory.

The uneasy relationship of rhetoric to truth has rarely come under closer scrutiny than in the perilous summer of 1940. Whether Churchill truly believed that the war was winnable is a moot point. His update is detailed and clear. He is at no point pretending that the threat is not grave. But his hopes for victory are not reportage; they are part of the quest for victory. If Churchill at times sounds more steadfast than he felt, that is the nub of his rhetorical task. This is a reminder that if we are too fastidious we can diminish our politics. A cynic who went through Churchill's 1940 speeches with an eye to convicting him of misleading the House of Commons might be able to do so. Churchill is most definite when he knows least, and in this passage he trades heavily on his John Bull status as the representative of the nation. He is convinced, with the victory in the air over Dunkirk his only evidence, that the British Air Force is greater than its German rival despite its numerical inferiority.

See too how Churchill decorates the speech with literature. He is quoting Andrew Marvell's 'An Horatian Ode upon Cromwell's Return from Ireland'. Churchill often quoted without footnotes. His 4 June speech ('We Will Fight Them on the Beaches') cites Tennyson's

Morte D'Arthur without acknowledging poet or poem. A man with a prodigious memory, Churchill had a mind stocked with the reading of a lifetime. His love affair with Shakespeare lasted all his life, and Churchill's grand style, anachronistic even in his time, owes a lot to the metre he heard in Shakespeare. Violet Bonham Carter once complained that Churchill could not stop reciting the odes of Keats, which he had by heart. He could perform similar feats with long stretches of Dr Johnson and Byron's *Childe Harold's Pilgrimage*. When Churchill stretches sentences over too great a distance it is Gibbon, the most overrated stylist of them all, whom he echoes. He was also a devotee of Fowler's *Modern English Usage*.

The literary reference allows Churchill to move between the two different registers of this passage. One aspect of this speech is a calm and reasoned report that the military authorities have cause to expect victory. The second aspect is that this will not come without cost; the British will have occasion to show their virtue in giving themselves to the cause. There is an echo here of the epitaph speech that Pericles gives in the Funeral Oration. The conventional epitaph speech is comprised of praise for the dead and advice for the living. Churchill calls on the living to be worthy of that praise when their descendants look fondly back on them. But this is Pericles *before* the battle rather than after.

> *We may now ask ourselves: In what way has our position worsened since the beginning of the war? It has worsened by the fact that the Germans have conquered a large part of the coast line of Western Europe, and many small countries have been overrun by them. This aggravates the possibilities of air attack and adds to our naval preoccupations ... If Hitler can bring under his despotic control the industries of the countries he has conquered, this will add greatly to his already vast armament output. On the other hand, this will not happen immediately, and we are now assured of immense, continuous and increasing support in supplies and munitions of all kinds from the United States; and especially of aeroplanes and pilots from the Dominions and across the oceans coming from regions which are beyond the reach of enemy bombers. I do not see how any of these factors can operate to our detriment on balance before the winter comes; and the winter will*

impose a strain upon the Nazi regime, with almost all Europe writhing and starving under its cruel heel, which, for all their ruthlessness, will run them very hard. We must not forget that from the moment when we declared war on the 3rd September it was always possible for Germany to turn all her Air Force upon this country, together with any other devices of invasion she might conceive, and that France could have done little or nothing to prevent her doing so. We have, therefore, lived under this danger, in principle and in a slightly modified form, during all these months ... Therefore, in casting up this dread balance sheet and contemplating our dangers with a disillusioned eye, I see great reason for intense vigilance and exertion, but none whatever for panic or despair. During the first four years of the last war the Allies experienced nothing but disaster and disappointment. That was our constant fear: one blow after another, terrible losses, frightful dangers. Everything miscarried. And yet at the end of those four years the morale of the Allies was higher than that of the Germans, who had moved from one aggressive triumph to another, and who stood everywhere triumphant invaders of the lands into which they had broken. During that war we repeatedly asked ourselves the question: How are we going to win? and no one was able ever to answer it with much precision, until at the end, quite suddenly, quite unexpectedly, our terrible foe collapsed before us, and we were so glutted with victory that in our folly we threw it away.

This whole speech is a clever dance between the unsparing and the sentimental. We get a passage of worrying clarity salvaged by inspirational optimism. Here Churchill does it again. He understands an important principle about rhetoric that lesser speakers get wrong – soft-pedalling on a crucial point gets you a reputation as a fraud. A reward greets being candid. The sense of inspiration in the speech is the greater precisely because the threat has been genuinely posed.

In his first speech as prime minister, on 13 May 1940, Churchill had spoken briefly and had been unable to offer anything beyond 'blood, toil, sweat and tears' and the promise of victory no matter how hard the road might be. That speech was nothing more than a bag of tricks. But what a bag of tricks. Then, on 4 June 1940, Churchill returned to the House to describe the Dunkirk evacuation in all its sorry detail. In Churchill's voice, of course, the evacuation sounded like the prelude to the forward march of progress. The 4 June speech was the rallying cry in which Churchill declared that whether the fight was waged on the beaches, on the seas, the oceans or the landing grounds, the British would never surrender.

That is the background to the optimism in this speech which arrives fully formed at the end of this section. It is practically grounded in the military supplies from the United States and the fortitude of the Allied and Dominion men who had proved themselves in air battle. It is also based on asking his audience to recall the events of twenty-two years earlier when the Great War had been won, suddenly, against expectation. The implication is that the same will happen again.

We do not yet know what will happen in France or whether the French resistance will be prolonged, both in France and in the French Empire overseas ... However matters may go in France or with the French Government, or other French Governments, we in this Island and in the British Empire will never lose our sense of comradeship with the French people. If we are now called upon to endure what they have been suffering, we shall emulate their courage, and if final victory rewards our toils they shall share the gains, aye, and freedom shall be restored to all. We abate nothing of our just demands; not one jot or tittle do we recede. Czechs, Poles, Norwegians, Dutch, Belgians have joined their causes to our own. All these shall be restored. What General Weygand called the Battle of France is over. I expect that the Battle of Britain is about to begin. Upon this battle depends the survival of Christian civilization. Upon it depends our own British life, and the long continuity of our institutions and our Empire. The whole fury and might of the enemy must very soon be turned on us. Hitler knows that he will have to break us in this Island or lose the war. If we can stand up to him, all Europe may be free and the life of the world may move forward into broad, sunlit uplands. But if we fail, then the whole world, including the United States, including all that we have known and cared for, will sink into the abyss of a new Dark Age made more sinister, and perhaps more protracted, by the lights

> *of perverted science. Let us therefore brace ourselves to our duties,*
> *and so bear ourselves that, if the British Empire and its*
> *Commonwealth last for a thousand years, men will still say, 'This*
> *was their finest hour.'*

For the first time Churchill stops reporting and raises himself to his full rhetorical height. Note, though, that a grand message does not demand grandiose language. Three-quarters of the words in this section are monosyllables. The message is, in summary, the same one he gave in each of his magnificent speeches in the summer of 1940: we confront the face of evil in the world, we have to save not only ourselves but all civilisation, there can be no victory short of extinction for the enemy. Triumph will come hard, but we are Britain, we can do it and we shall.

That is a simple way of saying what Churchill says with consummate rhetorical effect. The ending teems with triplets and pairs in each sentence, the contrast between light and dark, alliterations and eight instances of the word 'we'. Read it yourself and you feel the blood begin to stir with the three successive sentences that feature the word 'battle'. The Battle of France is over, the battle of Britain (lower-case in Churchill's transcript because it was not yet an event in the world) is about to begin, and then he widens the frame because the third battle puts civilisation on the line. Three battles – past, present and a battle for the future. The effect is clinched by the prospect that the verdict will be entered by men, which is to say all of mankind, who will, with gratitude, note our finest hour.

The weight of events exerts its own pressure, but a poor speaker can throw the moment away. Here, every sentence is perfectly balanced. The sheet in front of Churchill at the despatch box had the text arranged with five-line paragraphs in indented type, as if it were the blank verse of the Old Testament Book of Psalms. The effect is as if 'under the wand of a magician', as the younger Pitt said of Fox. Look at the way each sentence sets up the next: the Battle of France is over; the Battle of Britain is about to begin. Then the final two sentences that flow inexorably on to their conclusion in the speech's title. This is his finest hour. You are on fire, sir.

RONALD REAGAN

Tear Down This Wall

The Brandenburg Gate, Berlin
12 June 1987

The most successful electoral politician of any era of American politics, Ronald Reagan was, to use a coinage of George W. Bush, the
most mis-underestimated president of modern times. He was also, as
much as Wilson and Eisenhower, a war leader. Reagan's war was the
Cold War and it ended in a decisive victory. The Cold War was a war
of ideas, a war conducted through cultural imperialism and fine
words. It ended with a victory for the abundance of Western capitalism over the poverty of the Soviet regime.

Ronald Wilson Reagan (1911–2004) was born into a poor family
in Tampico, Illinois. His early life was peripatetic until his parents
settled in Dixon, Illinois, where his father opened a shoe store.
Reagan began his career as a radio sports announcer in Iowa and
then, in 1937, signed a seven-year contract with Warner Brothers for
whom, over the next three decades, he appeared in more than fifty
films. At the outbreak of war he was excused combat on account of
his poor eyesight. He spent the war making training films and left
the military ranked as a captain.

From 1947 to 1952, Reagan, a liberal Democrat at the time, served
as the president of the Screen Actors' Guild. He was a fervent admirer
of President Franklin D. Roosevelt, whose New Deal he believed had
provided jobs for his father and brother during the Depression. Reagan
remained a Democrat until after he turned fifty, only switching his
registration in 1962, and he never lost his admiration for FDR.

The Screen Actors' Guild gave him a new mission, though,
namely to root out the communists, which began his rightwards drift.

Reagan first appeared in national politics in 1964 with a well-received speech introducing the Republican presidential candidate Barry Goldwater. To a remarkable degree this speech foreshadowed his later career. He argued that government was eroding the freedom of individuals within the United States. 'I have wondered at times', said Reagan once, 'what the Ten Commandments would have looked like if Moses had run them through the US Congress.' He also decried the weakness of the American government against an expansive Soviet Union.

Two years later Reagan won the governorship of California for the first time, and in 1970 he won a second term, although his presidential bids in 1968 and 1976 failed. When he did win the nomination, in 1980, he thrashed Jimmy Carter to become, at the age of sixty-nine, as yet the oldest president in American history. Reagan cut taxes and tried to lighten the burden of business regulation, and the economy boomed, but at the price of growing inequality between the rich and the poor and a large deficit. He was a charming advertiser of conservative values, but it was sleight of hand. His boom bust after he left office. His foreign adventures are a shambles. Reagan's anti-communism was so severe that he upheld all manner of dubious military regimes in Latin America. The regimes in El Salvador and Nicaragua were not exactly shining cities on a hill, and in October 1983 Reagan ordered US forces to invade the Caribbean island of Grenada after Marxist rebels overthrew the government.

But the most pressing issue for his presidency, with which Reagan will always be associated, was the Cold War. Reagan fortified the American arsenal of weapons and its reserve of troops against a Soviet Union that he described, in a speech in March 1983, as 'the evil empire'. Providing aid to anti-communist movements in Africa, Asia and Latin America became known as the Reagan Doctrine.

In November 1984 Reagan won a second landslide, carrying 49 of the 50 US states and 525 of the 538 electoral votes, the largest number ever won by an American presidential candidate. His second term was tarnished by the Iran–Contra affair, an arms-for-hostages deal with Iran to funnel money toward anti-communist insurgencies in Central America. Though he initially denied knowing about it, Reagan later announced that it had been a mistake.

It was, however, during his second term as president that Reagan forged a diplomatic relationship with Mikhail Gorbachev, chairman of the Soviet Union. This was the context in which Reagan gave the following speech at the Berlin Wall, on the 750th anniversary of the city of Berlin, in which he challenged Gorbachev to tear down the wall. The West German government requested that the president's schedule be adjusted to allow him to visit Berlin on his way back from an economic summit in Venice. Reagan's visit brought a protest to the Berlin streets. By some accounts, the 50,000 who gathered the day before Reagan spoke to protest about American foreign policy outnumbered the 45,000 Berliners who attended the speech. By way of comparison, 450,000 people had witnessed John F. Kennedy's '*Ich bin ein Berliner*' speech in 1963.

Reagan spoke at the Brandenburg Gate behind two panes of bulletproof glass. West Berlin was all but an armed fortress. The Tiergarten was coiled with barbed wire. Anyone who wanted to see the leader of the free world had to pass through four barriers manned by armed guards and policemen in plain sight and in plain clothes. Reagan knew the value of what he was defending. As he said on another occasion: 'democracy is worth dying for because it is the most deeply honourable form of government ever devised by men'.

Chancellor Kohl, Governing Mayor Diepgen, ladies and gentlemen: Twenty-four years ago, President John F. Kennedy visited Berlin, speaking to the people of this city and the world at the City Hall. Well, since then two other presidents have come, each in his turn, to Berlin. And today I, myself, make my second visit to your city. We come to Berlin, we American presidents, because it's our duty to speak, in this place, of freedom. But I must confess, we're drawn here by other things as well: by the feeling of history in this city, more than 500 years older than our own nation; by the beauty of the Grunewald and the Tiergarten; most of all, by your courage and determination. Perhaps the composer Paul Lincke understood something about American presidents. You see, like so many presidents before me, I come here today because wherever I go, whatever I do: Ich hab noch einen Koffer in Berlin. [I still have a suitcase in Berlin.] Our gathering today is being broadcast throughout Western Europe and North America. I understand that

it is being seen and heard as well in the East. To those listening
throughout Eastern Europe, a special word: Although I cannot be
with you, I address my remarks to you just as surely as to those
standing here before me. For I join you, as I join your fellow
countrymen in the West, in this firm, this unalterable belief: Es gibt
nur ein Berlin. [There is only one Berlin.]

Berlin is the crucible of European history in the twentieth
century. American presidents were drawn to it because it was where
the world turned. On 26 June 1963 John F. Kennedy had famously
declared himself a citizen of Berlin. The two other presidents to whom
Reagan refers are Nixon and Carter. All the Berlin speeches were
essentially the same; until Reagan they are all variations on a theme
by Kennedy. In February 1969, Nixon said that 'all the people of the
world are truly Berliners'. In July 1978 Carter described Berlin, in John
Winthrop's biblical phrase, as a city on a hill. After the wall came
down, Clinton in 1994 and Bush in 2002 came to congratulate Berliners
on their freedom, and Obama reminded them that the Soviet Union
had tried 'to extinguish the last flame of freedom in Berlin'.

As all the presidents said, the wall divided ideas as well as people.
Reagan states this case up-front and concludes his opening by prefig-
uring the dramatic purpose that brings him to Berlin. Echoing
Kennedy's famous German sentence, Reagan gets the songwriter
wrong. The composer of 'I Still Have a Suitcase in Berlin', later
recorded by Marlene Dietrich, was in fact Ralph Maria Siegel. The
sentence in German has become a presidential tradition. Kennedy
started it. Carter and Reagan did it and then Obama, in July 2008,
told Berlin, in German, that everyone in the world was, in a sense, a
citizen of Berlin. In this speech Reagan also slips into German too
often, but his central claim is clear, no matter what language it is in:
Es gibt nur ein Berlin. There is only one Berlin.

Behind me stands a wall that encircles the free sectors of this city,
part of a vast system of barriers that divides the entire continent of
Europe. From the Baltic, south, those barriers cut across Germany
in a gash of barbed wire, concrete, dog runs, and guard towers.
Farther south, there may be no visible, no obvious wall. But there
remain armed guards and checkpoints all the same — still a

*restriction on the right to travel, still an instrument to impose upon
ordinary men and women the will of a totalitarian state. Yet it is
here in Berlin where the wall emerges most clearly; here, cutting
across your city, where the news photo and the television screen
have imprinted this brutal division of a continent upon the mind of
the world. Standing before the Brandenburg Gate, every man is a
German, separated from his fellow men. Every man is a Berliner,
forced to look upon a scar.*

The wall itself was a physical demarcation between two worlds.
The distinction Reagan draws conceptually here is the philosophical
division between progress and backwardness, embodied in Berlin in
stone. The wall had been erected in 1961 to stop East Germans fleeing to the West. Reagan describes the apparatus of the totalitarian
state to show that it was not the wall that prevented free access
through the city. The wall symbolised the lack of free access that the
military police enforced at the point of a gun.

The Berlin Wall stood 12 feet tall and created a barrier between
two ways of life. On the Western side there was a riot of colours.
Crowds thronged the streets and the windows displayed the goods of
consumer capitalism that, on the Eastern side, were absent. The grey
buildings of the East still bore the marks of shelling and the streets
were thinly populated with shuddering cars and badly dressed pedes-
trians. East Berlin was heavily guarded, complete with dog runs and
rows of barbed wire. The wall split the city in two, split families in
two, it split the modern world in two. It is less controversial to say
now than it was then, that Reagan was, literally and philosophically,
on the right side of the divide.

*In the Reichstag a few moments ago, I saw a display
commemorating this fortieth anniversary of the Marshall Plan. I
was struck by the sign on a burnt-out, gutted structure that was
being rebuilt. I understand that Berliners of my own generation
can remember seeing signs like it dotted throughout the western
sectors of the city. The sign read simply: 'The Marshall Plan is
helping here to strengthen the free world.' A strong, free world in
the West, that dream became real. Japan rose from ruin to become
an economic giant. Italy, France, Belgium – virtually every nation*

in Western Europe saw political and economic rebirth; the European Community was founded. In West Germany and here in Berlin, there took place an economic miracle, the Wirtschaftswunder. Adenauer, Erhard, Reuter, and other leaders understood the practical importance of liberty – that just as truth can flourish only when the journalist is given freedom of speech, so prosperity can come about only when the farmer and businessman enjoy economic freedom. The German leaders reduced tariffs, expanded free trade, lowered taxes. From 1950 to 1960 alone, the standard of living in West Germany and Berlin doubled. Where four decades ago there was rubble, today in West Berlin there is the greatest industrial output of any city in Germany – busy office blocks, fine homes and apartments, proud avenues, and the spreading lawns of parkland. Where a city's culture seemed to have been destroyed, today there are two great universities, orchestras and an opera, countless theaters, and museums. Where there was want, today there's abundance – food, clothing, automobiles – the wonderful goods of the Ku'damm … In the 1950s, Khrushchev predicted: 'We will bury you.' But in the West today, we see a free world that has achieved a level of prosperity and well-being unprecedented in all human history. In the Communist world, we see failure, technological backwardness, declining standards of health, even want of the most basic kind – too little food. Even today, the Soviet Union still cannot feed itself. After these four decades, then, there stands before the entire world one great and inescapable conclusion: Freedom leads to prosperity. Freedom replaces the ancient hatreds among the nations with comity and peace. Freedom is the victor.

This is the measure of the freedom that really counted in the end. Reagan is smart enough, perhaps he is American enough, to know that the way freedom really bit was commercially. This section could easily have been, after the example of Cicero or Jefferson, a paean to the democratic virtues or the beautiful state of liberty. It could have been a long exposition of the value of a free press, of freedom of association and speech. All of these questions were present in a Berlin which had passed from Hitler to Stalin, a unique journey through unfreedom.

Yet Reagan makes a less conventional argument which is, for that reason, more profound still. He poses the question economically. He makes the explicit link between democracy and capitalism, each of which helps the other. Growth and prosperity, the fruits of freedom, are made permissible by liberty and measure out its true worth. This is no vulgarisation. The difference in both the quality and the supply of goods available in West Berlin compared with the East was a major component in the destruction not just of the wall but of the system that built and maintained it. It is a vital link in the argument precisely because it was not widely accepted. The Left in most nations upheld liberty in theory but regarded capitalism as part of the system of oppression, not the liberator. Reagan's defence of capitalism is full-throated, important and right. It is the pivot of the speech; the pivot of the historical change.

> *And now the Soviets themselves may, in a limited way, be coming to understand the importance of freedom. We hear much from Moscow about a new policy of reform and openness. Some political prisoners have been released. Certain foreign news broadcasts are no longer being jammed. Some economic enterprises have been permitted to operate with greater freedom from state control. Are these the beginnings of profound changes in the Soviet state? Or are they token gestures, intended to raise false hopes in the West, or to strengthen the Soviet system without changing it? We welcome change and openness; for we believe that freedom and security go together, that the advance of human liberty can only strengthen the cause of world peace. There is one sign the Soviets can make that would be unmistakable, that would advance dramatically the cause of freedom and peace. General Secretary Gorbachev, if you seek peace, if you seek prosperity for the Soviet Union and Eastern Europe, if you seek liberalisation: Come here to this gate! Mr. Gorbachev, open this gate! Mr. Gorbachev, tear down this wall!*

The chief writer of this speech, Peter Robinson, struggled to formulate the best line. His first draft read: 'Herr Gorbachev, bring down this wall.' In the second draft he wrote 'take down' instead. Then he tried it in German: '*Herr Gorbachev, machen Sie dieses Tor auf.'* Eventually, at a Berlin dinner party Robinson heard a lady called Ingeborg Elz almost supply the right phrase: take down that wall.

That was when the trouble really started. Reagan had to contend with the opinions of so many advisers, not a problem Pericles ever had. Officials from the State Department and the National Security Council, including the deputy security adviser Colin Powell, were adamant it should not be included. Reagan had in fact made similar speeches before in Berlin. In 1982 he had asked: 'Why is that wall there?' In 1986, on the twenty-fifth anniversary of the wall, he had declared: 'I would like to see the wall come down today, and I call upon those responsible to dismantle it.'

That did not impress the officials, all of whom thought it too provocative to preach to Mr Gorbachev in the midst of his campaign for *perestroika* (restructuring), *glasnost* (opening) and, the forgotten part of the trinity, *uskorenie* (acceleration). The assistant secretary of state for Eastern European affairs called Reagan to object. The National Security Council (NSC) sent a stiff memorandum and the American ambassador in Berlin suggested the president should say: 'One day this ugly wall will disappear' as if it were set to walk away by itself. The State Department and the NSC submitted their own drafts, which said nothing about tearing the wall down. Secretary of State George Shultz tried to delete the line. At the crucial drafting meeting the president himself smiled and concluded: 'Let's leave it in.' On the day of the speech itself, the State Department and the NSC tried again. In the limousine on the way to the Berlin Wall, the president said: 'The boys at State are going to kill me but it is the right thing to do.'

Reagan was right. The effect, when he delivered it, was electrifying, and it is worth considering why this should be so. If Kennedy had said it a quarter of a century earlier it would have been no more than an expression of an unlikely hope. It would have been a statement about American virtue: we think your wall is a prison wall. By the time Reagan comes to Berlin the prospect of change in Russia is real. This is why his set-up is important. He does not build to the famous injunction to tear down the wall with an attack on Russia. On the contrary, he is emollient and cajoling. He takes seriously the reports that Mr Gorbachev may be in the process of starting down a new path. The demand to tear down the wall then becomes the necessary conclusion to an argument begun in Russia rather than merely yet another statement of American and Russian Cold War hostility.

> *But we must remember a crucial fact: East and West do not mistrust each other because we are armed; we are armed because we mistrust each other. And our differences are not about weapons but about liberty ... We in the West stand ready to cooperate with the East to promote true openness, to break down barriers that separate people, to create a safe, freer world. And surely there is no better place than Berlin, the meeting place of East and West, to make a start. Free people of Berlin: Today, as in the past, the United States stands for the strict observance and full implementation of all parts of the Four Power Agreement of 1971. Let us use this occasion, the 750th anniversary of this city, to usher in a new era, to seek a still fuller, richer life for the Berlin of the future. Together, let us maintain and develop the ties between the Federal Republic and the Western sectors of Berlin, which is permitted by the 1971 agreement. And I invite Mr. Gorbachev: Let us work to bring the Eastern and Western parts of the city closer together, so that all the inhabitants of all Berlin can enjoy the benefits that come with life in one of the great cities of the world.*

Like his hero Roosevelt, delivering a fireside chat to the nation on the wireless, Reagan is masterfully conversational even in his solemn moments. The first president to come alive on camera, Reagan filled the screen and had a comforting speaking voice. As befits a former actor, Reagan knew how to hit the stresses in a line, but the fact that his words were so good means some credit is due to his writers. There has rarely been a clearer divide between speaker and writer than there was with Reagan. Henry Kissinger has noted that the only part of the job that Reagan sweated over was the preparation of speeches. Notoriously indolent, Reagan once said: 'It's true that hard work never killed anybody, but I figured why take the chance?' He employed, instead, writers like Peggy Noonan, the finest of modern speechwriters, author of Reagan's superb speech at Pointe du Hoc in Normandy on the fortieth anniversary of the D-Day landings.

This raises the perennial question of to whom the great lines are due – the writer or the speaker? The answer is that the fiction must be maintained. There was only one man behind the bulletproof glass partition at the Brandenburg Gate. It was Reagan who had the final say on whether to deliver the immortal line. He did and so it is his. So is the argument he makes here, which is a universal case for the trinity of liberty, capitalism and democracy. Reagan believed that everyone would draw the same conclusion he had, if given the opportunity. Reagan takes the conflict between East and West of the wall into the world. This is the world made safe by democracy, the extension of the argument begun seven decades before by Woodrow Wilson.

One final proposal, one close to my heart: Sport represents a source of enjoyment and ennoblement ... And what better way to demonstrate to the world the openness of this city than to offer in some future year to hold the Olympic Games here in Berlin, East and West? In these four decades, as I have said, you Berliners have built a great city. You've done so in spite of threats – the Soviet attempts to impose the East-mark, the blockade. Today the city thrives in spite of the challenges implicit in the very presence of this wall. What keeps you here? ... Something that speaks with a powerful voice of affirmation, that says yes to this city, yes to the future, yes to freedom. In a word, I would submit that what keeps you in Berlin is love – love both profound and abiding. Perhaps this gets to the root of the matter, to the most fundamental distinction of all between East and West. The totalitarian world produces backwardness because it does such violence to the spirit, thwarting the human impulse to create, to enjoy, to worship ... As I looked out a moment ago from the Reichstag, that embodiment of German unity, I noticed words crudely spray-painted upon the wall, perhaps by a young Berliner: 'This wall will fall. Beliefs become reality'. Yes, across Europe, this wall will fall. For it cannot withstand faith; it cannot withstand truth. The wall cannot withstand freedom. And I would like, before I close, to say one word. I have read, and I have been questioned since I've been here about certain demonstrations against my coming. And I would like to say just one thing, and to those who demonstrate so. I

> *wonder if they have ever asked themselves that if they should have*
> *the kind of government they apparently seek, no one would ever be*
> *able to do what they're doing again. Thank you and God bless you*
> *all.*

A slight whimper to end a speech so powerful which reminds me of the annual last-minute scramble, at the Labour Party conference, for a policy announcement to crowbar uneasily into the text. How can we make the news?, I can hear Reagan's writers say. Let's call for Berlin to have the Olympic Games. The judgement looks faulty in retrospect but the immediate reaction to the speech was underwhelming. The German weekly *Die Zeit* did not even quote the request to Gorbachev. The 1987 speech really only came to prominence after the wall came down in 1989. By then it had begun to sound like the words of a prophet. This invites us to wonder about how much a speech like this changes the course of history. Condoleezza Rice co-wrote a book about the end of the Cold War in which she gave the speech only a walk-on part. Former Secretary of State George P. Schultz does not mention it at all in 1,184 pages of his memoirs. The political theatre certainly seems to have helped Mr Gorbachev with *uskorenie*, with acceleration.

Two years later, in November 1989, the East Germans issued a decree for the wall to be opened, allowing people to travel freely into West Berlin. Families that had been separated for decades were finally reunited. On 13 June 1990 the people of Berlin began the joyous process of tearing down the 109 miles of wall. Communism collapsed in Eastern Europe and in Soviet Russia itself. The exact but crucial contribution of Mr Gorbachev was to do nothing. As the crowd tore down the wall, taking blocks as historic souvenirs, citizens danced on the wider section of the wall surrounding the Brandenburg Gate which became instantly the symbol of liberty. The Berlin Wall had been a deadly frontier. Before its construction something in the order of 3.5 million people had fled across the border from East to West Germany. It was quiet going the other way. The wall had stopped the human traffic, but dissidents tried anyway. Approximately 5,000 people had managed to make it over or under the wall but 260 people had been killed, most of them shot by East German border guards.

Reagan left office in January 1989 with the highest approval rating of any departing president since that of his hero Franklin D. Roosevelt. After he had left office, he took a return trip to Berlin, in September 1990, a matter of weeks before Germany was officially reunified. With a hammer in his hand he took a few swings at the remaining chunks of the wall.

There is one last twist to this speech. Reagan is just lifting himself to the full heights of his finale when he notices some graffiti spray on the wall and breaks from his script to read it aloud. 'This wall will fall. Beliefs become reality' it says. What a great ending this would have been. The president who reads the writing on the wall. Instead, he goes back to the text with a superfluous commonplace dig at those who had protested about his visit. It is a flaw in a speech that is otherwise brilliantly crafted, but it doesn't matter much. Ronald Reagan had seen the writing on the wall anyway.

JUST WAR

To start with David Lloyd George's arresting image, democracy is worth the scrap of paper it's written on. The system of democratic liberty is superior to its rivals and it is worth fighting for. This is a difficult argument to press these days. Populism has wormed its way into democratic politics and planted an insidious lack of confidence in the institutions of democracies. Western nations are oddly apt to blame themselves for the world's troubles. Self-criticism is, of course, one of the attributes of a democracy, but self-loathing is not. The colonial adventures of the nineteenth century, the anti-communist conflicts that upheld dubious regimes in the twentieth century and the various military disasters in the Middle East of recent years provide a ready historical roster of Western culpability.

It sounds vainglorious and imperial to state baldly that democratic societies are superior to their non-democratic counterparts, but it is true all the same and the arguments that democracies make for war show why it is true. Whenever a democracy is in military combat with an autocracy, we should favour the democracy. Hold it to a higher standard of conduct and never stint on warranted criticism, but do not forget which side is the moral victor. That argument needs to be articulated in fine public speech which summons the case for war in sorrow. War can never be a cavalier exercise and great care needs to be taken to ensure that the conflict is just.

The most thorough articulation of a just case for war of recent times was given by Tony Blair at the Economic Club in Chicago in April 1999 in response to NATO action against the ethnic cleansing, systematic rape and mass murder in Kosovo. I can confidently announce that it was a speech to which I contributed not a word, and that it is the most substantive speech Blair ever gave. I can only hope that these two facts are not related. War brought out the best in Tony Blair as a speaker. His second-best speech, which once again lacks my contribution, was the case he made on 18 March 2003 in the House of Commons, for military intervention in Iraq. Read today as it was heard at the time, which is in ignorance of the course of the war, it is the state of the art of rhetorical persuasion. The 2003 speech owes a lot, however, to the address in Chicago four years before in which Blair had given a public expression of the idea of the *iustum bellum*, the just war.

The philosophical tradition of the just war is explained to best effect in the unfinished thirteenth-century classic the *Summa theologicae* of Thomas Aquinas, and in three volumes by the Dutch jurist Hugo Grotius, published in 1625, called *De jure belli ac pacis* (*On the Law of War and Peace*). The just war has three components. The first, known as *ius in bello*, sets out the rules that govern the conduct of war. The battlefield was once a lawless realm in which, in Shakespeare's words from *Macbeth*, 'fair is foul and foul is fair'. However, the attempt to enforce an ethic of war goes back to the references in the Funeral Oration of Pericles to the Athenian code of honour. Homer's *Iliad* is full of such codes and so are the works of Cicero. Moral restraint in war now has legal expression in the Geneva Convention and the protocols of The Hague. The existence of a body of law will never entirely prevent depravity but, despite the shameful absence of the United States, the International Criminal Court has successfully tried war criminals. Court proceedings are a difficult and imperfect response to war crimes. They are also the only response that politics can take to war.

The second part of the just war tradition is an argument that we have seen laced through the speeches of David Lloyd George, Woodrow Wilson and Winston Churchill. *Ius post bellum* describes the moral reasoning that is required to define the peace once the war is won. A war fought to repair a wrong must put it right once peace is restored. The passage in Grotius about the importance of moderation in negotiating the terms of surrender and conquest should be required reading in all democratic states. If the victorious powers had followed this counsel as they drafted the Treaty of Versailles at the end of the Great War, the terrible course of twentieth-century European history might have been avoided. As John Maynard Keynes pointed out in *The Economic Consequences of the Peace*, imposing reparations of £6.6 billion on Germany simply incubated resentment because it was so widely regarded as unjust.

The third part of the idea of the just war is the one that, after the wars in Afghanistan and Iraq and the conflict in Syria, most clearly needs restating. This is the case for military action itself, the account of the fair war, the *ius ad bellum*. Both Aquinas and Grotius argue that a just war can only be waged on the basis of a legitimate sovereign in order to put right a clearly defined wrong.

Aquinas provides a list of relevant wrongs which he has largely derived from Saint Augustine: avenging wrongs, punishing a nation, restoring what has been seized unjustly. Grotius describes the same point as a cause that is designed to prevent or to repair an injury. On the final criterion Aquinas and Grotius differ. Aquinas stresses that a war can only be just if it is the expression of a rightful intention to promote good and forestall evil. He mentions securing the peace, punishing evildoers and uplifting the good as examples of rightful intention. Grotius places his emphasis on the prudential likelihood that good consequences will follow.

This distinction, between intention and consequence, is beautifully dramatised in the speech that Krishna makes in the Hindu epic the *Bhavagad Gita*. On the eve of battle the warrior Arjuna confesses to his adviser Krishna his anxieties about the great loss of life that will be an inevitable result of the fighting. Krishna offers advice of some moral purity that Arjuna must do his duty, no matter the consequences. Krishna's position is endorsed by T. S. Eliot in the *Four Quartets*:

And do not think of the fruit of action.
Fare forward.

[...]

Not fare well,
But fare forward, voyagers.

The distinction between moral intention and consequence, proves to be critical in the context of Blair's Chicago speech and the democratic case for a just war. In Chicago Blair was not especially concerned with the conduct of war. Instead, he provided the most important contemporary updating of the other two parts of the case, the just intervention and the just peace. The latter is the less controversial. Blair's *post bellum* vision for Kosovo would command widespread support even among those who had been sceptical about the case for military action: 'we need to begin work now on what comes after our success in Kosovo. We will need a new Marshall plan for Kosovo, Montenegro, Macedonia, Albania and Serbia too if it turns to democracy'.

The dispute turns on the case for the intervention itself, the *ius ad bellum*. Blair makes the case in Chicago that the rules of the international community need to be rewritten to provide a legitimate sovereign authority for a democracy to go to war. This was Blair's first serious statement in favour of open markets and the rule of international law and against protectionism and nativism. These precepts, he argued, have to be defended and that requires a viable United Nations that can both legitimate and enforce justice. In the event, the national vetoes within the United Nations mean that it has not been a serious protagonist in this process, let alone a source of legitimate authority. That task has been returned, not without controversy, to national legal process.

The main burden of Blair's just war argument is, in an echo of Aquinas, that war must be fought as a retaliation against a clear wrong. The just moral case for action in Kosovo was 'the evil of ethnic cleansing', and much of the Chicago speech is devoted to setting out the moral imperative. Blair's section on the clarity of the military objective, though, reveals a crucial part of the case for the just war that has been forgotten in the aftermath of Iraq. He says in Chicago, quite baldly, that military action should only be undertaken if it can be plausibly asserted that 'we have clear objectives and we are going to succeed'. The objective is very clear indeed: 'a verifiable cessation of all combat activities and killings; the withdrawal of Serb military, police and paramilitary forces from Kosovo; the deployment of an international military force, the return of all refugees and unimpeded access for humanitarian aid; and a political framework for Kosovo'.

In his Chicago account of the just war, Blair is including, quite rightly, an assessment of consequence. Granting free rein to the tyrant, he argues, will be calamitous and make further conflict unavoidable: 'we will have to spill infinitely more blood and treasure to stop him later'. Remember, though, the second half of Blair's just war formula. Action needed not just a clear objective but also the reasonable assumption that 'we are going to succeed'. The military adventures envisaged in the Chicago speech are subject to a prudential caveat. Action should follow, says Blair, only if 'there are military operations we can sensibly and prudently undertake'. He adds the further prudential requirement that intervention can be justified only with a commitment to the long term. The just war must be all three of morally correct, plausibly beneficial and viable.

It is intriguing to apply the Chicago doctrine to Britain's subsequent involvement in the conflict in Iraq. The opposition to that war comes from both a critique of intent and, with the benefit of hindsight unavailable to Blair himself, a reading of the consequences. When no weapons of mass destruction were unearthed the *casus belli* collapsed. In his much later defence of the conflict, Blair himself changed his argument. After the consequences had unfolded and it was hard to argue that the outcome had been beneficial, he often argued from rightful intention – 'I did what I thought was right'. The sophisticated critique of the Iraq war is not the absurd allegation that Blair lied or entered into the conflict for another nefarious reason, it is that he failed to follow his own just war axioms. He has slipped from consequence to rightful intention, from Grotius to Aquinas, Arjuna to Krishna. The Chicago speech makes it clear that both are required.

Blair does not live up to the standard he set in Chicago, which remains a brilliant and durable account of when and how a democratic nation can intervene in the affairs of a rival and retain the mantle of justice. But it would be a terrible dead end if we were to lose the insight of Chicago in the counter-example of Iraq. To intervene in a human catastrophe, such as the instance of Kosovo, can be a noble venture. As Lloyd George pointed out in 1918, it is ignoble not to act in aid of an oppressed nation which has been wronged, even though we fear the consequences.

The prudential clause can, however, be a charter for a tyrant to wreak havoc. It was the bargain that Chamberlain made at Munich.

But there is always a risk involved in the calculus of war. Not all circumstances are as clear as those that faced Churchill in 1940. With the Luftwaffe in the sky over the cities of Britain, fighting back was the only option, and Churchill spoke for the nation at such a moment: 'What is our aim?' he asked. 'Victory, victory at all costs, victory in spite of all terror; victory, however long and hard the road may be; for without victory, there is no survival.'

Most conflicts are not as clear-cut as this, but the Second World War is exemplary as a reminder that a war can be just. Blair's Chicago speech is a sophisticated account of the conditions under which intervention is a more potent moral imperative than absence. Today, in the Western democracies the confidence that we are acting with justice seems to have been mislaid. When we doubt our rightful intention we simply leave others to bear the consequences. We say, in effect, to the people of Syria, not fare forward but farewell.

A World Made Safe by Democracy

It is important to remember that peace and democracy are linked at their deepest points. This argument, which Pericles is the first to make, is common to Lloyd George, Wilson and Churchill, before Ronald Reagan provides its fullest expression in the midst of a cold conflict. The political speech is a statement of a faith in peace. A democrat making the case for war is performing a concession speech, sadly admitting that war is now necessary, to save and then confirm democracy. It is a temporary political ceasefire, to be replaced, until normal service can resume, by gunfire.

The man who pioneered international cooperation was President Wilson. His quest to persuade America failed, as we have seen, and the failure is due in part to the fact that he got his central message exactly the wrong way around. The world does not need, as Wilson argued, to be made safe for democracy. It is democracy that will make the world safe. Democracy does not require, as Wilson suggests, a safe space to inhabit. The rule of law is itself the creation of that security. Liberal institutions are a guarantee of a lower likelihood of conflict. This is, at root, what all war speeches by democrats are about. Lloyd George and Churchill pass through national glory as a means of inspiration, but that is not their subject. Their true topic is democracy.

When democracies get entangled in conflict it is either a colonial adventure or a fight against a tyranny. Between two democracies the only wars are conducted with words. There are too many conflicts in the world today between ethnic rivals within the borders of a single nation-state. There are too many tyrants engaged in quelling popular uprisings. But there is no conflict anywhere, there never has been, and it is unlikely there ever will be, between two established democracies. This is not a curiosity; it is a point about the bedrock of politics. A democracy cannot wage war at the whim of an autocrat. The sceptical public has to be persuaded. This is as close to an empirical law as exists in international relations. In *Triangulating Peace*, Bruce Russett and John Oneal assigned every party to a conflict between 1816 and 2001 a score, on a decimal scale, for its approximation to a liberal democracy. They found that when one country was either a low-scoring democracy or an autocracy the chance of a quarrel between them doubled.

The spread of democracy has therefore been accompanied by an era of comparative peace. The quarter-century since the Berlin Wall was torn down in 1989 has been a time of great progress. The changed nature of warfare means there will never again be anything to compare with the Battle of the Somme or the siege of Leningrad. The last conflict between two great powers, the Korean War, effectively ended nearly sixty years ago. The last sustained territorial war between two regular armies, Ethiopia and Eritrea, ended a decade ago. Even civil wars, though a persistent evil, are less common than in the past; there were about a quarter fewer in 2007 than in 1990. In the first decade of the twenty-first century there were fewer deaths in war than in any decade during the preceding century. Worldwide, deaths caused directly by war-related violence in the same period have averaged about 55,000 per year, just over half of what they were in the 1990s (100,000 a year), a third of what they were during the Cold War (180,000 a year from 1950 to 1989), and a hundredth of what they were in the Second World War.

What democracies do instead of fight is talk and trade. As long ago as 1909 Norman Angell argued that commerce made war unprofitable and conflict was therefore, in the title of his book, *The Great*

Illusion. The richer a nation becomes the more likely to abandon dictatorship for democracy. Of the fifty-six nations with a GDP per capita of $15,000 or more, forty-five are democracies. The only general exception to this rule is the oil curse. When a ruling elite discovers the gift of lucrative natural resources it sees no need of democratic politics. Instant enrichment is simply a vast unearned dividend for the presiding ruling family. However, under a more usual economic development, gradual progress generates a demand for democratic representation. Private property within open markets creates a sphere of autonomy in which all people are granted certain liberties. The more that property ownership extends throughout a society, the more that power is spread. A resilient civil society, one more bulwark against the might of the state, is a characteristic of liberal democracies which, again, gives people something to value.

The great experiment to test this proposition took place in Berlin, the city that, as we have seen, became a Gettysburg away from home for American presidents. In the early hours of 13 August 1961, the people of Berlin had woken to the sound of heavy machinery. Soldiers were stringing barbed wire across a line that divided East and West Berlin. At the end of the Second World War, at the Potsdam Conference just outside Berlin, Germany had been split into quadrants. Berlin was deep within Soviet-controlled Germany. Armed troops stood sentinel over the city's crossing points. The barbed wire was soon replaced by a concrete wall 3.6 metres high which Walter Ulbricht's East German government called the *antifaschistischer Schutzwall*, the anti-fascist barrier. The wall wound through the city centre, encircling the Brandenburg Gate, the ostentatious arch that Friedrich Wilhelm II had modelled on the Acropolis in Athens. Sealed off from the West, the inaccessible Brandenburg Gate became the symbol of a divided and impassable Berlin. The Berlin Wall was the Cold War set in concrete.

It was here, on 26 June 1963, that John F. Kennedy gave one of the great war speeches. During a visit on foot to the Checkpoint Charlie crossing point on Friedrichstrasse, Kennedy had been deeply affected by the state of East Berlin. As he went through his last-minute preparations in the office of Berlin's mayor Willy Brandt, Kennedy was not happy with the speech he was about to deliver. Just before he took the stage, he remembered a phrase from Cicero's *In Verrem:*

Civis Romanus sum. I am a citizen of Rome, we are all citizens of Rome. Any such citizen was guaranteed safe passage across the Roman Empire, in the manner of Paul the Apostle claiming his right to be tried before Caesar. Kennedy wanted to link the Roman republic to the city of Berlin, and by implication to the province of freedom everywhere, by repeating the phrase in German. He added the famous four words to his script at the last minute, scribbling them on the text in his own hand, phonetically so that his pronunciation would be accurate: 'Ish bin ein Bearleener'.

On the way to the West Berlin City Hall at Rathaus Schöneberg, the president's entourage was showered with flowers, rice and torn paper. The schoolchildren of West Berlin were given the day off and a million Berliners, perched on signposts, balconies and rooftops, watched Kennedy pass through the streets in his open limousine on his way to speak to an ecstatic crowd 450,000 strong. He delivered a devastating critique of life on the communist side of the wall and the fundamental difference between a life lived at liberty and a life under state command. 'There are many people in the world,' said the president, 'who really don't understand, or say they don't, what is the great issue between the free world and the Communist world. Let them come to Berlin.'

Of Kennedy's 674 words, fifteen are either 'free' or 'freedom'. He then goes on to predict that the wall will fall and that democracy will in time spread through Eastern Europe. Democracy may not be perfect, says Kennedy, but 'we have never had to put a wall up to keep our people in'. He ended by repeating the best line: 'Today, in the world of freedom, the proudest boast is *Ich bin ein Berliner!* Most of the president's team, including National Security Adviser McGeorge Bundy, thought that Kennedy had gone too far, but the president's words were punctuated by rapturous rounds of applause. At the conclusion of the speech, the Freedom Bell tolled from the belfry of the Rathaus. 'We will never have another day like this one, as long as we live,' Kennedy told Sorensen on the flight home. Alas, that was true. The trip to Berlin was the last foreign excursion Kennedy would ever make before he was assassinated.

Kennedy's argument lived on and his successors came to Berlin to repeat it. Twenty-six years after Kennedy's triumphant day in Berlin, the results of the experiment came in. The Cold War had been won emphatically by liberal democracy and market capitalism, for the reason that Ronald Reagan had the insight to point out. It was an old point. In 1795, in the midst of the French revolutionary wars, Immanuel Kant published an essay called *Perpetual Peace*, in which he made the case that trade between nations will preserve peace in the world, especially in concert in a league of nations. It is still true. Military conflict does not take place between trading nations, and trade helped to win the Cold War. Between the West and the East, it was the quality of the goods in the shops that mattered as much as it was the military hardware, the diplomatic manoeuvres and the philosophical traditions. When Khrushchev took power in 1953 the American economy was three times as large as its Soviet counterpart. Armed with specially computed statistics that drastically overstated the Soviet growth rate, Khrushchev declared that the Soviet economy would overtake America by 1970. The year the Berlin Wall came down, annual GDP growth in the USSR was −3 per cent. In the USA it was 1.9 per cent. By 1991 Soviet GDP per capita had still not reached the level that America had reached in 1945.

When put to the test, in the laboratory conditions of a city divided by a wall into ideological segments, liberal democracy had triumphed over communism. The claim that runs through the rhetoric of Pericles, Lloyd George, Wilson, Churchill and Reagan is that democracy is the crucible of peace. The history of war speeches exhibits the politician who has turned, fleetingly, into a warrior although the only weapons wielded are words. The arguments they all prosecute for the war is to commend the procedures of politics. Pericles turned a eulogy for the war dead into a paean for the *polis*. Wilson echoed Kant's insight that international relations are better conducted in the chambers of conversation. Churchill mobilised the English language for free politics over tyrannical command. Reagan clarified that capitalist prosperity would help to win the war of ideas against communism.

In the annals of war rhetoric the most lasting image of what politics can do that war cannot is Lloyd George's scrap of paper. The words on that paper are those scribbled at the last moment on Kennedy's script. *Ich bin ein Berliner.* I am a citizen of the world. They are the words that guarantee peace and the promise of rules rather than *force majeure*. These are the words that democratic politicians have to use to justify the war they advocate.

The Fog of War

There is a lot of fog out there on the battlefield, said Clausewitz. The public arguments for war in democracies are also now lost in a fog. The beneficial consequences of the intervention in Kosovo, which provided the context for Blair's Chicago speech, have been overwhelmed by the contrary instance of Iraq. The verdict on the great speeches is always hard to separate from the verdict on the wars they justify. It is generally thought that, if the Great War had the poetry, the Second World War took the prize for rhetoric. Yet Lloyd George and the great pinnacle of sacrifice shows this is as much an account of our retrospective view of the war as it is an appreciation of Churchill. As the historical scholarship revises our view of the Great War as a necessary conflict, then the speeches that were made in its defence will be subject to a reassessment.

Yet stasis has its consequences too. Whereas the consequences of action can be visibly appalling, inaction can likewise do harm. The free reign of terror granted to President Assad in Syria might, conceivably, be marginally less gruesome than the upshot of Western intervention, but it is in the nature of such calculations that no answer will ever be known. It is not obvious that we are doing, or not doing, the right thing. Cowed by sins of commission and shamed by sins of omission, democracies seem unsure how to respond to this, the most grave of perils they ever encounter. The template is broken. We await the great speech setting out the circumstances in which it is just not to act. We are now, more than ever, in need of the tradition of the just war which lay dormant in the academy for centuries until the prospect of nuclear annihilation revived it. The terrorist attacks on New York of 11 September 2001 made the just war a required concept again.

A just war must be the last resort, after the exhaustion of diplomatic good faith. The power of words must have been thoroughly explored first before physical force can be justified, and only then with reluctance. But when the cause is just, the words will be noble as well as memorable. War is the opposite of politics, but sometimes politics has to be fought for. This is a point that Woodrow Wilson makes in his book *Man Will See the Truth*. The very idea of the war speech is to declare war with regret and commend politics with relish. In *Just and Unjust Wars* Michael Walzer argues that states, the power that protects the rights of individuals, have a right to defend themselves against external threat. People have the right to develop a common life together and to live in concert in a political community.

Pericles gives birth to that idea of the political community in a speech ostensibly dedicated to those who fell in battle. He inaugurates the idea that the war has the noble purpose of strengthening the commitment to democracy. At a remove of twenty centuries, it is astonishing how similar David Lloyd George and Woodrow Wilson sound amid the thunder of the Great War, and then again what echoes ring from the resounding rhetoric of Winston Churchill in the summer of 1940. By the time Ronald Reagan implores Mikhail Gorbachev to tear down the Berlin Wall, democratic politics has become not just the purpose of the war but the method by which it is fought. The aim is always the same. It is, at the final and in the finest hours, to create, through the expedient and unfortunate necessity of war, a land fit for heroes.

3

NATION:
THROUGH POLITICS THE
NATION IS DEFINED

Imagined Communities

A nation has to be spoken into existence. That arresting phrase from John Quincy Adams from his speech to the House of Representatives on Independence Day 1821 rightly puts the nationalism before the nation. No country exists before people talk about it. It is not providence, or nature, or blood or culture that defines a nation in its origins. It is speech. It is the proclamation that the people are identical with one another in one crucial respect – they share a nationality. This means the articulation of a common history, shared stories of origin and symbols of national belonging. This claim is then recognised by the panoply of civic laws and attendant rights and this conjunction creates the modern nation-state. Citizenship becomes a legal fact, but nationhood starts as a political claim, in speech.

Nations are, in the title of Benedict Anderson's fine book, *Imagined Communities*. That does not mean they are not real. Linda Colley's *Britons: Forging The Nation 1707–1837* is the story of a conscious process of historical creation. A nation is an achievement before it is a place. In the case of the strange multinational state of Britain this is an especially precarious task. Nationhood is the expression of solidarity rather than the discovery of a common race of men. Anderson dates national consciousness to the invention of the printing press, the creation of the novel and the appearance of newspapers. For the first time, men and women could experience the stories of people like themselves, being lived out in their own day.

Nationhood remains the most potent form of allegiance in modern politics. Affiliation to the nation has always trumped the claim of class and has always stood in the way of durable multinational institutions. Woodrow Wilson's dream of a League of Nations lasted just twenty-seven years. It is revealing that no great speech has ever been made in defence of the United Nations, which ought to be a promising subject. As the Remain campaign unwittingly showed in Britain in 2016, it is also hard to find elevated rhetoric in defence of the idea of the European Union. Almost all of the memorable speeches about the European Union, certainly in Britain, as we shall see, have been in defence of the nation-state.

In the history of speeches there are two stories of nationalism. The first was told, as we have seen, by Winston Churchill, whose speeches helped to bind the nation against the threat of a predator. This is the rhetoric of *risorgimento* nationalism which was the signature tune of the Greek and Latin American independence wars and the struggles in Indochina and Eastern Europe. The nation in this incarnation always marches in the pageant of progress.

But thereby hangs the other, darker story of nationalism. Churchill's eloquence was only required because it was a response to the egregious ethnic expansionism of Adolf Hitler's German nationalism. Before Hitler, and before modern amplification, no speaker had ever used the ritualistic occasion of the speech to greater or more malign effect. The European Union was formed in 1957 precisely because of the excesses of blood-and-thunder nationalism. Its founding purpose was to ensure that war would be impossible in the European theatre again. Its assembly of nations would restrain the exclusive claim of superiority that had brought Europe to the brink of catastrophe. Whatever else can be said subsequently of the European Union, it succeeded in that noble and historic aim.

As a community of the imagination, the nation needs to be enacted in rituals. A great deal of drama goes into embodying a nation in moments of communion. The oldest ritual of them all is the political speech. In each of the speeches that follow, the leader's address defines the virtues of belonging to the nation. No individual personifies the invisible state more completely than a monarch. *L'état, c'est moi.* Louis XIV's famous identification applies perfectly to Elizabeth I, whose rhetoric of indomitability was directed at two

potent enemies – the Spanish Armada which was gathering menac-
ingly in the English Channel and the sexism that greeted her claims
to authority.

There has never been a more consciously created nation than
the United States of America. The founding documents of the
American constitution do not verify nationhood that had already
been achieved. They were themselves the formation of that nation.
The founding fathers are the Romulus and Remus of the modern
age. Chief among them was Benjamin Franklin, one of the most
remarkable men of his or any other time, who spoke vitally in favour
of the constitution at a moment of peril.

America was not the last time that separate states had to decide
whether or not to join together in the more perfect union of a nation.
The same task befell Jawaharlal Nehru, India's first prime minister,
whose words helped to usher into being a steadfast new nation out of
its disparate principalities and competing ethnic and religious identities. The seventy-year story of Indian democracy has not lacked its
travails and setbacks, but a nation resembling Nehru's vision is still
there, and there is something unlikely and magnificent about that.

Nehru's instinct to bring people together is too often denied in
favour of a shrunken and exclusive idea of who truly belongs to the
people. In the dock in Rivonia, South Africa, Nelson Mandela gave a
magnificent retort to a racial definition of who belongs in his country.
As a former resident returning to Burma from exile abroad, Aung San
Suu Kyi was also denied standing in her own country. Swapping exile
in Oxford for exile in Rangoon, she spoke to reclaim power for the
Burmese people from the military dictatorship that had usurped
their authority.

It follows from the fact that nations are invented that there can
be better or worse nationalisms. Some countries tell generous stories
about who can be included in the definition of the nation. Others are
more exclusive. Even though nations are usually described in the
language of kith and kin, they are not natural human categories, and
they need to be argued into life. The members of even the smallest
nations on earth will never know most of their fellow citizens. Yet
somehow in the minds of all citizens of the nation there is the idea
of something shared with people they will never meet. That bond is
more than obedience to a common authority. It is an idea of a

country, a shared mental space. 'There are two countries, real and fictional, occupying the same space,' said Salman Rushdie in *Shame*. Unfortunately, in the history of nationalism, shame is too often the appropriate emotion.

ELIZABETH I OF ENGLAND

I Have the Heart and Stomach of a King

Tilbury

9 August 1588

Elizabeth I of England (1533–1603) was the first English monarch to lend her name to an age. In the Elizabethan era, England first gained a national consciousness. Her reign was the time that launched England as a major sea power and saw the greatest flourishing of English literature yet and probably since. Elizabeth was queen of England and Ireland from 1558 until her death in 1603, the last monarch of the Tudor dynasty.

A life less extraordinary had looked likely when Elizabeth lost her claim to the throne after the execution of her mother Anne Boleyn by her father Henry VIII for alleged adultery and treason. Elizabeth was just two years of age. Later, after the tempest of the English Reformation, she was imprisoned by her Catholic half-sister Mary, who accused her of taking part in a Protestant plot. Following Mary's death in 1558, Elizabeth was restored to the line of succession and acceded to the throne.

She became only the third woman ever to hold the office of Queen Regnant in England, and there was a strong presumption that her time on the throne would be precarious and fleeting. Elizabeth's two predecessor queens, her cousin Lady Jane Grey and her half-sister Mary I, had not lasted long. Their short reigns were ascribed at the time to their gender. The monarch was commander-in-chief of the army, the head of the English Church, and suzerain over a court that was fashioned to uphold a man ruling among his peers. It was simply assumed that a woman would struggle with such work. The obvious solution, much canvassed, would have been marriage. But

Elizabeth refused to bow to the expectation, instead cultivating a reputation for being wedded to her subjects or, as we would now say, married to the job.

It was a turbulent reign and Elizabeth needed all of her great strength and fortitude. This was an age of religious controversy, with England in the earliest stages of becoming a Protestant nation. The tumult led to constant, although mostly ineffectual, plotting in France, Spain and the Papal court to invade England and restore Catholicism. For the same reason, Elizabeth's reign was punctuated by a string of revolts and assassination attempts, all of which, mercifully, failed.

The speech that follows survives as a written text, transcribed from its Elizabethan idiom into English that is more readably comprehensible to us today. We cannot be sure, in truth, whether the speech as we now have it was ever delivered. The surviving text derives, rather unsatisfactorily, from a letter by Dr Leonel Sharp, a churchman and courtier later imprisoned for sedition, to the duke of Buckingham thirty-five years after the event. There are rhetorical echoes in the writing of other speeches Elizabeth gave, which is some nebulous evidence to suggest that the text is close enough to genuine. There is, however, no contemporary attesting evidence, so it is impossible to know.

If the speech was ever delivered, it was given to the English troops who had assembled in Tilbury to resist invasion by the Spanish Armada. Relations between England and Spain had been tottering for years, and Philip II of Spain had twice supported plans to invade England and place Mary Stuart on the throne. Elizabeth hadn't exactly eased the tension with her refusal of Philip's courtship. It broke after the execution of Mary Stuart, who shortly before her death had written to Philip to make her claim on the English throne. He greeted her death as the invitation to enforce that claim.

On 28 May 1588, Philip's naval fighting force left Spain for England. As the Spanish Armada gathered in the North Sea there was also a large and professional Spanish army in the Low Countries. The force of the words that follow derives from the troubling fact that, as Elizabeth steps up to speak, England faces genuine peril.

My loving people, we have been persuaded by some that are
careful of our safety, to take heed how we commit ourselves to
armed multitudes, for fear of treachery; but I assure you I do not
desire to live to distrust my faithful and loving people. Let tyrants
fear.

This speech is a telling example of the idea of character in rhetoric, and the character Elizabeth is playing, to great effect here, is the nation itself. There is a scholarly controversy about whether Elizabeth created this sense of formidable character by her physical image. Many of the historical and pictorial accounts of the occasion depict the queen on the back of a white steed in, variously, different types of armour, a white gown with a steel corselet, wielding a truncheon and sporting a helmet with a plume of feathers. The typical armoured representation is Britomart, an allegorical character in Spenser's epic poem *The Faerie Queen* who stands for English virtue and military power. It is more than likely that these representations depict the character Elizabeth was displaying rather than the clothing she actually wore.

In his famous trinity of rhetorical virtues, Aristotle distinguished the appeal to rational argument (*logos*) from the call on the emotions (*pathos*). But the hardest of the three elements to manufacture was *ethos*, the character of the speaker, the sense of the personal communicated when a speaker stands alone. The word 'character' has an important dual connotation. Character is a set of virtues we display which add up to who we are. But we also use the word 'character' to describe a figure in fiction. That usage too is relevant to rhetoric, and it is highly relevant to the imagined community of the nation.

In the case of Elizabeth, the character on display is an enhanced version of the actual person who had stood nervously at the mouth of the river Thames a few moments before. Elizabeth Tudor has one major advantage over any other speaker. She is the Queen of England. She is the nation. She uses this immediately to define her character. She identifies here at once with the people, seeking authority from the subjects she is addressing. She does this by refusing to doubt their fidelity to a task that is, by implication, bound to be onerous. She transfers the fear that she will be feeling and that her audience and soldiers will have been feeling onto the absent tyrant.

I have always so behaved myself that, under God, I have placed my chiefest strength and safeguard in the loyal hearts and good-will of my subjects; and therefore I am come amongst you, as you see, at this time, not for my recreation and disport, but being resolved, in the midst and heat of the battle, to live and die amongst you all; to lay down for my God, and for my kingdom, and my people, my honour and my blood, even in the dust.

The peril is so grave that a sacrifice may be called for. Victory is by no means assured, and Elizabeth makes it clear that she is prepared to pay the price herself. That is a vital message, as her purpose here is to rally the troops. Before speaking, Elizabeth had watched a mimicked battle in which the English were victorious. She then seeks to inspire the troops by conjuring the spirit of her people. They are not citizens, of course. The word *subjects* also conjures the shadow of the monarch who makes them so, but it is still notable that Elizabeth's appeal to the troops is done not in the name of power and the prestige of office but in that of service to the nation, which she evokes by asserting her own. This is a democratic form of address for a monarch to make, an association with the nation. No political institution is so wrapped up in the personal as the monarchy. The queen, in time of war, is the embodiment of national mythology.

I know I have the body but of a weak and feeble woman; but I have the heart and stomach of a king, and of a king of England too, and think foul scorn that Parma or Spain, or any prince of Europe, should dare to invade the borders of my realm: to which rather than any dishonour shall grow by me, I myself will take up arms, I myself will be your general, judge, and rewarder of every one of your virtues in the field.

This is the critical question that has, until this point in the speech, been unspoken. Elizabeth knows that the most barbed criticism of her reign, at a time of military crisis, is that she is a woman who does not have the strength to command the armed forces. The contrast with the excessively masculine Henry VIII lay like a shadow over the scene. Instead of stepping around the problem, Elizabeth confronts it by articulating the criticism. There is a general lesson here. Criticism is better countered if it is named honestly. Elizabeth describes exactly the thought the objector will have. She takes the opposing view seriously by seeming to accept it before she renders it irrelevant. It is not the body that matters but the spirit, and the confrontation shows that she has plenty of that. Call me weak and you call this nation weak. The nation in question was, of course, England.

Then, at the end of the counter-attack, she associates herself directly with the king. This is the king in general, the attributes that men might hitherto have regarded as a male preserve, but also the king in particular, Elizabeth's father Henry. In a single sentence she has turned an apparent weakness into a signal strength.

That shift of tone allows her to name the enemy. The duke of Parma was the governor-general of the Netherlands and leader of the Spanish army. He had a plan that the Armada would pick up his troops there before crossing the Channel to invade England. The Armada was already, at this point, assembled in the North Sea, but neither Elizabeth nor anyone else knew exactly where. The danger was palpable and the men at Tilbury would have been scared. So would the monarch. The rhetorical moment demands that she betrays no fear and countenances no prospect of defeat. The question of Elizabeth's gender is pertinent here. The fear of a king might conceivably have been attributed to realism. A queen's fear would certainly have been ascribed to her gender.

I know already, for your forwardness you have deserved rewards and crowns; and we do assure you in the word of a prince, they shall be duly paid you. In the meantime, my lieutenant general shall be in my stead, than whom never prince commanded a more noble or worthy subject; not doubting but by your obedience to my general, by your concord in the camp, and your valour in the field, we shall shortly have a famous victory over those enemies of my God, of my kingdom, and of my people.

And there, after two and a half minutes and two hundred and fifty words, she concludes. It was customary for Elizabethan orators to speak, in church and in Parliament, for at least an hour. Elizabeth was known at the time for appreciating good writing and the speech is elegantly put together. She was also known not to like long disquisitions, but this speech is short even for her.

Of course, once she has established her credentials as a national leader, Elizabeth has the perfect way of ensuring that her words are heeded. As queen she is the sovereign authority and the embodiment of the law. That is a quite an advantage when, as a speaker, you are asking for attention. To refuse to countenance defeat is a risky strategy because it is, after all, a defiance of the truth. No such certainty is warranted. But rhetoric is not a strict observation of the facts. It is an attempt to inspire. Elizabeth is saying here not what is but what must be. She strives to elicit the outcome she desires, to define the national characteristics that will prevail.

The end of the speech was greeted, according to contemporary reports, with great acclamation from the men in the battalion. The queen stayed near the camp for a week, and then learnt, soon after she had left, that the Armada had been scattered and the plan for an invasion abandoned. It was a defining moment in her reign. To the extent that Elizabeth I remains an English icon today, her reputation is owed largely to this speech, this moment at Tilbury.

BENJAMIN FRANKLIN

I Agree to This Constitution with All Its Faults

The Constitutional Convention, Philadelphia

17 September 1787

Benjamin Franklin (1706–90) was the only man to sign all three of the Declaration of Independence (1776), the Treaty of Paris (1783) and the American Constitution (1787). A man of polymathic capacity, he was an author, a printer, a scientist, an inventor, and a diplomat. He was, in the title given to him by Immanuel Kant in 1753, 'the modern Prometheus'.

Franklin was born into a devout Puritan family in the Boston of the early eighteenth century, the fifteenth child of his father's seventeen children. He learnt the art of printing and gained an acquaintance with the political classics as an apprentice to his older brother James. In 1721 the Franklins published the Whig bible, Henry Care's *English Liberties.* James Franklin also published a newspaper, *The New England Courant*, which was notably critical of the secular and religious authorities. Work as a printer in Philadelphia and London followed before Franklin established his own enterprise in Philadelphia. His newspaper and almanac soon became the best-selling periodical in colonial America.

At the age of forty-two Franklin retired to devote himself to the pursuit of civil life, science and literature, in all three of which endeavours he was accomplished to an almost incredible standard. Franklin was the first American to become internationally famous. He became renowned as the greatest scientist of the mid-eighteenth century. He was a fellow of the Royal Society in London and a foreign member of the French Royal Academy of Science. Franklin's proof that lightning was electrical opened a new frontier of knowledge. For his studies in electricity he won the 1753 Copley Medal of the Royal Society of London, the nearest contemporary equivalent of which would be the Nobel Prize for Physics. Crossing the two cultures seemingly without strain, Franklin was also regarded by David Hume as the first great American man of letters and the outstanding literary propagandist of his time. His reputation was forged by his essays, satires, letters, bagatelles and an *Autobiography* that became the most popular of the century.

In the spare time he found when he wasn't adding to knowledge through his scientific invention or to the culture through his writing, Franklin was active in public life. He threw himself into the civic life of Pennsylvania, founding hospitals and insurance companies and introducing street lighting. He was elected to the Pennsylvania Assembly, became the state's representative to Great Britain and was a personal and political success as minister plenipotentiary to France.

The speech that follows comes at the end of this long, vigorous and almost incredibly successful life. The Constitutional Convention, which was held in closed sessions at Independence Hall, Philadelphia, was the crowning act of the American Revolution. Under George Washington as president, fifty-five delegates devised a permanent framework for the government of the American nation. Success, though, was not guaranteed. After more than three months of deliberation, a draft was finally agreed on 15 September. Two days later the convention was due to meet to sign the official parchment version. If agreement could not be reached, the convention leaders were anxious that delegates might revisit the grievances that had accumulated in the course of discussion and refuse to sign the final document.

Franklin had written to Jefferson a month before the meeting to insist that if the convention could do no good then he, Jefferson, must ensure that it did no harm. Franklin had been active in the Constitutional Convention, in which he had proposed the Great Compromise that would ensure that election to the House of Representatives was by population while election to the Senate was by state. The leaders of the convention therefore approached him to ask Franklin to speak last, to make a plea for unity, to speak for the fledgling nation of America. On 17 September 1787 that was what he did.

> *Mr. President, I confess that there are several parts of this constitution which I do not at present approve, but, Sir, I am not sure I shall never approve them: for having lived long, I have experienced many instances of being obliged by better information, or fuller consideration, to change opinions even on important subjects, which I once thought right, but found to be otherwise. It is therefore that the older I grow, the more apt I am to doubt my own judgment, and to pay more respect to the judgment of others.*

This was meant to be Franklin's final public speech. In the event it almost was. At the age of eighty-one, Franklin was frail, and these opening lines were the only ones he got to speak. Then, his voice faltering, he had to hand his script to the lawyer James Wilson to read the rest. It is apparent at once that the tone of the speech is going to be conciliatory. This is a clever, almost sly, opening. On a first reading it seems humble – the style is plain and the idiom demotic – but there is more under the surface. Alan Bennett gave a line to George II that we should keep in mind with brilliant speakers: 'I have remembered how to seem'. Or 'pretending to be me', as Larkin said. James McHenry, delegate to the convention from Maryland, described the speech afterwards as 'plain, insinuating, persuasive', three epithets that point in three different directions.

The revisions in the extant manuscripts of Franklin's speech show how hard he worked for exactly the desired effects. In his original draft Franklin's first sentence was blunter: 'I must own that there are several Parts of this Constitution which I do not at present approve, but I am not sure I shall ever approve them'. The change of *ever* to *never* reverses the meaning. It adds humility; doubt replaces the original certainty. Franklin inserts the word 'confess' in the first sentence, rather than 'must own', which adds gravity to his deliberation. Throughout he is trying to be soft. The original drafting had Franklin saying that 'I do not approve' the Constitution. This gets muffled, on reflection, to 'I do not at present approve', thereby permitting the possibility of change. Franklin's labour shows that speechwriting is a poorly named discipline. The real tasks – thinking and editing – come before and after the writing. The craft and the rewriting here produce the insinuating effect.

The last important drafting revision is the insertion of the word 'Sir' into the first sentence. This is both a direct address to the man at the top and, in the presence of an exclusively male audience, a way of binding the assembled to the president. The word 'Sir' breaks the sentence nicely, pays homage to the office and signals the complicity of the audience in the request that is about to come. Franklin introduces his governing theme, which is flexibility, tolerance of dissent, a spirit of compromise. There is a pleasing symmetry of content and style throughout. Look at the odd usage of 'otherwise' in counterposition to 'right', when the obvious word, begging to be used, is the more straightforward 'wrong'. But though 'wrong' has the right meaning it has the wrong effect. Franklin is not only *talking* about an open mind. He is *dramatising* an open mind. The axiom of the novelist and the screen-writer – show, don't tell – applies to the good speechwriter too.

> *In these sentiments, Sir, I agree to this Constitution with all its faults, if they are such; because I think a general Government necessary for us, and there is no form of Government but what may be a blessing to the people if well administered, and believe farther that this is likely to be well administered for a course of years, and can only end in Despotism, as other forms have done before it, when the people shall become so corrupted as to need despotic Government, being incapable of any other. I doubt too whether any other Convention we can obtain, may be able to make a better Constitution. For when you assemble a number of men to have the advantage of their joint wisdom, you inevitably assemble with those men, all their prejudices, their passions, their errors of opinion, their local interests, and their selfish views. From such an assembly can a perfect production be expected? It therefore astonishes me, Sir, to find this system approaching so near to perfection as it does; and I think it will astonish our enemies, who are waiting with confidence to hear that our councils are confounded like those of the Builders of Babel; and that our States are on the point of separation, only to meet hereafter for the purpose of cutting one another's throats.*

Franklin gets democratic theory and democratic practice into a sentence: 'I agree to this Constitution with all its faults'. Democracy is never perfect. The ideal is a standard against which we gauge our practice, not a measure of our fidelity. A nation is a living process and all citizens will find something to quarrel with. The task, which Franklin captures, is not agreement but consensus; an acceptable deal rather than total satisfaction.

It is important, though, not to be taken in by Franklin's highly crafted rhetoric. The style is, ultimately, a pose. He is making the case for compromise, in a spirit of rapprochement, and yet this is still a partisan exercise. Every speech ever made has one of three possible functions: to change knowledge, perception or behaviour. Franklin knows what he wants his audience to do and is seeking to induce them to act after his instruction. His studied moderation is feigned. This is the art that Cicero called *concessio*; appearing to give way then, having won the right to speak by deliberately losing an unimportant battle, joining the war. Don't forget that the reason Franklin has prepared this speech is so that delegates may sign the document. He longs for the nation to be born. It is not an exercise in academic inquiry.

The influence of Cicero on the Founding Fathers was substantive as well as stylistic. The men who gathered in Freedom Hall in Philadelphia during the sweltering summer of 1787 were the beneficiaries of a classical school curriculum. *The Federalist Papers*, written by James Madison, Alexander Hamilton and John Jay, borrowed the form of a speech by Demosthenes and were published under the name of Publius. In the constitutional debates of May to September 1787, delegates had invoked the heroes and the institutions of the Roman republic as models for their utopian task. The early revolutionary pamphlets had been strewn with Latin and Greek tags and quotations from Thucydides and Cicero. In his *Defence of the Constitutions of Governments of the United States of America*, John Adams had applauded Cicero's case for a mixed government of monarchical, aristocratic and democratic elements.

Cicero's argument was that the consuls were a form of monarchy, the senate a form of aristocracy, and the masses were the element of democracy. Adams and James Madison both attributed the falls of Greece and Rome to the imbalance between the different estates of the realm. This was why the Constitution was replete with checks on power. It was why the Founders inserted a provision to prevent the rule of a demagogue which they regarded as instrumental in the decline of the Roman Republic. Article Two of the constitution, which limits the term and powers of the president, was precisely designed to prevent a Caesar-like figure from assuming command.

> *Thus I consent, Sir, to this Constitution because I expect no better, and because I am not sure, that it is not the best. The opinions I have had of its errors, I sacrifice to the public good. I have never whispered a syllable of them abroad. Within these walls they were born, and here they shall die. If every one of us in returning to our Constituents were to report the objections he has had to it, and endeavour to gain partisans in support of them, we might prevent its being generally received, and thereby lose all the salutary effects & great advantages resulting naturally in our favour among foreign Nations as well as among ourselves, from our real or apparent unanimity.*

Often a good speech is a series of variations on a single theme. Franklin really has one point – men should not allow the fictional perfect to be the enemy of the acceptable good. To do so imperils the nation that we are here to constitute. His variation here is to point out that, as a diplomat in Britain and France, he had always been loyal to the republic.

Yet, as there usually is with Franklin, there is a clever subtext. There is an ingratiating, cleverly coded, second argument. On the surface Franklin is requesting acquiescence with an imperfect constitution. At the same time, his stylistic conceit, of admitting to doubt, also has the effect of making those doubts plain. If the constitution passes, Franklin can claim to have convinced the doubters. If it does not pass, there is plenty of evidence that Franklin never really believed in the constitution anyway. There are two speeches written through every line, one that is saving the constitution and the other that is saving face.

This can only be done because Franklin is who he is. The character of the Grand Old Man of American politics lends authority to the argument. Quite outrageously, Franklin claims to stand above the fray, like a surveying monarch. He is, at once, an ingratiating activist and an impartial spectator. This touches on one of the perennial paradoxes of democratic power and of nationhood. The association of Franklin and Washington, the two titans of the revolutionary struggles, was critical to the success of the convention. So the system of government that enshrined the power of the people was, at the same time, built on a cult of leadership. The nation has always needed its heroes.

> *Much of the strength and efficiency of any Government in procuring and securing happiness to the people, depends, on opinion, on the general opinion of the goodness of the Government, as well as of the wisdom and integrity of its Governors. I hope therefore that for our own sakes as a part of the people, and for the sake of posterity, we shall act heartily and unanimously in recommending this Constitution (if approved by Congress and confirmed by the Conventions) wherever our influence may extend, and turn our future thoughts and endeavours to the means of having it well administered. On the whole, Sir, I cannot help expressing a wish that every member of the Convention who may still have objections to it, would with me, on this occasion doubt a little of his own infallibility, and to make manifest our unanimity, put his name to this instrument.*

Suddenly, with the conclusion looming, Franklin makes a personal appeal. The rest of the speech would lead us to expect him to say, in biblical fashion, 'Let us hope'. But he doesn't. He says, much more directly, 'I hope ...' He then increases the stakes by enfolding future generations, for the sake of posterity. Note then how artfully Franklin changes his demand. The whole speech has been a request for a hearing, for tolerance, for a spirit of reason to allow the nation to come to fruition. The speech has been a set-up, a kind of verbal larceny, because here, in a sentence, Franklin undercuts the dominant ethos and demands unanimity for his brand of tolerated dissent.

The extent to which Franklin intended this speech as an act of persuasion is shown by the fact that it was printed and published widely in America. It was an appeal to the republic as well as to its leaders, and it became a touchstone in the debate in the states over ratification. This was a more common tactic in an age before electrification, in which the distinction between the oral and the written was not marked. First television and then the internet have remade the connection now that speeches are cut up and disseminated in bites digestible in different formats.

This is the one defence of the accusation that modern political rhetoric is a slave to the soundbite. A speech is going to be edited down to a six-second definition by a broadcaster in any case, so it's better that the writing, by encapsulating the main thought in a witty maxim, should be a guide to that editing. The other defence is that soundbites are as old as writing. To be or not to be – that really was the question of the play, and if Shakespeare were to be given a quick segment of the six o'clock news he would have been disappointed if that line was not picked up in the report.

Franklin then goes on to make the critical point that politics begins rather than ends with signatures on a Constitution. The nation starts with those signatures; the job is simply beginning. Political wisdom is a process of governing well, not the words of a blueprint. But the first step in the process is to sign the document.

The speech inspired personal vituperation. Some correspondents took issue not just with the words Franklin wrote for the convention but the course of his whole career. As Franklin later wrote to his French friend Le Veillard: 'Much party heat there was, and some violent personal abuse'. Read now, there seems to be a strain of valedictory melancholy to Franklin's words. This was the culmination of a distinguished life as a propagandist and persuader. It would be too much to ascribe the outcome to this speech alone. Assessing the contribution of a single rhetorical moment is always hard. In any event, the constitution was signed by thirty-nine out of the fifty-five delegates. It was then submitted to the states for approval, which did emerge. The Constitution was eventually ratified by the required nine states in 1788. The eloquence of all the early founders had contributed a chapter to the creation of the American nation, but Benjamin Franklin merits his place in that pantheon.

JAWAHARLAL NEHRU

A Tryst with Destiny

Constituent Assembly, Parliament House, New Delhi

14 August 1947

Jawaharlal Nehru (1889–1964) was the hero of the generation of the midnight's children who saw India from colonialism into democracy. When he was born, in 1889, Queen Victoria was empress of India. By the time he died, in 1964, he had served for almost two decades as the first prime minister of an independent India. Nehru fathered a dynasty as well as a nation. His daughter, Indira Gandhi, and his grandson Rajiv both became prime ministers of India, although both were assassinated. The Nehru family remains a significant presence in the Congress Party to this day.

The transition to democracy in India was in defiance of immense scepticism that a country so varied, a nation with no tradition of democracy, could govern itself after its freedom from rule as a distant outpost of the British Empire. An experiment with democracy perhaps even more extraordinary than the formation of the United States began on 15 August 1947. With a brief hiatus under a state of emergency in 1975, this nation of multiple languages and religions found a solvent in democracy. This achievement is owed in no small part to Jawaharlal Nehru.

Nehru was drawn into active political opposition to the British Raj, inspired by Mahatma Gandhi's vision of an India reborn and his strategy of non-violent non-cooperation with the imperial rulers. In 1919 he joined the Indian National Congress, which was fighting for greater autonomy from the British. During the 1920s and 1930s he was repeatedly imprisoned by the British for civil disobedience. In 1929 he was elected president of the Congress Party. By the end of the Second World War, he had become Gandhi's designated successor, though they drifted apart on a question of tactics. Gandhi regarded peaceful methods as indispensable, conferring a spiritual benefit on the practitioner as well making an irresistible persuasive case. Nehru, always more radical, had come to see peaceful cooperation as one method among others.

Jawaharlal Nehru was born in Allahabad, the son of a wealthy civil lawyer who had moved from Kashmir. In 1905, at the age of sixteen, Jawaharlal left the family mansion and his father's collection of vintage cars to take up the education of an English gentleman of the upper class, at Harrow School, Trinity College, Cambridge, and the Inner Temple. Nehru developed some expensive habits in London and regularly wired home to ask his father to send more money. The style and attitudes of England were a constant touchstone in later criticism of his rule. Nehru paid a high personal price for his politics. As his biographer Judith Brown has written, he sacrificed his life, his family and friendships, and in the end his health, to his political project. Nehru's private life was, in fact, a tableau of tragedy. He endured the death of both parents, of a baby son and, in 1936, of his wife, which left him to bring up his only daughter, Indira, alone.

The context for the speech is the breakdown of constitutional negotiations between Nehru's Congress Party and the British Raj. The tactic of civil disobedience had resumed and its leadership was in jail. The willingness of the British government to resist the claim of independence had withered, though. By 1942, the British government had declared that India would be free. Nehru played a central role in the negotiations over Indian independence. As Gandhi was wrapped up in combating violence Nehru stepped into the void. He was re-elected Congress president in mid-1946, and from that position became the vice-president of the interim government that preceded independence. Nehru opposed the Muslim League's insistence on the division of India on the basis of religion, only reluctantly agreeing when Louis Mountbatten, the last British viceroy, decreed that partition was the quickest and most easily workable solution.

The road to independence was not without blood, and the future of Indian democracy was not a straight road either, yet 1947 was a unique historical moment. This was the first time that any European state had voluntarily handed authority over to its former colonial subjects. The barriers to success were high and its likelihood of success low. This year, 2017, is the seventieth anniversary of Indian democracy.

> *Long years ago we made a tryst with destiny, and now the time comes when we shall redeem our pledge, not wholly or in full measure, but very substantially. At the stroke of the midnight hour, when the world sleeps, India will awake to life and freedom. A moment comes, which comes but rarely in history, when we step out from the old to the new, when an age ends, and when the soul of a nation, long suppressed, finds utterance.*

One of rhetoric's tempting dangers is its music. A euphonious phrase can have an emotional effect even if it doesn't, on reflection, stand scrutiny. Here Nehru is turning the phrase towards the light. 'Tryst with destiny' is a delicious phrase, but in what sense is a tryst needed if an event is destined? Nehru goes on to say that the nation made a pledge to destiny which it shall now redeem. Yet if there is any choice in the matter of whether or not to redeem, then it is not destiny we are dealing with. Indeed, destiny has not turned up 'wholly or in full measure', which is Nehru's first lament for partition.

But the philosophical contradiction doesn't matter much. A phrase is fleeting and one goes straight from utterance into the memory. In any case, the Indian audience would have been appreciative of the idea of a destiny. Independence was set for 15 August, but the astrologers declared 14 August more auspicious. Nehru's compromise was that India's assembly would be convened on the afternoon of 14 August and continue in session until Nehru's speech, which would begin shortly before midnight.

This gave his claim that the world was sleeping a touch of poetic licence, as it was early evening in Britain, for example. Then, to the chiming of an English clock and the blowing of Indian conch shells, independent India would be born. It is certainly a momentous occasion. Nehru's claim is a vast one – that a new age has begun – and in almost all such instances it would be excessive. Here it is nothing of the sort. The weight of events lends gravity to the words, and Nehru delivers them with sober tranquillity.

> *It is fitting that at this solemn moment we take the pledge of dedication to the service of India and her people and to the still larger cause of humanity. At the dawn of history India started on her unending quest, and trackless centuries are filled with her striving and the grandeur of her success and her failures. Through good and ill fortune alike she has never lost sight of that quest or forgotten the ideals which gave her strength. We end today a period of ill fortune and India discovers herself again. The achievement we celebrate today is but a step, an opening of opportunity, to the greater triumphs and achievements that await us. Are we brave enough and wise enough to grasp this opportunity and accept the challenge of the future? Freedom and power bring responsibility. The responsibility rests upon this assembly, a sovereign body representing the sovereign people of India. Before the birth of freedom we have endured all the pains of labour and our hearts are heavy with the memory of this sorrow. Some of those pains continue even now. Nevertheless, the past is over and it is the future that beckons to us now.*

'Getting its history wrong is part of being a nation,' said Ernst Renan, one of the best thinkers on nationalism. India, as a nation, does not really have any centuries to track, and it certainly did not begin with the dawn of history. There has indeed been a civilisation in this territory for ages past, but the idea of India is being born with this speech. The unending quest is coming to a beginning, not an end. 'It is the magic of nationalism to turn chance into destiny,' said Nehru on another occasion. Nehru is not describing India here; he is creating it.

There is, though, an air of trepidation in his words that comes in part from the sorrow at partition and its dreadful human toll. Nehru is referring to the slaughter between Hindus and Muslims that was raging in cruel fashion as he spoke. As Nehru rose he would have been aware that Sir Cyril Radcliffe, working under Mountbatten, had delivered the report that would draw the boundary between India and Pakistan. An explicit reference would have changed the tone from triumph to elegy, but Mountbatten insisted the report be kept secret until after 15 August in any case.

There is more to Nehru's trepidation though than partition, as important as it was. Nehru is about to pass from the exciting era of protest into the grind of administration. A generation of dissidents is about to learn the statecraft of running a nation of which it has, until this moment, been critical. Nehru effects what is, in rhetorical terms, a rather brutal shift here from the past to the future. It comes with a lurch, as if to say, there is no point dwelling on anything. We have a tryst with destiny.

> *That future is not one of ease or resting but of incessant striving so that we may fulfil the pledges we have so often taken and the one we shall take today. The service of India means the service of the millions who suffer. It means the ending of poverty and ignorance and disease and inequality of opportunity. The ambition of the greatest man of our generation has been to wipe every tear from every eye. That may be beyond us, but as long as there are tears and suffering, so long our work will not be over.*

In this passage Nehru both embraces Gandhi and distances himself from him. The compliment to 'the greatest man of our generation' is all the better for not including his name, but there is a back-hand. Gandhi's aim, to wipe the tears from every eye, is gently slighted as probably beyond human capability.

To Gandhian utopianism Nehru contrasts what he regards as the more earthly delights of social democracy. In time those delights were to prove more elusive than he envisaged. Though the economic growth rate of India after independence was much better than the collapse that had been overseen by the British, it remained stuck stubbornly at an average of 2.5 per cent per annum. The rest of Nehru's ambition is still unfulfilled. Seventy years on, a third of the world's poor live in India and inequality blights the nation. In particular, India's growth as a nation will be curtailed as long as it fails to properly educate the majority of its citizens, especially in basic literacy.

> *And so we have to labour and to work, and work hard, to give reality to our dreams. Those dreams are for India, but they are also for the world, for all the nations and peoples are too closely knit together today for any one of them to imagine that it can live apart. Peace has been said to be indivisible; so is freedom, so is prosperity*

now, and so also is disaster in this one world that can no longer be split into isolated fragments. To the people of India, whose representatives we are, we make an appeal to join us with faith and confidence in this great adventure. This is no time for petty and destructive criticism, no time for ill will or blaming others. We have to build the noble mansion of free India where all her children may dwell. The appointed day has come – the day appointed by destiny – and India stands forth again, after long slumber and struggle, awake, vital, free and independent. The past clings on to us still in some measure and we have to do much before we redeem the pledges we have so often taken. Yet the turning point is past, and history begins anew for us, the history which we shall live and act and others will write about. It is a fateful moment for us in India, for all Asia and for the world. A new star rises, the star of freedom in the east, a new hope comes into being, a vision long cherished materialises. May the star never set and that hope never be betrayed!

The process of persuading the various maharajahs and regional princes to sign up to the new independent entity 'India' had been fraught. The settlement was precarious. The very idea of 'India' as a unitary body was still a novelty. Nehru approached the task of defining the nation by placing it in a global context. The story of India is written into the world, which is depending on us. Again, he glosses over the contradiction of destiny. A fate that is ordained cannot be betrayed.

It cannot be stressed enough what a difficult task Nehru has in this speech and just how much scepticism there was that the nation could endure. But this is the first intimation of the remarkable way in which democracy itself becomes the unifying element of Indian society. India had long been a land but never a nation. It was and is split across many of the dimensions which are usually required to foster coherent nationhood. By religion and language it was many-sided.

Consciously and in defiance of all expectations, Nehru launched the process of constructing the idea of democracy as the very thing that bound Indians of all regions and all creeds. Seventy years later it is hard but important to recall how audacious that claim was at the time. There are many people who would deny it still. Nehru says that the star of democracy has risen in the East. There is a strong school of thought that democracy is an intrinsically Western idea. India is a standing rebuke to this cultural pessimism, and Nehru the first disciple of optimism.

> *We rejoice in that freedom, even though clouds surround us, and many of our people are sorrow-stricken and difficult problems encompass us. But freedom brings responsibilities and burdens and we have to face them in the spirit of a free and disciplined people. On this day our first thoughts go to the architect of this freedom, the father of our nation, who, embodying the old spirit of India, held aloft the torch of freedom and lighted up the darkness that surrounded us. We have often been unworthy followers of his and have strayed from his message, but not only we but succeeding generations will remember this message and bear the imprint in their hearts of this great son of India, magnificent in his faith and strength and courage and humility. We shall never allow that torch of freedom to be blown out, however high the wind or stormy the tempest.*

This is Nehru's acknowledgment of his split with Gandhi, which was both stylistic and intellectual. Nehru erects a bridge between his own beliefs and Gandhi's by describing them both, rather flatly, as lovers of freedom. As long as the torch is alight then Gandhi's legacy is preserved. This is studiedly vague.

Gandhi was not in the chamber. He was in Calcutta trying to quell the riots. Gandhi had suggested that a Muslim be appointed the ruler of an undivided India, something Nehru regarded as an unrealistic proposition. This was the culmination of a rupture that had been a long time in the making. It was a split about method rather than about objective. Nehru was, in the end, a conventional politician, albeit a highly gifted one. This is the kind of artful rhetoric that Gandhi, a purer thinker, would not have countenanced.

The distance between the two was symbolised by a dispute over how the president of the Indian republic should live. Gandhi wanted a frugal lifestyle but Nehru preferred to retain the imperial style. Releasing a people from the shackles of imperial domination needed the doctrinal purity and idealistic commitment of Gandhi, but the next stage, the piecemeal change of democratic politics, called for different skills. To that extent, the rift between Gandhi and Nehru is really a description of different stages of democratic development. India was lucky to have them both, the prophet of liberation and the analyst of politics. The new nation needed them both. All nations do.

> *Our next thoughts must be of the unknown volunteers and soldiers of freedom who, without praise or reward, have served India even unto death. We think also of our brothers and sisters who have been cut off from us by political boundaries and who unhappily cannot share at present in the freedom that has come. They are of us and will remain of us whatever may happen, and we shall be sharers in their good and ill fortune alike. The future beckons to us. Whither do we go and what shall be our endeavour? To bring freedom and opportunity to the common man, to the peasants and workers of India; to fight and end poverty and ignorance and disease; to build up a prosperous, democratic and progressive nation, and to create social, economic and political institutions which will ensure justice and fullness of life to every man and woman.*

Partition was a brutal tragedy. It caused 15 million people to leave their homes, the largest migration in human history. In total one million people died. It is true that the transfer of power from Britain to India was, in comparative historical terms, peaceful, but we should spare the congratulations. While Gandhi 'celebrated' the tragedy of partition by fasting in Calcutta, the Punjab erupted into flames. The fatal flaw of the whole enterprise was that there were no borders. Cyril Radcliffe, who had never before been to Asia, had arrived in India only thirty-six days before the date of the partition. He finished drawing the map on 9 August, but the viceroy insisted that the details stay secret. Two days later the boundaries were announced. They became the focus of four wars and seven decades of animosity between India and Pakistan. For many millions on the subcontinent today, all the promise that came with independence remains unfulfilled. These words, on the lack of social justice in India, a country with so many malnourished children, would still read like a hope for the future seventy years after they were written.

We have hard work ahead. There is no resting for any one of us till we redeem our pledge in full, till we make all the people of India what destiny intended them to be. We are citizens of a great country, on the verge of bold advance, and we have to live up to that high standard. All of us, to whatever religion we may belong, are equally the children of India with equal rights, privileges and obligations. We cannot encourage communalism or narrow-mindedness, for no nation can be great whose people are narrow in thought or in action. To the nations and peoples of the world we send greetings and pledge ourselves to cooperate with them in furthering peace, freedom and democracy. And to India, our much-loved motherland, the ancient, the eternal and the ever-new, we pay our reverent homage and we bind ourselves afresh to her service. Jai Hind [Victory to India].

Destiny makes its final appearance, this time in individual form. Destiny has designs on every Indian and its objective is to make them free. This is a gesture towards an overtly religious idiom, in a devotional country, from a secular man. The peroration befits the moment. It is grand and momentous, as well it might be. The style has two functions. It is grand to meet the moment and it is grand to unite the nation. This speech is the beginning of the post-colonial world and the founding document of Indian democracy. The tryst with destiny is a far more famous document than the Indian constitution itself. It names Indian democracy in a spirit of optimism which, against so many predictions of doom, thrives today in a diverse land of more than one billion people.

This was a fitting soundtrack to an extraordinary day on which at midnight, after 163 years of British rule, India set out on an adventure. Outside the Assembly, Delhi rang to the sound of guns, temple bells and fireworks. The rejoicing in the streets included the burning of an effigy of imperialism. In Bombay, the sirens of hundreds of mills and factories, the whistling of railway engines and hooting from ships ushered in independence at midnight. There was, indeed, a mountain of hard work ahead, and it is not done yet, but Nehru's words defined the possibility of the nation that India is in the constant process of becoming.

NELSON MANDELA

An Ideal for Which I Am Prepared to Die

Supreme Court of South Africa, Pretoria

20 April 1964

Nelson Mandela (1918–2013) became, for a generation of people, within South Africa and far beyond, the captain of their soul. There is a case for suggesting that Mandela's incarceration was a blessing for his political reputation. Deprived of the capacity to speak and make public errors, Mandela emerged from a quarter of a century in prison as a candidate for sainthood, which his subsequent grace justified.

Mandela's magnanimous and generous response to the loss of twenty-seven years of his life to imprisonment helped keep the fissiparous nation of South Africa together. Mandela's essentially peaceful revolution elevated him to the presidency of his nation, which he served between 1994 and 1999. When Mandela died in 2013 his death shook the world like that of no politician since John F. Kennedy.

Nelson Mandela was born in Mvezo, near Umata, in the native reserve of the Transkei in the Eastern Cape, into the royal house of the Thembu people, though his father's branch did not stand in the line of succession of the Xhosa tribe and it was not a luxurious childhood. 'Apart from life, a strong constitution and an abiding connection to the Thembu royal house, the only thing my father bestowed upon me at birth was a name,' he recalled in his autobiography, *Long Walk to Freedom*.

Mandela was the first member of his family to go to school, and it was one of his teachers who gave him the name Nelson. On the death of his father, the nine-year-old Nelson was entrusted to the care of the Thembu regent, David Dalindyebo, who brought him up as his own child and groomed him to become a counsellor to the future king. From there he proceeded through Methodist schools to Fort Hare University College, South Africa's only black university. He ran away to Johannesburg in 1941 to escape an arranged marriage and took work as a night watchman guarding the compound entrance of a goldmine.

It was the future ANC leader Walter Sisulu who introduced Mandela to the legal profession and also to radical politics. In 1948, the exclusively Afrikaner Nationalist Party won the whites-only general election, and began to institute its policy of apartheid across South Africa. Every individual was categorised by race and it became illegal to marry across the colour line.

Mandela was by this time the deputy leader of the ANC's youth movement. He had also set up the only black legal firm in South Africa with Oliver Tambo. The failure of conventional politics to make any headway led Mandela to the conclusion that the ANC had no alternative but to take up armed resistance. In December 1956 he was arrested for high treason. The prosecution dragged on for years trying to prove violent intent, and was still going on when, on 26 March 1960, sixty-nine Africans demonstrating against the pass laws were shot dead by the police in Sharpeville, near Johannesburg. Mandela went underground, earning himself a reputation as 'the black pimpernel'. He was captured in August 1962 while masquerading as a chauffeur and sentenced to three years for incitement and another two years for leaving the country without a passport.

With this speech we see Mandela in court after the police had raided the headquarters of the resistance movement in Rivonia, a northern suburb of Johannesburg. Mandela was one of ten men charged with sabotage and faced the prospect of death by hanging. All ten pleaded not guilty: 'My lord, it is not I, but the Government that should be in the dock today. I plead not guilty.' Mandela was imprisoned, for much longer than anyone had ever imagined, in a tiny cell on Robben Island with a slop bucket for company and no proper bed. The emotional pain of imprisonment was always intense, but it would hit its peak when Mandela received the news, by telegram, that his eldest son Madiba had died in a car crash. Mandela's vulnerability is evident in his prison letters, which are exquisitely written records of pain.

Throughout his imprisonment Mandela was offered the chance of release, but always with unacceptable conditions attached. Finally, in 1989, in a meeting with President P. W. Botha shortly before he was succeeded by F. W. de Klerk, Mandela sensed a change of attitude. It was de Klerk who had the courage to concede, as he put it in the speech with which the two accepted a shared Nobel peace prize in 1993, that 'a terrible wrong had been done to our country'. On 4.14 p.m. on 11 February 1990, televised live, Mandela walked out through the gates of Victor Verster prison near Cape Town into a world that he did not recognise but that recognised him.

In May 1994, Mandela, a figure of immense bearing and dignity, was inaugurated as president after the first non-racial, democratic election in South Africa. He had missed the modern world. When Mandela was first imprisoned John F. Kennedy was still president of the United States of America.

Mandela was a hero with feet of clay, as all heroes are, and it does him a disservice to canonise him. He had many personal failings, and the ANC government under his command showed little imagination and even less competence. Behind the scenes, Thabo Mbeki was essentially running the show. But Mandela understood the importance of political theatre for a display of unity. His calls for calm as violence increased among rival political and ethnic groups was a crucial command. His decision to stand down, in 1999, was perhaps as important as his becoming president in the first place, because it showed that the fledgling democracy could transfer power without violence.

He was an extraordinary man and his was an extraordinary life. He was born Rolihlahla, a name that means 'troublemaker'. He died ninety-five years later as Nelson Mandela, in a time he had done so much to change, on 5 December 2013, for all his flaws a hero unmatched in his time.

I am the first accused. I hold a bachelor's degree in arts and practised as an attorney in Johannesburg for a number of years in partnership with Oliver Tambo. I am a convicted prisoner serving five years for leaving the country without a permit and for inciting people to go on strike at the end of May 1961. At the outset, I want to say that the suggestion made by the state in its opening that the

> *struggle in South Africa is under the influence of foreigners or*
> *communists is wholly incorrect. I have done whatever I did, both as*
> *an individual and as a leader of my people, because of my*
> *experience in South Africa and my own proudly felt African*
> *background, and not because of what any outsider might have said.*
> *In my youth in the Transkei I listened to the elders of my tribe*
> *telling stories of the old days. Amongst the tales they related to me*
> *were those of wars fought by our ancestors in defence of the*
> *fatherland. The names of Dingane and Bambata, Hintsa and*
> *Makana, Squngthi and Dalasile, Moshweshoe and Sekhukhuni,*
> *were praised as the glory of the entire African nation. I hoped then*
> *that life might offer me the opportunity to serve my people and*
> *make my own humble contribution to their freedom struggle. This*
> *is what has motivated me in all that I have done in relation to the*
> *charges made against me in this case.*

A trial defence rests more on the character of the plaintiff than any other rhetorical form. The connection is historic. Demosthenes was a pleader in court, as was Cicero. One of the most famous of classical speeches is Plato's account of the speech Socrates gave in his defence when he was accused of impiety. Socrates faced the death penalty as Mandela does here. Mandela does what Socrates refused to do and opens with his credentials. In a paragraph he summarises the case which, over more than four hours, he puts painstakingly to the court. His defence is to be highly personal, predicated on his status as an African. The prosecution was trying to paint Mandela as in some way a puppet of foreign forces and a man of violence. The speech, at its full length, is a detailed rebuttal of these charges.

Here Mandela presents his summary defence, evoking his African heritage as a way both to anchor him within it and to define the nation as widely as possible, a clearly vital tactic in a nation which has defined him and his kind out of existence. Mandela is also seeking to humanise his people. These are people too, he is saying, and these are their names. They are called 'Dingane and Bambata ...' His tone is sorrow rather than anger. This is going to be a humble submission, although always a proud one, and the style will be forensic, as befits an attorney making a case for a client in court. This time the attorney is speaking for himself, but also for all Africa and at the price of his own life.

Having said this, I must deal immediately and at some length with the question of violence. Some of the things so far told to the court are true and some are untrue. I do not, however, deny that I planned sabotage. I did not plan it in a spirit of recklessness, nor because I have any love of violence ... Firstly, we believed that as a result of Government policy, violence by the African people had become inevitable, and that unless responsible leadership was given to canalise and control the feelings of our people, there would be outbreaks of terrorism which would produce an intensity of bitterness and hostility between the various races of this country which is not produced even by war. Secondly, we felt that without violence there would be no way open to the African people to succeed in their struggle against the principle of white supremacy. All lawful modes of expressing opposition to this principle had been closed by legislation, and we were placed in a position in which we had either to accept a permanent state of inferiority, or to defy the government. We chose to defy the law. We first broke the law in a way which avoided any recourse to violence; when this form was legislated against, and then the government resorted to a show of force to crush opposition to its policies, only then did we decide to answer violence with violence. But the violence which we chose to adopt was not terrorism. We who formed Umkhonto[the organisation Umkhonto we Sizwe: Spear of the Nation] were all members of the African National Congress, and had behind us the ANC tradition of non-violence and negotiation as a means of solving political disputes. We believe that South Africa belongs to all the people who live in it, and not to one group, be it black or white. We did not want an interracial war, and tried to avoid it to the last minute. If the court is in doubt about this, it will be seen that the whole history of our organisation bears out what I have said, and what I will subsequently say, when I describe the tactics which Umkhonto decided to adopt ... In 1960 there was the shooting at Sharpeville, which resulted in the proclamation of a state of emergency and the declaration of the ANC as an unlawful organisation. My colleagues and I, after careful consideration,

> *decided that we would not obey this decree. The African people*
> *were not part of the government and did not make the laws by*
> *which they were governed. We believed in the words of the*
> *Universal Declaration of Human Rights, that 'the will of the*
> *people shall be the basis of authority of the government,' and for us*
> *to accept the banning was equivalent to accepting the silencing of*
> *the Africans for all time ... What were we, the leaders of our*
> *people, to do? Were we to give in to the show of force and the*
> *implied threat against future action, or were we to fight it and, if*
> *so, how?*

One of the charges against Mandela is that he committed the ANC to violence. He had been in prison for almost the whole period since the Sabotage Act was passed. He might have been expected to seek exoneration on those grounds. Here he signals that he is going to do the opposite. He affirms he was a leader of the ANC and the small splinter group that settled on violent means. This is, at least in the language and the logic of the court, a guilty plea.

With the court, according to contemporary reports, spellbound and silent as Mandela read from his script, the accused went to great lengths to clarify exactly what happened. He candidly concedes that he did advocate a shift to violence from pacifism, but enters two extenuating points. The first is that the violence was always directed against buildings and symbols of the apartheid state rather than against people. The targets were power lines, railway tracks and public buildings. The state responded brutally with arrest, killings and torture. The intention never to hurt anyone, says Mandela, was a conscious and important choice. If resistance is confined to sabotage, as Mandela argued it was, the prospect of a transition to democracy is left open. The second defence is that the resistance movement was left with no viable option beyond an armed struggle. The Sharpeville massacre was a pivotal moment. The black demonstrators killed by the police had been protesting about the pass laws that required them to carry identification.

Mandela therefore goes through, for the benefit of the court, the legislation enacted by the white supremacist government, which makes it impossible to live a free and dignified life in South Africa as a black person. This legislation has led Mandela, regretfully and sorrowfully, to the conclusion that armed resistance cannot be avoided. Black people cannot join the nation in any other way.

Another of the allegations made by the state is that the aims and objects of the ANC and the Communist party are the same. I wish to deal with this and with my own political position, because I must assume that the state may try to argue from certain exhibits that I tried to introduce Marxism into the ANC ... The ideological creed of the ANC is, and always has been, the creed of African nationalism. It is not the concept of African nationalism expressed in the cry, 'drive the white man into the sea.' The African nationalism for which the ANC stands is the concept of freedom and fulfilment for the African people in their own land. The most important political document ever adopted by the ANC is the 'freedom charter.' It is by no means a blueprint for a socialist state. It calls for redistribution, but not nationalisation, of land; it provides for nationalisation of mines, banks, and monopoly industry, because big monopolies are owned by one race only, and without such nationalisation racial domination would be perpetuated despite the spread of political power ... The ANC, unlike the Communist party, admitted Africans only as members. Its chief goal was, and is, for the African people to win unity and full political rights. The Communist party's main aim, on the other hand, was to remove the capitalists and to replace them with a working-class government. The Communist party sought to emphasise class distinctions whilst the ANC seeks to harmonise them. This is a vital distinction ...

To foreign observers of the apartheid regime the vital distinction at issue seemed to be obvious. It was there in black and white: it was racism. The Rivonia trial was in fact more complex than that, which explains why Mandela is so careful to distance his own world view from that of the communists, though he is generous enough to acknowledge that the South African communists were allies of the black people when almost nobody else was. The charges Mandela was forced to answer included aiding foreign military units in their attempt to invade the Republic, acting in ways to further the objects of communism, and soliciting and receiving money from named foreign sources. He was up on a charge of being a traitor to the nation and of being a communist. He had been imprisoned under the Suppression of Communism Act.

There is a Cold War aspect to the trial which is easily forgotten but which it is imperative for Mandela to deal with. This is what he is doing here. The Cold War comparison may go further still. In his reflections on the time, F. W. de Klerk noted that apartheid was not really defeated by protests, boycotts or sanctions. It fell because millions of educated black South Africans had become economically indispensable and the prejudice of a generation of young whites had been quelled by working with black colleagues. The apartheid generation were succeeded by their more liberal children. This is the case that Mandela is making. He is not enlisting Africans in the international fraternity of the working man. He is instead seeking to harmonise class interests under a heading of prior importance: African nationalism.

I have always regarded myself, in the first place, as an African patriot ... The basic task at the present moment is the removal of race discrimination and the attainment of democratic rights on the basis of the Freedom Charter. In so far as that party furthers this task, I welcome its assistance. I realise that it is one of the means by which people of all races can be drawn into our struggle. From my reading of Marxist literature and from conversations with Marxists, I have gained the impression that communists regard the parliamentary system of the west as undemocratic and reactionary. But, on the contrary, I am an admirer of such a system. The Magna Carta, the Petition of Rights, and the Bill of Rights are documents which are held in veneration by democrats throughout the world. I have great respect for British political institutions, and for the country's system of justice. I regard the British Parliament as the most democratic institution in the world, and the independence and impartiality of its judiciary never fails to arouse my admiration. The American Congress, that country's doctrine of separation of powers, as well as the independence of its judiciary, arouses in me similar sentiments. I have been influenced in my thinking by both west and east. All this has led me to feel that in my search for a political formula, I should be absolutely

*impartial and objective. I should tie myself to no particular system
of society other than of socialism. I must leave myself free to
borrow the best from the west and from the east …*

Mandela here identifies himself historically and decisively as a
democrat. He completes the task of distancing himself from
communism but then goes much further to establish his credentials
as a patriot as well. It is essential to do this because Mandela was
aware that white South Africans feared that the universal franchise
would extinguish their capacity to determine their own future. It was
not just communism that the whites were scared of. They feared
majoritarian democracy too, perhaps even more so, as it seemed
possible.

That is why Mandela allies himself so explicitly with the democratic systems. The naming of Magna Carta, the British Parliament
and the American Congress has the effect of making a case that
cannot be gainsaid. A Marxist could never say any such thing, representative democracy being strictly inferior to historical destiny as a
route to power. Mandela instead yokes the Freedom Charter to the
history of democratic institutions to defend himself against the
trumped up charge of being a communist but also to reduce the
atmosphere of fear in which the trial was held. This is an account of
an authentic liberal democratic nation. It is a long way from the
manifesto of a terrorist.

*Africans want to be paid a living wage. Africans want to perform
work which they are capable of doing, and not work which the
government declares them to be capable of. Africans want to be
allowed to live where they obtain work, and not be endorsed out of
an area because they were not born there. Africans want to be
allowed to own land in places where they work, and not to be
obliged to live in rented houses which they can never call their own.
Africans want to be part of the general population, and not
confined to living in their own ghettoes. African men want to have
their wives and children to live with them where they work, and not
be forced into an unnatural existence in men's hostels. African
women want to be with their menfolk and not be left permanently
widowed in the Reserves. Africans want to be allowed out after*

*eleven o'clock at night and not to be confined to their rooms like
little children. Africans want to be allowed to travel in their own
country and to seek work where they want to and not where the
labour bureau tells them to. Africans want a just share in the whole
of South Africa; they want security and a stake in society.*

A passage of fine rhetorical technique in which Mandela speaks
of the nation he wants to exist. Ten successive sentences begin either
with 'Africans', 'African men' or 'African women'. The repetition
builds momentum as the listener is on guard for the next item in the
list. The importance of the litany of demands is precisely that they
are quotidian. Everyone wants a living wage from work they are
capable of doing. Everyone wants to live where they choose and own
their own home. Everyone wants to live with their family rather than
be separated from them and everyone wants to be free to pass through
the streets and travel unhindered and safe through the country. There
is nothing 'African' about these demands. Mandela is pointing out,
with exemplary gentleness, that black Africans do not currently enjoy
these basic liberties.

Mandela shows in this passage how a resounding point can be
made *sotto voce*. He could have ascended the heights and lamented
the absence of justice in tones of anguish. The result is all the more
impressive for being so routine. The court is simply invited to draw
its own conclusions about a land in which such everyday freedoms
are denied to one set of its people. He is simply saying that we black
Africans, we are ordinary too. There is nothing transgressive about
the lives we wish to lead. Unjust nations define sections of their
people out of the fraternity of the citizenry. This is Mandela's simple
and effective claim for the black Africans to be readmitted.

*Above all, we want equal political rights, because without them our
disabilities will be permanent. I know this sounds revolutionary to
the whites in this country, because the majority of voters will be
Africans. This makes the white man fear democracy. But this fear
cannot be allowed to stand in the way of the only solution which
will guarantee racial harmony and freedom for all. It is not true
that the enfranchisement of all will result in racial domination.
Political division, based on colour, is entirely artificial and, when it*

disappears, so will the domination of one colour group by another. The ANC has spent half a century fighting against racialism. When it triumphs it will not change that policy. This then is what the ANC is fighting. Their struggle is a truly national one. It is a struggle of the African people, inspired by their own suffering and their own experience. It is a struggle for the right to live. During my lifetime I have dedicated myself to this struggle of the African people. I have fought against white domination, and I have fought against black domination. I have cherished the ideal of a democratic and free society in which all persons live together in harmony and with equal opportunities. It is an ideal which I hope to live for and to achieve. But if needs be, it is an ideal for which I am prepared to die.

This is one of the greatest endings to an important speech of all time, perhaps second only to Martin Luther King. The draft of this speech made Mandela's lawyers apprehensive that he would antagonise the judge. They begged him, in particular, to excise the last paragraph. Mandela refused. He spoke the last paragraph from memory, looking directly at Judge De Wet. Mandela expected to hear the death sentence declared, as twenty-year sentences had been issued for relatively minor offences.

Mandela was not really a renowned speaker. None of his other speeches are liable to make it to anthology. These are brave words on an extraordinary occasion, which is the essence of the great speech. Mandela's life was on the line. Peril sharpens his words, which are lent their resonance because of the injustice they describe. The concrete writing makes the case reasonably and the emotion is better evoked by being implicit.

But there is, in retrospect, a supplementary beauty to the words because we know they were sincere. We know this because of the grace that Mandela showed, a quarter of a century later, when he was released and we know how he acted as the president of the recovering republic.

So much can be said in silence, and in one of history's great rhetorical gestures, Mandela showed how it can be done. Rugby in South Africa had always been the sport of the Afrikaner, the sport of the oppressor, the sport of the white man. In 1995 South Africa hosted and won the Rugby World Cup and Mandela, in defiance of his closest aides, strode out onto the pitch in Ellis Park in Johannesburg, wearing the Springbok shirt with a 6 on his back, the number of the captain, Francois Pienaar. In one moment, with that gesture, Mandela brought the country together. When South Africa beat New Zealand in the game, Mandela presented the trophy to Pienaar, with whom he had forged a close friendship. The beautiful story is told in the film *Invictus*. It is an enduring image that stands for what Mandela is talking about in this passage: the captain and the captain of the soul.

It sounds like a happy ending, but all happy endings are provisional in a democracy. Half the black population of South Africa still live below the poverty line. At least 6 million South Africans are HIV-positive. Twenty per cent of the white population has emigrated. Utopia has not arrived in South Africa. It could, however, have been much worse. Mandela could have delivered the other speech he had ready. His handwritten notes to counsel, returned to him after his release from jail twenty-six years later, show that the prisoner had prepared some remarks in the event that he was handed down a sentence of death. 'If I must die, let me declare for all to know that I will meet my fate like a man.' The words were never spoken, mercifully never needed.

As Mandela ended with the amazing words 'an ideal for which I am prepared to die' there was silence in the courtroom for as much as half a minute. Thirty seconds of silence in a crowded room is an eternity. Only the sound of heavy breathing broke the silent tension until, in the gallery, a woman broke into tears. After a minute the judge broke the spell by saying to the defence team: 'You may call your next witness'.

AUNG SAN SUU KYI

Freedom from Fear

European Parliament, Strasbourg
10 July 1991

The demand for liberty cannot always be voiced. The dangers of nationhood are evident in the fact that Jawaharlal Nehru, Nelson Mandela and Aung San Suu Kyi were imprisoned by governments that wanted to silence them. Words that cannot be spoken can still be read, however, and these words of Aung San Suu Kyi, Burma's pro-democracy leader and Nobel Peace laureate, written when she was under detention, are what she would have said had she been free to speak. These words are her definition of the idea of Burma.

Aung San Suu Kyi was born on 19 June 1945, the daughter of Burma's independence hero, Aung San, and of Khin Kyi, her stern and principled mother who founded the Burmese Girl Guides. Hers was a childhood of some propriety. Biscuit-dunking was banned and Suu Kyi was not allowed to lick stamps, which were to be wetted with a sponge. Years later, friends in Oxford noted her habit of enforcing the rules of children's games with unyielding exactitude. Her father was assassinated when she was only two years old, leaving his daughter with the burden of his legacy. She was educated in Burma, India and the United Kingdom. While studying at Oxford University, she met Michael Aris, a Tibet scholar whom she married in 1972. They had two sons, Alexander and Kim.

In 1988 Suu Kyi returned to Burma to nurse her dying mother, and she soon became engaged in the country's nationwide democratic uprising. The Burmese military suppressed that uprising with brutal force, killing up to 5,000 demonstrators in August 1988 and establishing a military regime the following month. This prompted the formation of a pro-democracy party, the National League for Democracy (NLD), of which Suu Kyi was appointed general secretary. The pressure on the regime forced a general election in 1990, but the process was a sham. Aung San Suu Kyi was detained for campaigning for the NLD and banned from standing as a candidate. The NLD won 82 per cent of the vote, whereupon the regime refused to recognise the result and clung to power regardless.

Suu Kyi was held under house arrest until July 1995 and faced restrictions on her ability to travel when she was released. In 1999 her husband died of cancer in London. His request to visit his wife one final time had been rejected by the Burmese authorities. If Suu Kyi had left Burma she would not have been permitted to return. In 2000 she was again placed under house arrest after repeated attempts to leave Rangoon to attend political meetings. In 2002 the regime gambled that Suu Kyi would have been forgotten by the population and so ended her detention. When tens of thousands of people turned out to see her, the generals devised a political front, the Union Solidarity and Development Association (USDA), to harass NLD meetings. On 30 May 2003, the USDA attacked Suu Kyi's convoy in a disguised attempt to assassinate her. Suu Kyi's driver managed to drive her to safety, but more than seventy of her supporters were beaten to death. The attack became known at the Depayin Massacre and the incident has never been investigated.

Following the attack, Suu Kyi was returned to detention, then placed back under house arrest under far stricter conditions than had been imposed in the past. Her phone line was cut and her post stopped. In May of that year, days before her house arrest was due to expire, she was arrested and charged with breaking its terms, which forbade visitors, after John Yettaw, a United States citizen, swam across Inya lake and refused to leave her house. In August 2009 she was convicted, and sentenced to three years' imprisonment, later reduced to eighteen months under house arrest.

Finally, in 2010, Suu Kyi was released. In November 2015, the first openly contested elections in twenty-five years were held, and Suu Kyi's party, the National League for Democracy, won a landslide victory. A clause in the constitution prevented her from becoming the president, but she is now state counsellor, a role analogous in power to prime minister, a title her father held before his assassination in 1947.

Throughout this to-and-fro of detention, the world has been watching. Aung San Suu Kyi has been awarded the Nobel Peace Prize and the Presidential Medal of Freedom. The occasion of this essay was her award of the Sakharov Prize for Freedom of Thought from the European Parliament. The award, named after Andrei Sakharov, the Russian nuclear physicist who faced state persecution for his advocacy of civil rights, took place in Suu Kyi's absence in Strasbourg. In 1991 it was published as the title work in a volume of her writings.

> *It is not power that corrupts but fear. Fear of losing power corrupts those who wield it and fear of the scourge of power corrupts those who are subject to it. Most Burmese are familiar with the four a-gati, the four kinds of corruption. Chanda-gati, corruption induced by desire, is deviation from the right path in pursuit of bribes or for the sake of those one loves. Dosa-gati is taking the wrong path to spite those against whom one bears ill will, and moga-gati is aberration due to ignorance. But perhaps the worst of the four is bhaya-gati, for not only does bhaya, fear, stifle and slowly destroy all sense of right and wrong, it so often lies at the root of the other three kinds of corruption. Just as chanda-gati, when not the result of sheer avarice, can be caused by fear of want or fear of losing the goodwill of those one loves, so fear of being surpassed, humiliated or injured in some way can provide the impetus for ill will. And it would be difficult to dispel ignorance unless there is freedom to pursue the truth unfettered by fear. With so close a relationship between fear and corruption it is little wonder that in any society where fear is rife corruption in all forms becomes deeply entrenched.*

To begin with the four Burmese types of corruption is not just a colourful opening, although it is also that. One of Suu Kyi's weaknesses as a political figure in Burma has always been that she was seen as a foreigner coming back from a long spell abroad to reclaim her birthright. A similar example of the way this can be exploited by political opponents has been documented by Michael Ignatieff in *Fire and Ashes*. After many years as a celebrity academic in Harvard and Cambridge, Ignatieff returned to Canada, where he became the leader of the Liberal Party. The adventure ended in electoral disaster, and chief among the reasons was that the Conservative Party denied Ignatieff what he called 'standing' in his own country.

This had always been a vulnerability for Suu Kyi. When, in 1988, she returned to Burma to nurse her ailing mother, she played no active part in demonstrations against the junta, but that August she was persuaded to speak, at a rally at the Shwedagon Pagoda, the symbolic heart of Burma. Introduced by a Burmese film star, Suu Kyi spoke solemnly about the desire of the people for a multi-party democratic system of government before turning to the real subject of the day, which was herself. She confronted the questions about being married to a foreigner and having lived abroad. She concluded: 'Another thing which some people have been saying is that I know nothing of Burmese politics. The trouble is that I know too much.'

Suu Kyi uses a number of techniques to gain standing in her essay, and this is the first. Root it in a native idiom. Make the founding metaphor of the essay something that requires a Burmese education and sensibility. The central idea is fear and its intimate relationship with freedom. Suu Kyi therefore makes *bhaya-gati* the most important form of corruption, embodying and opening the way for the others. Fear is the currency of tyranny. It is through the fear of reprisals that the regime's power is maintained. The fear is, in part, physical; hence courage is required.

With this device Suu Kyi distinguishes between good and bad political power. Power is the currency of politics but it can be spent well or badly. Self-flagellating critics in the West are apt to pretend they live in corrupt states, by which they tend to mean only governments they do not like. To live in Burma was to encounter the reality of a corrupt state, and the agent that corrupts is not power but fear. This is also, of course, a neat way of saying, clearly and yet still by implication, that the regime governs by fear, and that regime therefore could not be more corrupt. In situations of political oppression and adversity much has to be said by implication and allusion, in allegory or metaphor. It would be dangerous to spell out the implications. A metaphor requires the listener to rewrite the speech's meaning as he or she listens, or in this case reads.

Public dissatisfaction with economic hardships has been seen as the chief cause of the movement for democracy in Burma, sparked off by the student demonstrations [of]1988. It is true that years of incoherent policies, inept official measures, burgeoning inflation and falling real income had turned the country into an economic shambles. But it was more than the difficulties of eking out a barely acceptable standard of living that had eroded the patience of a traditionally good-natured, quiescent people – it was also the humiliation of a way of life disfigured by corruption and fear. The students were protesting not just against the death of their comrades but against the denial of their right to life by a totalitarian regime which deprived the present of meaningfulness and held out no hope for the future. And because the students' protests articulated the frustrations of the people at large, the demonstrations quickly grew into a nationwide movement. Some of its keenest supporters were businessmen who had developed the skills and the contacts necessary not only to survive but to prosper within the system. But their affluence offered them no genuine sense of security or fulfilment, and they could not but see that if they and their fellow citizens, regardless of economic status, were to achieve a worthwhile existence, an accountable administration was at least a necessary if not a sufficient condition. The people of Burma had wearied of a precarious state of passive apprehension where they were 'as water in the cupped hands' of the powers that be. 'Emerald cool we may be/ As water in cupped hands/ But oh that we might be/ As splinters of glass/ In cupped hands'. Glass splinters, the smallest with its sharp, glinting power to defend itself against hands that try to crush, could be seen as a vivid symbol of the spark of courage that is an essential attribute of those who would free themselves from the grip of oppression.

Hereby hangs a major argument, to which we shall return in chapter 5, and Suu Kyi makes an emphatic case on one side. It is often argued that democracy is a luxury that poor nations cannot afford. Better to settle the knife-and-fork questions first. The people do not want liberties, the argument runs, because liberties get nobody fed. What they want instead is that the basics of life should be catered for, even if that is achieved through enlightened despotism.

At the time that Suu Kyi was writing the question of democracy was urgent, and not just because the generals of the Ne Win regime had denied the outcome of the 1990 election. The Soviet empire had just crumbled and fledgling democracies were emerging from its ruins. Suu Kyi counters the Asian values argument with a universal riposte. The regime in Burma was, in fact, unable to provide economic prosperity. But that, says Suu Kyi, is not the sole source of dissatisfaction. Life under a totalitarian regime is meaningless, she argues. Even the wealthy businessmen could find no satisfaction in a state that was not accountable to them and that did not recognise their rights to hold it to account. Democracy and indigenous values flow together freely.

Václav Havel pointed out, in his introduction to the collected edition, *Freedom from Fear*, that Suu Kyi had written that 'it is a puzzlement to the Burmese how concepts which recognise the inherent dignity and the equal and inalienable rights of human beings, which accept that all men are endowed with reason and conscience and which recommend a spirit of brotherhood, can be inimical to indigenous values'.

The memorable metaphor at the end of this passage also contains a profound point about the nature of popular power. The promise that a despotism makes is that life will be simple. It is reduced to the task of economic management. If there is food on the table and material satisfaction, then the job of government is fulfilled. If the water flows through the cupped hands all is well. Suu Kyi says, in lyrical verse, that this is not enough. Democracy will be difficult at times, even as splinters of glass in the hand are painful, but it is desirable all the same. The splinters of glass are, at the same time, a form of defence, a point to which Suu Kyi will return.

The effort necessary to remain uncorrupted in an environment where fear is an integral part of everyday existence is not immediately apparent to those fortunate enough to live in states governed by the rule of law. Just laws do not merely prevent corruption by meting out impartial punishment to offenders. They also help to create a society in which people can fulfil the basic requirements necessary for the preservation of human dignity without recourse to corrupt practices. Where there are no such laws, the burden of upholding the principles of justice and common decency falls on the ordinary people. It is the cumulative effect on their sustained effort and steady endurance which will change a nation where reason and conscience are warped by fear into one where legal rules exist to promote man's desire for harmony and justice while restraining the less desirable destructive traits in his nature ... The quintessential revolution is that of the spirit, born of an intellectual conviction of the need for change in those mental attitudes and values which shape the course of a nation's development. A revolution which aims merely at changing official policies and institutions with a view to an improvement in material conditions has little chance of genuine success. Without a revolution of the spirit, the forces which produced the iniquities of the old order would continue to be operative, posing a constant threat to the process of reform and regeneration. It is not enough merely to call for freedom, democracy and human rights. There has to be a united determination to persevere in the struggle, to make sacrifices in the name of enduring truths, to resist the corrupting influences of desire, ill will, ignorance and fear. Saints, it has been said, are the sinners who go on trying. So free men are the oppressed who go on trying and who in the process make themselves fit to bear the responsibilities and to uphold the disciplines which will maintain a free society. Among the basic freedoms to which men aspire that their lives might be full and uncramped, freedom from fear stands out as both a means and an end. A people who would build a nation in which strong, democratic institutions are firmly established as a guarantee against state-induced power must first learn to liberate their own minds from apathy and fear.

There are two points at work in this passage that sit rather uneasily together, yet are united in the contradictory character of Aung San Suu Kyi herself. The first point is that democracy is more than a legal framework, it is a living culture. It requires commitment, desire and participation from the people for it to work. Ask not what your country can do for you. But this seems to contradict, or at least to exist in tension with, a claim that Suu Kyi has made earlier in the essay, namely that democracy is the recognition of a universal spirit in human beings. Now she is demanding a revolution of the spirit which, it seems, needs to be cultivated in action.

There is more than a hint of autobiography in this passage. Suu Kyi had endured cramped and unpleasant conditions but, unlike dissidents like Mandela and Sakharov, she had been free to go at any point, although she would not then have been allowed to return. The psychological cost of displacement from her family must have been acute. At first Suu Kyi received letters and food parcels from home, until Khin Nyunt, the junta's intelligence chief, found that one contained lipstick and a Jane Fonda workout video. They were photographed and disseminated by the state media to show the luxury in which Suu Kyi still lived. After that she refused all deliveries and stopped eating. In 1999, when her husband was diagnosed with advanced prostate cancer, he was denied a visa to visit her. When Suu Kyi refused to leave Burma the authorities cut off the phone line between them. The regime had already revoked the Burmese passports held by Suu Kyi's sons. So it is important for her to feel that a saint can be made from a sinner who refuses to give up. Suu Kyi's courtship letters to Michael Aris, written before they were married, offer a portent of this: 'I only ask one thing, that should my people need me, you would help me to do my duty by them.'

Suu Kyi will also have felt fear, as well as sadness. Soon after she committed to the cause, she toured Burma to meet devotees of her new party. She was by no means welcomed everywhere. In the town of Danubyu in the Irrawaddy Delta, she defied an order to leave and walked alone down the middle of the street. She was, in effect, daring the line of soldiers ahead of her to open fire. The captain on duty was quite prepared to shoot but Suu Kyi kept on walking. It was only at the last moment when a senior officer arrived and stood the soldiers down that Suu Kyi's defiance did not lead her into deep, perhaps even fatal, danger.

This essay is every bit as uncompromising. It is definitive in its claims for the virtues of democracy over the vices of tyranny. It is of a piece with Suu Kyi's political strategy. Even some of her allies urged her to compromise a little, perhaps by granting the junta some of the treasure it had hidden, but she always refused. The junta responded by placing her under house arrest.

Always one to practise what he preached, Aung San himself constantly demonstrated courage – not just the physical sort but the kind that enabled him to speak the truth, to stand by his word, to accept criticism, to admit his faults, to correct his mistakes, to respect the opposition, to parley with the enemy and to let people be the judge of his worthiness as a leader. It is for such moral courage that he will always be loved and respected in Burma – not merely as a warrior hero but as the inspiration and conscience of the nation. The words used by Jawaharlal Nehru to describe Mahatma Gandhi could well be applied to Aung San: 'The essence of his teaching was fearlessness and truth, and action allied to these, always keeping the welfare of the masses in view.' Gandhi, that great apostle of non-violence, and Aung San, the founder of a national army, were very different personalities, but as there is an inevitable sameness about the challenges of authoritarian rule anywhere at any time, so there is a similarity in the intrinsic qualities of those who rise up to meet the challenge. Nehru, who considered the instillation of courage in the people of India one of Gandhi's greatest achievements, was a political modernist, but as he assessed the needs for a twentieth-century movement for independence, he found himself looking back to the philosophy of ancient India: 'The greatest gift for an individual or a nation … was abhaya, fearlessness, not merely bodily courage but absence of fear from the mind.' Fearlessness may be a gift but perhaps more precious is the courage acquired through endeavour, courage that comes from cultivating the habit of refusing to let fear dictate one's actions, courage that could be described as 'grace under pressure' – grace which is renewed repeatedly in the face of harsh, unremitting pressure.

Here is Aung San Suu Kyi's main technique for gaining standing. The survival of dynastic politics, turning democracy into hereditary monarchy, is one of the oddities of our age. Suu Kyi invokes the memory of her father, Aung San, whose charm, flair, and talent for exquisitely timed changes of side saw him progress from student communist and anti-colonial to Japanese-trained guerrilla, then to British ally and negotiator (with Attlee) of Burma's independence.

Burmese politics never recovered from the loss of Aung San. In the early 1960s, the latest in a series of sickly governments was first dominated, then overthrown in a coup by Aung San's former deputy, General Ne Win, who was soon nationalising industry, stifling the press, expelling foreigners and shooting protesting students in the name of something called the Burmese Way to Socialism. The failure of this programme was important to the rise of Aung San Suu Kyi. Under General Ne Win, the once fertile and mineral-rich country of Burma had been turned into a shabby backwater. A demonetisation in 1987 had wiped out the nation's savings without any compensation. In December of that year the UN declared that Burma was one of the world's 'Least Developing' countries.

Suu Kyi quite naturally positions herself as the heir to her late father's never-completed nation-building. In her speech at the Shwedagon Pagoda, Suu Kyi had said that 'this national crisis could in fact be called the second struggle for national independence'. Since Ne Win's coup, Burma's development, education and influence had all fallen. The regime had no feats to exhibit so it fell back on force and its claim to his anti-colonial legacy. Coming back to reclaim the mantle of her father stripped the generals of any right to associate their way with his. Suu Kyi's implicit comparison, in the Shwedagon speech, of the generals to the British colonisers her father had fought to displace changed her life for ever and did so in a contest about the meaning of her father's work and the rights of ownership to that work. There was also a rupture between Suu Kyi and her father. Unlike Nelson Mandela Suu Kyi had always rejected armed struggle. When her mother Khin Kyi accepted privileged exile in Delhi as Burma's first female ambassador, the teenage Suu Kyi met the Nehrus and became acquainted with the lives and writings of Tagore and Gandhi. Placing grace under pressure as the most important response to fear is to side with the gentler resistance. Her father had not always eschewed the gun, whereas Suu Kyi's prominence and reputation as a dissident rests on her quiet stoicism in the face of military intransigence.

Detention brought a change in her. In addition to the exercise, housework, the BBC World Service and the detective fiction that helped her cope, Suu Kyi took up the Burmese practices of meditation. Her solitude introduced her to the concept of *metta*, or loving

211

kindness, which became an important part of her political method. While evoking her father for the standing he offers in her country, and stressing the continuity of aim, she nevertheless signals a break with him here.

Within a system which denies the existence of basic human rights, fear tends to be the order of the day. Fear of imprisonment, fear of torture, fear of death, fear of losing friends, family, property or means of livelihood, fear of poverty, fear of isolation, fear of failure. A most insidious form of fear is that which masquerades as common sense or even wisdom, condemning as foolish, reckless, insignificant or futile the small, daily acts of courage which help to preserve man's self-respect and inherent human dignity. It is not easy for a people conditioned by fear under the iron rule of the principle that might is right to free themselves from the enervating miasma of fear. Yet even under the most crushing state machinery courage rises up again and again, for fear is not the natural state of civilized man. The wellspring of courage and endurance in the face of unbridled power is generally a firm belief in the sanctity of ethical principles combined with a historical sense that despite all setbacks the condition of man is set on an ultimate course for both spiritual and material advancement. It is his capacity for self-improvement and self-redemption which most distinguishes man from the mere brute. At the root of human responsibility is the concept of perfection, the urge to achieve it, the intelligence to find a path towards it, and the will to follow that path if not to the end at least the distance needed to rise above individual limitations and environmental impediments. It is man's vision of a world fit for rational, civilized humanity which leads him to dare and to suffer to build societies free from want and fear. Concepts such as truth, justice and compassion cannot be dismissed as trite when these are often the only bulwarks which stand against ruthless power.

This is a fine statement of an important democratic principle expressed beautifully in Albert Camus's observation that democracy is more valuable for what it prevents than for what it achieves. It is important to remember the depravity to which the Burmese military

AUNG SAN SUU KYI

regime was partial. The parodic name, the State Law and Order Restoration Council, cannot hide a propensity for violence that was, if not quite first-division, then at least in the upper reaches of the second. A foreign diplomat who took too great an interest in Suu Kyi came home one evening to find that his dog had had its eyes burned out. This tyranny was all maintained by the apparatus of a police state, the cameras, the spies, the informers, the absence of a free press. In 1988, the army shot over 3,000 unarmed civilians on a single day. Thousands of members of the NDL were detained and many were tried, summarily, before military tribunals. Some of them were tortured with cigarette burns to the flesh, electric shocks to the genitals and beatings that inflicted permanent damage to the eyes and ears.

If the preservation of order cannot be left to the courage of individuals acting on their own behalf, and if the will to misuse power is as strong as it has always been, then the only bulwarks against brutality are democratic institutions and the democratic habits that are instilled within them. The greatest virtue of a democratic society is that people can live lives no longer at the mercy of others. This is the nation that Suu Kyi is envisaging and talking into life. At the time of their writing her words sounded like utopia, and in a nation in which expression remains tightly controlled and journalists regularly find themselves threatened and imprisoned, they do not sound greatly more realistic yet.

THIS BLESSED PLOT

'The people are blowing the trumpets round the city walls. Are we listening?' These are my favourite lines of all those in which I had any hand. Quite who first concocted the idea of a biblical cadence to round off Tony Blair's speech to the European Parliament in 2005 I do not recall. Resonant turns of phrase have many authors while flat lines are orphans. Good speechwriting is often like comic writing. Without all the feed lines the punchline would never be found. The credit should usually be shared.

Blair was seeking, as many of his predecessors had done and his successors were to do, to define Britain's vexatious relationship with the European Union. This was a story, as we shall see, that had run through British politics, first one way and then the other, ever since the Second World War. It was Britain's turn to take up the presidency of the European Union, and I had prepared a speech full of pieties and protocols. It was competent, well ordered, and numbingly dull. Worthy but not worth much.

This will go down as one of those speeches that were written but never made, such as the speech drafted for John F. Kennedy declaring nuclear war on Cuba, Richard Nixon's remarks commending the sacrifice of Neil Armstrong and Buzz Aldrin on the moon landing that went wrong, or Eisenhower's jotted scribble about what to say in the event that the Normandy landings had gone awry. The European speech that Tony Blair might have delivered mattered a good deal less than any of these prepared-but-never-given remarks. Indeed, it is not even the best speech-never-given that I have myself drafted. That honour must go to David Miliband's victory speech in the 2010 Labour Party leadership contest.

The world was spared this crushing courteous nullity due to the intervention of Jean-Claude Juncker, at that time the prime minister of Luxembourg and the outgoing incumbent of the rotating presidency. The day before Blair was due to speak, Juncker had used his valedictory speech, on the floor of the European Parliament, to excoriate the British, and Blair in particular, for their recalcitrance in the recent attempt to settle the European budget. When, in 2017, Juncker gave a withering account of his dinner with Theresa May, his behaviour was simply a reversion to type. Junker's 2005 address is a checklist of the evergreen European complaints about British detachment from their project. Every cliché of British exceptionalism is polished and personalised. Juncker's attack invited one of two responses: ignore or retaliate. At the last moment, Blair decided to breathe fire.

My deathless prose was replaced with a work of passion. The speech Blair delivered to the European Parliament on 23 June 2005 was a defence of the British social model, a renunciation of the lazy notion that Britain was a mere economic mimic of America, and also a clear statement that Britain saw its destiny as a nation within the fold of the European Union. The speech carried a sting from top to tail. From a position of comparative economic strength, Blair turned Juncker's critique around. With youth unemployment at staggering levels, job creation negligible and growth stagnant, the European Union, he said, wasn't working. It was time Europe fell in with Britain's model rather than the other way round. His words were withering, and they were heard with great respect by an audience of MEPs who knew, those honest among them, that Blair was right. The speech ended with a warning that an alarming gap was opening up between the political class and the electorates. Not long before, the French and the Dutch had rejected the Constitution for Europe in referendums. 'The people are blowing the trumpets round the city walls. Are we listening?' Read back twelve years on, there is an uneasy prophecy in these words. They invite the obvious answer: No.

The idea of Britain as a nation has always been complex. Whether Britain is really an identity, rather than a political transaction, is a contested point. Most of the attributes that are said, by outsiders, to be essentially British can be further subdivided into the constituent identities that come from England, Scotland, Wales and Northern Ireland. Great Britain is, strictly speaking, a state that contains four nations, none of which come equipped with a state. It is the most peculiar and convoluted nation-state in the world, and its assorted nationalisms often threaten to pull it to pieces.

Since the end of the Second World War, the principal story of British nationalism has been the alternating repulsion from and attraction to the European Union. That story has been told in ten speeches – eight by prime ministers, one by the leader of the Opposition, and one by an embittered former chancellor of the exchequer – that between them run the gamut of European options from a united state to departure. These are the speeches in which British leaders have tried to settle the definition of the nation amid its relationship with its most important supranational alliance. These were the speeches in which the idea of Britain was spoken into being. The story begins with Winston Churchill in 1946.

United States of Europe

On 19 September 1946, at the University of Zurich, Britain's war-hero leader delivered his most notable speech since the summer of 1940. 'I want to speak', said Churchill, 'about the tragedy of Europe.' This blessed continent, the foundation of Christian faith and ethics, was also the source of the frightful nationalistic quarrels that had threatened a civilisation with extinction. Churchill was speaking before the creation of the European Economic Community about the Council of Europe whose main role was to ensure that its forty-seven member states abide by the European Convention on Human Rights. Churchill proposed a remedy for what he described as 'a vast, quivering mass of tormented, hungry, careworn and bewildered human beings, who wait in the ruins of their cities and homes and scan the dark horizons for the approach of some new form of tyranny or terror'. The remedy was to provide a structure under which the nations of Europe could live in peace, safety and freedom: 'we must build a kind of United States of Europe'.

Churchill lamented the failure of Woodrow Wilson's League of Nations and blamed its demise on the negligence of the states who brought it into being but failed to take it seriously and secure its future. He foresaw a world comprised of multinational blocs – the Commonwealth, the United Nations, the United States of Europe. There is a crucial plural in that phrase united *states* of Europe. Churchill was envisaging a union of sovereign states, a voluntary rapprochement of independent nations. He was not proposing a singular, federal state. Europe required, said Churchill, an act of faith, an act of oblivion against all the crimes and follies of the past.

Churchill's proposed act of faith astonished his audience: a partnership between France and Germany. Rather than merely punish Germany, which had been the mistake made at Versailles in 1919, Churchill concluded that the British should welcome the new family of Europe into existence, although he was careful not to suggest that the British should go so far as to actually join it. Britain was, as Churchill put it in a newspaper article at the time, 'linked but not combined', 'interested and associated but not absorbed'. His Zurich speech gave the idea of Europe gravity at a crucial moment in its early formation. It remains the most eloquent expression of the noble founding purpose of the European Union – to prevent nationalist tyranny stalking through the continent again.

Eleven years later the 1957 Treaty of Rome established the rudiments of Churchill's envisaged plan. Britain was not a founder member, but the argument about joining, which has never really ended, then began. On 31 July 1961, Prime Minister Harold Macmillan gave a speech in the House of Commons in which he pushed for Britain to begin negotiations, under Article 237 of the Treaty of Rome, to join the 'The Six' founding signatories – Belgium, France, Germany, Italy, Luxembourg and the Netherlands. Macmillan shifts the focus from Churchill's stress on security to the benefits of the European *Economic* Community (EEC). He attributes the reconciliation of France and Germany to their economic progress and recommends with some relish the prospect of 'a single market of approaching 300 million people'. He concluded his case by insisting that membership of the EEC would be complementary to the British Commonwealth rather than a threat to it. Macmillan's speech was a failure because his words failed to persuade the only man who mattered. President Charles de Gaulle of France vetoed the British application for membership in 1963 and then did the same again in 1967.

From the beginning, the definition of Britain in Europe had the power to rend parties apart. There was strong opposition in the Conservative Party to Macmillan's overture, but the Labour Party was the first to split open on the question. On 3 October 1962, Hugh Gaitskell gave the third notable European speech by a British politician. The annual party conference speech is usually the occasion for a *tour d'horizon* of the political landscape and a burst of obligatory cheerleading for party morale. Gaitskell instead devoted his entire speech to his reasons for opposing accession to the EEC. After a peculiar opening in which he mocked the low calibre of the debate ('It should not be decided because on the one hand we like Italian girls, or on the other, we think we have been fleeced in Italian hotels'), Gaitskell denied that Britain and the Commonwealth would be stronger for joining. The speech is a litany of reasons for staying out of the EEC which is a template for the Euro-scepticism to come, even when it migrated to the Conservative Party.

Gaitskell disputed the argument, common at the time, that Europe was competitive and modern in contrast to the sclerotic and antiquated Britain. He demanded control of employment policy at national level and commended exports to the Commonwealth, which were seven times their value, over exports to the Common Market. Gaitskell's passage on the movement of capital shows how little this debate, up to and including its vocabulary of taking back control, has changed in half a century: 'I know that some people are frightened lest, if we do not go into the Common Market, British industrialists will move their plants abroad, invest in Europe, with bad effects upon us at home. These are not easy things to decide, but you must know this – that at the moment while we are outside the Common Market that process is subject to Government control. It will no longer be subject to Government control if we go into the Common Market.'

Then Gaitskell raised the scariest phantom of all Britain's dealings with Europe. He predicted that political union would follow from economic cooperation. Gaitskell expressed the concern that the EEC was not just a customs union, that it was in fact a prelude to a political union he did not want, a united *state* of Europe.

Not acknowledging the contradiction in his own text, he also supplied the reason why such anxiety was always an exaggeration. The federal idea would never be likely to progress, he rightly said, so long as General de Gaulle remained in charge of France. Gaitskell quoted Churchill from 'their finest hour' by using one of those strange phrases that only politicians use when he noted that de Gaulle 'will not give up any jot or tittle of French independence'. Gaitskell was right about that, a point the British Euro-sceptics have never fully grasped. The pull of nation has always been strong in France and Germany, always strong enough to resist the countervailing pressure towards a single state. The limits of domestic opinion in France and Germany have always curtailed the European ambitions of federal politicians.

There is one last contemporary resonance when Gaitskell repeated his final demand: 'if when the final terms are known, this Party ... comes to the conclusion that these terms are not good enough, if it is our conviction that we should not enter the Common Market on these terms ... then the only right and proper and democratic thing is to let the people decide the issue'. Gaitskell pointedly accused the Macmillan government of elitism and a refusal to trust the people. His argument was, in all its rhetorical exaggeration, virtually without change, that of the most Euro-sceptic of observers more than half a century later. For Gaitskell it was a question of national power: 'it does mean the end of Britain as an independent nation state ... it means the end of a thousand years of history'. In summary, keep control. The speech dismayed many of Gaitskell's natural supporters in the Labour Party. As the Left applauded, Gaitskell's wife Dora observed at the time: 'all the wrong people are cheering'.

Despite the reservations of Gaitskell and the Labour Party, Britain joined the EEC on 22 January 1972. After ten years of arduous negotiation, Prime Minister Edward Heath signed the Treaty of Accession in Brussels, following which he gave a short speech to mark the occasion. Heath echoed Churchill in his case for the contribution that a stable and united Europe would make towards security. He paid lip service to Britain's proud attachment to national identity but spoke in glowing terms of 'our common European heritage, our mutual interests and our European destiny'. Heath made it plain that Europe faced a complex task in devising new institutions, but he had no doubt that Europe was where Britain belonged. He believed the question of Britain's place in the world was now settled, describing the day as an end rather than a beginning. In that he was set to be disappointed. This wasn't even the end of the beginning, let alone the beginning of the end.

Indeed, the decision might easily have been reversed only three years later. Labour's fault line on Europe had not closed, so when Harold Wilson came to power in 1974 he hit upon the ruse of a referendum, confirming or reversing membership of the EEC, as a device to bridge the division in his party. Three years and a day after Britain's entry, Wilson told the House of Commons that a referendum would be held on the EEC on the basis of revised terms that he would himself negotiate. In response to an intervention from Heath, by now the leader of the Opposition, Wilson described the referendum as 'a very special situation which I do not think anybody will take as a precedent'. With his usual chutzpah, the prime minister demanded that the question, which he had only raised to heal a rift in the Labour Party, be settled now definitively.

Wilson said very little about Europe during the campaign. His crucial statement came in the House of Commons on 9 June 1975, the Monday after the Thursday on which the British people had voted by 67 per cent to 33 per cent to Stay (that, rather than Remain, was the word on the ballot) in the European Community. The debate, Wilson declared optimistically, 'is now over'. His statement was a reiteration of what he had said during Labour's deliberations about whether to accept the original Conservative proposal to join the EEC. British nationhood, he argued, was enhanced rather than compromised by membership. Wilson's arguments were, in fact, usually narrowly economic. He set out a cost–benefit analysis of the balance of payments, the effect on the Commonwealth trade in sugar which he was not prepared to swap for 'a marginal advantage in selling washing machines in Düsseldorf', employment levels and capital movements. Wilson's echoes of Gaitskell were clearest when he criticised Heath, which he did regularly, for straying into the territory of defence and security. This Wilson regarded as a resolutely national question.

Margaret Thatcher, replying as the new leader of the Opposition, could hardly have been more effusively content, firing off compliments to her predecessor Heath and commending the vision of Winston Churchill. Her joy did not last. Although Thatcher, following rather than creating her party line, made plenty of pro-European noises that, to her embarrassment, would later be quoted back at her, by 1988 her position had hardened into nationalistic objection. The speech she gave to the College of Europe in Bruges on 20 September 1988 was a turning point. This is the speech that begins the transition by which the Conservative Party ceased to be the party of Europe. The term 'Euro-sceptic' was coined in the discussion sparked by the Bruges speech. It was the first time since Britain's entry into the EEC that the merits of membership began to come under question.

The speech was given at the instigation of the Foreign Office, which had been seeking an opportunity for the prime minister to make a positive statement on Europe. The original plan was to focus on economic issues, but as soon as Thatcher agreed to speak, that shifted. The early drafts strayed through an assortment of themes, ranging from the state and the individual in Europe to the fact that European cuisine apparently spurred British cooks to higher endeavours. The prime minister's adviser on Europe, John Kerr, suggested focusing on enterprise and the need for greater European efforts on defence. There was a long to-and-fro between the Foreign Office and Downing Street over the draft. At one point, after Geoffrey Howe, the foreign secretary, had raised substantive objections to the tone of the text, there were two drafts in circulation. Rather like Tony Blair's European Parliament drafts in 2005, one observed the protocols of the European Community, the other assaulted them.

During the preparation of the speech Thatcher was irritated by Jacques Delors, the president of the European Commission. During an appearance on the Jimmy Young Show on Radio 2 in July she slapped down what she took to be a hint from Delors in the direction of a single European government. On 8 September Delors won a standing ovation at the Trades Union Congress in Bournemouth for suggesting that collective bargaining should take place at European level. On the same day Delors informed David Hannay, Britain's permanent representative to the European Community, that he would be unable to attend the prime minister's speech in Bruges. He probably knew what was coming.

Thatcher opened by acknowledging the likelihood of controversy. The invitation to her to speak, she said, 'must seem rather like

inviting Genghis Khan to speak on the virtues of peaceful coexist-
ence'. But not all of her speech can be described as anti-European.
The Bruges speech was not the case against Europe at its full-throated
loudest. Thatcher maintained that 'our destiny is in Europe, as part
of the Community'. She included a far-sighted reference to extending the European community beyond the Cold War boundary to the
East: 'we shall always look on Warsaw, Prague and Budapest as great
European cities'.

The burden of her critique was practical rather than philosophical. Europe was not 'an institutional device to be constantly modified
according to the dictates of some abstract intellectual concept'.
Europe, for Thatcher, was either a means of securing prosperity or it
was nothing. In effect she said, much as Blair was to do seventeen
years later, that the people were blowing the trumpets around the city
walls, largely because the Community was not working practically
and because it had proved to be so poor at encouraging enterprise.
The Treaty of Rome', she said, 'was intended as a Charter for
Economic Liberty'. The original impulse towards freedom, she
continued, was being stifled in a panoply of regulations inspired by
social democratic centralisation.

Thatcher's solution, though, was not no Europe but a better
Europe. Her guiding principle in the Bruges speech was the willing
cooperation between independent sovereign states – 'France as
France, Spain as Spain, Britain as Britain'. She went on that this
proclamation of national independence did not preclude speaking as
one where that was in the common interest, citing trade, defence and
international relations as examples. Thatcher had an intriguing story
to symbolise cooperation. The printing press made possible the novel
and the newspaper, the two forms that helped incubate national identity. The first book printed in the English language was produced, she
recalled, in Bruges by William Caxton.

Like all political rhetoric, the speech was soon reduced to its
headline. Thatcher pulled down the standard of the United States of
Europe that Churchill had raised in 1946. The famous passage, in
which she attacked the tendency of the European Commission to
interfere, soon became all the speech was known for. Thatcher was
doomed to become her admirers, as Auden said in memory of W. B.
Yeats. Which is not to say that the words in question are not

heroically direct in their own way because they are: 'Let me say bluntly on behalf of Britain: we have not embarked on the business of throwing back the frontiers of the state at home, only to see a European super-state getting ready to exercise a new dominance from Brussels.' Margaret Thatcher took the conventional view that a nation was a unit in which the culture and the legal status were in large part congruent. She did not believe there was a European people or that Europe could command popular allegiance. A free trade alliance was desirable, and so was cooperation on defence, but, for her, concentrated power in Brussels was illegitimate.

Blowing the Trumpets

The Bruges speech began the process that would bring Thatcher down. The trigger for her resignation was another speech on Europe by the foreign secretary whose views she had discarded during the drafting of the Bruges speech, Geoffrey Howe. Twelve days after resigning as deputy prime minister, Howe got his own back in the House of Commons on 13 November 1990. He quoted both Churchill from 1946 and Macmillan from 1962 to echo the idea that Britain should not 'retreat into a ghetto of sentimentality about our past and so diminish our own control over our own destiny in the future'. It was clear that he saw that destiny, as Macmillan had, within the European Community.

In Howe's version, Thatcher held a Manichean view of Britain and Europe. He was withering on the false choice he said she posed between independent sovereign states on the one hand and a federal superstate on the other. He disliked the talk of 'surrendering' sovereignty and dismissed Mrs Thatcher's supposition that national identities were dissolving into a solvent called Europe. Howe's is one of the least well written of devastating speeches. He was far too fond of clichés like 'style not substance', 'two sides of the same coin', or 'at all costs'. His peroration contained a cricket metaphor that did not work in its own terms, would not travel and was hardly relevant to Mrs Thatcher: 'It is rather like sending your opening batsmen to the crease only for them to find, the moment the first balls are bowled, that their bats have been broken before the game by the team captain.'

The effect, though, was cataclysmic. Howe's assault triggered a leadership challenge. Margaret Thatcher resigned days later.

The fault line over Europe exposed by Howe's resignation speech opened into a chasm into which John Major fell after Thatcher. The Blair government came to power in 1997 with the intention of changing the mood. Blair's European Parliament speech was a warning to the capitals of Europe, but he was also the most unequivocally pro-European prime minister since Heath. The 2005 speech did not just make the case for union as a transaction of mutual benefit. It went further than that, with a suggestion of an identity of kinship: 'This is a union of values, of solidarity between nations and people, of not just a common market in which we trade but a common political space in which we live as citizens.'

Those words did not change much. The call of nation proved too strong. In 2013, David Cameron chose the same day, 23 January, that Harold Wilson had chosen thirty-eight years earlier, to announce another referendum on Britain in Europe. Like Wilson before him, Cameron dressed up a party fix as a noble calling. He paid the obligatory tribute to the original purpose of the European Union, which was to preserve the peace in the theatre of twentieth-century conflict. The task now, he declared, was to secure prosperity, competition and enterprise within a single market. Cameron confirmed that his objective was to stem the flow of powers from the national to the European level and sometimes to send it into reverse. He demanded more power for national parliaments and expressed the fear that a European state, Thatcher's phantom, was still viable. Cameron's passages on the economic failure of European nations were an echo of Blair's concerns that the people were blowing the trumpets round the city walls, though, if I may say so, without quite the turn of phrase.

The speech really turned, as did the history of the nation, on the announcement that a referendum would take place. Eleven years to the day after Tony Blair had delivered his lecture on the values that were shared in solidarity between Britain and other European nations, Britain voted to leave the European nation, by 52 per cent to 48 per cent of those who voted, in a referendum. Mr Cameron became the latest Conservative prime minister to find his words turned against him. As soon as it became clear he had lost, he resigned. The chain of events led to the tenth and, at least so far, the final speech in this sequence, which was delivered by the new prime minister, Theresa May, at Lancaster House, London, on 17 January 2017.

May summarised where this long debate about the nation had brought Britain, which was to a point of some confusion. Britain needed to ask again, she said, what kind of country it wanted to be. In a strange anachronism she included a section on the future of trade with the Commonwealth, the issue that had so occupied Gaitskell and Wilson. She left the impression of a nation going round in circles, or perhaps coming full circle. The vote to leave, said May, was in essence a demand for control to be exercised at the level of the nation-state.

One Nation

'I have sat through Council Conclusions after Council Conclusions', Tony Blair told the European Parliament in 2005, 'describing how we are "reconnecting Europe to the people". Are we?' Clearly not; no leader, in this rhetorical litany, succeeded in defining the European Union in a way that resonated as powerfully as the call of nationhood. The European Union, like Great Britain, is an imagined community. It is just that one was imagined long before the other and excites an allegiance that no international body has ever commanded.

The lesson of these ten speeches on the European Union is therefore that the idea of the nation is tenacious and important. The vital question is, then, just how that nation is defined. The speeches in this chapter defined it in the face of a threat from an external aggressor, in the case of Elizabeth I, and from an internal aggressor, in the case of Aung San Suu Kyi. In the cases of Benjamin Franklin and Jawaharlal Nehru the nation is defined as the prize to be won after the departure of a colonial power. Nelson Mandela defined the nation generously in defiance of an exclusive account of who belongs to it.

The nation is constituted by the people, and belonging therefore needs to be widely drawn. By contrast, the populist understanding of the nation is always narrow. The claim of the populist to have a mystical understanding of the genuine will of the people leads, in a straight line, to the claim that those who disagree are not really part of the true and faithful nation. This dismal version of nationalism is an exercise in exclusion. The history of Britain's half-hearted engagement with the European Union in its various incarnations shows that the desire for rootedness and a sense of place cannot be wished away. But it does need to be spoken about with care.

Nationalism stands astride the division that runs throughout this book. On one side of the chasm, there is the generosity of the democrat; on the other the angry exclusivity of the populist. Nationalism has taken both forms, and the real history of any nation is complex and winding. The real identities of actual citizens are plural and changing, especially in a world shrunk by travel and technology. National identity, like everything else that has political value, needs to be wrestled from the clutches of the populists.

The populist always starts with the claim that the country has suffered some dreadful decline, to which the only viable answer is the populist himself. Only he can Make America Great Again. Only he can Put the Great Back into Britain. Substitute the name of any nation and there is another populist making the same unhistorical, unsubstantiated, unwarrantable claim. The core claim of the populist is that only some people are truly *the* people. Only some people count. The nation is some but not all. The populist argues that there are two nations – the elite and the common people. To which argument, authentic speech needs to assert that there is but one nation and that *all* citizens compose it.

The speeches in this chapter are arguments about who counts. The answer has to be that everyone counts and that the idea of the people has to be generous. Amid the comparatively gentle arguments about Europe, in which the only harm will be economic rather than physical, we still need to take care to carve out a single British nation. All countries are imagined and forged by words. The act of saying that someone is included is also the act of including them. It is very dark down at the other end of the spectrum. The egregious twentieth-century nationalisms were murderously exclusive. Colonial conquerors and racist regimes have always sought to define the people out of existence. The best retort to them is the one that runs through this book. It is the creation and defence of a democratic and free society, an ideal for which one should, *in extremis* and if one has the requisite moral courage, be prepared to die.

4

PROGRESS:
THROUGH POLITICS THE
CONDITION OF THE PEOPLE
IS IMPROVED

The Guy Next Door

I never expected Les Dawson to be such an important voice for improving the condition of the people. The setting was the Labour Party conference in Manchester Central on 26 September 2006. Prime Minister Tony Blair had made it plain that this was to be his last address to the conference. In truth, the party had tired of him and allegiance was moving, by slow degrees but inexorably, to his main rival, the chancellor of the exchequer, Gordon Brown.

The previous day, Brown's own conference speech had been pushed down the news schedule by a remark allegedly made by Blair's wife Cherie to the effect that he, Brown, was less than sincere in his demand, from the podium, for a more equal society. If this seems a trivial dispute a decade on, it was big news on the day. I had prepared an address on how globalisation, trade between nations and the movement of people brought with it both great prosperity but also the test of ensuring that the rewards were evenly distributed. That message would be lost entirely if we could not divine a way to close down the Cherie and Gordon story.

We knew that the solution was a joke. Scriptwriters and playwrights hide plot twists in a joke. In the midst of laughter an audience drops its guard. The smuggled plot twist they notice only in retrospect. A joke in a speech has the same dual function. A Greek joke book called *Philogelos* (*The Laughter-Lover*) survives from the fourth century BC, and three books of Cicero's jokes, which he was thought to use too much, were published after his death, though they are sadly lost to posterity. As long as it works as a joke, it simultaneously allows a contested point to be gently made, or a concession to be granted, as it was in this case. Searching frantically for the right line with the clock running down, it struck me that the circumstances had all the elements of music hall. There was a wife too candid for her own good whose truth-telling embarrassed the put-upon husband and a rival man who lived next door. Looking up all the comedians of the right vintage, I found nothing suitable in Arthur Askey or Max Miller, but then I hit upon this, from a local boy, Les Dawson of Collyhurst, Manchester: 'My wife's run off with the guy next door. And, do you know what, I'm really going to miss him.'

The prime minister, not to my knowledge much of a Les Dawson fan, liked the joke, and so we tried to make it work. In its unvarnished form the gag was too vulgar, too obviously seaside-postcard for a prime minister, so we had to turn the line. The final version was left out of the script released to the press and did not appear on the autocue. It was left to Blair himself, in the spotlight on the stage, to read the mood of the audience. He decided to risk it and the customised version of a Les Dawson joke brought the house down: 'At least she won't run off with the guy next door.'

A joke carries more risk than the rest of the speech. Say the line to yourself. If you stumble at the punchline you lose the effect. As the joke is often the only point in a speech where the speaker asks the audience for an instant verdict, a silence bare of laughter can be devastating. It is no accident that comedy shares a language with mortality. The comedian corpses if she laughs. The line dies a death. Plato thought a sense of humour was the last thing a statesman needed, and the anthologies of the great speeches contain very few funny moments. A turning point of history, when an injustice is named, is rarely a moment for levity. But when it works the effect is memorable, and, like Lloyd George calling attention to his own size, it only works when the comedy has a serious intent. The Manchester joke conceded the point that Cherie Blair had indeed said something disobliging about Gordon Brown. The story dissolved into the laughter and Blair gained permission to give a disquisition on the condition of the people. The rest of the speech anticipated the problems, as well as the benefits, of globalisation. It was a serious analysis of the social forces which, years later, contributed to the election of Donald Trump as president of the United States and to Britain's departure from the European Union. It was fitting that such a speech should have been made in Manchester, which is the first place that the question of the condition of the people was raised.

The Dream of Progress

The material condition of the people is a standard subject for the political speech. Many speeches have been made on the topic, but only the rare ones survive in the canon. The best recent example was made by the man who made Blair's leadership of the Labour Party possible, Neil Kinnock. In Llandudno in 1987, Kinnock described the dream of equal life chances in poetic style. As a speaker, Kinnock is the apotheosis of the reformist Left, in that he reserved his most magnificent scorn for the battle against the revolutionaries in his own party. Kinnock might, though only might, have been gentler on Dolores Ibárruri, the Spanish revolutionary who went under the rhetorical guise of La Pasionaria. Ibárruri was the voice of justice when the alternative was the military fascism of General Franco. She was the voice of a desire for liberation which, as we shall see, can easily lead in the opposite direction from the one intended: away from progress.

This is a battle within the Left that continues until the present day. The Labour Party fought the 2017 general election with a leader, Jeremy Corbyn, and an organisational faction, Momentum, both of whom preferred doctrinal purity to piecemeal progress. It would be wrong, though, to suppose that questions of justice and equality have been the sole preserve of the political Left. Indeed, One Nation Conservatism was defined by Benjamin Disraeli, in a speech in 1872 in the Free Trade Hall in Manchester, a short walk from where Blair spoke in 2006. Both before and after Disraeli there is an honourable Conservative tradition of social reform.

In Piccadilly Circus in London stands the Angel of Christian Charity, more commonly known as the statue of Eros. This is a commemoration of the Tory social reformer Earl Shaftesbury, author of the Factory Acts of the 1840s, which reduced working time for women and children and introduced the idea of state responsibility for health and safety. Disraeli's Factory Act of 1874 made education compulsory for children up to the age of ten, and the Public Health Act of 1875 forced councils to clear refuse and sewage and to provide an adequate water supply. The same year, the Artisans' and Labourers' Dwelling Act started the clearance of the urban slums.

The Conservative tradition of progress is represented in this book by two people not usually associated with the political Right. William Wilberforce is the Conservative Party's best retort to the claim, often levelled by opponents, that it is always and only the party of the rich. He devoted his political life to the cause of the abolition of slavery. Looking back from today, the opprobrium that rained down on Wilberforce seems hard to credit. His speeches on slavery made him one of the most hated men in England. But, after two decades of ceaseless effort and disappointment, his day dawned. Despite feeling very unwell, Wilberforce spoke for three and a half hours on the theme of 'Let Us Put an End at Once to This Inhuman Traffic'.

Even less representative of the Conservatism of male merchants, Emmeline Pankhurst devised radical methods to win the right to vote for women. Since the granting of democratic rights to the propertied male in the *acropolis* in Athens, people had campaigned to widen the enchanted circle of the entitled. The franchise in Britain had been extended in 1832, 1867 and again in 1884, but even then the responsibility of voting was thought to be a burden too much for women. Emmeline Pankhurst's oratorical talent was roused by the moral offensiveness of excluding anyone from democracy on the mere basis of being a woman.

The other false criterion of moral worth that has been invoked to deny people equal weight in the consideration of their condition has been race. Perhaps the most famous, and perhaps even the greatest, of the speeches in this book is a passionate plea for the equal treatment of little black boys and little black girls in a racially divided America. In words taken from the Bible and given political immortality, Martin Luther King delivered, at the March for Freedom in Washington in August 1963, the most eloquent demand for equal worth that anyone has yet put into words. It is hard to resist the judgement that this speech contains the most irresistible closing in all rhetorical history.

King's words are passionately delivered, sincerely held and sadly still appropriate. But they would not merit their status as a statement of progress if they had not led to change. The ultimate verdict on the speeches that follow is that they show that progress is possible. They do not just record progress; they propel it and make it happen. The speech is the public argument for progress. Political change is slow and failure is part of the process but, measured both by material prosperity and expanded liberty, tomorrow in the democracies has always been marginally better than today, which is, in turn, marginally better than it was yesterday. That is a prosaic way of making a poetic point. The even better way is in the words that now follow.

WILLIAM WILBERFORCE

Let Us Make Reparations to Africa

House of Commons, London

12 May 1789

William Wilberforce (1759–1833) showed that a member of the British Parliament can change the world. Without the words of Wilberforce, people who lived in freedom would have been indentured as slaves in the British Empire.

Wilberforce was born on 24 August 1759 in Hull, the son of a wealthy merchant. William was a sickly child with poor eyesight, but he was blessed with a generous and kind nature. At Cambridge, he began a lasting friendship with the future prime minister William Pitt the Younger. In 1780, at the tender age of twenty-one, Wilberforce became MP for Hull, at a cost of £8,000 to buy the necessary votes, as was the custom then. He later represented Yorkshire in more tolerably democratic fashion. As a young MP in London, he lived a dissolute life. He was an habitué of gambling clubs such as Goostree's and Boodle's, his particular vices cards and late-night drinking dens. Wilberforce was described at this time, by the writer Madame de Staël, as the 'wittiest man in England'.

The great rupture in Wilberforce's life came with a sudden conversion to evangelical Christianity in 1785. From then onwards he approached politics from a position of strict Christian morality. This led him down some strange paths. He was deeply opposed to trade unions, approved of government limitations on public meetings and, convinced that British society was descending into moral turpitude, occasionally suggested that the spread of profanity was as important as slavery. His efforts to ban adultery and Sunday newspapers came to nothing, but Wilberforce's moralistic fervour could be damaging as well as eccentric. Thomas Williams, the London printer of Thomas Paine's *The Age of Reason*, was imprisoned at the instigation of the Society for the Suppression of Vice, which Wilberforce helped to found.

The more laudable side to his passion was expressed in an interest in the poor conditions in the factories of newly industrialised Britain. Wilberforce campaigned to provide all children with regular education in reading, personal hygiene and religion. He was closely involved with the Royal Society for the Prevention of Cruelty to Animals and campaigned for better salaries for curates. But, inspired by the abolitionist Thomas Clarkson, his evangelical zeal found its greatest cause in the slave trade. Legend has it that Wilberforce's decision to devote himself to the cause derives from a meeting with Pitt, by now the prime minister, under a tree in Croydon in May 1787. Wilberforce later declared that: 'God has set before me two great objects: the suppression of the slave trade, and the reformation of manners.' There may still be work to do on the latter cause, but the former gives him a place in history.

Britain was at the time the world's foremost slave-trading nation. The introduction of plantations in the American colonies, especially those growing sugar, had led to the extensive use of African slaves. Some 70 per cent of all enslaved Africans shipped across the Atlantic were destined to work in the sugar fields. Pioneered by the Spaniards and perfected by the Dutch, sugar plantations were eagerly adopted by the English from the 1620s. They were followed by tobacco plantations. The slave ventures were episodic at first, but were soon licensed and chartered from London. By the time Wilberforce came to be involved in the argument, British ships were regularly carrying black slaves from Africa, in the most appalling conditions, to be bought and sold in the West Indies as chattels.

For nearly two decades Wilberforce repeatedly introduced anti-slavery motions in Parliament. The abolitionists published pamphlets and books, held rallies and issued petitions. The twenty-year campaign made him simultaneously one of the most loved and one of the most loathed men in the country. The speech that follows was delivered in Parliament in May 1789, a month before the French Revolution, as the House of Commons considered a Privy

Council report, commissioned by Pitt, on the effects of the slave trade on British commerce.

Wilberforce, who was never the most robust of men, had been feeling unwell before he spoke. It didn't stop him speaking for three and a half hours which, though it would be unacceptable today, was not an unusual length for the House of Commons in the late eighteenth century. As a sign of the support of his friend Pitt, the prime minister, he was permitted to speak from the dispatch box, despite not being a member of the government.

The text we have is not an official record, there being no such office at the time. It was the practice of contemporary newspapers to print their own versions of speeches, not always exactly verbatim. This speech, however, was printed and circulated afterwards as part of the continuing campaign against slavery. It is consistent with everything else we know about Wilberforce and likely, therefore, to be faithful to his intent.

When I consider the magnitude of the subject which I am to bring before the House – a subject, in which the interests, not of this country, nor of Europe alone, but of the whole world, and of posterity, are involved: and when I think, at the same time, on the weakness of the advocate who has undertaken this great cause – when these reflections press upon my mind, it is impossible for me not to feel both terrified and concerned at my own inadequacy to such a task. But when I reflect, however, on the encouragement which I have had, through the whole course of a long and laborious examination of this question, and how much candour I have experienced, and how conviction has increased within my own mind, in proportion as I have advanced in my labours – when I reflect, especially, that however averse any gentleman may now be, yet we shall all be of one opinion in the end – when I turn myself to these thoughts, I take courage. I determine to forget all my other fears, and I march forward with a firmer step in the full assurance that my cause will bear me out, and that I shall be able to justify upon the clearest principles, every resolution in my hand, the avowed end of which is, the total abolition of the slave trade.

For once the traditionally modest opening, in which the speaker claims to be inadequate for the scale of the task before him, is something more than standard technique. This is not to say that Wilberforce was not a noted orator of his day, for he was. Striking oratory at Castle Yard in York had won him political control of Yorkshire in 1784. William Pitt said that Wilberforce possessed 'the greatest natural eloquence of all the men I ever knew', which, from a man who himself carried quite a reputation as an orator and who was by this time prime minister, was a verdict not to be taken lightly. Wilberforce became known as the nightingale of the House of Commons – a reference both to his mellifluous speaking voice and his habit of attending evening debates. It was said of him, by a parliamentary reporter, that he had a speaking voice so attractive to the ear that if he talked nonsense the audience would feel obliged to listen nonetheless. That is by no means a virtue shared by all the speakers of famous words. Lincoln, Churchill and John F. Kennedy all had reedy, weak voices; all worried about the effect this had on their impact.

Wilberforce's modesty is therefore a reasonable recognition of the gravity of the occasion. He might also have been worried by the fact that his time for preparation had been cut short by illness. Wilberforce was known at the time for a style that was more conversational than the orotund contrivances of Burke or Pitt, but this speech is looser than it ought to have been. It is a classic example of Pascal's adage that he would have written a shorter letter, only he didn't have the time. Every speechwriter knows that editing is the greater part of writing, and anyone with a facility for language can write a long speech quickly. Writing the correct and appropriate short speech takes time. Wilberforce ran out of time and so turned up at the House with a structure scribbled on a piece of paper and a complete command of the facts about slavery. By the time he entered his third hour on his feet he was exemplifying another principle – the speaker who knows too much can be as great a menace as the one who knows too little.

> I wish exceedingly, in the outset, to guard both myself and the
> House from entering into the subject with any sort of passion. It is
> not their passions I shall appeal to – I ask only for their cool and
> impartial reason; and I wish not to take them by surprise, but to

deliberate, point by point, upon every part of this question. I mean not to accuse any one, but to take the shame upon myself, in common, indeed, with the whole Parliament of Great Britain, for having suffered this horrid trade to be carried on under their authority. We are all guilty — we ought all to plead guilty, and not to exculpate ourselves by throwing the blame on others; and I therefore deprecate every kind of reflection against the various descriptions of people who are more immediately involved in this wretched business. In opening the nature of the slave trade, I need only observe, that it is found by experience to be just such as every man, who uses his reason, would infallibly conclude it to be. For my own part, so clearly am I convinced of the mischiefs inseparable from it, that I should hardly want any further evidence than my own mind would furnish, by the most simple deductions. Facts, however, are now laid before the House. A report has been made by His Majesty's Privy Council, which, I trust, every gentleman has read, and which ascertains the slave trade to be just such in practice as we know, from theory, it must be.

This slightly deceptive passage introduces the tone that Wilberforce is largely, though not entirely, going to deploy. This was an era, before the discipline of the party whip made such a prize of loyalty, in which Members of Parliament would routinely change their minds and their votes on the persuasive merits of a fine speech.

Wilberforce knows his audience well and he wishes to move it to act. Plenty of MPs shared the view that slavery was wrong in the abstract. They just worried about the impact of abolition on trade and prosperity. Addressing a group of men who had, for the most part, bought their way into the House in order to stand for commercial and propertied interests, Wilberforce calculated that an argument predicated on the human worth of the individual slave might fail to carry the debate. He is thus, throughout, reasonable beyond measure towards the Liverpool slave merchants, some of whom he mentions by name. He could have laid the blame for slavery on them, but this would have lost him the argument. Instead, he says the shame belongs to everyone in the nation, himself included.

The tone here is instructively moderate, cautious and generous to opponents and their arguments. Indeed, Wilberforce is at great pains to go through the commercial case for the status quo and knock it over. The speech relies more on clear argument and detailed factual commentary than it does on an evocation of moral horror or even appeals to Christian compassion. Wilberforce is clear that complete abolition of slavery was the eventual aim. The objective of this speech, though, was to win the battle to end the trade in new slaves. He therefore exhibits a primary skill of democratic politics – the patience to argue for a secondary item as a preliminary to the principal aim. This takes some of the drama out of the rhetoric but it is the stuff of how progress is made.

> *I must speak of the transit of the slaves in the West Indies. This I confess, in my own opinion, is the most wretched part of the whole subject. So much misery condensed in so little room is more than the human imagination had ever before conceived. I will not accuse the Liverpool merchants. I will allow, them, nay, I will believe them, to be men of humanity. And I will therefore believe, if it were not for the multitude of these wretched objects, if it were not for the enormous magnitude and extent of the evil which distracts their attention from individual cases, and makes them think generally, and therefore less feelingly on the subject, they never would have persisted in the trade. I verily believe, therefore, if the wretchedness of any one of the many hundred negroes stowed in each ship could be brought before their view, and remain within the sight of the African merchant, that there is no one among them whose heart would bear it. Let anyone imagine to himself six or seven hundred of these wretches chained two and two, surrounded with every object that is nauseous and disgusting, diseased, and struggling under every kind of wretchedness! How can we bear to think of such a scene as this? One would think it had been determined to heap on them all the varieties of bodily pain, for the purpose of blunting the feelings of the mind.*

The self-denying ordinance cracks here. Wilberforce has been making a practical case against the slave trade, painstakingly rebutting each case that had been made for its retention. But it is impossible to make a case about the forced bondage of a human being and his trafficking in servitude without mustering some passion. This was a campaign to which Wilberforce had devoted his adult life. Some of his evangelical fervour was bound to get into the speech. Perhaps if he had crafted the speech properly in advance he might have excised all passion in favour of pragmatism. Speaking extempore, the truth barges in.

The evidence that had been collected by his friend Thomas Clarkson for the Privy Council inquiry was harrowing. Here Wilberforce makes an appeal to common humanity to consider the appallingly wretched conditions the slaves had to endure. Note, though, that he is once again, even at the moment of high emotion, not condemning the status of the slave: a slave is still living at the mercy of others even if he is kept in hospitable conditions. The true, deep horror of the institution is the lack of liberty. Disgusting conditions are an added insult, but the real injury to the self is to be unfree. Indeed, that was the case usually made by the campaigners. Josiah Wedgwood had created an image, one of the prototype logos and mottos, which depicted a kneeling slave above the rhetorical question 'Am I not a Man and a Brother?' That phrase might have been a good addition here, but Wilberforce instead avoids sinking into the philosophical argument. Even at his most impassioned his target is a subsidiary position rather than the horror itself. Even at the height of his revulsion he is holding himself back. This passage is emotional at the level of rhetorical performance but still disciplined at the level of content.

> *I have in my hand the extract from a pamphlet which states in very dreadful colours what thousands and tens of thousands will be ruined; how our wealth will be impaired; one third of our commerce cut off for ever; how our manufactures will drop in consequence, our land-tax will be raised, our marine destroyed, while France, our natural enemy and rival, will strengthen herself by our weakness ... There is one other argument, in my opinion a very weak and absurd one, which many persons, however, have much dwelt upon. I mean that, if we relinquish the slave trade, France will take it up. If the slave trade be such as I have described it, and if the House is also convinced of this, if it be in truth both wicked and impolitic, we cannot wish a greater mischief to France than that she should adopt it. For the sake of France, however, and*

*for the sake of humanity; I trust, nay, I am sure, she will not.
France is too enlightened a nation to begin pushing a scandalous as
well as ruinous traffic, at the very time when England sees her
folly and resolves to give it up. It is clearly no argument whatever
against the wickedness of the trade, that France will adopt it. For
those who argue thus may argue equally that we may rob, murder,
and commit any crime, which anyone else would have committed,
if we did not. The truth is that by our example we shall produce the
contrary effect.*

At the point that Wilberforce suggested that France would be strengthened by Britain's absence from the slave trade, there was a cry of assent from the back benches. Anti-French feeling was common in Parliament, and Wilberforce is careful to stay just the right side of it by suggesting that Britain (naturally) can be an example to France from a position of moral superiority.

He pursues at length the argument that abolition would not be calamitous economically. Pointing out that trade revenues would survive the rupture is like a more substantive version of the argument made by some on the Leave team about Britain's place in the European Union. Wilberforce is well briefed on the tonnage of trade that comes in and out of Liverpool and does not spare his audience much of his learning. There are sections of this speech that are, not to put too fine a point on it, boring. Wilberforce needs to keep the traders on his side, though. Slavery was lucrative and it was not just the fruits of the bonded labour where the rewards lay. Outbound slave ships to Africa were laden with British metal, firearms, textiles and wines, all to be exchanged for human cargo. The ships eventually returned to Britain full of produce from the plantations. This trading network was overseen and approved by Parliament. The City of London's Corporation, the Bank of England, Lloyd's insurance and a host of other banking facilities had all thrived on the Atlantic trades.

Wilberforce was ranged against some serious vested interests. Again, though, he cares too much to be able to sustain a cold demeanour all the way. Emotion breaks in when he points out that the real cost of the trade is human. The lives of both British seamen and traded servants are lost in the unfolding of transactions that are by any measure awful.

Let us recollect what Europe itself was no longer ago than three or four centuries. What if I should be able to show this House that in a civilized part of Europe, in the time of our Henry VII, there were people who actually sold their own children? What if I should tell them that England itself was that country? What if I should point out to them that the very place where this inhuman traffic was carried on was the city of Bristol? Ireland at that time used to drive a considerable trade in slaves with these neighbouring barbarians; but a great plague having infested the country, the Irish were struck with a panic, suspected (I am sure very properly) that the plague was a punishment sent from Heaven, for the sin of the slave trade, and therefore abolished it. All I ask, therefore, of the people of Bristol is, that they would become as civilized now as Irishmen were four hundred years ago. Let us put an end at once to this inhuman traffic. Let us stop this effusion of human blood. The true way to virtue is by withdrawing from temptation. Let us then withdraw from these wretched Africans those temptations to fraud, violence, cruelty, and injustice, which the slave trade furnishes.

This is the most withering section in the speech, yet it contains an argument that is in fact curiously crafted for this audience. The passionate conclusion to which it appears to lead – 'Let us put an end to this inhuman traffic. Let us stop this effusion of human blood' – lends the speech a title by which it is sometimes now known. This is hugely effective both as description and as an expression of the anguish inflicted, but these should be the closing words. Instead, Wilberforce undercuts their effect with a rider about the beneficial effect abolition would have on the otherwise recidivist Africans.

Once again the argument is not joined at the level of principle but for its attendant consequences. In this case, ending the slave trade is described as an incentive for better behaviour. The first part of this passage has described a transition from barbarism into civilisation. The daring aspect is that it is the odyssey taken by the people of Bristol, engineered by the Irish. Slavery is therefore the handmaiden of barbarism not on account of the bondage and the indentured labour but because it does not allow a society to give up its appalling habits.

242

The complex addition to the argument does, to some extent, lessen the impact of the magnificent moral authority of the best words in the speech. But only to some extent. This is Wilberforce showing how good he is. The balanced symmetry of the famous two sentences adds even more grandeur than is contained in the message. It is hard to resist the claim and hard to resist the call.

I have one word more to add upon a most material point. But it is a point so self-evident that I shall be extremely short. It will appear from everything which I have said, that it is not regulation, it is not mere palliatives, that can cure this enormous evil. Total abolition is the only possible cure for it ... We see then that it is the existence of the slave trade that is the spring of all this internal traffic, and that the remedy cannot be applied without abolition ... I trust, therefore, I have shown that upon every ground the total abolition ought to take place. I have urged many things which are not my own leading motives for proposing it, since I have wished to show every description of gentlemen, and particularly the West India planters, who deserve every attention, that the abolition is politic upon their own principles also. Policy, however, sir, is not my principle, and I am not ashamed to say it. There is a principle above everything that is political; and when I reflect on the command which says, 'Thou shalt do no murder,' believing the authority to be divine, how can I dare to set up any reasonings of my own against it? And, sir, when we think of eternity, and of the future consequences of all human conduct, what is there in this life that should make any man contradict the dictates of his conscience, the principles of justice, the laws of religion, and of God. Sir, the nature and all the circumstances of this trade are now laid open to us; we can no longer plead ignorance, we cannot evade it, it is now an object placed before us, we cannot pass it. We may spurn it, we may kick it out of our way, but we cannot turn aside so as to avoid seeing it; for it is brought now so directly before our eyes that this House must decide, and must justify to all the world, and to their own consciences, the rectitude of the grounds and principles of their decision. A society has been established for the abolition of this trade, in which dissenters, Quakers, churchmen, in which the most conscientious of all persuasions have all united, and made a

common cause in this great question. Let not Parliament be the
only body that is insensible to the principles of national justice. Let
us make a reparation to Africa, so far as we can, by establishing a
trade upon true commercial principles, and we shall soon find the
rectitude of our conduct rewarded by the benefits of a regular and
a growing commerce.

It is always important to end well. The effect of a speech is
destroyed by a speaker who mumbles words to the effect that: 'OK,
that's it, thanks for listening.' The end needs to be signalled by content
and by style. There are two ways to finish. One is with elevation, the
other is with pathos, but either way, the audience needs to be prepared,
with the progress of the argument and the inflection of the voice, for
the approaching conclusion. If Wilberforce had ended here he would
have achieved this elementary task of the orator. Indeed, the speech
is so loosely structured that the full text contains a number of points
at which he gestures towards completion.

Unfortunately, despite detaining his audience for more than
three hours and despite coming to an obvious terminus, he was not
done yet. Instead he resumed with 'I shall now move to several
Resolutions', which were like dry footnotes to his own speech, or a
maths homework in which points are awarded for showing working.
The Resolutions, which the prime minister had asked Wilberforce to
move, concerned the number of slaves annually carried from the
coast of Africa and the West Indies in British vessels, the high mortality rate both among British seamen employed in the slave trade and
among the transported slaves either in transit or in the harbours of
the West Indies, the various restraints on slaves having a family and
the high mortality rate of slaves in Jamaica, Barbados and the
Leeward Islands. It is all historically fascinating and every word of it
should have been saved for one of the parliamentary committees, at
which Wilberforce was a renowned master.

The appendix to the speech was an intellectual error, though the
blame attaches to Pitt rather than Wilberforce. Having taken the
House to the brink of the conviction that abolition is the natural step,
he then complicates the issue with a set of procedural questions. This
is poor oratorical technique, but there is a political lesson, which is
that a democracy can move but slowly. Wilberforce had won the

debate but not yet the issue. In blatant defiance of his request, the House of Commons lost the question in its labyrinthine procedures for a year. The motion was not carried.

To his credit, Wilberforce did not waver in his commitment to the cause. He brought forward further motions in 1791 and 1792, but with Parliament preoccupied by the war against Napoleon, progress was minimal. The French Revolution ate up the available attention span of politicians and a slave uprising in Saint-Domingue, a French colony in the West Indies, did not help. Progress stalled until the death of Pitt in 1806 and the campaign for the Foreign Slave Trade Abolition Bill. During the vital debate in the House of Commons on 23 February 1806, the speech of the solicitor-general, Sir Samuel Romilly, concluded with a long and emotional tribute to Wilberforce in which he contrasted the peaceful happiness of Wilberforce in his bed with the tortured sleeplessness of the guilty Napoleon Bonaparte. Wilberforce was overcome by Romilly's tribute. He sat with his head in his hands, tears streaming down his face. As Romilly concluded, the House of Commons rose to give Wilberforce a standing ovation. The slave trade had been abolished.

Slavery still remained in British colonies, although that story too has a heartening ending. The Emancipation Bill received its final Commons reading on 26 July 1833. Progress can take a long time. There were more than four decades between Wilberforce's great speech and final success. Mercifully, Wilberforce had lived to witness the event and celebrate it. He died three days later and was buried in Westminster Abbey.

EMMELINE PANKHURST

The Laws That Men Have Made

The Portman Rooms, London
24 March 1908

Emmeline Pankhurst's campaign to win the right for women to vote is a drama about the appropriate method in a parliamentary democracy. The suffragettes were at times violent, and yet the purpose of their radicalism was to be permitted entry to the democratic system. They were the radicals knocking down the door because they wanted to get in. She was the middle-class girl from finishing school who ended up with detectives in plain clothes transcribing her speeches on the pretext of public safety.

Emmeline Pankhurst (1858–1928) was born Emmeline Goulden to a Manchester family with a tradition of radical politics. She opens her autobiography, *The Making of a Militant*, with a story about a bazaar in Manchester to raise funds for emancipated American slaves. Her father Robert Goulden was on the committee that greeted the abolitionist clergyman Henry Ward Beecher when he visited Britain. Henry's sister Harriet Beecher Stowe's *Uncle Tom's Cabin* was the young Emmeline's bedtime reading.

She was sent to finishing school at the École Normale Supérieure in Paris, which provided a full curriculum that was at least as much science as embroidery. In 1879 she married Richard Pankhurst, a lawyer and supporter of the women's suffrage movement and the author of the Married Women's Property Acts of 1870 and 1882, which allowed women to keep earnings or property acquired before and after marriage. Emmeline was both heartbroken and impoverished when her husband died in 1898. She sold all her books, paintings and furniture and took a job as the registrar of births and deaths in Manchester to make ends meet. She also opened a shop selling silks and cushions in King Street, Manchester. The overburdened mothers whose children she registered in her new occupation were an important influence on Emmeline's growing sense that the treatment of women was insufferable. In October 1903, persuaded by her daughter Christabel, she helped found the Women's Social and Political Union (WSPU).

The WSPU was the first organisation to be given the title of suffragette, and it soon attracted criticism born of bafflement. Demonstrations, window smashing, arson, cutting telephone lines, interrupting the proceedings in Parliament, damaging Velázquez's *Rokeby Venus*, throwing yourself under the king's horse at the Derby and going on hunger strikes was not the behaviour expected of respected bourgeois gentlewomen. Emmeline herself was arrested and imprisoned on numerous occasions. During one incarceration, her hunger strike was ended with violent force-feeding. She ended up living like a fugitive, flitting between friends' houses when she was not spending time in prison. She was even detained as an undesirable alien at Ellis Island, New York, in 1913, until President Wilson intervened.

It is telling that so many of the orators in this book – Nehru, Mandela, Aung San Suu Kyi – spent time in prison. Ideas are dangerous and the authorities regularly wish to have them silenced. The speech that follows was given five days after Pankhurst was released from jail. The cause of her February 1908 imprisonment was trying to enter Parliament to deliver a resolution of protest to the prime minister. She was released on 19 March and went straight to a suffragette meeting at the Albert Hall to mark the end of 'Self-Denial Week', a fundraising initiative in which women had abstained from butter, sugar, meat and sweets. The audience at the Albert Hall was not expecting her because she was not due to be released until the following day. Unannounced, Pankhurst walked slowly onto the stage, removed the placard that said 'Mrs Pankhurst's chair' and sat down to a tremendous ovation. 'It was some time before I could see them for my tears,' she wrote in her autobiography, *My Own Story*.

What I am going to say to you tonight is not new. It is what we have been saying at every street corner, at every by-election during the last 18 months. It is perfectly well known to many members of my audience, but they will not mind if I repeat, for the benefit of those who are here for the first time tonight, those arguments and illustrations with which many of us are so very familiar. In the first place, it is important that women should have the vote in order that in the government of the country the women's point of view should be put forward. It is important for women that in any legislation that affects women equally with me, those who make the laws should be responsible to women, in order that they may be forced to consult women and learn women's views when they are contemplating the making or the altering of laws. Very little has been done by legislation for women for many years — for obvious reasons ... There are many laws on the statute-book today which are admittedly out of date, and call for reformation: laws which inflict very grave injustices on women. I want to call the attention of women who are here tonight to a few acts on the statute-book which press very hardly and very injuriously on women. Men politicians are in the habit of talking to women as if there were no laws that affect women. 'The fact is,' they say, 'the home is the place for women. Their interests are the rearing and training of children. These are the things that interest women. Politics have nothing to do with these things, and therefore politics do not concern women.' Yet the laws decide how women are to live in marriage, how their children are to be trained and educated, and what the future of their children is to be. All that is decided by Act of Parliament.

Emmeline Pankhurst deals with the canard that women cannot be good speakers. The motto of the WSPU was 'Deeds, not words', but Pankhurst was so good with words that she became a professional, being paid £200 a year touring the country as the WSPU's star orator. Every witness to her speaking style remarked on her air of authority on stage. She was always nervous before speaking but never used notes. She was invariably still, using few gestures and refusing to use a microphone, even at the Albert Hall. Every witness recalls the contrast between her physical fragility and beauty and her verbal aggression.

The case she opens here is radical in one sense. How extraordinary it is that, as late as 1908, it was still thought defensible that women should be denied the vote. Yet her words are not those of a revolutionary. This is the case of someone who wants to join the system, not smash it to bits. Pankhurst makes it plain here that she wants the right to participate in the drafting of the law rather than dispute the legitimacy of doing so.

This speech is one of a series, published as penny pamphlets, which Pankhurst collected under the title *The Importance of the Vote*. The whole case is pragmatic. There is an assumption in this opening that a change in the franchise will produce a change in the sexist law which will, in turn, produce the desired effect in the status of women. The case for women being given the vote is cast in terms of its beneficial consequences for women rather than due to the moral equality that women human beings have with men human beings. Pankhurst makes this case because she wants to be, rhetorically, the soul of reason to show that violent methods attach to valid ends. She is also a single-issue campaigner who has chosen a battle she might win — the franchise — rather than start a forlorn fight for everything, which yields nothing.

It is interesting to note, with the vantage point of almost a century of legal equality, that the law is a guideline but not a guarantee. On pay and progression at work, for example, the story of gender equality has not been concluded yet. It is interesting too that Pankhurst's opening foreshadows so many of the arguments for gender equality that follow in the decades to come. Though she bridles at the insult that politics is no place for women, later in this speech and elsewhere in her rhetoric she was at pains to suggest that the traditional role of the wife and mother would not be threatened by the vote. Again, she is trying to reassure the public that she is not a revolutionary breathing fire. To this extent, in raising the expectations of her radicalism, her violent methods are a significant drawback and force her into this concession.

> *Let us take a few of these laws, and see what there is to say about them from the women's point of view. First of all, let us take the marriage laws. They are made by men for women. Let us consider whether they are equal, whether they are just, whether they are*

wise. What security of maintenance has the married woman? Many a married woman having given up her economic independence in order to marry, how is she compensated for that loss? What security does she get in that marriage for which she gave up economic independence? Take the case of a woman who has been earning a good income. She is told that she ought to give up her employment when she becomes a wife and a mother. What does she get in return? All that a married man is obliged by law to do for his wife is to provide for her shelter of some kind, food of some kind, and clothing of some kind. It is left to his good pleasure to decide what the shelter shall be, what the food shall be, what the clothing shall be. It is left to him to decide what money shall be spent on the home, and how it shall be spent; the wife has no voice legally in deciding any of these things. She has no legal claim upon any definite portion of his income. If he is a good man, a conscientious man, he does the right thing. If he is not, if he chooses almost to starve his wife, she has no remedy. What he thinks sufficient is what she has to be content with. I quite agree, in all these illustrations, that the majority of men are considerably better than the law compels them to be, so the majority of women do not suffer as much as they might suffer if men were all as bad as they might be, but since there are some bad men, some unjust men, don't you agree with me that the law ought to be altered so that those men could be dealt with? … By English law, no married woman exists as the mother of the child she brings into the world. In the eyes of the law she is not the parent of her child. The child, according to our marriage laws, has only one parent who can decide the future of the child, who can decide where it shall live, how it shall live, how much shall be spent upon it, how it shall be educated and what religion it shall profess. That parent is the father. These are examples of some of the laws that men have made, laws that concern women. I ask you, if women had had the vote, should we have had such laws? If women had had the votes men have had, we should have had equal laws. We should have had equal laws for divorce, and the law would have said that as nature has given to children two parents, so the law should recognise that they have two parents.

Passion does not always have to be exclaimed. This is a passionate case, fired by deep conviction, but articulated *sotto voce*. The
extended litany of rhetorical questions skirts the border between
forensic analysis and mockery but the effect is to focus on the injustice. It was common in 1908 as it is now for men to denigrate women
with the slur that they were high on passion but low on reason. This
is the exordium of a lawyer before the judge, patiently assembling
the rudiments of the case, seeding the important questions, leading
the jury towards the inevitable answer to each rhetorical question.

The contrast with Pankhurst's tolerance of violent protest could
hardly be more total. During her trip to New York five years later,
she defended herself in a speech called 'Why We Are Militant'.
Bending historical accuracy to breaking point, she argued that the
extensions of the franchise in 1832, 1867 and 1884 would never have
happened if not for violent protest. Victory, she said, was won by
resistance. In her autobiography she was thoroughly unrepentant,
claiming that 'militancy never set the cause of suffrage back but, on
the contrary, set it forward at least half a century'. The debate about
method split the women's movement just as every civil rights
campaign has been split. Is violence permissible or not? In pre-inde-
pendence India, apartheid South Africa and the segregated states of
America, the same argument takes place. The choice for women in
the early twentieth century was Millicent or militant. Pankhurst's
militant line was opposed by the more moderate National Union of
Women's Suffrage Societies (NUWSS), under the slogan 'Law-abiding
suffragists' and led astutely by Millicent Fawcett, whose statue will
soon adorn Parliament Square in London. Fawcett argued that the
violent outbursts of WSPU members harmed the case for the suffrage
because they turned public opinion against the cause and alienated
sympathetic members of Parliament. The NUWSS had 50,000
members compared with the 2,000 members of the WSPU, so the
moderate line held for most campaigners.

But this shows the perennial power of spectacle and theatre in
politics. The suffragettes left us with dramatic moments and fine
speeches. Though the moderate and the immoderate campaigners
are always at loggerheads, they may well need each other. Fawcett's
suffragists gained their reputation for moderation partly because
they were a contrast to Pankhurst's suffragettes. The analytical and

measured tone of this speech shows that there was a meeting point between the two factions. Besides, their objective was the same. Fawcett did not want to break the law, but Pankhurst only wanted to break the law so that she could make the law.

I have spoken to you about the position of the married woman who does not exist legally as a parent, the parent of her own child. In marriage, children have one parent. Out of marriage children have also one parent. That parent is the mother – the unfortunate mother. She alone is responsible for the future of her child; she alone is punished if her child is neglected and suffers from neglect. But let me give you one illustration. I was in Herefordshire during the by-election. While I was there, an unmarried mother was brought before the bench of magistrates charged with having neglected her illegitimate child. She was a domestic servant, and had put the child out to nurse. The magistrates – there were colonels and landowners on that bench – did not ask what wages the mother got; they did not ask who the father was or whether he contributed to the support of the child. They sent the woman to prison for three months for having neglected her child. I ask you women here tonight, if women had had some share in the making of the laws, don't you think they would have found a way of making all fathers of such children equally responsible with the mothers for the welfare of those children? ... If it ever was important for women to have the vote, it is ten times more important today, because you cannot take up a newspaper, you cannot go to a conference, you cannot even go to church, without hearing a great deal of talk about social reform and a demand for social legislation. Of course, it is obvious that that kind of legislation – and the Liberal government tells us that if they remain in office long enough we are going to have a great deal of it – is of vital importance to women. If we have the right kind of social legislation it will be a very good thing for women and children.

There is the shadow of something darker here. When the law offers no protection women are at the mercy of men. Not all women were as lucky in their marriages as Emmeline Pankhurst knew herself to be. The welfare of children was also a far bigger question than could be fixed by granting their mothers the vote, and Pankhurst knew that very well. Her experience in Manchester as a Poor Law guardian and the registrar of births and deaths and her various spells in prison gave her an acute sense of the social deprivation in which many women reared their children. She routinely returned to this question in her speeches, seeing the franchise as the first step towards a larger emancipation that would encompass better material conditions. She also campaigned for an end to female prostitution and the sexual exploitation of girls. Elsewhere in *The Importance of the Vote* Pankhurst lamented the plight of women who were forced, through servitude, to do back-breaking work at the behest of men and women who did the same work as men but were paid less.

This section of this speech also raises the question of what we would now call the culture in which men and women live. Those were days in which a child born out of wedlock created a scandal, as Pankhurst herself discovered. Late in Emmeline's life her daughter Sylvia had a daughter by a man to whom she was not married. The prospect of the scandal it would cause if the nature of the birth was revealed ended the parliamentary ambitions that, even as a woman in her sixties, Pankhurst still nursed. She was never reconciled with her daughter.

Illegitimacy was a cultural norm given legal expression, and sometimes attitudes have to shift before the law can follow. Pankhurst's argument, like that of Roy Jenkins when he was liberalising British life at the Home Office in the 1960s, is that the law is an important signal both of a cultural change that is happening and a cultural change that is desirable. Men will not all behave like Richard Pankhurst if the law decrees they should, but the blackguards among them can be more easily prevented from making women live at their mercy. Note, though, that Pankhurst has maintained throughout the tone of forensic rhetorical reasonableness. All of this is below the surface, deeply implicit.

> *The more one thinks about the importance of the vote for women, the more one realises how vital it is. We are finding out new reasons for the vote, new needs for the vote every day in carrying on our agitation. I hope there may be a few men and women here who will go away determined at least to give this question more*

consideration than they have in the past. They will see that we
women, who are doing so much to get the vote, want it because we
realise how much good we can do with it, when we have got it. We
do not want it in order to boast of how much we have got. We do not
want it because we want to imitate men or to be like men. We want
it because without it we cannot do that work which it is necessary
and right and proper that every man and woman should be ready
and willing to undertake in the interests of the community of which
they form a part.

The tone of moderation continues to the conclusion, which is an appeal to the powers-that-be to engage with the cause. After delivering this speech, Pankhurst then went on to the Peckham by-election where the WSPU's hostility to the unyielding Liberal government made it, *faute de mieux*, a supporter of the Conservative Party. In Peckham a Liberal majority of 2,339 was converted into a Conservative majority of 2,494. The newspapers attributed the swing to the 'lady suffragists', as the *Pall Mall Gazette* described them.

Pankhurst's heritage was on the Liberal and Labour Left, but she ended up in the Conservative fold. This was not the drift rightwards of a person growing older but a pragmatic search for success. Pankhurst's patience with the Liberal Party, which had been stretched by Gladstone's lack of interest, snapped when Asquith, a noted anti-suffragist, became prime minister in 1908, a fortnight after this speech. Labour she regarded as a bastion of male trade unionism and a party too preoccupied with questions of class to pay much attention to gender. Her sympathy for the Independent Labour Party had evaporated in 1903 when a hall built in her husband's name for the meetings of members declined to admit women. Besides, she had no sympathy with the Labour Party's pacifist and anti-imperial bent or its state socialism.

Pankhurst was also a distinctly enterprising radical. The extensive WSPU operation was funded by a commercial organisation that marketed suffragette china, jewellery, soap, handkerchiefs, board games and Christmas cards. The big London department stores sold coats, shoes and underwear in suffragette colours – purple for dignity, white for purity and green for hope.

Pankhurst was selected by the Conservative Party in 1928 as the candidate for Whitechapel and St George's. The same year, Baldwin's Conservative government passed the Representation of the People (Equal Franchise) Act 1928, giving women over the age of twenty-one the right to vote on equal terms with men. Emmeline Pankhurst did not, alas, quite live to see that day. She died on 14 June 1928, three weeks before the bill that equalised the franchise passed into law. Her last days were sad ones, marked by the dispute with her daughter Sylvia. Pankhurst suffered greatly, as did La Pasionaria and Aung San Suu Kyi, from the common accusation that she was a bad mother. The accusation was all the more painful because it came from Sylvia in her book *The Suffragette Movement*.

Pankhurst here leaves us with the central question when she pledges that 'we women, who are doing so much to get the vote, want it because we realise how much good we can do with it, when we have got it'. The question is whether women politicians are women first and politicians second. Most would find this idea patronising, to use the appropriately male term. The pivotal figure is Margaret Thatcher, who became Britain's first female prime minister in 1979. Like the suffragettes, who were dismissed as mannish, Thatcher was often denigrated by her opponents as being in some way not really a woman. She was, for example, famously portrayed by the satirical programme *Spitting Image* standing in line for the urinals.

Pankhurst's argument in this speech is that the vote is an instrument of power and that power is the handmaiden of progress. Yet she would surely have greeted two female prime ministers, both Conservatives, as a triumph irrespective of the character of their governments. Not that Margaret Thatcher and Theresa May mark the end of the road down which Emmeline Pankhurst embarked. Equality is never really finished. There are always injustices to be remedied. But we are some of the way down the road. Today, nations in the developing world are in every way held back because those societies have yet to learn to value properly the contribution their women make. As Vera Brittain put it, 'more certainly than Latimer in the days of Mary, Mrs. Pankhurst lighted a candle in England which neither change nor circumstance is likely to put out'.

ISIDORA DOLORES IBÁRRURI GÓMEZ (LA PASIONARIA)

No Pasarán

Mestal Stadium, Valencia

23 August 1936

Isidora Dolores Ibárruri Gómez (1895–1989) both exemplifies why there are so few women in this, or any other, anthology of great speeches and also rebuts that idea. If it is true that the women who gain greatness have to be more remarkable than the men, Isidora Dolores Ibárruri Gómez is in the first rank of the remarkable. She should be more famous than she is. Such fame as Ibárruri has is not under her given name but under her revolutionary sobriquet of La Pasionaria. The passion flower.

Dolores Ibárruri was the eighth of eleven children born into a mining family in the village of Somorrostro, in the mountains near Bilbao in the Basque country. As a child of delicate health, she was of disappointing economic value and so attended school until she was fifteen, two years longer than the law required. Her parents had hoped that she might become a teacher, but their poverty closed off that opportunity and Dolores was instead apprenticed to a dressmaker. She then worked for three years as a maid and, at the age of twenty, married a migrant miner from Asturias.

Ibárruri's memoir, published in 1962 under the misleading translation of *They Shall Not Pass* (the Spanish title had been *El Unico Camino* – the only way), was written in exile in Russia, probably with the authorities looking over her shoulder. The book contains little in the way of detail about her husband or the six children she bore, including triplets, all girls, born in 1923. There must have been great pain in her life because all but two of her six children died in infancy. In one of the rare lapses into intimacy in her revolutionary boilerplate, La Pasionaria recalls her pain at seeing her two surviving children turn up at the prison gates every day trying to catch a glimpse of their mother. She asks herself: 'Did I have a right to sacrifice my children, depriving them of a secure and warm home, of a mother's care and affection that they needed so much?' Ibárruri's only son, Ruben, born in 1922, is believed to have died in the Second World War, fighting on the Russian side.

By then, Ibárruri had been on a remarkable odyssey. She had lost her deep Roman Catholic faith on contact with the writings of Karl Marx, and in 1918 she started work on the miners' newspaper *El Minero Vizcaino*. Her first piece, published during Holy Week, was heavily critical of the Catholic Church, so she disguised herself with the *nom de plume* that would attach to her for the rest of her life and beyond: La Pasionaria.

Throughout the 1920s La Pasionaria folded herself into radical politics. No story better illustrates her immersion than her revelation in her memoir that, 'as I rocked my baby to sleep', she thought of the recent 1917 revolution in Russia and what came to her lips were 'not the old lullabies I had learned from my mother, but revolutionary songs which I had learned in my village and which had lain dormant in my memory'. She was a member of the founding provincial committee of the fledgling Spanish Communist Party and was elected a delegate to the first national communist congress, which led to the formation of the party proper in 1921. La Pasionaria soon became known as a brilliant agitator, organiser and orator of spellbinding capacity. In public, in pursuit of her official duties, she always dressed all in black. But it was her words, rather than her dress, on which her reputation rests.

In 1930, La Pasionaria was elected to the central committee of the party and she was soon placed in charge of its official organ, *Mundo Obrero*. She first visited the Soviet Union in 1933 and was elected to the Spanish Parliament as a deputy for Asturias in 1934. As the civil war intensified, she made numerous speeches in which she urged the country to resist the nationalist insurgents the way it had resisted Napoleon in 1808. As the republic's voice to the world, she became the personification of the Spanish Civil War. Her face appeared, usually in an expression of anguish, in thousand of posters and her words adorned a million leaflets. She came to stand for the beleaguered but defiant Spain, the symbol of hope that democracy might prevail.

During the bitter siege of Madrid in October and November 1936, La Pasionaria had her greatest moments. The government had abandoned Madrid and the communists stepped in to take up its defence. They did so with heroic resolve, and none more so than La Pasionaria. There were reports that her eloquence had inspired retreating troops to turn around and continue the fight. Against all likelihood, the fascist forces were repelled and Madrid was saved. For the time being. The Republican front held in Madrid only until 1939, when it fell to Franco. By then La Pasionaria had fled Spain for Russia, where she spent the next thirty-eight years in exile. In her memoir she says sadly there was never a day when she did not think of home.

The speech that follows was delivered at a mass meeting organised by the People's Front at the Mestal Stadium, Valencia, on 23 August 1936. Something in the order of 100,000 people were present. It is testament to the ability that made her one of the finest orators of her century, a woman with a gift of cadence to turn phrases that passed straight into the language and into legend. Her gift for political language gained Dolores Ibárruri a place in the canon of rhetoric and also immortality in fiction. In *For Whom the Bell Tolls*, Ernest Hemingway describes a gathering of Republican leaders in the Hotel Gaylord in Madrid, one of whom recalls how the news travelled of the fighting near Segovia: 'Dolores brought the news herself. She was here with the news and was in such a state of radiant exultation as I have never seen ... Goodness and truth shine from her as from a true saint of the people. Not for nothing is she called La Pasionaria.' Truth and goodness is rather much, given the beastly nature of the regime to which La Pasionaria gave her loyalty. The historical verdict is more complex than this fiction, but it must at least contain it.

Comrades, people of Valencia! You must not be surprised if at this deeply moving moment, when I see before me this huge mass of people filled with sacred enthusiasm and the determination to defend their national freedom, I may perhaps be unable to express the feelings that overwhelm me, that well up from the bottom of my heart, and clothe them in simple and convincing words. This is an

> *occasion when I should like more than ever to possess the eloquence*
> *to express the full force of my convictions, so as to prove to you how*
> *necessary it is to unite our ranks more closely than ever — for the*
> *danger today, too, is greater than ever.*

This is another self-refuting passage of solemn humility. Flatter the audience and mark the gravity of the occasion by suggesting that the chosen speaker is inadequate to the task. As it was all the way back to Pericles, and via Wilberforce, the real import of the moment is to say that 'Such an occasion is this that not even one such as I can hope to rise to its full height.' There is nothing in what she says in this speech that, if we did not know her gender, identifies La Pasionaria as a woman. She was and is, of course, a feminist hero, the woman who led the way in a society and a conflict for which the Spanish word *machismo* might have been invented. And La Pasionaria was indeed deeply concerned with the issues faced by Spanish women, but she was too smart to allow herself to be categorised as interested only in those things.

'La Pasionaria' is, of course, itself a rhetorical construction of identity. The idea of the passion flower suggests delicacy but also resilience and pathos. The sobriquet refers explicitly to the religious celebration of the suffering of Christ, a sense that reinforces her given name, Dolores, which itself means 'suffering'. Throughout all her speeches, Dolores takes this symbolism to stand for the plight of the Spanish proletariat. In this way, just as Elizabeth did at Tilbury, she cleverly constructs a character out of her own life. Inevitably, she was seen at the time in cartoon style, either as an indomitable Mother Courage tending to the poor and the dispossessed or as an evil enchantress whose mysterious wiles were turned to malign effect. La Pasionaria always received notices that no man would. Like a Stalinist Elizabeth Tudor she was the 'communist virgin'. Ransacking the treasure-house of female stereotype, she was a Spanish Joan of Arc, the Earth Mother of War, a Medusa, even, in the fascist newspaper *Gringoire*, a vampire. This latter image brings together her threat as a sexual and political predator with her apparent loathing of religion.

For all these reasons, it is important to insist that La Pasionaria is a political speaker and leader first, a revolutionary second and a Stalinist third, in order not to make a fetish of the other remarkable fact about her, which is that she was a woman taking on the men. In her memoir, she describes the life of a woman in the Spain of her youth: 'Woman's goal, her only aspiration, had to be matrimony and the continuation of the joyless, dismal, pain-ridden thralldom that was our mother's lot; we were supposed to dedicate ourselves wholly to giving birth, to raising our children and to serving our husbands who, for the most part, treated us with complete disregard.'

The early days of the republic were days of progress. Divorce and abortion were both legalised, and after the lobbying of the feminist Clara Campoamor, a women's suffrage law was passed in 1931. Conscious that all this was in peril from the thought-vandals of fascism, women came out onto the streets in support of the republican resistance. They were right to be concerned. When Franco triumphed in 1939, the liberal laws on divorce and abortion were repealed. The danger, as La Pasionaria says here, was greater than ever.

> *I have come to you in these tragic and gloomy hours, when the fate of Spain and especially the future of the working masses is being decided. I have come to you, my mouth filled with the acrid taste of gunpowder, my mind filled with the impressions of the difficulties facing our comrades who are fighting on the summits and slopes of the Guadarramas, who realise the importance of our struggle and who are prepared to die rather than fall into the clutches of fascism. I have come to you from the field of battle, from that great fight which is assuming the character of a heroic epic, for we entered battle armed only with enthusiasm, self-sacrifice and supreme devotion to the cause of the people in order to fight an enemy furnished with all the means of warfare, which he has stolen from the people ...*

These rather graphic images of violence refer to the civil strife between the fascists and the rebel forces. The republican side was riven with disputes between forces of different political persuasions. Orwell's *Homage to Catalonia* is the most famous account of the conflict between the anarchists and the communists. La Pasionaria was an uncompromising advocate of the party line, and so the echo of violence in these words does not only refer to the fascists.

La Pasionaria is not one of those national liberation fighters, like Gandhi, Martin Luther King or Aung San Suu Kyi, who eschewed the use of arms. She is not even in the company of Nelson Mandela, whose turn to armed struggle was weighed down with caveats. La Pasionaria could talk of the fight with an emotion that sounded rather too close to relish. As it always has been, the shocked reaction to this was all the more intense because it was thought an unbecoming attitude for a woman. The truth is that it is scary stuff whoever says it. On one occasion La Pasionaria told women to fight with knives and burning oil.

In the spring before this speech was delivered, La Pasionaria had helped to bring down the Socialist prime minister, Francisco Largo Caballero. In a dramatic parliamentary session on 11 July 1936, she had shouted at the finance minister and monarchist leader, José Calvo Sotelo: 'This is your last speech!' Two days later Mr Calvo Sotelo was kidnapped and slaughtered by left-wing terrorists. This was the murder that began the civil war. La Pasionaria was accused of having instigated the killing, a charge she always denied. Whatever she did or did not do, she was almost certainly acting on orders from Moscow. Rhetoric's reputation for duplicity did not spring up from nowhere. La Pasionaria was a talent, but she wasn't always the sole scriptwriter.

If, when entering the firing line to fight the enemy who is threatening our national liberty, we have such enthusiasm in the rear, then I say to you, the working people of Valencia, what I said when I saw the weapons in the hands of the militia, when I saw the rifles in the hands of the troops loyal to the government: Fascism shall not pass! Fascism shall not pass because the wall of bodies with which we have barred its way is today strengthened by weapons of defence we have captured from the enemy – a cowardly enemy, because he lacks the ideals that lead us into battle. The enemy therefore has no dash and impetuosity, whereas we are borne on the wings of our ideals, of our love, not for the Spain that is dying along with the enemy, but for the Spain we want to have – a democratic Spain. When we speak of Spain, we mean not only the name; we mean a democratic Spain, not the Spain that is clinging to her old traditions; we mean a Spain that will give the

peasants land, that will socialise industry under the control of the
workers, that will introduce social insurance so that the worker
may not be condemned to a homeless old age; we mean a Spain that
will completely and comprehensively, and in a revolutionary spirit,
solve the economic problems that lie at the foundation of all
revolutions.

It is always good to have a watchword, to embody the message in a single phrase. *No Pasarán* – They shall not pass – became La Pasionaria's line and the rallying cry of the dying Republic, especially when a fine speech of hers in defence of the Second Spanish Republic in the Government Ministry building in Madrid on 19 July 1936 was broadcast on Madrid radio. These two words define the defiance and hope for which La Pasionaria was seen to stand.

When La Pasionaria speaks of Spain, hers is not the nation of tradition. It is a nation of socialised industry. There is also a clear political message in her final claim that the revolution will everywhere be driven by deprivation. There is a case to be made for that, but it does need to be made rather than asserted, as it is here. This is ideological thought which, transmuted into soaring rhetoric, is masquerading as analysis. This part of the speech was greeted with long and loud applause. La Pasionaria had the ability to rouse an audience and to command respect even from opponents. There were Franco supporters who regarded her as a great Spaniard. If you can look past the off-the-shelf politics there is, without question, heroism and courage in the assertion that they shall not pass. The speech has to be judged in its moment, not with the wisdom of retrospect, under whose light La Pasionaria's politics have not worn well.

On all fronts communists, anarchists, socialists and republicans
are fighting shoulder to shoulder. We have also been joined by
non-party people from town and country, because they too have
realised what a victory for fascism would mean to Spain. The
struggle, started within the frontiers of our country, is already
assuming an international character, because the working people
of the whole world know that if fascism were to triumph in Spain,
every democratic country in the world would be confronted with
the fascist danger. The working people have realised this, as is

borne out by the messages of solidarity we are constantly receiving from all parts of the world. International fascism, too, has realised the significance of the struggle of the Spanish people against the enemies who have violated their oath of loyalty to the country and to the country's flag. These violators of their vows have broken their promises and have rebelled in vile alliance with seditionary priests and debauched sons of the aristocracy, and are committing endless crimes in all the inhabited places through which they pass. One needs the brush of Goya and the eloquent pen of Blasco Ibáñez to depict the horrors and revolting crimes committed by these elements led by arrogant fascist generals who have long ago revealed who they are and what they are capable of.

There is no doubting the passion with which La Pasionaria opposed fascism. She and Franco loathed one another and the mutual detestation lasted for forty years. She does not need the brush of Goya or the pen of Ibáñez to depict the horrors of fascism. She does it on her own, depicting Spain as the heroic workers minus the treacherous priests and the debauched aristocrats who are collaborating with the alien idea of fascism.

But this is where a leap in the argument prefigures what La Pasionaria gets horribly wrong. The first tip-off is the worrying praise for the 'non-party people' who, no doubt fleetingly, are complimented for joining the march towards historical destiny. The error is to suppose, as La Pasionaria says, that the working class of every nation will join up in international solidarity, assuming their chosen status as the agents of the revolution. This is the utopian moment of arrival. It was easy to believe the moment had come in 1936, especially as idealistic young volunteers from many nations were turning up in Spain to join the International Brigades.

It was an illusion, though, and behind it there lurks a major philosophical mistake, which has ramifications for the rest of the twentieth century, everywhere. It was such a common mistake on the left that even a writer of stature such as George Orwell, could make it. The error was to think that capitalism was the midwife to fascism. The craven behaviour of many capitalists, bending to the will of authority, convinced many on the left that their classical texts were correct to say that capitalism itself was always a fellow traveller with tyranny.

It is an axiom of La Pasionaria's rhetoric, here, in every speech she gives and in her writings, that she is more vivid and alive when she decries the injustice done to women than she is when she adopts the revolutionary bromides of the Left. Because there is nothing in the socialist texts about feminism La Pasionaria sounds like every other socialist, except when she talks about women. Compare the passage above with this, one of many such examples from La Pasionaria's memoirs: 'Was life worth living? My companions in misery and I often asked this question as we discussed our situation, our wretchedness. They spoke with resignation; after all, what could we women do? I rebelled against the idea of the inevitability of such lives as ours; I rebelled against the idea that we were condemned to drag the shackles of poverty and submission through the centuries like beasts of burden – slapped, beaten, ground down by the men chosen to be our life companions'.

La Pasionaria's autobiography is a largely tedious defence of a calamitous political vision which is redeemed by the few passages that strike the reader in the heart, where it hurts. Writing of the deaths of four of her six children in infancy, she recalls that 'every day, when I took lunch to my husband at the mine, I had to pass the cemetery where they were buried; each time my heart was torn with anguish'. After she left her husband, she often had to leave her children in the care of others and eventually made the painful decision to send them to live in Russia while she carried on the struggle in circumstances she did not feel were propitious for bringing up a family. Perhaps she made choices we might not make, but the question of the sacrifice is rarely mentioned when the man is the revolutionary absentee.

As she nears her conclusion, La Pasionaria's voice falters. Despite calls from the audience that she should cease, she goes on, and the words that follow are audible only to the platform. There is, all the same, a storm of applause.

> *Dante's inferno is but a pale reflection of what happens in places*
> *through which these modern vandals pass. The slaughtered*
> *children and old people, the raped and hacked bodies of women, the*
> *demolished monuments of art ... Wherever they pass they sow*
> *death and desolation. And what is taking place in the districts*
> *captured by the fascists would have taken place all over Spain, if*
> *they had not been opposed by a people inspired by faith in its own*
> *strength. We shall very soon achieve victory and return to our*
> *children ...*

La Pasionaria was fond of a metaphor from hell. In her autobiography she describes the industrial history of the Basque country,
where she was radicalised, in such terms: 'At night, when the miners
went to bed, the interior of their bunkhouses looked like a scene from
Dante'. Hell was the appropriate location, but not in the way she ever
thought. La Pasionaria could see right through the fascists but she
was blind to the communists. In March 1938, shortly before the fall
of Madrid, she left for the Soviet Union, where she spent the next
thirty-eight years. In Moscow La Pasionaria met, among others, Mao
and Ho Chi Minh. Asked in an interview in 1983 which of the leaders
she had known had been the most impressive, she answered without
hesitation but with sinister emphasis: 'Logically, Stalin.'

Admiration for La Pasionaria as a speaker and an anti-fascist, at
which she showed by turns brilliance and courage, has to be tempered
by the fact that she remained a devotee of Stalin long after even the
Communist Party itself began to recognise his crimes. During her
four decades in the Soviet Union she provided a reliable stream of
propaganda at choreographed congresses throughout the Soviet bloc.
She was always an apologist for the attitude Auden named in his
poem 'Spain' and that he later disavowed as dishonest and rhetorical:
'the conscious acceptance of guilt in the necessary murder'.

La Pasionaria returned to Spain in 1977, two years after the
death of Franco. She was greeted on her return by crowds who
chanted '*Sí sí, sí, Dolores está aquí*'. The Spanish Communist Party
was made legal once again in 1975 and La Pasionaria was re-elected
to the Spanish Parliament, for Asturias, the region she had represented forty years before. Age and infirmity meant she did not last
long. Neither did her beloved party. By 1982, the Spanish Communist

Party had been decisively rejected by voters and promptly split into three amid the usual arcane quarrels.

For all the failure, though, it was a mark of her impact that there were still people who thought that it was only with the return of La Pasionaria that the Spanish Civil War could be said to be over. She died on 12 November 1989, three days after the Berlin Wall fell, three days after the cause to which she had devoted her life suffered its desperate defeat. The literal translation of her autobiography was *The Only Way*. But communism was not the only way. It was a *via dolorosa*. La Pasionaria's was a remarkable life, on the right side of the century's first great rift but then on the wrong side of the second. She became a symbol of the reconciliation of the Spanish nation but, for all her rhetorical brilliance, the link she never understood was the one between freedom and capitalism. She thought that the system of enterprise and fascism were allies and that communism was the cure for both. La Pasionaria never understood that she had traded one sickness for another.

MARTIN LUTHER KING

I Have a Dream

The March on Washington
28 August 1963

If there is a single person who answers Cicero's description of the ideal orator then that man is Martin Luther King. If there is one speech that stands above all the others then it is this one, at the Freedom March in Washington in August 1963. Between 1955 and 1968 Martin Luther King was the inspiration of the American civil rights movement during a decade in which America made more progress towards racial equality than it had in the previous history of the republic.

Martin Luther King, Jr (1929–68) was born Michael Luther King, Jr, but later changed his name to Martin. He attended segregated schools in Georgia, before following his grandfather and father into the family trade as a pastor of the Ebenezer Baptist Church in Atlanta. After theological college in Pennsylvania, King received a doctorate from Boston University in 1955, in which year he was recruited to serve as spokesman for the Montgomery Bus Boycott, a campaign to force integration on the buses which had been started a year earlier by Rosa Parks. This led, in time, to a Supreme Court judgement that segregation on transport was unconstitutional. Taking up the presidency of the Southern Christian Leadership Conference, a position he held until his death, King became the most important of all the leaders of the civil rights movement.

Drawing inspiration from his faith and the teachings of Mahatma Gandhi, Dr King resisted the calls to demand freedom by any means necessary. For that decision alone, Martin Luther King must be reckoned, in a time of tempest, as one of the greatest of politicians. To demand non-violent resistance and distinctly civil disobedience, seen to best effect in his *Letter from a Birmingham Jail*, was a historic choice for which Dr King merits the laurels of posterity. The provocation, we have to remember, was severe.

In 1963, King led a coalition of civil rights groups through Birmingham, Alabama, probably the nation's most segregated city. The television pictures of that night, which showed young black men being assaulted by dogs and policemen with water hoses, shamed the nation. Later the same year, King helped to convene the March for Jobs and Freedom, which drew over a quarter of a million people to the national mall, where he delivered this speech, the one that immortalised him. In 1964 Congress passed the Civil Rights Act, ending legal segregation in the United States and making discrimination illegal in hiring, public accommodation and transport. In 1965 Congress passed the Voting Rights Act which removed the remaining barriers to the franchise which, remarkably, had existed until then.

On 3 April 1968, King spoke at the Mason Temple Church in Memphis. He spoke about the struggle for equality and, humbly, about his own role in it: 'We've got some difficult days ahead. But it doesn't really matter with me now, because I've been to the mountain top. And I don't mind. Like anybody, I would like to live a long life. But I'm not concerned about that now.' The following day Dr Martin Luther King, Jr was assassinated at the Lorraine Motel in Memphis, Tennessee.

He remains the only non-president to have a national holiday dedicated in his honour, and the only non-president memorialised on the Great Mall in Washington DC, the scene of his greatest rhetorical triumph. The competition for that honour is fierce because King delivered many fine speeches in his career, of which the second-best was given to accept the Nobel Peace Prize in 1964. On that occasion he delivered the words that we might hope, without great expectation, ring out in his homeland to this day: 'I believe that unarmed truth and unconditional love will have the final word in reality. This is why right temporarily defeated is stronger than evil triumphant.'

I am happy to join with you today in what will go down in history as the greatest demonstration for freedom in the history of our nation. Five score years ago, a great American, in whose symbolic shadow we stand today, signed the Emancipation Proclamation. This momentous decree came as a great beacon light of hope to millions of Negro slaves who had been seared in the flames of withering injustice. It came as a joyous daybreak to end the long night of their captivity. But one hundred years later, the Negro still is not free. One hundred years later, the life of the Negro is still sadly crippled by the manacles of segregation and the chains of discrimination. One hundred years later, the Negro lives on a lonely island of poverty in the midst of a vast ocean of material prosperity. One hundred years later, the Negro is still languished in the corners of American society and finds himself an exile in his own land. And so we've come here today to dramatize a shameful condition.

King places himself in the tradition of the American republic with his reference to Lincoln. His craft is evident in this opening, which summons Lincoln to his side and makes plain that the promise of America has yet to be redeemed. Note that the construction of the speech is classical. Proceeding in stately fashion through this exordium (introduction) to his narration (narrative) and passing through a refutation of dissenting voices before rising to a flourish in his peroration, King's structure is exactly that set out by Cicero. With one major difference at the end, as we shall see.

There is, though, nothing histrionic about his words. The truth makes the words apocalyptic and strangely tranquil both at once. By the centennial of Lincoln's Emancipation Proclamation, a host of derivative injustices held back the black person in America: high levels of unemployment, work at minimal wages, poor job mobility, systematic disenfranchisement and the persistence of racial segregation in the South. After invoking Lincoln, the Declaration of Independence, freedom for the thirteen original colonies, the Emancipation Proclamation, freedom for nearly 4 million black slaves – all of which has the air of ritual – King then changes the register to great effect.

When he moves on to say that a century later the negro still is not free, his diction is less formal, more direct. This is now the stark present, cut off from the abstract dignity of the past. The point established, King reaches for metaphor and his box of fireworks. 'The flames of withering injustice' evokes images of cross-burnings by the Ku Klux Klan, and he places the negro in manacles to make the point graphically that genuine freedom remains a dream, even as prosperity is widely enjoyed in white society. The pathos is established early. This is not going to be a forensic dissection of the civil rights programme. It is a call to arms against an injustice that offends the spirit of the nation.

> *In a sense we've come to our nation's capital to cash a check. When the architects of our republic wrote the magnificent words of the Constitution and the Declaration of Independence, they were signing a promissory note to which every American was to fall heir. This note was a promise that all men, yes, black men as well as white men, would be guaranteed the 'unalienable Rights' of 'Life, Liberty and the pursuit of Happiness'. It is obvious today that America has defaulted on this promissory note, insofar as her citizens of colour are concerned. Instead of honouring this sacred obligation, America has given the Negro people a bad check, a check which has come back marked 'insufficient funds'. But we refuse to believe that the bank of justice is bankrupt. We refuse to believe that there are insufficient funds in the great vaults of opportunity of this nation. And so, we've come to cash this check, a check that will give us upon demand the riches of freedom and the security of justice.*

Two of the preliminary titles of this speech were 'Normalcy, Never Again' and 'A Cancelled Check', neither of which has the resonance of 'I Have a Dream'. The original idea was that the rather bureaucratic metaphor of bankruptcy would carry the speech. It is demotic and recognisable to a mass audience, but also the opposite of poetic, and it grows even less poetic as King drags out the metaphor over five sentences. By the end of that it is starting to die: the image of the cancelled check is too thin to bear the weight of injustice it is being asked to carry.

This section is designed to set up the purpose of the speech, which is to help President Kennedy introduce a comprehensive civil rights bill. That bill was intended to do away with segregated public accommodation, protect the right to vote and the panoply of constitutional rights, desegregate all public schools and introduce a Federal Fair Employment Practices Act to debar discrimination in all employment. King's scripted moderation is in deference to the anxieties of the president. When the civil rights activist James Bevel proposed a march from Birmingham, Alabama, to Washington, modelled on Gandhi's famous Salt March to the Sea, President Kennedy was worried that bad publicity, maybe from violence on the day, could set back the cause. 'The only effect is to create an atmosphere of intimidation,' he said at the time, 'and this may give some members of Congress an out.' King therefore sets out to define the cause, to inspire the congregation but, at the same time, to soothe.

> *We have also come to this hallowed spot to remind America of the fierce urgency of now. This is no time to engage in the luxury of cooling off or to take the tranquilizing drug of gradualism. Now is the time to make real the promises of democracy. Now is the time to rise from the dark and desolate valley of segregation to the sunlit path of racial justice. Now is the time to lift our nation from the quicksands of racial injustice to the solid rock of brotherhood. Now is the time to make justice a reality for all of God's children. It would be fatal for the nation to overlook the urgency of the moment. This sweltering summer of the Negro's legitimate discontent will not pass until there is an invigorating autumn of freedom and equality. Nineteen sixty-three is not an end, but a beginning.*

The locution 'now is the time' is always hard to justify. This, along with the entire vocabulary of the speeches of the Kennedy family, has become a staple cliché of British political rhetoric, especially on the left, where the effect is bathetic or ridiculous. King, of course, is neither bathetic nor ridiculous, because he has at least taken care to open with a memorable phrase – the fierce urgency of now. Then the tone shifts, gesturing to the grand style, but for the moment at the level of cliché. Each of these iterations says, essentially, the same thing. There is a sense that the speech is naming an injustice but not quite developing it. At this stage the response in the crowd is muted.

PROGRESS

The rather derivative writing does, however, conceal a clever movement in time in the speech. All speeches can be analysed by their use of time. Some speeches settle scores with the past. Some describe a current predicament and some project perfection into the future. King has been conjuring up a sense of urgency by convincing his audience of the injustice to which the black man and woman is heir and which continues, shamefully, into the present. He does nothing with this for the moment, but it does raise high the platform on which he will stand in the famous passage at the end. The speech until this point has been flat, but high-octane rhetoric has to be justified. Like all drama, a speech needs valleys and peaks. You cannot jump from summit to summit. An audience will be carried along with a passage of rhetorical grandeur if it seems to derive from an argument and bring it to a resolution. Like a joke requiring the set-up, or the *recitative* between the arias, the duller sections matter in the construction and, even though they may not dwell in the mind, the speech would suffer for their absence. A brilliant speech is a whole entity and its more prosaic passages cannot be dismantled without doing violence to its finer parts.

And those who hope that the Negro needed to blow off steam and will now be content will have a rude awakening if the nation returns to business as usual. And there will be neither rest nor tranquillity in America until the Negro is granted his citizenship rights. The whirlwinds of revolt will continue to shake the foundations of our nation until the bright day of justice emerges. But there is something that I must say to my people, who stand on the warm threshold which leads into the palace of justice: In the process of gaining our rightful place, we must not be guilty of wrongful deeds. Let us not seek to satisfy our thirst for freedom by drinking from the cup of bitterness and hatred. We must forever conduct our struggle on the high plane of dignity and discipline. We must not allow our creative protest to degenerate into physical violence. Again and again, we must rise to the majestic heights of meeting physical force with soul force. The marvellous new militancy which has engulfed the Negro community must not lead us to a distrust of all white people, for many of our white brothers, as evidenced by their presence here today, have come to realize that

272

their destiny is tied up with our destiny. And they have come to realize that their freedom is inextricably bound to our freedom. We cannot walk alone. And as we walk, we must make the pledge that we shall always march ahead. We cannot turn back. There are those who are asking the devotees of civil rights: 'When will you be satisfied?' We can never be satisfied as long as the Negro is the victim of the unspeakable horrors of police brutality. We can never be satisfied as long as our bodies, heavy with the fatigue of travel, cannot gain lodging in the motels of the highways and the hotels of the cities. We cannot be satisfied as long as the Negro's basic mobility is from a smaller ghetto to a larger one. We can never be satisfied as long as our children are stripped of their selfhood and robbed of their dignity by signs stating: 'For Whites Only'. We cannot be satisfied as long as a Negro in Mississippi cannot vote and a Negro in New York believes he has nothing for which to vote. No, no, we are not satisfied, and we will not be satisfied until justice rolls down like waters, and righteousness like a mighty stream.

This is a long and important passage of refutation. King takes three genuine anxieties seriously and deals with them in turn. The first accusation is the anxiety, from civil rights activists, that the march on Washington will be the end of the process rather than the start. King answers explicitly that there can be no rest until full rights of citizenship are extended. The second anxiety is that the civil rights movement wants too much and will keep returning for more. Here, King specifics police brutality, discrimination in motels and voting rights as the conditions of satisfaction. Finally, he answers the fear that violence is in the air by insisting that the protesters 'must not be guilty of wrongful deeds'.

This is an important plea for forbearance, summarised in the striking contrast between 'physical force' and 'soul force'. Like the president, the organisers of the March on Washington had been anxious that the day should not descend into violence. Here King, who was greatly influenced by Gandhi's concept of *satyagraha*, makes a dignified case for soulful resistance. It is worth noting what a remarkable feat of civic protest it was that 210,000 people should have gathered on the Mall in Washington, to protest against an historic injustice. There was, in the event, almost no reported violence.

It is an achievement, in a speech designed to inspire through evoked injustice, to be able, at the same time, to make a successful appeal for calm. This is not the least of King's gifts.

I am not unmindful that some of you have come here out of great trials and tribulations. Some of you have come fresh from narrow jail cells. And some of you have come from areas where your quest for freedom left you battered by the storms of persecution and staggered by the winds of police brutality. You have been the veterans of creative suffering. Continue to work with the faith that unearned suffering is redemptive. Go back to Mississippi, go back to Alabama, go back to South Carolina, go back to Georgia, go back to Louisiana, go back to the slums and ghettos of our northern cities, knowing that somehow this situation can and will be changed. Let us not wallow in the valley of despair, I say to you today, my friends. And so even though we face the difficulties of today and tomorrow, I still have a dream. It is a dream deeply rooted in the American dream. I have a dream that one day this nation will rise up and live out the true meaning of its creed: 'We hold these truths to be self-evident, that all men are created equal.' I have a dream that one day on the red hills of Georgia, the sons of former slaves and the sons of former slave owners will be able to sit down together at the table of brotherhood. I have a dream that one day even the state of Mississippi, a state sweltering with the heat of injustice, sweltering with the heat of oppression, will be transformed into an oasis of freedom and justice.

This is the pivot, the moment the speech changes, the moment the arc of history is bent. The words that have preceded this passage are too well constructed to be dismissed, but none of them have quite caught the light. Even granting licence for the nature of the subject, the writing has been a little too consciously rhetorical. King had been working until 4 a.m., scribbling longhand, and had missed the deadline for submitting his text. When he had finally left his text alone the famous section about the dream was not in it. His team had drafted this speech because they were all, King himself included, as he admits in his autobiography, bored with the 'dream' sequence they had heard too often. In *Behind the Dream*, his memoir of his time as

King's speechwriter, Clarence B. Jones quotes another adviser, Wyatt Walker, as saying: 'Don't use the lines about "I have a dream". It's trite. It's cliché. You've used it too many times already'.

The script King had written was good but not his best. The tropes and metaphors are either a little obvious and too frequently repeated (the storm, the winds) or overworked (the blank cheque and the insufficient funds). It is at this point that King begins the section in which he talks himself into immortality. Each speaker was under strict instruction to take no more than five minutes. King breaks the rules and speaks for sixteen. The immediate credit has to go to Mahalia Jackson, a gospel singer who often travelled with the entourage and who had heard King deliver the dream sequence in Detroit that June. Jackson was standing behind the podium as King spoke. As King was, rather flatly, imploring the congregation to 'go back to Louisiana', Jackson cried out 'Tell 'em about the dream, Martin.' King grabbed the podium and set his prepared text to his left. The act transformed him into a Baptist preacher. 'Aw, shit', said Walker. 'He's using the dream.'

The section that follows is improvised in the sense that it is not in the script. But King's campaign technique was to work passages over and over, with varying modulations, so he had, at any one moment, a vast array of possible passages available to him. King was renowned not so much for writing his speeches as assembling them from poetic fragments. He had a voracious memory and had developed an allusive style drenched in references to the Hebrew prophets and the idioms of King James's Bible. This was a vocal style, rich and melodic, that King had forged in the theological seminary and in the pulpit in the early years of his ministry. It is probable, then, that the extraordinary rhetoric that follows is being spoken out loud here, in this exact form, for the very first time. That breaks all the sensible rules of rehearsal and preparation. Should you be invited to speak at the Lincoln Memorial do not on any account do it like this. In fact, don't even try this at home. It will never work. It shouldn't have worked for Martin Luther King. But it is something of an understatement to say that it worked. How it worked.

I have a dream that my four little children will one day live in a nation where they will not be judged by the colour of their skin but by the content of their character. I have a dream today! I have a dream that one day, down in Alabama, with its vicious racists, with its governor having his lips dripping with the words of 'interposition' and 'nullification' — one day right there in Alabama little black boys and black girls will be able to join hands with little white boys and white girls as sisters and brothers. I have a dream today! I have a dream that one day every valley shall be exalted, and every hill and mountain shall be made low, the rough places will be made plain, and the crooked places will be made straight; 'and the glory of the Lord shall be revealed and all flesh shall see it together.'

Is there any more shaming sentence in American rhetoric, or that of any nation, than King's demand that his children be judged not by the colour of their skin but by the content of their character? Here he gets the idea of a popular democracy into a sentence, along with a critique of a nation, which was falling so far short of its promise. The effect is clinched with the image of the little white boys and girls joining hands with little black boys and girls. An image so innocent and yet so evocative; a plainsong with the power to move even at this distance.

Remember that King is on the high wire here, with no safety net. He is quoting the King James's Version of the Bible, Isaiah 40: 4–5, from memory, with perfect recall. He is a pastor; it is his book. There is a case, in fact, for regarding the latter part of this speech as a sermon. King never failed to say that he was a 'preacher' when asked what he did. He is envisaging the realisation of the heavenly dispensation on earth. Most of the lines in the speech, spoken separately, end on a dying intonation which acts as an invitation for the audience to participate. Even in the opening half of the address the audience is audible in a call and response sequence. 'Yeah' and 'My Lord', they say. This is a sermon in the southern Baptist tradition.

All that said, King's fluency is still astonishing. At this moment, building to a crescendo, any stutter or pause breaks the torrent. The delivery has to flow, which is hard enough to pull off when it is intensely rehearsed and scrolling in front of you on the autocue. King is doing the biggest moment of his life off the cuff. It is a bravura effort.

Contrast it with his planned peroration, the text he had in the script: 'And so today, let us go back to our communities as members of the international association for the advancement of creative dissatisfaction. Let us go back with all the strength we can muster to get strong civil rights legislation in this session of Congress. Let us go down from this place to ascend other peaks of purpose. Let us descend from this mountaintop to climb other hills of hope.' The original draft is a highly rhetorical piece of work. It has allusions to Shakespeare, Donne and the Bible. It uses plenty of rhetorical figures, antitheses and alliterations and regular use of anaphora, the repetition of crucial words. However, if the speech had ended by climbing the hills of hope and the peaks of purpose it is unlikely to have entered the anthologies.

This is our hope, and this is the faith that I go back to the South with. With this faith, we will be able to hew out of the mountain of despair a stone of hope. With this faith, we will be able to transform the jangling discords of our nation into a beautiful symphony of brotherhood. With this faith, we will be able to work together, to pray together, to struggle together, to go to jail together, to stand up for freedom together, knowing that we will be free one day. And this will be the day — this will be the day when all of God's children will be able to sing with new meaning: My country 'tis of thee, sweet land of liberty, of thee I sing. Land where my fathers died, land of the Pilgrim's pride, From every mountainside, let freedom ring! And if America is to be a great nation, this must become true. And so let freedom ring from the prodigious hilltops of New Hampshire. Let freedom ring from the mighty mountains of New York. Let freedom ring from the heightening Alleghenies of Pennsylvania. Let freedom ring from the snow-capped Rockies of Colorado. Let freedom ring from the curvaceous slopes of California. But not only that: Let freedom ring from Stone Mountain of Georgia. Let freedom ring from Lookout Mountain of Tennessee. Let freedom ring from every hill and molehill of Mississippi. From every mountainside, let freedom ring. And when this happens, and when we allow freedom to ring, when we let it

> *ring from every village and every hamlet, from every state and*
> *every city, we will be able to speed up that day when all of God's*
> *children, black men and white men, Jews and Gentiles, Protestants*
> *and Catholics, will be able to join hands and sing in the words of*
> *the old Negro spiritual: Free at last! Free at last. Thank God*
> *Almighty, we are free at last!*

Goodness and heavens above but that is good. Just pause to hear the emotion in the stress on the final *all*. Listen to the way King makes the sense climb up to that word and then descend from it. This is a peak of purpose. This is how to say everything in a single word. The word *all* contains the full injustice and the full force of the call for progress. The momentum is maintained through 'the words of the old Negro spiritual' to the brilliant thrice-repeated invocation of freedom at the end. There is no more uplifting a conclusion to a speech in the history of rhetoric.

The key to its greatness may be that, notwithstanding the pulpit style and the practised ministry-rhetoric of its improvised and inspirational coda, this speech is not an exclusively black speech or a speech addressed to a Christian audience. It is a consciously American speech that ranges, as the American speech book does and as Lincoln had done in the first sentence of the Gettysburg Address, from the Declaration of Independence through the Emancipation Proclamation and from the American constitution to the Bible. King was not questioning the values of the founding fathers. On the contrary, he was asking that their promise be extended to all. Equal and exact justice to all men.

There is one break in the river-like flow of the rhetoric, and it is crucial to the effect. The pause comes with the apparently incongruous, prosaic throat-clearer: 'but not only that ...' King is doing two things with this break. First, he is granting the audience a brief rest before he strikes out for the next summit, this time the peak of the range. But, more important, he is also bracketing off the North from the South. The revolution for liberty must extend to the South, he is saying. To the places of most contention. It breaks the passage into two, both in time and in substance.

The river of King's prose then begins again, flowing like the righteous stream. The elimination of legal segregation is perhaps the last historic moral victory in America for which there is still a national consensus. This was the last victory before the start of the culture wars. King gives the definitive account of this impulse towards justice and equality. It is for this reason that this speech has become scriptural in American history. Greil Marcus called it 'a rhetorical Woodstock', so perfectly did it come to stand for the times. The Dream speech has entered the annals along with Gettysburg. Martin Luther King was a well-regarded figure when he stood up to the podium. By the time he stepped off he was a legend.

NEIL KINNOCK

Why Am I the First Kinnock in a Thousand Generations?

Welsh Labour Party conference, Llandudno

15 May 1987

Neil Kinnock was the saviour of the Labour Party, at least temporarily. To anyone who grew up caring at all about Labour in its dark days in the 1980s Kinnock was a hero. Migrating from left to right in the party, he took it from the brink of the abyss to the threshold of power. He was not able to take it further, but the governments that followed, led by Tony Blair and Gordon Brown, would have been inconceivable without the preparatory work done by Neil Kinnock.

Kinnock was born in 1942 in Tredegar, Wales, to a coal miner and a district nurse. After a short spell as a tutor for the Workers' Educational Association he became Labour MP for Bedwellty in 1970. His talent was clear and by 1979 he had been appointed by James Callaghan as shadow education spokesman. Two years later the leftward swing of the Labour Party led to the creation of the Social Democratic Party (SDP) as a direct competitor for Labour's vote. Labour responded with an unrepentant manifesto for the 1983 general election, which one of its leading politicians, Gerald Kaufman, described as 'the longest suicide note in history'. An unelectable leader, Michael Foot, was offered to the public on a manifesto of narrow appeal in the most chaotically organised campaign in modern political history.

This was the fiasco that Kinnock inherited when he became Labour leader on the resignation of Foot in 1983. No one in British history has held the position he inherited, leader of the Opposition, as long as Kinnock. He took the hard road as well as the long road. The trouble began when Kinnock set himself against the National

Union of Mineworkers, the praetorian guard of the Labour movement, in the strike of 1984. This, though, was just a prelude to the
great struggle of his career, which was the quest to expel the hard-left
pressure group Militant from the Labour Party. The fight-back was
conducted in the constant grind of organisation, but it was defined
and given momentum in a magnificent speech that Kinnock gave at
the Labour Party conference in 1985 when he denounced Militant
for its irresponsible conduct in refusing to set a budget in Liverpool:
'the grotesque chaos of a Labour council – a *Labour* council – hiring
taxis to scuttle round a city handing out redundancy notices to its own
workers'.

Kinnock modernised the Labour Party's communication methods. His changing the party logo to a red rose, for example, was a
dalliance with newfangled methods that the elders of the party
regarded as tantamount to betrayal. Kinnock himself featured very
prominently in the 1987 general election campaign, which produced
what *Private Eye* described as 'Labour's brilliant defeat'. In retrospect, Kinnock's victory in 1987, and it was significant, was to see off
the threat of the SDP.

After 1987 Kinnock oversaw a more vigorous attempt to change
party policy, jettisoning some of the sacred tenets of the socialist Left,
notably the outworn promise to nationalise industry and the commitment to unilateral nuclear disarmament. As Mrs Thatcher's government fell into a trap of its own making with the community charge
system for local finance, Labour moved into an opinion-poll lead that
was, at its height, more than 20 points. The Conservatives acted with
ruthless dispatch against Mrs Thatcher in November 1990 but, after
a sharp recession, most Labour figures expected Kinnock to beat the
new prime minister, John Major. Defeat sent a tremor through the
Labour Party. Broken, and blaming adverse media coverage for his
defeat, Kinnock resigned. There was then a second act to his political
life as one of the UK's European commissioners. From 1999 to 2004
he served as vice-president of the European Commission under
Romano Prodi.

The speech that follows was used as the basis for a renowned
party-political broadcast in the election campaign of 1987. Entitled
simply 'Kinnock', it was directed by Hugh Hudson and it is one of
the few examples of its genre that bears repeated viewing. It was not

nearly enough for Labour to win, but it was in its way magnificent, as was the speech. When he first become MP for Bedwellty, Kinnock's father Gordon had said to him: 'Remember Neil, MP stands not just for Member of Parliament, but also for man of principle.' He never forgot. Kinnock had his flaws. He didn't take the Labour Party far enough down the long, hard road and the nation never found him prime ministerial. But in the history of the Labour Party he is a giant.

> *Mrs Thatcher said this week that she was full of ideas for continuing in the direction they have been going. We know what she means: new ideas like privatising schools; new ideas like decontrolling rents; new ideas like paying for health care. Wonderful new ideas. But anyone attracted to them had better ask themselves why every single one of these new ideas was abandoned fifty and more years ago. If payment for schooling was so wonderful, why was free schooling celebrated as a leap forward for this country? If uncontrolled rents did so much for housing, why were they ever ended? If paying for health care was such a blessing, why was the ending of that system hailed as the greatest step forward in post-war history? The reason is simple: the system that existed before that – the system that Margaret Thatcher wants to return to – was wrong and wretched, it was squalid and brutal. It was rotten with injustice and misery and division. That is why it was discarded. That is why it must never be restored.*

There isn't much sign in this opening passage of the brilliance that is to come. Here Kinnock opens with a section of standard party-political name-calling that works much less well than the protagonists think it does. The trouble with this opening – and in this respect its faults are representative of many such instances – is that it is not even a cartoon truth. There is a place for clever caricature in political knockabout, but this is too far from the truth to be persuasive. Thatcher was not really proposing to privatise schools and the audience in the country knows this. The accusation therefore says more about Neil Kinnock than it does about Margaret Thatcher.

It is overwrought to reach straight for 'wrong and wretched, squalid and brutal' in the opening paragraphs. A verdict so harsh needs building up to. This is like melodramatic characterisation in a poorly conceived opera. The drama starts in histrionic mood without any justification. The audience senses at once that this is Kinnock's starting assumption rather than his reasoned conclusion. If you do not already share his starting assumption then the bald assertion is unlikely to be persuasive.

Here is a paradox of political rhetoric. Kinnock needs to win people over to the Labour cause who, not long ago, voted for the Tories he is disparaging. Telling them they are associated with, or even to blame for, something squalid and brutal, something wrong and wretched, is not exactly an enticing invitation.

> *And that is why the election is just in time. Just in time for those whose lives and skills are wasted by unemployment. Just in time for the children in a school system that is being deprived and derided by an Education Secretary who won't send his own children to local schools. Just in time for the old who are being cheated out of pensions and housing benefits. Just in time for our health service with its three quarters of a million list of people who wait in pain. The election has come in time for all those who are not poor, do not have children going through school, and are not old and anxious, not young and unemployed, not badly housed, not waiting for an operation. All the people who are not badly off but who know that Tory Britain has become an increasingly divided, deprived and dangerous place. They know, as you know, that when Britain has a Prime Minister who has allowed unemployment and poverty and waiting lists and closures and crime to go up and up and up, Britain cannot afford such a Prime Minister to go 'On and on and on'.*

This should have been the opening. It is more measured than the beginning Kinnock actually uses because here he largely confines himself to description. He mostly (with the exception of loaded errors such as the use of the word 'cheat') allows the listener to supply the verdict. The rhetorical tactic here, on first glance, appears to be a separation between those benighted people for whom the election has come just in time and who can therefore be saved, and the implied others who would be just fine with no election.

On closer inspection, there is no real tension here because the whole population is included in Kinnock's first category and literally nobody is in the latter. So the election has come just in time for everyone, which makes a mockery of the long list of categories and doesn't sound especially likely. This is better than the opening but it is still overwrought. Kinnock sounds like he thinks the country is going to the dogs, and there are never enough people who think that to win an election.

Kinnock in truth always spoke more freely to the Labour movement than he did to the nation. It is the familiar dual audience for anyone who does a grand political speech. In his brilliant speech at the Labour conference in Bournemouth in 1985, Kinnock had let it be known where his heart, and also his talent, really lay: 'I speak to you, to this Conference. People say that leaders speak to the television cameras. All right, we have got some eavesdroppers. But my belief has always been this, and I act upon it and will always act upon it. I come here to this Conference primarily, above all, to speak to this movement at its Conference.' In this instance, the conference would have lapped up the idea that everyone was suffering from the Tory government, but that is not a message to take out to a nation. Kinnock makes Britain sound rather downtrodden and defeated, and he therefore, implicitly, associates Labour with those who are losing out from the current dispensation.

This is an important part of any political coalition and very much a part of the essential purpose of the Labour Party, but it is never enough to secure victory. Speeches can profitably be analysed according to their split between optimism and pessimism. A leader of the Opposition deals in pessimism, so it is important to add a shaft of sunlight too. Otherwise it is too gloomy, as it is here. When Kinnock spits out the words, as he did, it sometimes sounds as if he is relishing the pain.

> *They only care when they are cornered. That's the difference between us. We are democratic socialists. We care all the time. We don't think it's a soft sentiment. We think that care is the essence of strength. And we believe that because we know that strength without care is savage and brutal and selfish. Strength with care is compassion – the practical action that is needed to help people lift*

themselves to their full stature. That's real care. It's not soft or weak. It is tough and strong. But where do we get that strength to provide that care? Do we wait for some stroke of good fortune, some benign giant, some socially conscious Samson to come along and pick up the wretched of the earth? Of course we don't. We co-operate, we collect together, we co-ordinate so that everyone can contribute and everyone can benefit, everyone has responsibilities, everyone has rights. That is how we put care into action. That is how we make the weak strong, that is how we lift the needy, that is how we make the sick whole, that is how we give talent the chance to flourish, that is how we turn the unemployed claimant into the working contributor. We do it together. It is called collective strength, collective care. And its whole purpose is individual freedom. When we speak of collective strength and collective freedom, collectively achieved, we are not fulfilling that nightmare that Mrs Thatcher tries to paint, and all her predecessors have tried to saddle us with. We're not talking about uniformity; we're not talking about regimentation; we're not talking about conformity – that's their creed. The uniformity of the dole queue; the regimentation of the unemployed young and their compulsory work schemes. The conformity of people who will work under tough conditions and take orders and accept pay because of mass unemployment that they would laugh at in a free society with full employment. That kind of freedom for the individual, that kind of liberty can't be secured by most of the people for most of the time if they are just left to themselves, isolated, stranded, with their whole life chances dependent upon luck!

Much of the reason the Labour Party has been so historically good at losing general elections is wrapped up in the opening sentences of this passage. Hannah Arendt once asked why the Left is so preoccupied with motive. Kinnock locates the difference between Labour and its political rivals in their absence of good will. The Tories are not just wrong; they are also bad people who have to be forced to care. As well as being historically inaccurate, this insult is an absurd way to try to persuade Conservatives to vote Labour.

The difference between Labour and the Tories in fact lies in their differing levels of optimism about the efficacy of state power.

The hardest questions in politics, said Isaiah Berlin, are the conflicts between good and good. Here Kinnock makes a cartoon of politics by making it a contest between good and evil. In his 1985 speech he devotes a section to defining what he calls the 'enabling' or the 'opportunity' state. Most ordinary people don't ever think of the state as being enabling, or indeed of being anything else at all, expect occasionally intrusive and irritating. Speeches entitled 'The Something State' are a left-of-centre political obsession.

Still, that would have been better than the rest of this section, which is a dense and complex argument that could have been lightened by an example. Kinnock is arguing that genuine freedom is more than merely the absence of restraint. A person cannot be free, he is saying, unless certain prior conditions are satisfied, and those conditions always require collective provision of services. It might have been better to walk through an example of, say, an elderly man in receipt of social care. The services that are necessary in order to ensure that he is able to enjoy the elementary freedom of going for a walk would have made the same point quicker, more vividly, and probably more comprehensibly.

Think of the brilliant way Kinnock used metaphor in his famous speech to the Labour Party conference in Bournemouth in 1985. This was the speech in which he took on the Militant entryists in public, to devastating effect, decrying the habit of the leaders of Liverpool council of hiring taxis to deliver redundancy notices to workers. The inspired verb Kinnock chose for the journey of the taxis was 'scuttle'. The image is that of insects, the black cabs feeding on something grotesque, the word he had used to introduce the image. By contrast, a lot of the audience will have been lost in this passage. An audience can only bear so much philosophy.

A story would also have been a better answer to the charge that Kinnock places against himself. It is often said by the political Right that the political Left's commitment to equality will in fact end up in a state of uniformity. If Kinnock had illustrated his point with a dramatised example he would have sounded less defensive than he does here. He ends on a theme that could have been developed more – the role of brute luck in our life chances. Making a fortune is too often a matter of good fortune; our life chances depend too much on chance.

Why am I the first Kinnock in a thousand generations to be able to get to university? Why is Glenys the first woman in her family in a thousand generations to be able to get to university? Was it because all our predecessors were 'thick'? Did they lack talent – these people who could sing, and play, and recite and write poetry; those people who could make wonderful, beautiful things with their hands; those people who could dream dreams, see visions; those people who had such a sense of perception as to know in times so brutal, so oppressive, that they could win their way out of that by coming together? Were those people not university material? Couldn't they have knocked off their A Levels in an afternoon? But why didn't they get it? Was it because they were weak – those people who could work eight hours underground and then come up and play football? Weak? Those women who could survive eleven childbearings, were they weak? Those people who could stand with their backs and their legs straight and face the people who had control over their lives, the ones who owned their workplaces and tried to own them, and tell them: 'No. I won't take your orders.' Were they weak? Does anybody really think they didn't get what we had because they didn't have the talent, or the strength, or the endurance, or the commitment? Of course not. It was because there was no platform upon which they could stand; no arrangement for their neighbours to subscribe to their welfare; no method by which the communities could translate their desires for those individuals into provision for those individuals.

Here Kinnock hits gold. This is what can happen when a speaker finds a theme and their rhythm and imagery coming together in harmony. We feel we are there, living with those previous Kinnock generations. So many memorable rhetorical passages come in threes, and this one almost does too. Kinnock in fact mashes two of his three together. He asks three questions of the previous Kinnock generations: did they lack brains, talent and endeavour? In the writing he runs the first two together so he moves from brain power to hand craft and back again, merging talent with intelligence. Whether or not this was deliberate, it works neatly because one of the abidingly foolish distinctions in British life has been the gap between those who work by hand and those who work by brain. Ever since the technical schools that were promised in Butler's 1944 Education Act failed to appear, the British schools system has been thoroughly inhospitable to those whose talents are not conventionally academic. By merging the two notions Kinnock brings them together rhetorically and creates the widest possible canvas on which he paints the idea of talent.

And how vividly he does so too. This is a good example of another general rule about speechwriting, indeed about all writing: write in particular, not in general. Kinnock could have made the point about opportunity with statistics on social mobility. Plenty of politicians had done so before and plenty have done so since. I have written this speech myself more than once. Every one of these mathematical treatises combined is not worth a single sentence of this passage.

The most important word here is 'Kinnock'. In that one word he defines a family of real people who then live and breathe as we hear the account of their lives. It is important too that Kinnock does not feel sorry for them. He is not recounting a tale of woe and loss. The Kinnocks were strong people who lived with brio. Such people deserve better. The idea that one generation should do better than the next could be described as the British political dream. It has been the implicit bargain of post-war British politics, although the bargain appears to have been compromised in recent years. There has been no more eloquent expression of it than this passage in this speech. Indeed, so memorable was this refrain that Joe Biden, later Barack Obama's vice-president, delivered what might generously be described as a tribute and less generously as a rip-off at a debate in Iowa in September 1987, during his bid for the presidency. Biden blatantly repeated Kinnock's structure without any attribution. 'Why is it', he asked unoriginally, 'that Joe Biden is the first in his family ever to go a university? ... Is it because our fathers and mothers were not bright? ... Is it because they didn't work hard? My ancestors who worked in the coal mines of north-east Pennsylvania and would come home after twelve hours and play football for four hours? It's because they didn't have a platform on which to stand.' The revelation of the cover version led directly to Biden's withdrawal from the race.

There is one last point to make to demonstrate why this passage is so good. Kinnock asks a series of questions about his ancestors which we assume to be rhetorical. Were they thick; did they lack talent; were they weak? But the source of the emotional impact is that he then answers the questions, which turn out not to be rhetorical at all. It was because they were denied a platform upon which they could stand.

Note how Kinnock's version is so much better than Biden's. That is because Kinnock builds the suspense for longer, and the answer comes as the conclusion to a problem that sounds, by the time Kinnock has finished, intractable. Biden compresses the whole section and his answer comes too easily. Note too that *this* is the difference between political traditions that Kinnock got so wrong before. Politics is not ill will on one side versus good will on the other. The real divide is over how fatalistic people are and how optimistic they feel about the capacity of the state to improve individual lives. By locating the source of his ancestors' lack of progress in poor public policy and support, Kinnock places himself so much more cleverly as a social democrat than he ever does when he is insulting Tories. There is a lesson here: the critique of your opponent is implicit in a clear description of your own view. You don't help yourself when you serve up insults on a trowel.

I think of the youngsters I meet. Three, four, five years out of school. Never had a job and they say to me 'Do you think we'll ever work?' They live in a free country but they do not feel free. I think of the fifty-five-year-old woman I meet who is waiting to go into hospital, her whole existence clouded by pain. She lives in a free country but she does not feel free. I think of the young couple, two years married, living in Mam and Dad's front room because they can't get a home. They ask 'Will we ever get a home of our own?' They live in a free country but they do not feel free. And I think of the old couple who spend months of the winter afraid to turn up the heating, who stay at home because they are afraid to go out after dark, whose lives are turned into a crisis by the need to buy a new pair of shoes. They live in a free country. Indeed they are of the generation that fought for a free country but they do not feel free. How can they – and millions like them – have their individual freedom if there is not collective provision? How can they have strength if they do not have care? Now they cannot have either because they are locked out of being able to

> *discharge responsibilities just as surely as they are locked out of being able to exercise rights. They want to be able to use both. They do not want feather-bedding, they want a foothold. They do not want cotton-wooling, they want a chance to contribute. That is the freedom they want. That is the freedom we want them to have. Freedom with fairness; that is our aim.*

The technique of citing real examples in political speeches is fraught with danger, which is perhaps why Kinnock avoided it earlier. The stories are impersonal, the characters close to abstractions. It is not quite clear whether he has really met these people or if they are constructs from what he surmises must be the case in a country under the yoke of Thatcherism. The effect is therefore muffled because it feels as though he may have invented his *dramatis personae* to make the point of his story. Citing a real person in a speech closes the distance between the politician and the people and interrupts the barrage of statistics and conceptual argument. But it is hard to pull off, because even when the politician cites a real person the audience is suspicious that the speechwriters have engineered the meeting with the express purpose of using it in the speech. A bit like school-children being astonished when they see their teacher in real life, we do not imagine that politicians have any encounters with actual voters that are not choreographed.

That is what leads to passages like this one which lies somewhere between abstract and personal. It works well enough, and it is important that it does, because it carries an argument of genuine weight. The political Left has always maintained that freedom must be a question of the capacity to act rather than merely the absence of coercion. The married couple cited by Kinnock are formally free, but their freedom is less useful to them because they cannot afford a home. The fifty-five-year-old woman lives a free life but one that is limited by pain. This directly recalls (not that Kinnock was a great reader of philosophy) a famous passage by Thomas Hobbes in which he writes of being fastened to his bed by sickness. Hobbes maintains that sickness is not really a curtailment of freedom. The ill person is free to leave but unable to do so, which is a different thing. No, says Kinnock, it is not a different thing. The only freedom worth having is the freedom that can in fact be exercised.

Vividly and colloquially, Kinnock also devotes his words, as he did his career, to the attempt to secure a majority in Parliament. In Bournemouth he had chided the purists in his party — 'the people will not, cannot, abide posturing. They cannot respect the gesture-generals or the tendency-tacticians' — and quoted Aneurin Bevan's dictum that the victory does not have to be complete to be convincing. Bevan and Kinnock were *democratic* socialists. At a time when the Labour Party has collapsed into theoretical barrenness it is an elementary lesson that will have to be learned all over again.

> *The Tories have fixed upon a future dominated by financiers. They have nothing to put in place of the oil and in their low-tech, no-tech future of teashops and warehouses there is no place for an industrial strategy. There is just more asset-strip and sell-off, more run-down and redundancy, more dependence on imports and less commitment to exports. That has been their record in the past eight years. It is the prospect of their future. There is no prudence or progress in that. There is no patriotism in it either. They are literally shouting down, selling off and selling out Britain. And everyone in this country, whoever they are, wherever and however they live, must ask themselves: 'How do we pay our way if that is our future?' How do we pay out way in the world? How do we get the necessities? How do we help the needy? How do we influence others? How do we buy when we do not sell? How too do we pay our way at home? How do we generate the wealth necessary to give employment, to provide education and health care, to finance decent pensions? And the answer is, at home and abroad, if we do not make goods and market goods then we do not pay our way. That is not a future which I am prepared to accept. It is not one I am prepared to offer my children or my contemporaries. For it is a future of great fortunes for the few and of decline and insecurity for the many. That is where we have been heading through industrial contraction and trade loss and unemployment ever since Margaret Thatcher went into 10 Downing Street. It is among the greatest reasons for putting her out of 10 Downing Street. And that is exactly what we and the British people will do.*

Unfortunately, for Kinnock, they didn't. Just under a month later, on 11 June 1987, the Conservatives won a handsome victory, their third in succession. Only 31 per cent of the nation was persuaded to vote for the first Kinnock in a thousand generations who had been to university. The Conservatives were returned with the loss of just 21 seats on their 1983 victory and an overall majority of 102. Clearly, Kinnock's invective had not worked. The harsh lesson shows the limitations of political rhetoric, of course, but it shows something deeper than that. It shows that rhetoric is duplicity if it is not matched to an underlying reality. After delivering this speech, Kinnock was filmed, with his wife Glenys, walking in the hills above Llandudno. The footage became the basis for the celebrated film directed by Hugh Hudson in which this speech was laid over shots of the Kinnocks and the Welsh landscape. As a landmark in party-political broadcasting it is famous. So is all of the communications effort of the 1987 Labour Party campaign. Led by Peter Mandelson, it was cleverly conceived, perfectly executed and entirely futile, because Labour wasn't ready to win.

There is only one story in Labour politics. Attlee promised to rebuild Britain after the war. Wilson promised the white heat of technology. Blair said he would modernise for the information age. By 1987, Labour had not modernised enough and the electorate sniffed it. Kinnock was still too prone, as he had been in Bournemouth in 1985, to call Labour 'the party of production'. He thought he meant manufacturing; the country heard trade union influence. It is a reminder that the same message sounds different according to the identity of the speaker. Kinnock often outlined an industrial strategy that Theresa May has more or less endorsed. When May says it, the industrial strategy sounds like the one aberrant foray into left-wing tendencies in the otherwise conventional life of a Tory vicar's daughter. When Kinnock said the same it sounded like his first step on the road to socialism. Rhetoric has an intrinsic content, but it also points in a certain direction, and every speaker needs to calculate where the passage fits within the overall impression. It is a common tactic for all Labour politicians to describe expenditure as 'investment', which sounds laudable rather than profligate. Tories counter by describing the same event as mere 'spending', which by implication is reckless and wasteful.

A lot of politics is a battle over words. I once drafted a speech in defence of university tuition fees which can just as accurately, in fact more accurately, be described as a capped graduate tax. Labour MPs prefer the title of tax, which the public hates. However, re-description only goes so far. Labour's policies of the 1980s were not credible and Kinnock knew it. Between 1988 and 1992 incredible policies on unilateralism, nationalisation, Europe, council house sales and the closed shop were abandoned. It was still not enough and in 1992 Kinnock lost again.

Neil Kinnock thus stands as something of a case study in the caveats that must be applied to the power of speech. Kinnock was the best public speaker in British political life in the latter part of the twentieth century. He had a command of imagery unrivalled among his contemporaries and a better speaking voice than any of them. He also had something important to say. He could be long-winded, to be sure. John Major cruelly said of Kinnock that he talked so much because, as he had no idea what he was trying to say, he could never tell when he'd finished. But there were days, magnificent days, like 11 October 1985 in Bournemouth and 15 May 1987 in Llandudno, when Kinnock knew exactly what he was trying to say and he said it with a power matched by none of his peers. It was still not enough. Magnificent though this speech was, it could not mask the facts. Rhetoric never does, at least not for long

THE PHILOSOPHICAL CAPITAL
OF THE WORLD

The material and political progress of Britain can be told without ever venturing far from a small site in Manchester called St Peter's Field. The story of democratic politics, its best answers and its false trails, can be found in words that were either spoken at St Peter's Field, inspired by it or written about it. In his novel *Coningsby*, Benjamin Disraeli, one of the protagonists in the great drama of Manchester, summarised its leading role in modern British history: 'a great city, whose image dwells in the memory of man, is the type of some great idea. Rome represents conquest; Faith hovers over the towers of Jerusalem; and Athens embodies the pre-eminent quality of the antique world, Art ... In the minds of men the useful has succeeded to the beautiful. Instead of the city of the Violet Crown, a Lancashire village has expanded into a mighty region of factories and warehouses. Yet, rightly understood, Manchester is as great a human exploit as Athens.' Manchester, Disraeli went on to say, was the philosophical capital of the world.

This sounds like the hyperbole that Disraeli could rarely resist, but just for once it is not. The claim that liberal democracy can best represent the people and improve the condition of their lives has had some persuasive advocacy at St Peter's Field. So have the rival claims from the extreme left and right of the political spectrum, traditions of thought that have been voiced but never fixed in British public life. The demands for individual recognition that inspired the passion of William Wilberforce, Emmeline Pankhurst and Martin Luther King are all requests for equal moral worth to be respected by making everyone a political citizen. This has been achieved in Britain through a tradition of slow adaptation, rather than violent cataclysm.

There are two traditions that have been heard here, two routes towards progress. The first is the demand for inclusion in the parliamentary franchise. The second is the many answers that have been heard to what Disraeli defined in the Free Trade Hall, Manchester, as the condition of England question. These are speeches that changed an argument and therefore change the world. They show the glacial pace at which democratic politics progresses towards a utopia that is always receding. The first instance combined both demands. On 16 August 1819 more than 60,000 people assembled in Manchester at a patch of empty ground known as St Peter's Field. They had come to demand parliamentary representation and a better standard of living and for the promise of hearing the renowned speaker Orator Henry Hunt.

Later in life Hunt would be an entrepreneur who produced a roasted corn breakfast powder in a vain bid to replace tea and coffee, and shoe-blacking bottles that carried the slogan 'Equal Laws, Equal Rights, Annual Parliaments, Universal Suffrage and the Ballot'. But Hunt's early renown was as a magnetic public speaker. In a series of speeches at assemblies of radicals, his was the most eloquent voice of the early nineteenth century for universal suffrage on the grounds that extending the vote to working men would lead to the better use of public money, fairer taxes and an end to the restrictions on trade, which damaged industry and were a cause of unemployment. Protesters descended on St Peter's Field from all over Lancashire to hear him speak. In the event, Orator Hunt is best known for a speech that was never given.

The Patriotic Union Society had organised the assembly to protest against material conditions and exclusion from representation. In 1815, at the end of the Napoleonic Wars, Lord Liverpool's Conservative government had introduced the Corn Law which imposed a tariff on foreign grain to protect native merchants. The 1815 Corn Law prohibited the importing of wheat, except under a vast duty, until the price of domestic wheat had reached 80s per quarter. The obvious consequence was that wheat then sold on the home market at an artificially inflated price – 112s 8d per quarter by 1817

– which caused great hardship among the poor, who could not live without paying the price.

The 'bread tax' as it became known was the cause of riots. By 1818 weavers and spinners in Manchester and its surrounding mill towns were earning a third of their 1803 wages. Parliament would not hear their demands because in 1819 Lancashire had just two MPs to cover the rapidly growing industrial centres of Manchester, Salford, Bolton, Blackburn, Rochdale, Ashton-under-Lyne and Oldham, which between them had a population of almost one million people. Not that any of these industrial workers were permitted to do anything as democratic as vote. The franchise was restricted to adult male owners of freehold land with an annual rental value of 40 shillings or more.

The purpose of the St Peter's Field meeting was peaceful protest for the franchise and better conditions. The publicity material for the event stated explicitly its aim 'to consider the propriety of adopting the most LEGAL and EFFECTUAL means of obtaining a reform in the Common House of Parliament'. Instructions were issued to attendees that 'Cleanliness, Sobriety, Order and Peace' were expected and all weapons prohibited. The crowd did proceed in an orderly way to St Peter's Field on a hot day under a cloudless blue sky. They gathered under banners demanding 'No Corn Laws', 'Annual Parliaments', 'Universal Suffrage' and 'Vote By Ballot'.

Orator Hunt, accompanied by Mary Fildes, the leader of the Manchester female reform movement, arrived at 1 p.m and made his way up to the hustings amid a rapturous ovation. He arrived under the watchful observance of the Manchester magistrates who had arranged the presence of 600 men from the 15th Hussars, several hundred infantrymen, a Royal Horse Artillery unit with two six-pounder (2.7 kg) guns, 400 men of the Cheshire Yeomanry, 400 special constables and 120 cavalry of the Manchester and Salford Yeomanry, the grand title granted to a motley band of local volunteer businessmen. The ovation that Hunt received on the way to the podium was enough to convince William Hulton, chairman of the magistrates, who was watching from a house on the perimeter of St Peter's Field, to issue a warrant for his arrest. The chief constable, Jonathan Andrews, replied that military assistance would be required to disperse the crowd. The first contingent to receive the order were the erratic Manchester and Salford Yeomanry, stationed a few streets away in Portland Street and led by a local factory owner, Captain Hugh Hornby Birley.

Trying to pick their way on horseback through a narrow channel formed by two lines of special constables, the Yeomanry induced panic in the crowd and then responded in kind by striking with sabres. The arrest warrant was duly issued to Orator Hunt. When the Yeomanry set about destroying the banners and flags on the podium, the crowd threw brickbats, at which provocation Hulton sent in the Hussars to disperse the meeting. With uncoordinated contingents of Hussars and Yeomanry attempting to restore order, at least eleven people were killed and more than 600 injured in scenes of shocking chaos.

The incident was at once notorious. James Wroe, the editor of the *Manchester Observer*, gave his report of the day the headline 'the Peterloo Massacre', to link it to the 1815 Battle of Waterloo, which was still fresh in the memory. Lord Liverpool's government responded with authoritarian stupidity, passing what became known as the Six Acts to suppress radical meetings and publications of a free press. James Wroe was charged and found guilty of sedition and imprisoned for twelve months. Orator Hunt and eight others were tried at York Assizes on 16 March 1820 and charged with sedition. After a two-week trial, Hunt was sentenced to thirty months in Ilchester Gaol, where he served two years.

Despite the restrictions placed on free publication after Peterloo, one legacy of the massacre was the foundation, in 1821, of the *Manchester Guardian* by John Edward Taylor, who had been in St Peter's Field the day Orator Hunt was arrested. Taylor's prospectus for the new publication was a manifesto of defiance. The *Manchester Guardian* would 'zealously enforce the principles of civil and religious Liberty ... and warmly advocate the cause of Reform'. Percy Bysshe Shelley offered a more poetic expression of the same impulse. Shelley was away in Italy at the time of Peterloo and only heard reports a month later but when he did his response was to write *The Masque of Anarchy*, subtitled *Written on the Occasion of the Massacre at Manchester*. State prohibition of the radical press meant that the following famous lines were not published until 1832, ten years after Shelley's death:

Rise like lions after slumber
In unvanquishable number.

The Manchester School

The lions were to roar eventually, and none more potently than John Bright, the man described by the Conservative prime minister Lord Salisbury as 'the greatest master of English oratory that this generation has produced ... At a time when much speaking has depressed and almost exterminated eloquence, he maintained robust and intact that powerful and vigorous style of English which gave fitting expression to the burning and noble thoughts he desired to express'. Bright was trying to emulate the best. His interest in politics and in rhetoric in particular had been first kindled by the election in Preston in 1830 in which the winner, after a long battle, was one Henry Hunt. Bright then learned his trade among the Quakers in the Rochdale Juvenile Temperance Band. At his first open-air event he got into a muddle with his notes and had to stop. During a musical interlude, the chairman told him to say what came into his mind, which is truly terrible advice for anyone who doesn't happen to be a rhetorical supernova in the making. Bright, typically, was magnificent, but it is not advisable to try public speaking that way.

The great insight of Bright and his colleague and friend Richard Cobden was to realise that, when a state seeks to protect its industries, it is the wealthy who are protected and the vulnerable who suffer the cost. Cheaper food, they reasoned, meant higher real wages. Cobden and Bright understood that free trade should be a doctrine of the downtrodden. This is the axiom of the Manchester school. It was to uphold that principle that the Anti-Corn Law League was founded at the York Hotel, Manchester, on 24 September 1838. Bright gave his first notable speech on the issue to an open-air meeting in his home town of Rochdale on 2 February 1839. The price of corn, he said, was not a party question, it was a pantry question. The working classes, he argued, had been grievously injured by the monopoly enjoyed by the landed classes.

The early years of the League were devoted to petitions, circulars, handbills and all manner of written persuasion. Bright and

Cobden embarked on a speaking tour to take the case for abolition of the Corn Laws to the nation. They spoke everywhere but they always came back to their campaign headquarters in Manchester. On 29 December 1840, Bright told the Corn Exchange in the city that towns all over Britain now looked to Manchester rather than to London for leadership to lessen the distress of the daily struggle for bread. Cobden then gave his new association a significant gift. He bought the land at St Peter's Field. Here, on the site of the Peterloo massacre, a temporary pavilion was built in 1840 and was named the Free Trade Hall after the cause.

Bright and Cobden spoke at the Free Trade Hall many times, and they flattered Manchester, but their main audience was in Parliament. When Cobden became MP for Stockport in 1841 and Bright MP for Durham in 1843 they were able to speak directly to Prime Minister Robert Peel, a man from just down the road in Bury. In his speech 'You Are the Gentry of England' in March 1845 Cobden spoke for the consumer exploited by the plutocratic merchants. Cobden and Bright complemented one another ideally. Cobden provided the calm reasoning of the philosopher and Bright brought the passion and emotion of the great speaker. He was universally recognised as the chief orator of the free trade movement.

Bright sat in the House of Commons between 1843 and 1889 as the MP for Durham, then Manchester and then Birmingham, where he gave some of the greatest parliamentary speeches ever heard. They include his unheeded warning about the risks of war in the Crimea, 'The Angel of Death Has Been Abroad throughout the Land', and 'If All Other Tongues Are Silent Mine Shall Speak', his visionary speech against British support for the slave-owning South in the American Civil War, which ranks with the rhetoric of Wilberforce on the same subject and earns him a place in the first tier of parliamentary orators. It is, though, his campaign against the Corn Laws and the eloquence he first displayed in its cause that earned Bright the statuesque immortality he now enjoys in Manchester's Albert Square.

Between 1841 and 1846 the prime minister had been hard to move. Peel's government introduced a sliding scale for corn in 1842, but the triumphant reaction among the landowners and Tory protectionists, chief among them Benjamin Disraeli, showed that it did little to bring prices down for the consumer. Eventually, though, the rhetorical torrent broke Peel's resolve. One of the great virtues of a democracy is that it allows a politician to change his mind. Peel's career can be marked out by the significant problems on which he changed his mind. He was the opponent of extending the franchise who, in the Tamworth Manifesto of 1834, provided the apostate's template for conservatives. He was the resolute ally of the merchants who realised that reform was necessary no matter the political price to be paid.

Bright always attributed the change of heart to the speeches that Cobden gave in the House of Commons, and they did have an effect, as did Bright's own rhetoric. But speeches alone change nothing unless the background events are grand enough to warrant the rhetorical indignation. The event that really moved Peel was the Irish potato famine. In August 1845 a potato disease blackened thousands of acres of the crop and threatened the lives of millions of people. A meeting of the Anti-Corn Law League was held in the Free Trade Hall on 28 October at which Cobden pointed out that the remedy was to remove the impediments on imports. Bright said that the Corn Law was now having its desired effect, of taking from the starving poor and handing 'the bounty of Providence' to the rich. In a speech in London, Cobden called Peel 'a criminal and a poltroon' for hesitating and Bright predicted that the prime minister had concluded the Corn Law had to be abolished but that he as yet lacked the courage to say so.

In due course, Peel found the courage. On 4 December 1845, *The Times* announced that Parliament would be recalled for the first week of the new year and that a Royal Speech would be brought forward that would give immediate consideration to the Corn Laws, prefatory to their total repeal. Peel resigned because he did not believe he had the numbers in Parliament to implement his policy, but the Liberal leader Lord John Russell was unable to form a government after Cobden refused the post of vice-president of the Board of Trade, so Peel remained prime minister. On 22 January 1846 Peel came to the House of Commons and conceded that, in part due to the failure of the potato crop in Ireland, he had changed his mind on the question of agricultural protection, on which he had voted in favour every year up to and including 1845.

Five days later, in a speech that lasted three and a half hours, Peel proposed that total repeal would follow within three years, leaving only a 1 shilling duty per quarter. On 15 May 1846 Disraeli gave a cruel *ad hominem* speech in which he denounced Peel for the proposal to abolish the Corn Laws. Peel tried a personal counter-attack but, with tears in his eyes as his claim to integrity was jeered in the House of Commons, his voice broke and he had to stop. He took a moment to compose himself and then delivered an explanation of his change of course that was as dignified and impressive as any speech he ever gave.

The split between Peel and Disraeli was irreparable. Peel pushed through the abolition of the Corn Laws with the help of the Whigs in Parliament and tore his own party in two for the first and only time in its history. The division has never gone away, though. Free trade has ever after been the fault line between the liberals and the traditionalists in the Conservative Party, and it was Cobden, Bright and Peel, the men of Manchester, who opened it up. The Peelites merged with the Whigs and the Radicals in 1859 to form the Liberal Party. The legacy of the battle over the Corn Laws was the origin of the party-political system as we know it today. In his resignation speech Peel had attributed the success of the repeal case to Cobden. On 2 July 1846, at a meeting in Manchester, Cobden moved a motion, which Bright seconded, to dissolve the Anti-Corn Law League. A library of twelve hundred volumes was presented to Bright as a memorial of the struggle.

The Condition of the English Working Class

At precisely the same moment that free trade was winning its first decisive victory in British politics two young men were working half a mile away, in the library at what would become the music school Chetham's, on a system to rival commercial enterprise. The rivalry that was brewing in Manchester in 1846, the competition between market enterprise and communism, would eventually convulse the world.

In the years of the tumult over the Corn Laws, the Manchester mill owner Friedrich Engels received regular visits from his friend

Karl Marx. Engels had been sent to Manchester from Germany by his father in December 1842 to work at the family firm of Ermen and Engels in the hope that commercial experience would rid the young Friedrich of his radical opinions. In the three decades he stayed there, Manchester had the opposite effect. Engels spent his days as a cotton merchant in the Exchange earning the money he then sent to Marx to finance the latter's work. He spent his evenings scouring the Manchester slums for the evidence that, in 1844, he would accumulate and publish in *The Condition of the Working Class in England*, which is still the most pertinent description of the dismal fate to which factory work condemned the Manchester working class at the height of the industrial revolution.

Manchester had grown rapidly in the late eighteenth and early nineteenth centuries. Between 1773 and 1801 the population quadrupled in size from 22,500 inhabitants to 84,000, but the city's housing could not expand to cope. Cholera tore through large families in small spaces. Of the slums just off Oxford Street, Engels writes: 'The cottages are old, dirty, and of the smallest sort, the streets uneven, fallen into ruts and in part without drains or pavement; masses of refuse, offal, and sickening filth lie among standing pools in all directions ... The race that lives in these ruinous cottages, behind broken windows, mended with oilskin, sprung doors, and rotten door-posts, or in dark, wet cellars, in measureless filth and stench must surely have reached the lowest stage of humanity.'

These days the slums that Engels reported in *The Condition of the Working Class in England* are no longer there. But it wasn't the research that Marx and Engels did together in the library at Chetham's that made the difference. The work of Marx and Engels went to the heads of political radicals all over Europe, inspiring a great speaker like La Pasionaria to her rhetorical heights and her political lows. But Britain never had much taste for their economic eschatology. The answer to the condition of England question did not lie there. It lay instead, improbably, in the argument of another Conservative prime minister who changed his mind.

Benjamin Disraeli had led the opposition to the abolition of the Corn Laws and was widely regarded as a Tory chancer to whom rhetorical fluency came too easily. The most conspicuous legacy of the Anti-Corn Law League had been set in stone when, between 1853 and 1856, a grand Free Trade Hall was constructed, on the site of St Peter's Field. It was here, of all places, in April 1872, that Disraeli came to define Conservatism as a creed of social reform. This was the speech that advocated moderation in all things yet made a series of bold promises that politics would deal with the condition of England question better than radical anger ever could.

On 3 April, Disraeli gave a disquisition that lasted three and a quarter hours during which he got through two bottles of brandy. He opened by pondering why Britain, alone of European nations, had not experienced a genuine revolution and therefore enjoyed an unbroken history of 'that long established order which is the only parent of personal liberty and political rights'. Though there is something of the Pollyanna in his uncritical reflections on the appeal of republicanism, the status quo in the House of Lords and the relationship between Church and State, Disraeli's main point is a sound one. Referring to the 1871 Paris Commune, he asked why, as the latest French revolution unfolded, 'yet not five men were found to meet together in Manchester and grumble. And why? Because the people had got what they wanted.'

What they had wanted and what they had got, said Disraeli, were the two demands of St Peter's Field: the parliamentary franchise and more congenial living conditions. It was the latter to which he devoted most of his remarks. During the forty years after the Great Reform Act, Disraeli noted of working people, 'their wages have been raised, and their hours of daily toil have been diminished'. He then named the next task for a public policy that has a claim on the title of One Nation, which is better public health. Without 'pure air, pure water, the inspection of unhealthy habitations', the glories of the nation collected in museums and galleries matter little.

It is remarkable how close a model this speech was for Disraeli in government. The Manchester speech is, in effect, a prospectus for the government that he was to lead between 1874 and 1880. The 1875 Public Health Act laid down minimum standards for drainage, sewage disposal and refuse. The 1875 Artisans' and Labourers' Dwellings Act gave local authorities the power to buy, clear and redevelop the slums. The 1875 Conspiracy and Protection of Property Act meant that trade unions could no longer be prosecuted if they were doing something that would be legal if done by an individual. This, in effect, legalised peaceful picketing. The 1875 Employers and Workmen Act introduced a contract of service that granted terms to employees that were the equal of those offered to employers. The campaign of Lancashire MPs for a maximum nine-hour working day was successful and the six-day working week of women and children was reduced by half a day, to a maximum of fifty-six hours. The minimum legal working age was raised from eight to ten.

By the standards of the early twenty-first century some of these improvements seem minor and from a base so low that it seems like an injustice. But this creeping piecemeal process is exactly how progress in the material conditions of the people of England has come about. *The Condition of the English Working Class* is, as the name implies, a classic study of the condition of England question. The rhetoric of Orator Hunt at St Peter's Field provided the stimulus to seek representation in Parliament. The rhetoric of John Bright and Richard Cobden in the Free Trade Hall and in Parliament provided the answer that comes from the good will of commerce. A notable speech by a Conservative prime minister in the Free Trade Hall and his legislation in Parliament provided the good will of government. Between them they described the means by which the condition of the working class was improved.

The Mother of Parliaments

Orator Hunt had made two demands – material progress and parliamentary representation – and they were linked. Bear in mind that the Manchester radicals never wanted to break the parliamentary system. They wanted to join it so that they could partake of progress. It was John Bright who, in a speech in Birmingham in January 1865 in support of extending the franchise, had coined the phrase 'the mother of Parliaments'.

On 24 September 1866 Bright had returned to the Free Trade Hall to make a captivating case for universal suffrage; 'It is a fact worth knowing', he argued, 'that five millions of men in the United Kingdom have no vote ... I call it a stupendous fraud upon the people.' Once again, Disraeli was the villain of the hour, organising the opposition to Gladstone's attempt to extend the franchise. But, here as with everything else, Disraeli's substantive political views owed more to his own status than to any enduring conviction. It is a strange but salutary happenstance of democracies that volatile prag- matists can get a lot of good done when the national interest coin cides briefly with their own. Once he was installed as chancellor of the exchequer, Disraeli introduced his own Reform Bill. The 1867 Reform Act did not bring universal suffrage and a property qualifi- cation remained, but it did double the electorate in England and Wales from one to two million men.

The operative word was the last one. The extension of the fran- chise in 1867 and the further extension in 1884 took the electorate to two-thirds of the men in the country. Women, however, remained entirely outside the fold of democratic politics. The demand for the representation of women had always been part of Manchester's radi- calism. It had been notable how many women had been at Peterloo. Female reformers had appeared at St Peter's Fields dressed in white as a symbol of their virtue. In Manchester, the unjust absence of women from the electorate fuelled a radical response. It was there, in 1903, that Emmeline Pankhurst formed the Women's Social and Political Union (WSPU) to prosecute the case for women being given the vote. The controversy excited by the WSPU for the militancy of its methods derived largely from two speeches given in the Free Trade Hall. The first was at a meeting of the Free Trade League on 2 February 1904, and was delivered by a young MP who had recently switched from the Conservative to the Liberal Party. His name was Winston Churchill. The promising young MP gave a speech of impeccable Liberal credentials, citing Cobden and Bright by name and putting the traditional case for free trade that was the raison d'être of that chamber. Emmeline's daughter Christabel attended the meeting and refused to sit down when her amendment with regard to women's suffrage was not put. In her memoir *Unshackled: The Story of How We Won the Vote*, Christabel Pankhurst gives her account of the 1904 speech under the title 'The Actual Start of Militancy'.

The second speech took place in October 1905 when Sir Edward Grey, soon to be the Liberal foreign secretary, spoke at the Free Trade Hall in the election campaign. The WSPU had written to Grey to ask him to receive a deputation but had received no reply. Christabel and her friend Annie Kenney, a mill worker from Oldham, joined the audience intending to heckle with a view to getting themselves arrested. As Grey spoke, Pankhurst unfurled a banner on which they had inscribed 'Votes for Women' and Kenney shouted out: 'Will the Liberal government give women the vote?' The two of them were dragged from the hall and, after giving an impromptu speech outside the Free Trade Hall, did indeed contrive to get arrested.

The next day they appeared in court, were fined but refused to pay. Pankhurst received a sentence of seven days' imprisonment and Kenney was confined for three. According to the account of Christabel's sister Sylvia in *The Suffragette Movement*, Churchill turned up at Strangeways prison and tried to pay the fines but the governor refused to take his money. Pankhurst and Kenney were released a week later and on 20 October, ten days after they had been dragged out, addressed a crowded meeting at the Free Trade Hall. Keir Hardie, who four months later became the Labour Party's first official leader, also spoke. This was the beginning of the Votes for Women campaign that led, eventually, to universal suffrage in Britain. The 1918 Representation of the People Act gave the vote to men over the age of twenty-one, all women over thirty and women over twenty-one who were householders or married to householders or university graduates over twenty-one. Ten years later, the 1928 Representation of the People Act granted women the vote on the same basis as men. The demands that had begun at St Peter's Field over a century earlier had finally been met.

The populist and the utopian always, though, seek to accelerate progress. The various stamps of Manchester radicals and visiting Conservative prime ministers had all seen the slow road to material comfort that passed through Parliament. The anti-democratic radicalism of which Marx and Engels became the international prophets gained no traction in England which, uniquely amongst the European democracies, experienced no serious communist party. As a more realistic German economist, Werner Sombart, said, 'all socialist utopias come to nothing on roast beef and apple pie'. From the other end of the political spectrum, with equally negligible effect, in 1931 Sir Oswald Mosley offered himself as the man of the hour, England's own native dictator.

The road that runs down to the site of St Peter's Field in Manchester is called Mosley Street. The first Sir Oswald Mosley had been created a baronet in Ancoats in Manchester by George I in 1720, upon which he inherited the manor of Manchester. The third Sir Oswald Mosley then sold the manorial rights to the mayor and corporation of Manchester in 1846, the year of the repeal of the Corn Laws. The sixth baronet, who succeeded to the title on his father's death in 1928, was the Sir Oswald Mosley who, having already gone through the Conservative and Labour parties, came to the Free Trade Hall on 26 October 1931 to launch his New Party. Rather like Donald Trump's self-obsessed lament at Gettysburg, there could hardly have been a more inappropriate venue for Mosley's confection of high protective tariffs and corporatist optimism.

When the New Party failed to win a single seat in the 1931 general election, Mosley gave up on democratic politics altogether. In 1932 he formed the British Union of Fascists (BUF), and in March 1933 he returned to the Free Trade Hall for a rally that ended in a riot and a fight with the Communist Party of Great Britain. By September of that year Mosley was copying the theatre of fascism. At a rally at Belle Vue in Manchester, he gave a speech which, in a different country at the same time, might have sounded like the call of a frightening future. Marching through a mass of cheering supporters all dressed in black, Sir Oswald mounted a stage and, more than a little hysterical, declaimed: 'If you think the present system of things can really see you through then it's idle for our new and virile faith of fascism. I come to you with a new and revolutionary conception of politics, of economics and of life itself. We have another doctrine to put before you ... We say that England is not dead. We say, and I ask you to say with us, lift up you mighty in this great meeting in the heart of England, send to all the world a message, England lives and marches on.'

Mosley never found a way to speak that was not a ventriloquist version of Hitler. But Britain already had its Manchester school doctrine and it was tempted by no other. The ascent of Sir Oswald Mosley was about as likely as the tale in the *Superman: War of the Worlds* comic in which Mosley became prime minister after a Martian invasion in 1938, or Philip Roth's fantastic imaginative notion in *The*

Plot against America that Hitler installed Mosley as his puppet in Britain.

Mosley's military display caused consternation for a short time. For six months during 1934 the BUF gained the support of the *Daily Mail*. His fascist rallies rattled the government enough to pass the 1936 Public Order Act banning political uniforms and organisations of a military type. The thuggish anti-Semitism of Mosley's support- ers was nasty and must have been horrible to be on the receiving end of, but in the end his attempt to bring the politics of the extreme Right to Britain was a total failure. The BUF collapsed into acrimony and squabbling. Mosley was interned during the Second World War along with his wife Diana Mitford, whom he had married in October 1936 in the Berlin home of Joseph Goebbels. Adolf Hitler was one of the guests.

After his release, Mosley was a figure of some disrepute in the nation, so much so that he lived out most of the rest of his life in France, occasionally essaying a rather bathetic comeback. The best commentary came from P. G. Wodehouse, whose Sir Roderick Spode was a mockery of Mosley: 'The trouble with you, Spode, is that just because you have succeeded in inducing a handful of half-wits to disfigure the London scene by going about in black shorts, you think you're someone. You hear them shouting "Heil, Spode!" and you imagine it is the Voice of the People. That is where you make your bloomer. What the Voice of the People is saying is: "Look at that frightful ass Spode swanking about in footer bags! Did you ever in your puff see such a perfect perisher?"'

The Rise of the Meritocracy

England, or rather Britain, had sent out a message to the world, as Sir Oswald Mosley had asked. England did live and it did march again. It did so slowly, democratically, quietly. It achieved something for which it is hard to give thanks, which is a rather temperate, dull political life. The condition of England has improved slowly but this utopia like every other is elusive and the quest goes on.

Britain is still not a thoroughgoing meritocracy. Birth still accounts for too great a part of destiny, as Neil Kinnock pointed out.

The time of perfect racial equality, of which Martin Luther King dreamt, has not arrived in Britain yet, let alone in America. But there has been great progress since the people of what is now called Greater Manchester marched to St Peter's Field to demand representation in Parliament and their economic due. The life chances of their descendants are also significantly greater than theirs. The improvements are owed to three things: to social reform pursued through politics, to the prosperity generated by free enterprise, and to the liberties of association and speech. These were the values of the magazine *The Economist* which was founded by the Liberal politician James Wilson in 1843 to propagate the doctrines of the Manchester school. Wilson's son-in-law, Walter Bagehot, was one of its first editors. It was, to cite the title of Bagehot's famous 1867 work, the English constitution to which progress is owed rather than the works of Marx and Engels or ersatz political heroes of the political Right like Sir Oswald Mosley. The real heroes of the story are Orator Hunt, John Bright, Richard Cobden, Robert Peel and Benjamin Disraeli. Taken together, their words describe a country gradually moving forwards.

That term comes from Michael Young's 1958 book *The Rise of the Meritocracy*, and it was not meant kindly. Young's book is a parable of a society in which intelligence has become the governing criterion of society and the bedrock of a new, self-satisfied elite. The poor, who previously had their misfortune to blame for their benighted circumstances, are now told that they merit their lowly status. Although Young projects his narrative forward to 2034, he was in fact taking issue with the education system introduced by the 1944 Butler Act which separated, in the words of Matthew's gospel, the sheep from the goats, by shepherding the cleverest children into grammar schools and leaving the rest in second-class secondary moderns. At the end of *The Rise of the Meritocracy*, the helots rise in rebellion against the new hierarchy. The riot takes place at St Peter's Field, Manchester.

After a spell as a concert hall, home to the Hallé Orchestra and the place where Bob Dylan reacted to a cry of 'Judas!' as he plugged in the guitar to play 'Like a Rolling Stone', the Free Trade Hall is a hotel these days. It was there, in the hotel on St Peter's Field, that Tony Blair's Les Dawson joke was conceived. They hardly count as among the most edifying words associated with that spot. Indeed, of all the words delivered in the Free Trade Hall, perhaps the most complete account of what politics can achieve was given by the visiting American president Woodrow Wilson on 30 December 1918. Wilson flattered his audience by knowing his history: 'This is a doctrine which ought to be easy of comprehension in a great commercial centre like this. You cannot trade with men who suspect you. You cannot establish commercial and industrial relations with those who do not trust you. Good will is the forerunner of trade, and trade is the great amicable instrument of the world on that account.'

The process of democratic politics is never perfect. The authorities reacted brutally to the protesters at Peterloo. Generations struggled with contagious diseases and high infant mortality. It took a party to split apart for the interests of the consumer to prevail over those of the merchants. The addition of the working class and women to the franchise was scandalously late. It took the vision of Disraeli to see that the working men and women, the 'angels in marble', might conceivably reward him with their vote. But slow as politics is, there is no way faster.

Recognition that the individual must be taken seriously as a moral agent, the idea that unites the passionate arguments of Wilberforce, Pankhurst, King and Kinnock, arrives through political progress. There is a story about the sculptor Jacob Epstein which is a telling metaphor both for the process of writing speeches and the method of politics. At the unveiling of his bust of the Labour foreign secretary Ernest Bevin, Epstein was asked how he managed such a perfect likeness. 'I just take a block of marble,' he said, 'and chip away all the bits that don't look like Ernest Bevin.' The angel is in the marble somewhere. The process of sculpting is called politics.

5

REVOLUTION:
THROUGH POLITICS THE
WORST IS AVOIDED

The Rebel

'Tyrants conduct monologues above a million solitudes,' said Camus. *The Rebel*, from which that magnificent line is taken, is a set text of liberal democracy. It says so much about the relationship between the speaker and the spoken at. It describes the distinction, which runs through every part of this book, between the open and plural society and the missionary men who believe they have located the route to utopia. Too many people in the rich, fortunate democracies are tempted by easy ideologies that promise instant justice. It is critical, but it can be hard, to insist on the provisional virtues of the free society over the false pledge of the fantasist. One such fantasist, who has competed with Camus in French intellectual life for the title of the prince of glamour, was Jean-Paul Sartre.

Sartre and Camus first met briefly in June 1943 at the opening of Sartre's play *The Flies*, but did not get to know one another properly until Camus started to join Sartre and Simone de Beauvoir in the Café Flore and the two male writers discovered a shared passion for the theatre. Sartre even suggested that Camus play the lead in his new drama *No Exit*. Their friendship was cemented when each wrote appreciative reviews of the other's sense of the absurd, Camus on Sartre's *The Wall* and Sartre returning the compliment with a generous review of *The Stranger*. But the two men were to split, and it was on a fundamental question. It is important to say, since Sartre is a representative figure of a kind of Western self-loathing that persists into our time, that Sartre was a fluent fool philosopher while Camus was the true lover of wisdom.

Camus's contribution to the discussion went on in the pages of *Combat*, a resistance journal he edited during the Second World War. In truth, neither man did a great deal of resisting in occupied Paris, although Camus took more risks than Sartre and did at least have the grace to acknowledge his comparative safety afterwards. By contrast, during *l'épuration* (the purge) between 1944 and 1949, in which collaborationists were identified, tried and punished for treason, Sartre lied shamelessly about the extent of his resistance activities. He was still maintaining heroic status, quite wrongly, when he died. His status as a villain does not rest on his being a man of low moral repute, though. It rests on the errors of his politics.

Although throughout the 1940s the two men shared a superficial view of the political world, the division between them was actually fundamental. Camus came to understand that liberty can only be attained outside a fully-fledged all-explaining ideology, Sartre, by contrast, was always too ready to visit the latest revolutionary fashion on a grateful world. Their first clash came in 1948 in the pages of the left-wing journal *Caliban*. Sartre's piece, titled 'To Be Hungry Already Means You Want to Be Free', in which he argued that individual liberty was impossible in a democracy because the people are serfs to the bourgeoisie, inspired a caustic dismissal from Camus. Sartre thought that violence was the proletariat's natural response to humiliation. This was simplistic, crude and one-dimensional, thought Camus.

The split was confirmed in 1951 when Camus published his classic work *The Rebel*. This is the book in which he gives up on the idea that history has a purpose. Camus argues that revolutions start with noble intentions but lead to ignoble consequences. The revolution to overthrow a cruel regime goes full circle and installs a new tyranny. Freedom and justice are lost as regimes that believe in their own metaphysical truths 'make murder their tool'. The inexorable conclusion is that the end of communism is the Gulag and the Great Purge. Camus had the wisdom, in a time and a place when such ideas were *de rigueur*, to see that it was an arrogant error made, despite their manifest differences, by each of Maximilien Robespierre, Adolf Hitler and Fidel Castro, in supposing that history is tending towards a destination. Beyond human aspiration, there is no end and no point. There is only time and chance. Perhaps this makes life absurd but there we are. Politics is the system by which we gather to accept and negotiate this ineluctably tragic fact of human existence. Camus understood that the supreme political virtue was moderation; Sartre never did, and in politics, if you don't understand that you don't understand anything.

It was obvious from the review of *The Rebel* in Sartre's journal *Les Temps Modernes* that he was the philosopher-king of missing the point. The review was written by a junior editor called Francis Jenson, but Camus, like everyone else, took the contents to be the disguised view of Sartre. Jenson disparaged Camus's central thesis that revolutions are, by definition, bound to fail and liable to end in violence. Camus responded to Sartre, dismissing Jenson, with a choice selection of the term, as 'your collaborator', by asking him to address the central point of *The Rebel*, which is that murder is never a justifiable way to secure freedom from oppression. Sartre was not quite able to bring himself to say what followed from his immature view, which is that the Gulags must tend towards some ultimate good.

Sartre made do with *ad hominem* attacks on his former friend, and the two conducted an intellectual battle throughout the 1950s. While Sartre concocted elaborate insults, Camus continued to oppose totalitarian politics of both Left and Right. He resigned from UNESCO in 1952 when Franco's Spain was admitted. He criticised Soviet repression of strikes in East Berlin and in Poland and his 1957 speech 'The Blood of the Hungarians' is a pellucid statement of his political thought, applied to real life rather than, like Sartre, to some metaphysical fancy. The rift between the two former friends was never healed and ended only when Camus died tragically young at forty-six in a car crash in 1960.

The exchange between Camus and Sartre was, in one sense, a period piece. As they talked in the cafés of Paris they shared the table with Nazi and SS officers. Paris was, as Simone de Beauvoir put it, 'a vast Stalag'. After the war they both realised that a new battle had begun. Sartre thought he was on the right side of history, but Camus understood that history doesn't have a side. History does no work for us; we have to choose for ourselves. In this sense, the dispute between Camus and Sartre is timeless and it was Sartre, the intellectual who chose frivolously and wrongly, who was the more fêted of the two. The argument is with us still.

Despite an alliance that has lasted since 1778 and despite the gift of the Statue of Liberty, France has a claim to be the home of facile anti-Americanism. On the political Right, Gaullism is saturated with anti-American claims of French superiority. The political Left, and this was true not just in France, found in alleged American materialism an example of the decadence it detected under late capitalism. A loathing of the West, rooted equally in hatred of America and hatred of capitalism, is a constant temptation, especially on the political Left. There are plenty of people in rich, democratic societies who believe that all the evils in the world are merely the process by which the consequences swirl back on the real perpetrator, the United States of America. Sartre gave a distinguished voice to the idiotic thesis that violence from other nations is the inevitable, and justifiable, response to the humiliation they have received from America and the West. We should not be sentimental about where this argument leads. It leads to a baroque justification of the show trials such as can be found in Sartre's *The Communists and Peace*.

Wherever there is political power there is always a struggle about how to wield it between the moderates and the more extreme elements: a choice to be made between the Jacobins and the Girondins, between the dying embers of the Weimar Republic and the new force of National Socialism, between the Mensheviks and the Bolsheviks, between the liberal democrats and the historically destined communists. In retrospect the victors and the vanquished of these conflicts seem obvious to us, but we have to remember that they didn't at the time. In history as it is lived rather than as it is predicted, immoderate politics has always exerted a glamour. Liberal democracies demand patience and patience is usually in short supply. Many distinguished people have demanded a short cut to utopia.

Camus was one of the intellectuals to whom we should still look because he had the fortitude to be clear on the most important question of all, which is the contest between advanced dreams of utopia and the lesser virtues of liberal democracy. This question is still with us today and good guides are needed. The other guide in Camus's time was the unjustly neglected Raymond Aron, who resigned from the board of *Les Temps Modernes* in 1945 because of Sartre's communism and whose *The Opium of the Intellectuals* is a book-length devastation of the fatuity of Sartre and his kind. They were the thinkers, along with Léon Blum, the leader of the Popular Front and defiant opponent of the Vichy regime, who were prepared to take on, to cite the title of Tony Judt's study of the three heroes, the burden of responsibility.

The speeches that follow show the tragic consequences of the belief that history has a destiny. Camus's analysis of the French Revolution traces the source of the terror back to aggressive idealism. Nobody ever defined the philosophy of terror with such unrepentant candour as Maximilien Robespierre. But as gruesome as it was, the revolution gone wrong was only a prelude to hell. The unsurpassable example of Adolf Hitler cannot be avoided if the subject is the glamour of rhetoric. The speech as rally and ritual has never penetrated so far down into the dark recesses of the human mind. By that comparison, the allure of Fidel Castro is a gentle mistake, but it is an important one all the same, for the reason that Sartre gave us unwittingly, which is that utopian certainty can never be satisfied until perfection has been achieved. These are not speeches that we need, but we do need to understand them.

Then there are the rebels, the crucial figures who fought for justice without abandoning the political virtues. Neither Václav Havel nor Elie Wiesel would have chosen their status as, in the first case a velvet revolutionary and in the second case a witness, but they are the survivors who came through to tell the story. Communism and fascism were a living hell and the bombastic, destined certainty of Adolf Hitler and Fidel Castro contrasts vitally with Havel and Wiesel's resigned and sorrowful reflection on the past. That disenchanted tone — rhetoric without illusions — is also, however, the source of what is beautiful and elevating in their words. But the very fact that those words needed to be said is a tragedy without redemption. Camus says a lot in a single sentence in *The Rebel*: 'None of the evils that totalitarianism claims to cure is worse than totalitarianism itself.' Camus knew what it was and he named it. It was the plague.

MAXIMILIEN ROBESPIERRE

The Political Philosophy of Terror

The National Convention, Paris

5 February 1794

Thomas Carlyle famously called Maximilien Robespierre the 'sea-green incorruptible' of the French Revolution because he was so intellectually consistent and unyielding. Indeed, in his speeches, Robespierre pushes reason to an unreasonable extent. He also conducted a private life of conspicuous virtue, staying in simple, unfurnished rooms, walking everywhere and refusing even to take a carriage. His puritan lifestyle was devoid of any of the trappings of power or celebrity. But virtue cannot be read across from the private to the public, and it is for his record as a man of politics that Robespierre's capacity for corruption has to be judged. If the transformation from a provincial lawyer to the central figure in the Reign of Terror is not a clear example of corruption, then corruption no longer has any meaning. The odyssey of Robespierre from an ordinary man of reason, and a fierce opponent of the death penalty, into a man prepared to see opponents go to the scaffold for the sake of an idea requires some explanation. He was the finest orator of the Terror, the man who put forensic, lawyerly aptitude at the service of the perversion of an idea. There is perhaps no more pertinent example of utopian longing gone horribly, viciously wrong than in the rhetoric of Robespierre and the parable of revolution that, unwittingly, he tells.

Maximilien Marie Isidore de Robespierre (1758–94) was born in Arras, the son of a lawyer, the profession he entered himself after an education in Paris. Robespierre's mother died when he was six. His father could not cope with the grief or the responsibility and so fled, leaving young Maximilien to be brought up by elderly relatives. At twelve, he was awarded a scholarship to the Collège Louis-le-Grand in Paris. He qualified there as a lawyer at the age of twenty-three, and on graduation received a special prize for exemplary academic success and good personal conduct. He returned to Arras and began working to pay off his father's debts.

Robespierre's life changed when he was elected as a deputy in the Estates-General, the formal but essentially powerless body that met in the prelude to the Revolution in 1789. France was in severe debt and Louis XVI and his queen Marie Antoinette had become symbols of an authority that was no longer recognised. The Estates-General of 1789 demanded greater powers, the upshot of which was the creation of a new legislative body, the National Constituent Assembly. Two months after Robespierre's election to the Estates-General the French Revolution broke out. On 14 July citizens stormed the Bastille, the fortress that represented the idea of absolute monarchy in France. Rebellion spread from the city to the countryside and Robespierre took part in the drafting and dissemination of the revolutionary Declaration of the Rights of Man and of the Citizen.

In April 1790 Robespierre was elected the president of the Jacobin political club and then, after the monarchy fell in August 1792, the first deputy for Paris to the National Convention. He made his name as an orator with a series of assaults on the integrity and legitimacy of the monarchy. He became a vocal supporter of the declaration of France as a republic, the decision to put the king on trial for treason and the execution of King Louis in January 1793. The execution of the king began a struggle for pre-eminence in which the radical Jacobins prevailed over the more moderate Girondins whose leaders were arrested. Control of France passed to the Committee of Public Safety (a sinister title, in retrospect), of which Robespierre was a member. His rhetorical skill meant that he quickly came to dominate proceedings on the Committee.

Fearful of foreign invasion and with disorder in France rising, the Committee began to designate and eliminate enemies of the revolution. Tens of thousands of people were executed during what became known as the Reign of Terror. In the speech that follows, Robespierre tries to provide a philosophical justification for the terror he is practising. This speech is his attempt to purloin the revolutionary principles for degraded practice. It is hard to find any traces of liberty, equality or fraternity within it. By the time of this speech, the Federalist revolt and the Vendée uprisings had been pacified. The threat of invasion by the Austrians, British and Prussians had receded. Robespierre nevertheless conjures the threat of internal and external enemies to justify the terrible beauty of his prose.

There is a scholarly dispute about the extent to which Robespierre can be held to personal account for the Terror. As Orwell points out in his essay on Dickens, the average English reader's notion of the French Revolution as an unceasing frenzied massacre is owed to *A Tale of Two Cities*. In fact, fewer people were killed in the Terror than died in any one of Napoleon's battles in the quest for *la gloire*. There were also others, more brutal than Robespierre, whose guilt is lost because of their obscurity. This is the sort of unresolvable conflict between structure and agency that bedevils too much historical explanation. It might be better to read Robespierre's own words which, alas, condemn him well enough.

> *It is time to mark clearly the goal of the revolution, and the end we want to reach; it is time for us to take account both of the obstacles that still keep us from it, and of the means we ought to adopt to attain it: a simple and important idea which seems never to have been noticed. For ourselves, we come today to make the world privy to your political secrets, so that all our country's friends can rally to the voice of reason and the public interest; so that the French nation and its representatives will be respected in all the countries of the world where the knowledge of their real principles can penetrate; so that the intriguers who seek always to replace other intriguers will be judged by sure and easy rules. We must take far-sighted precautions to return the destiny of liberty into the hands of the truth, which is eternal, rather than into those of men, who are transitory, so that if the government forgets the interests of the people, or if it lapses into the hands of the corrupt individuals, according to the natural course of things, the light of recognised principles will illuminate their treachery, and so that every new faction will discover death in the mere thought of crime.*

A sinister tone is established from the opening. Robespierre has barely even bothered to set out the principles upon which the government is based before he is excoriating the corrupt individuals who will scupper the revolution. The argument is confidently stated and, on the page, betrays none of the nerves with which Robespierre shook before he had to speak. His voice was not strong, so he always struggled to command the attention of an audience. Early in his career, he was often shouted down. He lacked oratorical flourish or any great sense of theatre. His skill here is that of the lawyer, picking his way expertly, albeit somewhat aridly, through a case.

Whatever Robespierre's limitations as a speech-giver, he was a fine speechwriter. This section seeds everything that is to come. It is an accurate guide to what follows, both in content and mood. Or rather, moods, because this is a speech in which one ethos competes with another. Robespierre is speaking in an uplifting spirit of optimism about the virtues of the Revolution, a mood regularly undermined by the grisly insinuation that unnamed conspirators are threatening the promise of the future.

It is important to recall that Robespierre came to power in a context of violence on the streets. When, in September 1793, the *sans-culottes* invaded the Convention under the slogan 'make Terror the order of the day!' the Jacobins responded by passing the Law of Suspects. This gave sweeping powers of arrest to the ruling committees. The next month the Convention passed the Decree on Emergency Government that authorised the suspension of ordinary rights and the adoption of violence. Girondist leaders and Marie Antoinette were sent to the guillotine. In the last phrase of his opening – 'the light of recognised principles will illuminate their treachery' – Robespierre captures the paranoia of the times and anticipates what is to come. He is able to say something so abominable because of an important distinction, which he introduces in this opening. Truth is eternal but men are transitory. Truth is a property of the world, to which men must conform. This is the non-divine form of religious reasoning that revolutionaries everywhere have adopted.

What is the goal toward which we are heading? The peaceful enjoyment of liberty and equality; the reign of that eternal justice whose laws have been inscribed, not in marble and stone, but in the hearts of all men, even in that of the slave who forgets them and in that of the tyrant who denies them. We seek an order of things in which all the base and cruel passions are enchained, all the beneficent and generous passions are awakened by the laws; where ambition becomes the desire to merit glory and to serve our country; where distinctions are born only of equality itself; where the citizen is subject to the magistrate, the magistrate to the people, and the people to justice; where our country assures the well-being of each individual, and where each individual proudly enjoys our country's prosperity and glory; where every soul grows greater through the continual flow of republican sentiments, and by the need of deserving the esteem of a great people; where the arts are the adornments of the liberty which ennobles them and commerce the source of public wealth rather than solely the monstrous opulence of a few families. In our land we want to substitute morality for egotism, integrity for formal codes of honour, principles for customs, a sense of duty for one of mere propriety, the rule of reason for the tyranny of fashion, scorn of vice for scorn of the unlucky, self-respect for insolence, grandeur of soul over vanity, love of glory for the love of money, good people in place of good society. We wish to substitute merit for intrigue, genius for wit, truth for glamour, the charm of happiness for sensuous boredom, the greatness of man for the pettiness of the great, a people who are magnanimous, powerful, and happy, in place of a kindly, frivolous, and miserable people – which is to say all the virtues and all the miracles of the republic in place of all the vices and all the absurdities of the monarchy. We want, in a word, to fulfil nature's desires, accomplish the destiny of humanity, keep the promises of philosophy, absolve providence from the long reign of crime and tyranny. Let France, formerly illustrious among the enslaved lands, eclipsing the glory of all the free peoples who have existed, become the model for the nations, the terror of oppressors, the consolation of the oppressed, the ornament of the world – and let us, in sealing our work with our blood, see at least the early dawn of the universal bliss – that is our ambition, that is our goal.

This is a comprehensive list of what Robespierre sees as the virtues of the republic. The best of it is desirable and most of the rest is unobjectionable. There is a hint, at times, of the *Lucky Jim* axiom that nice things are nicer than nasty ones. Coming from another speaker, in a context not spattered with violence, much of this passage might stand as a banal litany of the democratic virtues.

But there are three verbal clues to alert the attentive listener. The first is the chiliastic language. The justice that will reign is 'eternal'. As long as France commands the right ideas, providence itself will be absolved from a reign of tyranny. The bliss on offer will be universal. The second clue is the call of destiny. Politics is cast as if it were the fulfilment of natural desire. It is a basic rule that whenever a speaker starts to confuse politics with nature it is time to run for the hills. That speaker will always be trying to smuggle in something undesirable in which other human beings are regarded as not worthy of equal consideration. The third tip-off comes at the end of the passage. After all the ambitions have been specified Robespierre lets slip that the universal bliss will come sealed in blood. Not his blood, but perhaps yours. Strip out those three clues to the oppressive nature of Robespierre's politics, perform a light edit, and you have an account of utopian hope. As they stand they are laced with threat.

Robespierre meant both sides of the Faustian bargain he struck. He read Rousseau's *Social Contract* as if it were a biblical text and his commitment to the ideals of the Revolution was total. He was a passionate and consistent opponent of slavery and played an instrumental role in abolishing it in France and her territories. He was regarded within France as a great defender of the poor and a man who spoke on behalf of oppressed minorities such as Jews, black people and (it was a different age) actors. He was the man who sought to rewrite the Declaration of Rights to limit private property and enshrine the right to life and subsistence for all.

And in a sense it was exactly this reasoned consistency that is the key to his tragic advocacy of terror. Robespierre's ardent republicanism was rooted in a genuine, even noble distaste for privilege. He really did believe that the cause was high enough to warrant the methods. He was an ideologue with political reflexes and no boundaries. It is a reminder that dark things can be done by people who believe they alone are walking in light.

> *What kind of government can realise these wonders? Only a democratic or republican government — these two words are synonyms, despite the abuses in common speech, because an aristocracy is no closer than a monarchy to being a republic. Democracy is a state in which the sovereign people, guided by laws which are of their own making, do for themselves all that they can do well, and by their delegates do all that they cannot do for themselves. Now, what is the fundamental principle of popular or democratic government, that is to say, the essential mainspring which sustains it and makes it move? It is virtue. I speak of the public virtue which worked so many wonders in Greece and Rome and which ought to produce even more astonishing things in republican France — that virtue which is nothing other than the love of the nation and its law. But as the essence of the republic or of democracy is equality, it follows that love of country necessarily embraces the love of equality. But the French are the first people of the world who have established real democracy, by calling all men to equality and full rights of citizenship; and there, in my judgment, is the true reason why all the tyrants in league against the Republic will be vanquished.*

Robespierre was renowned for his animus against the monarchy. The king and queen had been captured in August 1792 and by September France had become a republic and the king had been put on trial for treason. On 3 December 1792 Robespierre had spoken to the National Convention as it deliberated on the fate of the king. The Girondists were seeking to have the king tried in a ceremonial fashion, as an example of the true spirit of the revolution. Robespierre disdained clemency and the court and called on the revolutionary justice of the people: 'Louis must die in order for the Revolution to live'. He wrote in *Défenseur de la Constitution*, his own journal, that Louis could not plead in mitigation to a constitution that he had himself violated. Louis was found guilty and went to the blade on 21 January 1793 in the Place de la Révolution.

The puzzle is why Robespierre was so determined on the execution of the king and why he consented to the Reign of Terror. Danton gave one answer when he said 'Let us be terrible in order to stop the people from being so', but that was not really Robespierre's view. If anything, he had an idealised notion of the innate goodness of the French working class. The source of his radicalism is given here in his commendation of the republican form of government. Robespierre had idealised the Roman republic since his time at school. He was a student and an admirer of Cicero and found himself attracted to the idea of the virtuous self, the man who stands alone with only his conscience for guidance, which he also discovered in Rousseau. Robespierre's conception of revolutionary virtue is owed primarily to Rousseau's arguments about sovereignty and direct democracy. This passage reveals a kind of excess of commitment. Robespierre is so adamant that the ideals of the Enlightenment must prevail – something he often said during court hearings as a lawyer – that he was prepared to abandon them in his means to secure them in his ends.

Within the scheme of the French revolution, that which is immoral is impolitic, that which is corrupting is counter-revolutionary. Weakness, vice, and prejudices are the road to royalty. We deduce from all this a great truth – that the characteristic of popular government is to be trustful towards the people and severe towards itself. Here the development of our theory would reach its limit, if you had only to steer the ship of the Republic through calm waters. But the tempest rages, and the state of the revolution in which you find yourselves imposes upon you another task. We must smother the internal and external enemies of the Republic or perish with them. Now, in this situation, the first maxim of your policy ought to be to lead the people by reason and the people's enemies by terror. If the mainspring of popular government in peacetime is virtue, amid revolution it is at the same time both virtue and terror: virtue, without which terror is fatal; terror, without which virtue is impotent. Terror is nothing but prompt, severe, inflexible justice; it is therefore an emanation of virtue. It is less a special principle than a consequence of the general principle of democracy applied to our country's most pressing needs. It has been said that terror was the mainspring of despotic government. Does your government, then, resemble a despotism? Yes, as the sword which glitters in the hands of liberty's heroes resembles the one with which tyranny's lackeys are armed. Let the despot govern his brutalised subjects by terror; he is right to do this, as a despot.

*Subdue liberty's enemies by terror, and you will be right, as
founders of the Republic. The government of the revolution is the
despotism of liberty against tyranny. Is force made only to protect
crime? And is it not to strike the heads of the proud that lightning
is destined? To punish the oppressors of humanity is clemency; to
pardon them is barbarity. The rigour of tyrants has only rigour for
a principle; the rigour of the republican government comes from
charity.*

Rhetoric is rarely as unvarnished as this. You might expect some
elaborate euphemism or the ransacking of the techniques of classical
oratory to disguise the true intent in clever word-play. Not a bit of it.
Robespierre gives instead a brutally clear exposition of the philosophy of terror. The passage relies a great deal on the perennial populist opposition between the people and the enemies of the people.
The enemies pose such a threat that, though reason is warranted for
the people, terror must be applied to the enemies. As the enemies of
the republic deserve only terror, that terror is therefore just. It is not
really terror at all but ultimate truth in action.

Again, Robespierre does not seek to disguise what is a truly cruel
thought: 'Terror is nothing but prompt, severe, inflexible justice'.
Terror is not vice let loose in the world, it is, in Robespierre's
Manichean logic, 'an emanation of virtue'. These are not just words
either. Robespierre by now is guiding the policy of terror. The practical application of this rhetoric is one of the things that make it so
chilling. The other is the certainty of rectitude, the complete absence
of doubt or regret. This passage is spoken in conviction rather than
in sorrow.

The revolutionary trinity that Robespierre coined – *liberté, égalité, fraternité* – once had a fourth element: *liberté, égalité, fraternité et
la Mort!* This was not terrorism committed against an incumbent
regime. It was terrorism committed *by* an incumbent regime. Terror
as official government policy. The policy of terror was instituted by
the Convention on 5 September 1793 in a proclamation of extraordinary candour: 'It is time that equality bore its scythe above all heads.
It is time to horrify all the conspirators. So legislators, place Terror on
the order of the day! Let us be in revolution, because everywhere coun-
ter-revolution is being woven by our enemies. The blade of the law

should hover over all the guilty.' The republic was a utopian ideal and Robespierre could not permit anybody to fall short. As Auden wrote in 'Epitaph on a Tyrant', perfection, of a kind, was what he was after.

> *Glance over our true situation. You will become aware that vigilance and energy are more necessary for you than ever. An unresponding ill-will everywhere opposes the operations of the government. The inevitable influence of foreign courts is no less active for being more hidden, and no less baneful. One senses that crime, frightened, has only covered its tracks with greater skill. You could never have imagined some of the excesses committed by hypocritical counter-revolutionaries in order to blight the cause of the revolution. Would you believe that in the regions where superstition has held the greatest sway, the counter-revolutionaries are not content with burdening religious observances under all the forms that could render them odious, but have spread terror among the people by sowing the rumour that all children under ten and all old men over seventy are going to be killed? ... Whence came this sudden swarm of foreigners, priests, noble, intriguer of all kinds, which at the same instant spread over the length and breadth of the Republic, seeking to execute, in the name of philosophy, a plan of counter-revolution which has only been stopped by the force of public reason? Execrable conception, worthy of the genius of foreign courts leagued against liberty, and of the corruption of all the internal enemies of the Republic!*

Robespierre spends a long while setting out the evils to which terror is the only justified response. Time and again in the speech he lists the threat of tyrants of other nations who want to conquer the new republic, the threat of foreign intrusion in the republic. It is notable how contemporary this sounds and how many populists of today say the same thing. Structurally this passage might have been better before the philosophy of terror, so as to lead up to the conclusion in justification, but the effect is clear enough. Repetition of this tedious kind is usually an example of poor composition, but Robespierre is too good a writer to be so charged. His tedium is a tactic. He is creating the platform on which a murderous argument can rest.

what he meant, but it is a reminder of what can happen when a captivating speaker gets hold of an idea that leaps out of his control. Words have to be handled with care and Robespierre did not respect his talent enough to keep it disciplined. More than 2,500 people went to the scaffold in Paris and more than 40,000 in France as a whole. It is precisely because of the gruesome philosophy set out in this speech that Robespierre was one of them. His tragedy was not that he betrayed the ideals of the revolution. It was that he carried them out.

ADOLF HITLER

My Patience Is Now at an End

Berlin Sportpalast
26 September 1938

Adolf Hitler is the man who tests, to destruction, the idea that even the malignant think they are doing the right thing. Given the magnitude of the crimes committed with his connivance, under his instruction and in his name, it seems wrong to associate Hitler with ordinary concepts such as 'revolution' or 'rhetoric'. But Hitler thought of himself as a revolutionary who was ridding the world of error, and his use of the performative act of the speech to create the effect was more developed than in any of his contemporaries. There is no sense with Hitler, as there may be with Robespierre and Castro, that the revolution has somehow gone wrong. His revolution was pernicious from the start. But he didn't think so, and one of the ways we can be alert to the tragedy is to work out exactly what he did, and how he did it.

Adolf Hitler (1889–1945) was born in Braunau am Inn, Austria. His childhood in Austria was marked by a constant struggle with his father over the young Adolf's desire to be an artist. In 1905 Hitler moved to Vienna, where he repeatedly failed to get into the Academy of Fine Arts and lived a bohemian life of no great repute or promise. The Vienna of the first decade of the twentieth century was rife with prejudice, especially anti-Semitism, which became part of the brew of resentment that Hitler was slowly preparing. In *Mein Kampf* Hitler says that it was in Vienna he first became an anti-Semite, although it is probable that his full conviction did not emerge until after Germany's defeat in the First World War. He then become a full-bore advocate of the theory of the *Dolchstoßlegende*, the stab in the back. The obvious perpetrators, in his fevered mind, were the international Jews.

Hitler moved to Munich in 1913 and enlisted in the Bavarian army. He served as a dispatch runner on the Western Front in Belgium and France, was present at the battles of Ypres, Arras and Passchendaele and was wounded at the Somme. He was decorated for bravery, receiving the Iron Cross, First Class, in 1918. In October 1918, he was temporarily blinded in a mustard gas attack and while he was in hospital in Pasewalk he received the news that Germany had been defeated in the war. By his own account the terrible news induced a second attack of blindness. The Treaty of Versailles pinned responsibility for the war on Germany and imposed severe reparations. Hitler felt it as a keen humiliation.

Back in Munich after the war Hitler became the army's point man with the German Workers' Party (DAP). Its founder, Anton Drexler, was impressed by Hitler's skill as an orator and, as the DAP became the National Socialist Party (NSDAP), Hitler joined up. Even in these early days his polemical invective against the Versailles Treaty, Marxists and Jews was notorious in Munich. It was there, in 1923, that Hitler staged his ill-fated putsch in the Bürgerbräukeller beer hall. Its failure landed him in jail, and it was while in prison that he dictated the first volume of *Mein Kampf*, the manifesto in which his vain mixture of incoherence and viciousness would speak for itself if only he could organise a sentence to point in the right direction. *Mein Kampf* is a depressing testament to Hitler's paranoia about the perceived humiliation at Versailles and the various conspiracies supposedly practised by international Jewry, capitalism and communism. One of the puzzles of Hitler's rhetoric is how someone whose thinking was so disordered, in every sense of that term, could be so effective on the stage.

It was a tragedy that Hitler was always underestimated. The elders of the Weimar Republic believed that by embracing him they could contain him. The NSDAP became the second-largest party after the 1930 election, and when elections in 1932 produced no decisive result, President Hindenburg appointed Hitler as chancellor. In 1933, the Communist Party was blamed for the Reichstag fire and proscribed, and the NSDAP's share of the vote rose to almost 44 per cent, making it the largest single party. Bursting free of the weak shackles imposed on him, Hitler passed an Enabling Act in 1933, which gave him the power to pass laws without the consent of the Reichstag for four years. The official title of the Enabling Act shows the NSDAP gift for sinister euphemism: *Gesetz zur Behebung der Not von Volk und Reich* – the Law to Remedy the Distress of People and State. On 14 July 1933 the NSDAP was declared the only legal political party in Germany. When Hindenburg died in August 1934 Hitler merged the role of president with that of chancellor and formally named himself Führer und Reichskanzler, leader and chancellor.

Hitler proceeded to make himself the most notorious leader of modern times. His domestic programme was marked by antipathy to the Jews and vast infrastructure expenditure, including rearmament, which helped unemployment to fall from 6 million in 1932 to 1 million in 1936. The rearmament was in the service of a vaulting imperial ambition. In March 1936 Hitler reoccupied the demilitarised zone in violation of the Versailles Treaty. At all points in the process he protested his peaceful intentions and at all points he could not be trusted. The following speech is a classic of Hitler's fictitious reassurance. Hitler had convinced Neville Chamberlain, the British prime minister, that his claim on Czechoslovakia was both legitimate and the summit of his ambition. Determined to avoid conflict, Chamberlain consented. We know now that he was catastrophically wrong to have done so.

On 1 September 1939, Germany invaded Poland, which drew a declaration of war from Britain and France. The cost of the war that followed was savage. The Nazi regime was responsible for the genocide of at least 5.5 million Jews and millions of others designated by Hitler as *Untermenschen*, subhumans. The herding of human beings into cattle trucks for transportation to concentration camps where they faced almost certain execution is the most abhorrent episode in modern history, perhaps in all history.

Hitler's gruesome end befits that history. On the Wilhelmstraße in Berlin the last scenes of the European war played out. Hitler cowered in the damp Führerbunker, below the water table in the garden of the Reich Chancellery, waiting for the end, sitting under his large portrait of Frederick the Great, listening to radio broadcasts from the BBC. Overhead, the air droned with the sound of bombers. On 16 April the Red Army began the battle of Berlin; three days later they had encircled the city. By the evening of the 21st, Russian tanks had reached the outskirts of Berlin. At his afternoon conference the following day, Hitler fell into a tearful rage when he realised, for the first time, that the war was lost. He declared that he would remain in Berlin until the enemy arrived, whereupon he would shoot himself. At midnight, 29 April 1945, Hitler married his mistress Eva Braun. He then dictated his last will and testament to his secretary Traudl Junge. In the Führerbunker on 30 April, 1945 Hitler shot himself. His wife took cyanide. In accordance with Hitler's instructions their bodies were burnt in the garden of the Reich Chancellery.

The new head of government was one of the only other occupants of the Führerbunker, Joseph Goebbels, Reich minister of propaganda. The appalling grotesquerie of the Nazi regime is beyond ordinary symbolism, but if any wretched story approximates to the horror of the times it is the fate of Helga, Hildegard, Helmut, Holdine, Hedwig and Heidrun, the children of Joseph and Magda Goebbels. Loyal to the end, Goebbels was Hitler's closest adjutant. Committed to dying in the bunker rather than seeking to flee, he condemned his children to the same fate. In the late afternoon of 1 May 1945, he and Magda murdered their six children by arranging for an SS dentist to inject them with morphine. When the children lost consciousness, Magda crushed ampoules of cyanide in their mouths. After performing this dreadful benediction, Magda committed suicide with her husband. On 2 May the Soviet forces entered the bunker complex.

The line that led here can be traced back to the fateful speech that Hitler delivered in the Sportpalast in Berlin on 26 September 1938. The man who introduced him to the crowd on that day was his loyal propagandist, Joseph Goebbels.

Today I step before you to speak directly to the people for the first time just as in the days of our great struggles, and you know well what that means! The world may no longer have any doubts: it is not one Führer or one man who speaks at this point, rather it is the German people that speaks! As I now speak for this German people, I know that this people of millions joins in the chorus of my words, reaffirms them, and makes them a holy oath in its own right. Some of the other statesmen might do well to consider if this is the case

> *with their people as well. The question which has moved us so*
> *profoundly within the last few months and weeks is an old one.*
> *It reads not so much 'Czechoslovakia', but rather 'Herr Benes'.*
> *This name unites all that moves millions of people today and*
> *which lets them either despair or instils in them a zealous*
> *determination ...*

This is Hitler's rhetorical and political method perfectly defined. He simply asserts himself as the representative individual of Germanic experience. He is the nation and the nation is him. The German historian Friedrich Meinecke, himself an anti-Semite, called Hitler 'one of the great examples of the singular and most incalculable power of personality in historical life'.

At the NSDAP congress in Nuremberg two weeks before this speech, Hitler had preached about the German Reich to an already converted crowd. 'The German Reich has long been dormant,' he said. 'Now the German Volk has awakened and once more bears its crown of a thousand years high on its head'. The novelty in his rhetoric was to create a bound community, a *Volksgemeinschaft*, just by talking it into life. No speaker has ever used public performance as much, or to such effect.

One of the closest studies of Hitler's rhetorical skill was conducted by Goebbels, who published an essay called 'The Führer as a Speaker' in 1936. 'The Führer is the first person in Germany', says Goebbels, 'to use speech to make history.' He goes on, for once not exaggerating: 'it is also a classic proof for the outstanding rhetorical brilliance of the Führer that his word alone was enough to transform an entire period, to defeat an apparently strong state and to bring in a new era.' In German history, says Goebbels, only Fichte's addresses to the German nation and Bismarck's political speeches were of world-historical standard. Hitler 'has the amazing gift', said Goebbels, 'of sensing what is in the air'. He didn't mention that what you sense in the air is more likely to be in the air if the police are on hand to enforce it.

The 15,000 people in the Sportpalast hung on Hitler's every word. It is an unedifying but instructive practice to watch the Führer speak. The theatrical spectacle is obvious. Hitler always liked to speak at twilight, in the fading light of the *Götterdämmerung*. The language too is aggressive. George Steiner said that Hitler drew on a rhetorical power that might be peculiar to German, or at least enhanced in German. It is a mixture of abstract concepts and political violence. Hitler's coiled energy seems to manifest his meaning. He is a speaker who can easily be understood with the sound turned down. The setting and the demeanour say so much, even before the language intervenes. But when the language does come it is soon clear that the script has been written by the devil.

I have really in these years pursued a practical peace policy. I have approached all apparently impossible problems with the firm resolve to solve them peacefully even when there was the danger of making more or less serious renunciations on Germany's part. I myself am a front-line soldier and I know how grave a thing war is. I wanted to spare the German people such an evil. Problem after problem I have tackled with the set purpose to make every effort to render possible a peaceful solution. The most difficult problem that faced me was the relation between Germany and Poland. There was the danger that the conception of a 'hereditary enmity' might take possession of our people and of the Polish people. That I wanted to prevent. I know quite well that I should not have succeeded if Poland at that time had had a democratic constitution. For these democracies which are overflowing with phrases about peace are the most bloodthirsty instigators of war. But Poland at that time was governed by no democracy but by a man. In the course of barely a year it was possible to conclude an agreement which, in the first instance for a period of ten years, on principle removed the danger of a conflict. We are all convinced that this agreement will bring with it a permanent pacification. We realise that here are two peoples which must live side by side and that neither of them can destroy the other. A state with a population of thirty-three millions will always strive for an access to the sea. A way to an understanding had therefore to be found. And we did arrive at a settlement which is constantly being improved upon. What is decisive in this instance is that both governments and all reasoned and rational people in both countries have the firm will to increasingly improve relations. This deed was truly in the service of peace, worth substantially more than the idle talk in the League of Nations' Palace in Geneva.

The lying is breathtaking. The accusation that a speaker is lying should be levelled sparingly. It is more often the case that a speaker is deluded or foolish than that they are saying things with the conscious desire to deceive. There is no other word for this passage. Hitler has not been pursuing peace. The only circumstances in which his ambitions are compatible with peace are if his opponents simply allow him the *Lebensraum*, living space, that he demands. He has already claimed, just before this passage, that he does not want war with France and that his intuition that the people of Austria wanted to be reunited with the larger German nation had been vindicated in a plebiscite. In fact in March of 1938 Hitler had invaded Austria in the power-grab he called the *Anschluss*.

Later Hitler asks, with a cynicism that is still astonishing: 'Can there be anything more shameless than to compel folk of another people, in certain circumstances, to fire on their own fellow-country-men only because a ruinous, evil, and criminal government so demands it?' Can there be anything more shameless than that senti-ment? Shameless, of course, is hardly the word.

At the Nuremberg rally on 12 September Hitler had said brazenly that 'no European state has done as much as Germany in the service of peace'. Hitler's claim to peaceful desires with respect to Poland are a travesty in the light of what we know now, which is that, a year later, the German tanks would be rolling in. His contempt for democracy is evident in the suggestion that it was only the exist-ence of a single authority in Poland that allowed him to do the deal for peace he desired. Diplomacy is reduced to the conversations of great men. Throughout, Hitler poses himself against the single representatives of other nations, Poland and Czechoslovakia, in a strong-man contest. There is no doubt about the victor: 'I myself am a front-line soldier.' It is just about the only true statement in the passage.

> *And now before us stands the last problem that must be solved and will be solved. It is the last territorial claim which I have to make in Europe but it is the claim from which I will not recede and which, God willing, I will make good. The history of the problem is as follows. In 1918 under the watchword 'the right of the peoples to self-determination' Central Europe was torn in pieces and was*

newly formed by certain so-called crazy 'statesmen'. Without regard for the origins of the peoples, without regard for either their wish as nations or for economic necessities, Central Europe at that time was broken up into atoms and the new so-called states were arbitrarily formed. To this procedure Czechoslovakia owes its existence. The Czech state began with a single lie and the father of that lie was named Beneš. This Mr Beneš at that time appeared in Versailles and he first of all gave the assurance that there was a Czechoslovak nation. He was forced to invent this lie in order to give to the slender number of his own fellow countrymen a somewhat greater range and thus a fuller justification. And the Anglo-Saxon statesmen who were, as always, not very adequately versed in respect of questions of geography or nationality, did not at that time find it necessary to test the assertions of Mr Beneš. Had they done so, they could have established the fact that there is no such thing as a Czechoslovak nation but only Czechs and Slovaks and that the Slovaks did not wish to have anything to do with the Czechs. So in the end through Mr Beneš these Czechs annexed Slovakia. Since this state did not seem fitted to live, out of hand three and a half million Germans were taken in violation of their right to self-determination, and their wish for self-determination. Since even that did not suffice, over a million Magyars had to be added, then some Carpathian Russians and at last several hundred thousand Poles. This is the state which then later proceeded to call itself Czechoslovakia in violation of the right of the people to self-determination, in violation of the clear wish and will of the nation to which this violence has been done ...

Before he spoke Hitler always spent some time building himself up into a state of resentment, and here it is in all its ignobility. The signature emotion of a Hitler speech is anger, fuelled by the sense of being hard done by. The location of that injustice is the Treaty of Versailles and the settlement at the end of the First World War. In this instance 'the crazy statesmen' unversed in geography and nationality had created an unnatural territory called Czechoslovakia without regard for the truly German lineage of those who lived in the Sudetenland. Hitler simply does not acknowledge the right of Czechoslovakia to independent existence because his conception of a nation is entirely ethnic. He is the epitome of the definition of nation by blood rather than belonging. Look at how he tries to clinch the case against Czechoslovakia. How can any nation which has to be constructed out of Czechs, Slovaks, Poles, Carpathian Russians and Magyars be a nation? Hitler simply runs together the two separate categories of ethnic origin and national allegiance and presents it as the merest common sense.

In his encomium to his leader's speaking prowess, Goebbels distinguished between speakers who use reasoning – 'a master of dialectic as the pianist is master of the keyboard' – from a speaker who 'knows the secret corners and aspects of the mass soul'. It is hardly surprising that he thought Hitler uniquely combined the virtues of both, and this is how he does it.

This assertion of ethnic origin passes both for Hitler's mastery of the piano and his search for the secret corners of the soul. At Nuremberg on 12 September Hitler had delivered the full performance, denouncing in turn the atheistic Social Democrats and 'the alliance of Jewish capitalism with an abstract version of communist anti-capitalism'. The rhetoric in Nuremberg is still shocking: 'the burden has become overbearing and the nation is no longer willing to have its lifeblood sucked out of it by these parasites'.

And then I can only say one thing: now two men stand arrayed one against the other: there is Mr Beneš and here stand I. We are two men of a different make-up. In the great struggle of the peoples when Mr Beneš was sneaking about through the world, I as a decent German soldier did my duty. And now today I can stand over against this man as the soldier of my people! I have only a few comments still to make: I am grateful to Mr Chamberlain for all his efforts. I have assured him that the German peoples desire nothing else than peace, but I have also told him that I cannot go back behind the limits set to our patience. I have further assured him, and I repeat it here, that when this problem is solved there is for Germany no further territorial problem in Europe. And I have further assured him that at the moment when Czechoslovakia solves her problems, that means when the Czechs have come to terms with their other minorities, and that peaceably and not through oppression, then I have no further interest in the Czech state. And that is guaranteed to him! We want no Czechs! But in the same way I desire to state before the German people that with regard to the problem of the Sudeten Germans my patience is now at an end! I have made Mr Beneš an offer which is nothing but the carrying into effect of what he himself has promised. The decision now lies in his hands: Peace or War! He will either accept this offer and now at least give to the Germans their freedom or we will go and fetch this freedom for ourselves. The world must take note that in four and a half years of war through the long years of my political life there is one thing which no one would ever cast in my teeth: I have never been a coward!

This sounded frightening at the time. Hitler has already said that Germany's patience was at an end, so here, with the repetition, he makes again the link that is the thread of the whole speech between the German people and himself as their authentic voice. Now his patience is at an end. The point is thick with menace. The end of patience meant war. Chamberlain had visited Hitler twice in the ten days prior to this speech to offer a plan for the Sudeten districts of Czechoslovakia to be transferred to Germany without even the need for a plebiscite. On the day of the Berlin Sportpalast speech, Chamberlain sent Sir Horace Wilson to appeal directly to Hitler to moderate the tone of the speech and submit to negotiations with the Czechs, with the British as honest broker. Wilson found Hitler in his usual pre-oratory mood, which was nervous, intransigent and working himself up to a pitch of resentment. His mission was pointless. Hitler already had an assurance from Chamberlain that, as long as he promised the Sudetenland would be Germany's 'last territorial claim', Britain would cede the territory. Hitler therefore gave the speech as planned and the deadline for Czechoslovakia to cede the Sudetenland to Germany was set for 2 p.m. on 28 September.

On 29 September, with no Czech in attendance, Hitler, Chamberlain, the French premier Édouard Daladier and Italy's Benito Mussolini held a one-day conference in Munich which gave the disputed parts of the Sudetenland to Germany. The outcome was feted. Hitler was made *Time* magazine's Man of the Year for 1938. Chamberlain went home to a tumultuous ovation. He appeared triumphantly on the balcony of Buckingham Palace with George VI and Queen Elizabeth and then, from Downing Street, told the nation that he had secured peace for our time. 'Go home and get a nice quiet sleep,' he signed off, in one of the great misjudgements in all public speech.

It wasn't as if Chamberlain hadn't been warned, and not just by Churchill. At Nuremberg two weeks before this speech in Berlin, Hitler had been as clear as could be expected about his actual objectives and had then added for good measure: 'I am a National Socialist and as such I am accustomed to strike back at any attacker. Moreover, I know only too well that leniency will not succeed in appeasing.'

If at that time a wandering scholar was able to inject into our people the poison of democratic catchwords – the people of today is no longer the people that it was then. Such catchwords are for us like wasp stings: they cannot hurt us: we are now immune. In this hour the whole German people will unite with me! It will feel my will to be its will. Just as in my eyes it is its future and its fate which give me the commission for my action. And we wish now to make our will as strong as it was in the time of our fight, the time when I, as a simple unknown soldier, went forth to conquer a Reich and never doubted of success and final victory. Then there gathered about me a band of brave men and brave women, and they went with me. And so I ask you my German people to take your stand behind me, man by man and woman by woman. In this hour we all wish to form a common will and that will must be stronger than every hardship and every danger. And if this will is stronger than hardship and danger then one day it will break down hardship and danger. We are determined! Now let Mr Beneš make his choice.

Democracy is a sting from an insect to which, mercifully, the German nation is now immune. Hitler only really has one theme; all his invective is a variation on it. His purpose at the end is simply to stir the audience; no further content is added to the case. In his essay on Hitler's speeches Goebbels had written that 'a sure sign of a good speech is that it not only sounds good, but reads well'. It's not quite true that all good speeches both read well and sound well and it's not really true of this speech either. Hitler's method was regular repetition of well-worn themes, which reads rather badly. However, in the stadium the repetition serves to demonstrate deep feeling, to show that Hitler was, in Goebbels's phrase, one of 'the drummers of fate'. This is the trick of the shaman. He has created a need and a *Weltanschauung* and claimed it was what the people thought all along. It is the pinnacle of what every speaker would like to achieve; for rhetoric to be true as soon as I say it, and *because* I say it.

The achievement is not really, despite the advocacy of Goebbels, just Hitler's. There is a major scholarly dispute, and has been ever since the war, about the extent to which the conflict, and its squalid consequences, can be attributed to the man himself. In the lesser but related question of his speeches, Hitler was known to take great pains, editing each text at least five times. In *Mein Kampf* he had written: 'I know that men are won over less by the written than by the spoken word, that every great movement on this earth owes its growth to great orators and not to great writers.' He worked deep into the night, occupying three secretaries at a time in a bid to get the words right. He practised his body language and gestures in front of a mirror. Hitler knew that his command of the audience was his principal method. But other people can do this. Hitler possessed no demonic quality in his rhetoric or his public speaking that marks him out from anyone else. The demon lay in his thinking. It was the poison in the ideology that sends people, without so much as a second thought, to their deaths. Hitler bragged in this speech that nobody could call him a coward. In fact he was. He never visited a concentration camp. He let others do the vicious work. He knew that his words carried authority. Rhetoric was never more dangerous, and in the 5,000 speeches he gave, Hitler spoke himself into eternal infamy.

FIDEL CASTRO

History Will Absolve Me

Santiago, Cuba
16 October 1953

Fidel Alejandro Castro Ruz (1926–2017) was an example of how easily glamour can attract supporters and how readily it can go wrong. He was the attractive nationalist-cum-Marxist who overthrew a dreadful, illegitimate military government and who then nearly colluded in blowing up the world. He was the man who taught a whole nation to read but controlled too much of their curriculum. He is a one-man lesson in the cycle of the revolution.

Castro was born to a Spanish soldier who settled in Cuba, where he became a sugar-cane farmer on his own plantation. Fidel was educated at expensive schools run by the Jesuits and then enrolled as a law student at the University of Havana. Already his flair for dramatic gestures was clear, and he became a big figure in the political gangsterism running student politics in Cuba at that time. He was arrested several times and was suspected of killing one of his rivals. Already disposed by temperament to radical solutions, Castro began to search in the writings of Marx for a solution to Cuba's problems.

That path was confirmed when, in March 1952, many of Castro's comrades were murdered in General Fulgencio Batista's military coup. With his younger brother Raúl, Castro formed an underground military training unit, and in July 1953 he led his first attempted rising against Batista, the assault on a federal garrison at Moncada, Santiago. The rebels were forced to retreat and many of them were executed. The Castro brothers, though, were imprisoned. Batista made the mistake of turning the subsequent trial into a media spectacle that gave Fidel Castro his chance to attack the regime. Like Nelson Mandela before him, in this one respect at least Castro's greatest moment came in court, as the first accused. The speech that follows is a title Mandela could have used: 'History Will Absolve Me'. Whether or not history would, Batista did not. Castro was sentenced to fifteen years in prison. The speech we have now, which Castro reconstructed from memory after the event, became the point at which the Cuban Revolution was said to have begun. Castro had the text smuggled out of his cell in matchboxes. A lot of matchboxes, presumably.

Released after two years, Castro fled to Mexico, where he met an Argentinian doctor called Ernesto Guevara, known as Che. Together they formed the 26th of July Movement, named after the date of the assault on the Moncada Barracks. Just after midnight on 25 November 1956 Castro led his crew of eighty-two revolutionaries in their leaky wooden motor yacht, the *Granma*, down the Tuxpan River in the Gulf of Mexico, bound for Cuba, where they intended to overthrow the regime. Armed with no more than ninety rifles, two anti-tank guns, three machine guns and forty pistols, they stood in the darkness and sang the Cuban national anthem: 'To die for the motherland is to live'.

In the event, the coup was a fiasco so bad it was almost comical. The Mexicans told the Cuban embassy that Castro was coming. The *Granma* was horribly overcrowded and the revolutionaries felt seasick. The expedition was meant to take five days, but by the time it had taken seven they were almost out of food and water. They had also managed to miss an abortive uprising by their supporters in Cuba. When the *Granma* did come within sight of Cuba it ran aground far from the shore and the saviours of their nation had to leave most of their equipment in the boat and wade in to safety. Guevara described it as a shipwreck rather than a landing. The mission lost lots of men and the twelve surviving rebels were forced to take refuge in the Sierra Maestra mountains where a long armed guerrilla campaign began.

Slowly, with the help of the rural poor who gained little under Batista's corrupt regime, Castro took over large tracts of Cuba. He lived in the mountains for more than twenty months, issuing manifestos that called for free elections and justice. By 1958 he was ready to launch an attack on the major towns which caused Batista to flee. In January 1959 Fidel Castro marched into Havana to a hero's reception and took up residence in the Hilton Hotel garlanded with high expectations. He was thirty-two years of age.

Trouble with the United States, hatred of which was the pivot of Castro's politics, was inevitable. In January 1961, the United States severed diplomatic relations in response to the Cuban nationalisation of US-owned sugar plantations, banks and businesses. On 17 April 1961, 1,500 Cuban exiles armed by the CIA invaded near the Bay of Pigs. The mission met with none of the expected support in Cuba, and Castro won the battle within three days. Fearful of his hostile neighbour across the water, Castro then signed a deal with the Soviet leader Nikita Khrushchev to place nuclear missiles in Cuba. When American spies saw the missiles, President Kennedy threatened to attack the Soviet Union if they were not removed. After thirteen days in which the world teetered on the edge of nuclear conflict, the Russians backed down.

In Cuba itself, literacy and health care improved under Castro but at the cost of personal liberty. As the economy faltered during the 1980s there were severe jobs and housing shortages and a steady drift of disillusioned Cubans took the dangerous journey across the Gulf of Mexico in search of Florida. The Cuban economy suffered a further blow when the collapse of the Soviet Union deprived it of its $6 billion annual subsidy and the capacity to export sugar in exchange for oil. With his factories and agriculture in serious trouble, Castro imposed strict food rationing and made limited reforms to private enterprise, in particular to encourage tourism. In 1999 he signed a deal with Hugo Chávez in Venezuela to send doctors in exchange for oil.

Over the years, the Americans devised a series of bizarre ways to take Castro's life, which included exploding cigars, booby-trapped sea shells, cyanide-laced milkshakes and a fungus-infected scuba-diving suit. He survived them all. After a long period of poor health, he stood down as president at the age of eighty-one in February 2008, leaving power, in a mockery of his fine democratic words, to his 76-year-old brother Raúl. Castro and Guevara became poster boys for adolescent revolutionaries everywhere, some of whom never grew up. Their committed anti-Americanism and conviction that American imperialism was the world's enemy informed everything they did. It is possible both to note the immorality of a great deal of American foreign policy in Latin America and to shudder at what became of the high ideals with which Castro and Guevara began. But the last laugh, if there were any laughs to be had, is on Castro and Guevara, who have both ended up as icons of the consumer culture that they both so ardently despised.

I am going to make only one request of this court; I trust it will be granted as a compensation for the many abuses and outrages the accused has had to tolerate without protection of the law. I ask that my right to express myself be respected without restraint. Otherwise, even the merest semblance of justice cannot be maintained, and the final episode of this trial would be, more than all the others, one of ignominy and cowardice. I must admit that I am somewhat disappointed. I had expected that the Honorable Prosecutor would come forward with a grave accusation. I thought he would be ready to justify to the limit his contention, and his reasons why I should be condemned in the name of Law and Justice – what law and what justice? – to twenty-six years in prison. But no. He has limited himself to reading Article 148 of the Social Defense Code. On the basis of this, plus aggravating circumstances, he requests that I be imprisoned for the lengthy term of twenty-six years! Two minutes seems a very short time in which to demand and justify that a man be put behind bars for more than a quarter of a century ... Honourable Judges: Why such interest in silencing me? Why is every type of argument forgone in order to avoid presenting any target whatsoever against which I might direct my own brief? Is it that they lack any legal, moral or political basis on which to put forth a serious formulation of the question? Are they that afraid of the truth? Do they hope that I, too, will speak for only two minutes and that I will not touch upon the points which have caused certain people sleepless nights since July 26th? ... Fundamental matters of principle are being debated here, the right of men to be free is on trial, the very foundations of our existence as a civilised and democratic nation are in the balance. When this trial is over, I do not want to have to reproach myself for any principle left undefended, for any truth left unsaid, for any

> *crime not denounced ... My purpose is not to bore the court with epic narratives. All that I have said is essential for a more precise understanding of what is yet to come.*

Castro was not a speaker who ever troubled himself too much with how long he spoke. This address, which he practised in his cell until dawn, lasted four hours and it was by no means the longest speech he ever gave. Once he took power there was virtually no stopping him. Castro asks if the court hoped he would speak for only two minutes. No, but two hours would probably have done. It is all but impossible to speak for four hours without longueurs and these edited extracts do not do justice to the feat of listening required to get through the whole thing. Castro is the Wagnerian among the speakers in this book, and Rossini's remark about Wagner comes to mind: he had some brilliant moments but some truly awful quarter-hours.

Before we even get to this point Castro has already treated the court to a lengthy wrangle about whether he had been well enough to testify (the authorities had pretended he was ill to stop him using the court as his theatre) and his reasonable complaints that he had been kept in solitary confinement, unable even to communicate with his son.

Castro says he does not want, when all has been said and done, to reproach himself for having left anything he might have said unsaid. There isn't much chance of that as he launches into an exposition on Cuban history to show that it is the generals who are the aberration rather than the revolutionaries. After this section, rather like Nelson Mandela in the same situation, he goes into great detail about the chronology of the struggle and its battles. The extenuating factor is that this is a court of law and he is conducting his own defence. Forensic rhetoric of this kind, which requires a thorough grounding in the facts, is bound to date.

But the strategy is clear here. Castro is going to claim constitutional propriety. All the political virtues of a democracy, transparency, true liberty and justice, are his and all are threatened, indeed mocked, by the terrible government under which Cuba has been suffering. He turns the trial into a public relations disaster for the Batista regime. With all the skill of the lawyer that he once was, Castro sets out an impressive command of Cuban constitutional history and places himself as the scion of that tradition. It is an important and characteristic manoeuvre. Castro is not best understood as a Marxist pure and simple. He is also a Cuban nationalist and a patriot. He would not have commanded the loyalty in Cuba that he did if all his political thought came from the arid textbooks of Marxism–Leninism. It was warmer, more appealing, more homely than that. His objective is, as he goes on to say, not abstract justice but 'Justice in Cuba'.

Why were we sure of the people's support? When we speak of the people we are not talking about those who live in comfort, the conservative elements of the nation, who welcome any repressive regime, any dictatorship, any despotism, prostrating themselves before the masters of the moment until they grind their foreheads into the ground. When we speak of struggle and we mention the people we mean the vast unredeemed masses, those to whom everyone makes promises and who are deceived by all; we mean the people who yearn for a better, more dignified and more just nation; who are moved by ancestral aspirations to justice, for they have suffered injustice and mockery generation after generation; those who long for great and wise changes in all aspects of their life ... In terms of struggle, when we talk about people we're talking about the six hundred thousand Cubans without work, who want to earn their daily bread honestly without having to emigrate from their homeland in search of a livelihood; the five hundred thousand farm labourers who live in miserable shacks, who work four months of the year and starve the rest, sharing their misery with their children, who don't have an inch of land to till and whose existence would move any heart not made of stone; the four hundred thousand industrial workers and labourers whose retirement funds have been embezzled, whose benefits are being taken away, whose homes are wretched quarters, whose salaries pass from the hands of the boss to those of the moneylender; whose future is a pay reduction and dismissal, whose life is endless work and whose only rest is the tomb ... These are the people, the ones who know misfortune and, therefore, are capable of fighting with limitless courage! To these people whose desperate roads through life have been paved with the bricks of betrayal and false promises, we were

> *not going to say: 'We will give you ...' but rather: 'Here it is, now fight for it with everything you have, so that liberty and happiness may be yours!'*

This section leads in to Castro's five revolutionary laws, the manifesto he would have proclaimed if the assault on the Moncada Barracks had been successful. The five laws are a return to the 1940 Constitution, protecting popular power, transfer of land ownership to tenant farmers, a 30 per cent profit share of all industrial enterprises given to employees, sugar planters given a right to a majority share of production, and the confiscation of all gains attributable to fraud during the previous regime. The proceeds recovered would have been spent on subsidising retirement funds for workers, hospitals, asylums and charitable organisations. In addition, quoting his nationalist hero José Martí, Castro pledged that Cuba would be a link of solidarity in Latin America.

This section is Castro's definition of the people, and it is interesting that 'the people' rather than 'class' is the category that he uses throughout. There is, no doubt, a stress on those who have done less than well under the Batista dispensation. But that was, first, a lot of people and, second, it is a routine tactic for a political leader to appeal to those who feel neglected. There is, though, no attempt to draw on an explicit concept of class. Castro was never really a Marxist believer in the way that his comrade Guevara was. Like most utopians, Guevara wasn't happy with people as they are. He wanted to create what he called *el hombre nuevo*, the new man, a selfless individual equipped for the beautiful world of cooperation that he alone had the vision to see. Castro was less easily persuaded by this sort of rubbish. He was instead a Cuban nationalist defined by a heavy belief that American capitalism was the bane of his country.

The reality of Cold War politics did require Castro to make a choice, though, and Cuba become woundingly reliant on the Soviet Union. But whenever he came to talk about the nature of his revolution his words were particular rather than universal. This passage is also a glimpse down the path not taken. In Chile, Uruguay and Brazil brutal dictatorships were overthrown for liberal democracies. It was the alternate path in Latin America to the populist charlatan of the Chávez type in Venezuela. There was a fork in the road here and, although Castro used this speech to imply that he favoured the democratic route, he did, in the fullness of time, take the road populated with fellow travellers.

A revolutionary government backed by the people and with the respect of the nation, after cleansing the different institutions of all venal and corrupt officials ... would solve the housing problem by cutting all rents in half, by providing tax exemptions on homes inhabited by the owners; by tripling taxes on rented homes; by tearing down hovels and replacing them with modern apartment buildings; and by financing housing all over the island on a scale heretofore unheard of, with the criterion that, just as each rural family should possess its own tract of land, each city family should own its own house or apartment. There is plenty of building material and more than enough manpower to make a decent home for every Cuban. But if we continue to wait for the golden calf, a thousand years will have gone by and the problem will remain the same. On the other hand, today possibilities of taking electricity to the most isolated areas on the island are greater than ever. The use of nuclear energy in this field is now a reality and will greatly reduce the cost of producing electricity. With these three projects and reforms, the problem of unemployment would automatically disappear and the task of improving public health and fighting against disease would become much less difficult. Finally, a revolutionary government would undertake the integral reform of the educational system, bringing it into line with the projects just mentioned with the idea of educating those generations which will have the privilege of living in a happier land ... The soul of education, however, is the teacher, and in Cuba the teaching profession is miserably underpaid. Despite this, no one is more dedicated than the Cuban teacher. Who among us has not learned his three Rs in the little public schoolhouse? It is time we stopped paying pittances to these young men and women who are entrusted with the sacred task of teaching our youth. No teacher should earn less than 200 pesos, no secondary teacher should make less than 350 pesos, if they are to devote themselves exclusively to their high calling without suffering want ... Where will the money be found for all this? When there is an end to the embezzlement of

> *government funds, when public officials stop taking graft from the large companies that owe taxes to the State, when the enormous resources of the country are brought into full use, when we no longer buy tanks, bombers and guns for this country (which has no frontiers to defend and where these instruments of war, now being purchased, are used against the people), when there is more interest in educating the people than in killing them, there will be more than enough money.*

This is an epic exercise in willing the ends. Structurally, Castro is all over the place. He has done a summary of the case for Cuban justice after a long procedural section about the assault on the Barracks, to which he returns after this. In between two sections that really ought to go together, Castro lurches into great detail about policies he intends to enact which is itself sandwiched in between two separate accounts of the despotism that Cuban has been experiencing. This section on solutions is preceded by an account of Cuba's problems – the lack of suitable housing, the inflated price of rents, poor electricity coverage, education that extends to too few and a disgraceful health care system that allows children to be consumed by parasites as they walk to school. The morbid people of Cuba, says Castro, 'will have heard ten million speeches and will finally die of misery and deception' because the public hospitals only accept patients on the say-so of the powerful. Finally, he makes an implicit promise to bring jobs to Cuba when he laments that over a million people are without work.

Castro's policy manifesto is impressively detailed, though it is always a problem for a speechwriter to make policy commitments sound interesting. The details of schemes for improvement are not very easy to listen to. It is hard to be precise enough without numbers, and statistics usually slaughter interest in rhetoric. Yet in 1960, in a speech to the United Nations, Castro promised he would eliminate illiteracy in Cuba in a single year and he was almost as good as his word. A vast volunteer army reduced illiteracy from 23 per cent to 4 per cent. Unfortunately Castro had no real sense of how to pay the bills. The reforms to health and education were unaffordable in the context of a faltering economy. Despite having no credentials for the job, Guevara became finance minister and president of the National

Bank. With his usual flair, he liked to sign 'Che' on the currency, but his 'moral incentives' for workers caused a steep fall in productivity and a rise in absenteeism. The economic stand-off with America meant Cuba's export market was Russia and Eastern Europe, which, in time, proved to be a disaster. Castro asks himself a question on which the political Left has foundered too often: 'Where will the money be found for all this?' He doesn't really have an answer.

Let me tell you a story: Once upon a time there was a Republic. It had its Constitution, its laws, its freedoms, a President, a Congress and Courts of Law. Everyone could assemble, associate, speak and write with complete freedom. The people were not satisfied with the government officials at that time, but they had the power to elect new officials and only a few days remained before they would do so. Public opinion was respected and heeded and all problems of common interest were freely discussed. There were political parties, radio and television debates and forums and public meetings. The whole nation pulsated with enthusiasm. This people had suffered greatly and although it was unhappy, it longed to be happy and had a right to be happy. It had been deceived many times and it looked upon the past with real horror. This country innocently believed that such a past could not return; the people were proud of their love of freedom and they carried their heads high in the conviction that liberty would be respected as a sacred right. They felt confident that no one would dare commit the crime of violating their democratic institutions. They wanted a change for the better, aspired to progress; and they saw all this at hand. All their hope was in the future. Poor country! One morning the citizens woke up dismayed; under the cover of night, while the people slept, the ghosts of the past had conspired and has seized the citizenry by its hands, its feet, and its neck. That grip, those claws were familiar: those jaws, those death-dealing scythes, those boots. No; it was no nightmare; it was a sad and terrible reality: a man named Fulgencio Batista had just perpetrated the appalling crime that no one had expected … Cuba is suffering from a cruel and base despotism.

The contrivance of the fairy story comes as a welcome relief from the otherwise rather relentless rhetoric. It is a reminder that audiences cannot listen uninterrupted for long and they need the punctuation of a break or a story. Castro rarely breaks his flow, which makes this all the more notable. It is also a clever passage in the construction of the speech because it turns the main argument around. It is Batista who is the revolutionary, not him and his comrades. They are the patriots trying to restore legitimate constitutional government to Cuba.

Throughout the speech Castro has taken care to compile a chronicle of Cuban history so as to place himself within it and the generals outside of it. Batista has usurped the rightful place in the constitution and Castro is therefore a restorationist rather than a revolutionary. This is at least as much a speech about legal right and wrong as it is about political Right and Left.

Batista had come to power in a coup in 1952, and his government, which was dependent on dubious sponsorship from Washington and the favours of the local Mafia, was not popular. Under Batista, Cuba had become a haven for the rich, run by crime syndicates and awash with prostitution, gambling and drug trafficking. Batista claimed, absurdly, that his coup automatically cancelled the previous Cuban constitution and established a new legality which, retrospectively, made his coup legal. Castro had been one of the few who had attacked this from the start. He was in print denouncing the coup for its lack of legitimacy before anyone else. This speech would have been heard as a recapitulation of a reasonable view long held. Both in form and in content this is the most effective part of the address.

It is well known that in England during the seventeenth century two kings, Charles I and James II, were dethroned for despotism. These actions coincided with the birth of liberal political philosophy and provided the ideological base for a new social class, which was then struggling to break the bonds of feudalism. Against divine right autocracies, this new philosophy upheld the principle of the social contract and of the consent of the governed, and constituted the foundation of the English Revolution of 1688, the American Revolution of 1775 and the French Revolution of 1789. These great revolutionary events ushered in the liberation of the

Spanish colonies in the New World – the final link in that chain
being broken by Cuba. The new philosophy nurtured our own
political ideas and helped us to evolve our Constitutions, from the
Constitution of Guáimaro up to the Constitution of 1940 … The
right of insurrection against tyranny then underwent its final
consecration and became a fundamental tenet of political liberty.
As far back as 1649, John Milton wrote that political power lies
with the people, who can enthrone and dethrone kings and have the
duty of overthrowing tyrants. John Locke, in his essay on
government, maintained that when the natural rights of man are
violated, the people have the right and the duty to alter or abolish
the government. 'The only remedy against unauthorized force is
opposition to it by force.' Jean-Jacques Rousseau said with great
eloquence in his Social Contract: *'While a people sees itself forced*
to obey and obeys, it does well; but as soon as it can shake off the
yoke and shakes it off, it does better, recovering its liberty through
the use of the very right that has been taken away from it' …
Thomas Paine said that 'one just man deserves more respect than a
rogue with a crown' … The Declaration of Independence of the
Congress of Philadelphia, on July 4th, 1776, consecrated this right
in a beautiful paragraph which reads: 'We hold these truths to be
self-evident, that all men are created equal, that they are endowed
by their Creator with certain inalienable rights, that among these
are Life, Liberty and the Pursuit of Happiness' … The famous
French Declaration of the Rights of Man willed this principle to
the coming generations: 'When the government violates the rights
of the people, insurrection is for them the most sacred of rights and
the most imperative of duties.' 'When a person seizes sovereignty,
he should be condemned to death by free men.'

This is Castro's second long passage of intellectual history. He
has already invoked Montesquieu's distinction in *The Spirit of Laws*,
between the republican form of government in which the people are
sovereign and the despotic form where one man rules at will, the
Chinese tradition by which a king who governed 'rudely' should be
deposed in favour of a virtuous prince, the philosophers of ancient
India who upheld the principle of active resistance to arbitrary
authority on the grounds that 'a rope woven of many strands is strong

enough to hold a lion', the city-states of Greece and republican Rome, which meted out violent death to tyrants, Saint Thomas Aquinas's endorsement of the people overthrowing a tyrant, Martin Luther's argument that a people is released from the obligation to obey, and the same point emphasised by John Knox, George Buchanan and obscure German jurists of the seventeenth century.

It is an astonishing catalogue of allies to summon, and Castro is, as he said before, only just getting started. There follows here the main course. Castro's objective is to establish the deep constitutional roots of his case. He is explicitly not claiming himself as a revolutionary. He is claiming a kinship with an established tradition of thought that even extends to a fraternity with the founding fathers of the American constitution. For a man whose abiding hatred of America was, as Richard Nixon once said, 'incurable', this was quite a departure. Underpinning the long quotation of theorists from the Western tradition is the philosopher who Castro refers to throughout as 'the Apostle' and the 'Master': José Martí, the hero of Cuba's liberation from Spanish colonial power. Castro was familiar with the twenty-eight volumes of Martí's work and he thought of himself as more like Garibaldi than like Marx – the prophet with honour in his own country.

> *Still there is one argument more powerful than all the others. We are Cubans and to be Cuban implies a duty; not to fulfil that duty is a crime, is treason. We are proud of the history of our country; we learned it in school and have grown up hearing of freedom, justice and human rights ... We were taught to cherish and defend the beloved flag of the lone star, and to sing every afternoon the verses of our National Anthem: 'To live in chains is to live in disgrace and in opprobrium,' and 'to die for one's homeland is to live forever!' All this we learned and will never forget, even though today in our land there is murder and prison for the men who practise the ideas taught to them since the cradle. We were born in a free country that our parents bequeathed to us, and the Island will first sink into the sea before we consent to be the slaves of anyone ... I come to the close of my defence plea but I will not end it as lawyers usually do, asking that the accused be freed. I cannot ask freedom for myself while my comrades are already suffering*

*in the ignominious prison of the Isle of Pines ... The guilty
continue at liberty and with weapons in their hands – weapons
which continually threaten the lives of all citizens. If all the weight
of the law does not fall upon the guilty because of cowardice or
because of domination of the courts, and if then all the judges do
not resign, I pity your honour. And I regret the unprecedented
shame that will fall upon the Judicial Power. I know that
imprisonment will be harder for me than it has ever been for
anyone, filled with cowardly threats and hideous cruelty. But I do
not fear prison, as I do not fear the fury of the miserable tyrant
who took the lives of seventy of my comrades. Condemn me. It does
not matter. History will absolve me.*

This is defiant and rather magnificent. It is easy to see why
Castro commanded the Cuban people as he did. The reference to the
absolution of history at the end is not Marxist historicism. Castro does
not mean History with a capital H, he means the verdict of historians
and the judgement of time. The instant verdict of the judges was less
forgiving. Castro was sentenced to fifteen years in jail, although under
the terms of an amnesty he was to serve less than two years, which
were spent on the Isla de Pinos, south of the mainland.

Castro's testimony became a venerated script of the revolution,
but, for all the hopes vested in it, the historical verdict has to be that
the Cuban revolution went wrong. Castro had spoken of free elections, but in May 1961 he abolished multi-party elections. Hundreds
of Batista supporters were executed by firing squad after trials that
did not exceed in fairness the procedures Castro himself had criticised. Free media were suppressed. Priests and homosexuals were
jailed. The crumbling elegance of Havana in Castro's final years is a
metaphor for his regime, the decay of which can be measured
economically. After the collapse of the Soviet Union in 1991, the
Cuban economy shrank 40 per cent in two years. The power was off
for most of the day and night and basic provisions, such as bread,
were scarce. Cuban GDP today is the same as it was thirty years ago.

In the end, the allure of a nation can always be judged by the
net exporting of people. If nobody is clamouring to get in but the
ports are full of people trying to get out, then something is going
wrong. One of the only people taken into Castro's confidence during

the planning of the assault on the Moncada Barracks, the cause of this speech, was a supporter called Naty Revuelta. In the event that the attack succeeded it would have been Revuelta's job to broadcast the news over the radio. She did it anyway, seizing a radio station in Havana, playing *Eroica*, the symphony that Beethoven wrote for Napoleon, and then fleeing to avoid detection. Castro and Revuelta went on to have a daughter together, Alina, who was born in 1956. Alina Fernández Revuelta lived in Cuba until 1993, at which point, using false papers and disguised in a wig, she left for Spain and then Miami, where she too, like her mother, took a job in radio. Her show *Simplemente Alina* was a Wednesday afternoon discussion of Cuban politics. Her memoir, *Castro's Daughter*, was a distressing, critical account of the way that liberty in Cuba was inhibited, even for those inside Castro's court.

Castro's friend Gabriel García Márquez caught both sides of the revolutionary bargain: 'He is one of the great idealists of our times and perhaps this may be his greatest virtue, although it has also been his greatest danger.' It was, and the danger was not exclusive to Castro. By the end he had turned Cuba, in the words of his sister Juanita who defected to America, into 'an enormous prison surrounded by water'.

VÁCLAV HAVEL

A Contaminated Moral Environment

New Year's Address, Prague
1 January 1990

Václav Havel (1936–2011) was the tenth president of Czechoslovakia and the first president of the Czech Republic. He was the man who gave voice to a people emancipated from the moral slavery of communism. Havel was that rare creature, a man of letters whose eloquence turned towards politics without disappearing into the ether. He could craft words of hope that were rooted in the soil. A dissident since the Prague Spring, Havel lived most of his adult life either in prison or under surveillance from the police. When, in the speech that follows, he rose to his full intellectual height, Havel knew of what he spoke. He was a philosopher and he was a king.

Havel was born in 1936 to a wealthy entrepreneurial and intellectual family and started his career in the theatre as a stagehand at Prague's Theatre ABC. His absurdist works *The Garden Party* and *The Memorandum* brought international acclaim. Havel's participation in the Prague Spring led to him being blacklisted after the invasion of Czechoslovakia in 1968 and his plays were banned in his own country. This treatment radicalised him further and he helped found dissident initiatives such as Charter 77 and the Committee for the Defence of the Unjustly Prosecuted. He had several spells in prison, the longest between 1979 and 1983.

Communist rule in Czechoslovakia seemed impregnable right up until the moment it collapsed. The end when it came was astonishingly swift. The Communist Party, which had lost the will to go on, simply fell apart. Its leaders, Husák and party chief Miloš Jakeš, resigned in December 1989. Havel reluctantly agreed to stand for president as posters saying *Havel na Hrad* (Havel to the Castle) appeared in Prague. On 29 December he was installed as president by a unanimous vote of the Federal Assembly. In 1990 Czechoslovakia held its first free elections in forty-four years, which produced an overwhelming victory for Havel's Civic Forum and its Slovak counterpart Public Against Violence.

Havel did not especially enjoy politics. He kept his appointments on a scrap of folded paper and hated the pomposity of political life. But, as a citizen of the world, he proved to be a statesman of wisdom and subtlety. Havel dismantled the Warsaw Pact and expanded membership of NATO to the East, which in his memoir *To the Castle and Back* he counts as his most important accomplishment. He was feted and received the Presidential Medal of Freedom in the United States. But his reception abroad was not always repeated at home. His granting of a general amnesty to all those imprisoned under communism and his condemnation of the Czechoslovak treatment of Sudeten Germans after the Second World War were not popular. Havel resigned as president when the Slovaks issued a divorce decree in 1992. However, he did stand again in the new Czech Republic, and was re-elected president in January 1993 and then again in 1998 until his term ended in 2003.

Václav Havel died on 18 December 2011 at the age of seventy-five. The Czech prime minister declared three days of mourning and Havel was granted a state funeral at Saint Vitus Cathedral.

In 1982 Samuel Beckett dedicated a play to Havel, who was a political prisoner at the time, with the title of *Catastrophe*. Beckett's title is a reminder of the truth about Czechoslovakia, which is exactly what Havel dispenses in the speech that follows. It is his New Year's address, his first as the president of the newly free nation. He is live on television and radio. The context is the accumulated weight of dishonesty under which the people of Czechoslovakia had lived for four decades. Havel declines to bother with any of the usual parish notices or courtesies. He comes straight to the point – in his time, having lived his life, to vacillate would have been trivial. Havel had waited a long time to say what he says here and he had suffered a lot. Most of his life his country had been the victim of a catastrophe. Here he speaks at last, certain and unafraid.

My dear fellow citizens. For forty years you heard from my predecessors on this day different variations on the same theme: how our country was flourishing, how many million tons of steel we produced, how happy we all were, how we trusted our government, and what bright perspectives were unfolding in front of us. I assume you did not propose me for this office so that I, too, would lie to you. Our country is not flourishing. The enormous creative and spiritual potential of our nation is not being used sensibly. Entire branches of industry are producing goods that are of no interest to anyone, while we are lacking the things we need. A state which calls itself a workers' state humiliates and exploits workers. Our obsolete economy is wasting the little energy we have available. A country that once could be proud of the educational level of its citizens spends so little on education that it ranks today as seventy-second in the world. We have polluted the soil, rivers and forests bequeathed to us by our ancestors, and we have today the most contaminated environment in Europe. Adults in our country die earlier than in most other European countries.

After decades of double-speak and power politics and fictitious statistics, Václav Havel, at long last, stands up and tells the truth. There is no self-deprecation and no conventional flattery. It is unadorned, direct, and feels like a cleansing of the contaminated realm. It is so stark and so pellucid that no explanation feels necessary.

The history gives the words their resonance. The reference to forty years takes us back to February 1948, when the communists took power. Under Prime Minister Klement Gottwald, Czechoslovakia became a satellite state of the Soviet Union. Dissidents were purged, its economy centrally planned and private capital abolished. The communist hegemony was solidified under Antonín Novotný, who became president in 1957. In the 1950s the Stalinists arranged a series of show trials for any former communist leaders they accused of having an 'international' background, by which they meant Jews, Spanish Civil War veterans and anyone connected to the West. The 1960 rewriting of the constitution had declared the victory of social-ism and inaugurated the Czechoslovak Socialist Republic (CSSR). But the economy began to stagnate in the early 1960s, which led the

Communist Party to approve rudimentary free market disciplines in their 'New Economic Model'. The reform continued when Alexander Dubček became first secretary of the party in January 1968. Censorship was lifted and anti-Soviet polemics started to appear in the press in the spring of 1968. The Social Democrats began to form as a separate party. The seeds of plural politics were sprouting.

This was meant to be, in Dubček's famous phrase, 'socialism with a human face', but the idea of religious and political pluralism was too much for the Warsaw Pact countries. On the night of 20 21 August 1968, the Soviets invaded Czechoslovakia. The peace that Dubček negotiated produced the Brezhnev Doctrine, which ensured strict control of the media and the suppression of the Social Democratic Party. Dubček was removed from his post, political liberty repressed, the economy controlled and ideological uniformity enforced. With that gift for sinister language that was the preserve of the totalitarian regimes (one of the many ways in which we can describe them as Orwellian or perhaps Kafkacsque), this was labelled as a period of 'normalisation'.

There was no one more sensitive than Havel to the corruption of language that we see in all totalitarian regimes. His first full-length play, *The Garden Party*, was a parody of the meaningless clichés of communism. His next play, *Memorandum*, introduced a language invented, like Newspeak, to eliminate all ambiguity. In his collection of essays *The Power of the Powerless*, Havel described a society in which citizens were forced to 'live within a lie'. It is possible for the whole history of a country to be a tissue of lies, and this was the offence against truth that Havel was rebelling against when he stood up to speak: the clownish incompetence, the ubiquitous corruption. In a single, direct paragraph of searing honesty, in his first act as president, Havel told the truth about power.

Allow me a small personal observation. When I flew recently to Bratislava, I found some time during discussions to look out of the plane window. I saw the industrial complex of Slovnaft chemical factory and the giant Petr'alka housing estate right behind it. The view was enough for me to understand that for decades our statesmen and political leaders did not look or did not want to look out of the windows of their planes. No study of statistics available to me would enable me to understand faster and better the situation in which we find ourselves. But all this is still not the main problem. The worst thing is that we live in a contaminated moral environment. We fell morally ill because we became used to saying something different from what we thought. We learned not to believe in anything, to ignore one another, to care only about ourselves. Concepts such as love, friendship, compassion, humility or forgiveness lost their depth and dimension, and for many of us they represented only psychological peculiarities, or they resembled gone-astray greetings from ancient times, a little ridiculous in the era of computers and spaceships. Only a few of us were able to cry out loudly that the powers that be should not be all-powerful and that the special farms, which produced ecologically pure and top-quality food just for them, should send their produce to schools, children's homes and hospitals if our agriculture was unable to offer them to all.

The first casualty of the war on truth is morality. The statistics that Havel declares unnecessary would never have been accurate anyway. A factotum from the bureaucracy would always have been on hand to supply the desired number, which was always preferable to the real one. That is why looking out of the window of the plane would have told the leaders of Czechoslovakia something that was not in their dossiers. In that split second before their brain re-engaged and reinstated the ideological lie, their eyes could not deceive them. The visual imagery is effective here. We can see the unduly privileged *nomenklatura* enjoying the hospitality in their specially commissioned aircraft and we can see the brutal reality of the prison-like chemical factory and the brutalist housing estate from which they turn their gaze. What Havel is saying here, with great subtlety, in a single material image, is that if they had looked they would have *known.* He had only to look out of the window and the truth stared back at him.

But the conditions that allow men to keep their eyes fixed on falsehood leads him to the finest phrase in the speech: 'The worst thing is that we live in a contaminated moral environment.' This is as beautifully rendered an account of how human relationships are corrupted as Havel's compatriot Milan Kundera documented in his magnificent series of novels about Czechoslovakia, written from the safety of France. When there is no truth-telling there can be no effective moral life.

> *The previous regime – armed with its arrogant and intolerant ideology – reduced man to a force of production, and nature to a tool of production. In this it attacked both their very substance and their mutual relationship. It reduced gifted and autonomous people, skilfully working in their own country, to the nuts and bolts of some monstrously huge, noisy and stinking machine, whose real meaning was not clear to anyone. It could not do more than slowly but inexorably wear out itself and all its nuts and bolts. When I talk about the contaminated moral atmosphere, I am not talking just about the gentlemen who eat organic vegetables and do not look out of the plane windows. I am talking about all of us. We had all become used to the totalitarian system and accepted it as an unchangeable fact and thus helped to perpetuate it. In other words, we are all – though naturally to differing extents – responsible for the operation of the totalitarian machinery. None of us is just its victim. We are all also its co-creators. Why do I say this? It would be very unreasonable to understand the sad legacy of the last forty years as something alien, which some distant relative bequeathed to us. On the contrary. We have to accept this legacy as a sin we committed against ourselves. If we accept it as such we will understand that it is up to us all and up to us alone to do something about it. We cannot blame the previous rulers for everything, not only because it would be untrue, but also because it would blunt the duty that each of us faces today: namely, the obligation to act independently, freely, reasonably and quickly. Let us not be mistaken: the best government in the world, the best parliament and the best president, cannot achieve much on their own. And it would be wrong to expect a general remedy from them alone. Freedom and democracy include participation and therefore responsibility from us all. If we realise this, then all the horrors that the new Czechoslovak democracy inherited will cease to appear so terrible. If we realise this, hope will return to our hearts.*

This is a brave message to give to a newly free people. Havel uses the metaphor of the communist ideology as a machine that reduces individuals to cogs. But, daringly, he chooses not to develop that idea. It would have been safe to continue the critique of the Soviet years. Nobody would have contradicted him. Instead, he risks the charge that the guilt must attach to everyone. This passage is a counterpart to Kennedy's famous Inaugural which asked the American people not what he could do for them but what they could do for their country. It is a stark message: take responsibility. Do not allow yourself to be browbeaten into the belief that it was all the fault of the regime. The first step towards recovery is for the citizen body to take responsibility for some part of the past as a prelude to taking responsibility for the future.

The message was received as a painful truth, but it was by no means universally popular. Havel's own moral standing on this question gives him the moral authority to make the point. He had been involved in the first organised opposition to the regime under the auspices of Charter 77, a manifesto for freedom signed by artists and former public officials and published in West German newspapers on 6 January 1977. The Charter was critical of the communist government for its record on human rights. Signatories were arrested and interrogated and many dismissed from their employment. One of the three founding spokesmen of Charter 77, Jan Patocka, a philosophy professor, died during a gruelling eleven-hour interrogation. Havel spent five months behind bars in 1977, with a further three months in 1978.

Yet it is still a risky thing to say, and Havel is courageous to say it. It was an idea he had been harbouring for a long time. In 1975 he had written to the communist leader Gustáv Husák, saying the order that the authorities believed to be their great achievement was 'a musty inertia ... like the morgue or a grave'. The country, he thought, was rotting inside: 'It is the worst in us which is being systematically activated and enlarged – egotism, hypocrisy, indifference, cowardice, fear, resignation, and the desire to escape every personal responsibility.' Here, nobody escapes his attribution of responsibility.

*In the effort to rectify matters of common concern, we have
something to lean on. The recent period — and in particular the last
six weeks of our peaceful revolution — has shown the enormous
human, moral and spiritual potential, and the civic culture that
slumbered in our society under the enforced mask of apathy.
Whenever someone categorically claimed that we were this or that,
I always objected that society is a very mysterious creature and that
it is unwise to trust only the face it presents to you. I am happy that
I was not mistaken. Everywhere in the world people wonder where
those meek, humiliated, sceptical and seemingly cynical citizens of
Czechoslovakia found the marvellous strength to shake the
totalitarian yoke from their shoulders in several weeks, and in a
decent and peaceful way. And let us ask: where did the young
people who never knew another system get their desire for truth,
their love of free thought, their political ideas, their civic courage
and civic prudence? How did it happen that their parents — the very
generation that had been considered lost — joined them? How is it
that so many people immediately knew what to do and none needed
any advice or instruction? I think there are two main reasons for
the hopeful face of our present situation. First of all, people are
never just a product of the external world; they are also able to
relate themselves to something superior, however systematically the
external world tries to kill that ability in them. Secondly, the
humanistic and democratic traditions, about which there had been
so much idle talk, did after all slumber in the unconsciousness of
our nations and ethnic minorities, and were inconspicuously passed
from one generation to another, so that each of us could discover
them at the right time and transform them into deeds.*

Having charged the citizens of Czechoslovakia with complicity
in their fate, Havel compliments them, almost in contradiction, with
having the strength of purpose to rebel. This speech is a bit like
Philip Larkin's description of the English novel: it has a beginning,
a muddle and an end. Havel is not really clear about where the resistance has come from. This passage purports to excavate the sources of
the resistance to the oppressor but those sources never really come
into focus. The two reasons he gives for the survival of the urge
towards freedom are really one. The first is that an oppressed people

can retain the capacity to imagine a moral entity larger than themselves, even though the authorities try to kill it off. The second is that a democratic tradition has somehow survived the time of unfreedom in Czechoslovakia. But this tradition contains the moral capacity that was his first point; they are the same thing. It is also unclear how a tradition can really be passed down if nobody was articulating it or practising it. If the people really were as compliant and as complicit in the Soviet rule as he has just said they were, then they could hardly have been simultaneously harbouring the democratic tradition. The tip-off here is the word *unconsciousness*. Havel implies that the knowledge was hidden somewhere in the collective psyche; people both knew and did not know. Back in 1979 Havel had written of the process of rebelling: 'We never decided to become dissidents. We have been transformed into them, without quite knowing how.'

We had to pay, however, for our present freedom. Many citizens perished in jails in the 1950s, many were executed, thousands of human lives were destroyed, hundreds of thousands of talented people were forced to leave the country. Those who defended the honour of our nations during the Second World War, those who rebelled against totalitarian rule and those who simply managed to remain themselves and think freely, were all persecuted. We should not forget any of those who paid for our present freedom in one way or another. Independent courts should impartially consider the possible guilt of those who were responsible for the persecutions, so that the truth about our recent past might be fully revealed. We must also bear in mind that other nations have paid even more dearly for their present freedom, and that indirectly they have also paid for ours. The rivers of blood that have flowed in Hungary, Poland, Germany and recently in such a horrific manner in Romania, as well as the sea of blood shed by the nations of the Soviet Union, must not be forgotten. First of all because all human suffering concerns every other human being. But more than this, they must also not be forgotten because it is these great sacrifices that form the tragic background of today's freedom or the gradual emancipation of the nations of the Soviet Bloc, and thus the background of our own newfound freedom. Without the changes in the Soviet Union, Poland, Hungary, and the German Democratic

Republic, what has happened in our country would have scarcely happened. And if it did, it certainly would not have followed such a peaceful course … Let us not allow the sympathies of the world, which we have won so fast, to be equally rapidly lost through our becoming entangled in the jungle of skirmishes for power. Let us not allow the desire to serve oneself to bloom once again under the stately garb of the desire to serve the common good. It is not really important now which party, club or group prevails in the elections. The important thing is that the winners will be the best of us, in the moral, civic, political and professional sense, regardless of their political affiliations … In our country there are many prisoners who, though they may have committed serious crimes and have been punished for them, have had to submit – despite the good will of some investigators, judges and above all defence lawyers – to a debased judiciary process that curtailed their rights. They now have to live in prisons that do not strive to awaken the better qualities contained in every person, but rather humiliate them and destroy them physically and mentally. In a view of this fact, I have decided to declare a relatively extensive amnesty. At the same time I call on the prisoners to understand that forty years of unjust investigations, trials and imprisonments cannot be put right overnight, and to understand that the changes that are being speedily prepared still require time to implement. By rebelling, the prisoners would help neither society nor themselves. I also call on the public not to fear the prisoners once they are released, not to make their lives difficult, to help them, in the Christian spirit, after their return among us to find within themselves that which jails could not find in them: the capacity to repent and the desire to live a respectable life.

This is an important passage in which Havel sets out his hopes that the Velvet Revolution will not go awry. He approaches this in two ways. The first is to locate the revolution in Czechoslovakia in the context of a regional collapse of the idea of communism. By raising the stakes and making this a struggle of liberty versus tyranny, Havel is gathering moral authority to his side.

Havel also sets up his second stratagem, which is to signal a desire for clemency and forgiveness, a vital sentiment in the tumult of a change in regime. The generosity of these words conceals how controversial they were. It is one thing to ask people to forgive and another for them to do so. When Havel was as good as his word, when he enacted a general amnesty for some of the most serious criminals, when he apologised on behalf of Czechoslovakia for the expulsion of the Sudeten Germans after the Second World War and when he resisted the demands for a more draconian purge of secret police collaborators, he ran into strong opposition. Havel felt that the court verdicts of the previous regime could not always be trusted. He did not believe that most of those in prison had received a fair trial. He was probably right about that, but the most finely constructed words cannot brush off a troublesome reality. When the crime rate tripled in the four years after the Velvet Revolution, Havel faced the consequences of this first speech. Crony capitalism soon came to Czechoslovakia and, against Havel's wishes, Czechoslovakia split into the Czech Republic and Slovakia in 1993.

In conclusion, I would like to say that I want to be a president who will speak less and work more. To be a president who will not only look out of the windows of his airplane but who, first and foremost, will always be present among his fellow citizens and listen to them well. You may ask what kind of republic I dream of. Let me reply: I dream of a republic independent, free, and democratic, of a republic economically prosperous and yet socially just; in short, of a humane republic that serves the individual and that therefore holds the hope that the individual will serve it in turn. Of a republic of well-rounded people, because without such people it is impossible to solve any of our problems — human, economic, ecological, social, or political. The most distinguished of my predecessors opened his first speech with a quotation from the great Czech educator Komensk. Allow me to conclude my first speech with my own paraphrase of the same statement: People, your government has returned to you!

Havel was always keen to speak less. Though he was a fine writer, of speeches as well as of plays and essays, he was not a natural orator. His voice worked at too low a pitch and he had a recognisable but not especially attractive habit of rolling the r. He also took a while to come to terms with the demands of speech-making, particularly for television. For a playwright he had a strangely rarefied sense of theatre. His revolutionary speeches had been mostly extempore or given from scanty notes. All at once he had to read his speeches from a text, as neither the Czechoslovakian television company nor the office of the president owned a teleprompter, a device that Havel in any case regarded as a trick. He also found the necessary discipline of political speech limiting and frustrating. A political speech needs to repeat and emphasise. Points need to be hammered in, but he thought repetition was poor writing. He was also, as a writer, fond of irony and understatement, and these are lesser currencies in rhetoric.

The task for this speech was to inspire by telling the truth, so Havel was persuaded to harden his language. In an early draft he suggested ending the speech by saying simply 'goodbye'. He was persuaded that goodbye would not do and so chose a phrase that is famous in Czech national mythology and which is ascribed to the seventeenth-century Czech educator Jan Amos Komenský: 'People, your government has returned to you!' And it had.

Havel faced difficulties in office, but they stayed within the usual political frame. His great contribution was to oversee a peaceful end to the fantasy that had begun with utopia and ended in slavery. It had seemed, to cite the title of one of Havel's volumes of non-fiction, to be *The Art of the Impossible*. It proved to be gloriously possible, and some measure of the joy to be taken from the Velvet Revolution is found in the fact that one of the new president's first acts in office was to invite Frank Zappa to play a victory concert in Prague.

Havel had a simple, almost wilfully naive, motto that stands as a summary of his political career and of this, his first and best speech: 'Truth and love must prevail over lies and hate'. As Milan Kundera said, 'Havel's most important work is his own life.' Many more citizens can afford to fly into Prague these days and eat organic vegetables and look out of the window at a modern city as they arrive. When they touch down they will enter the Czech Republic through Václav Havel Airport.

ELIE WIESEL

The Perils of Indifference

The White House, Washington DC

12 April 1999

Eliezer Wiesel (1928–2016) was born into the close-knit Yiddish-speaking Jewish community in Sighet, a small town in the Carpathian Mountains in Hungary, the third child of Shlomo Wiesel and Sarah Feig. Before Elie there had been Hilda and Bea, his elder sisters. After him came a third sister, Tzipora. The young Elie was deeply studious and intensely religious. He loved the mystical tradition of the Hasidic sect of Judaism to which his mother's family belonged.

Sighet was insulated from the worst of the Second World War until 1944. Then the devil appeared in the form of German soldiers. The Sighet Jews were crammed into cattle cars and deported to concentration camps in Poland. When the Wiesel family arrived in Auschwitz, men were told to step to the left and women to the right. Wiesel went one way with his father; his mother and sisters went the other way. He recalled that as they walked away his mother was stroking the seven-year-old Tzipora's hair. He never saw them again. Hilda and Bea survived Auschwitz, though Wiesel would not discover this until years later.

Wiesel survived, as he says, in his memoir *Night*, by chance. He and his father were selected for slave labour by a monocled Dr Joseph Mengele 'with a wave of a bandleader's baton'. After moving from camp to camp either on unshod feet in the driving snow or in open cattle cars, Wiesel and his father ended up in a rubber factory. They were worked to the point of death, starved and beaten. As the Russian army drew close, Shlomo and Elie were moved to Buchenwald. Though neither of them knew it, when Shlomo Wiesel succumbed to dysentery, starvation, exhaustion and exposure, salvation was close at hand. In *Night* Wiesel describes witnessing his father's death. It is one of the most harrowing passages in all literature. The whole book is hard to read, but it must be read.

On 12 April 1945, American soldiers liberated the camp at Buchenwald. Wiesel was put on a train of 400 orphans that found its way to France, and he was assigned to a home in Normandy under the care of a Jewish organisation. There he mastered French by reading the classics, and in 1948 he enrolled in the Sorbonne. He became a journalist and wrote for French and Israeli newspapers. For ten years he said nothing of what had happened to him and his family. Then at the prompting of the French Nobel laureate François Mauriac, Wiesel started writing about his experience. The result was a 900-page manuscript, in Yiddish, called *Un die welt hot geshvign* (*And the World Kept Silent*). This version was published in Buenos Aires, but Wiesel struggled to find a publisher elsewhere. Finally, in a much-winnowed version, his memoir was published under the title of *Night*.

In 1956, Wiesel moved to New York, where he started to speak both about, and sometimes for, those who had survived the Holocaust. He wrote plays, novels, essays and short stories. He also became a prominent public advocate for the oppressed peoples of the world, in the Soviet Union, South Africa, Vietnam, Biafra and Bangladesh. In 1978 President Carter appointed him the chairman of the United States Holocaust Memorial Council. In 1985 he was awarded the Congressional Gold Medal and in 1986 the Nobel Prize for Peace. In 1992 Wiesel was presented with the Presidential Medal of Honor, the highest civilian award in America. Wiesel's words are engraved on the Holocaust Memorial in Washington DC: 'For the dead and the living, we must bear witness'. It is the terrible cause to which he had to dedicate his life. He died at home in Manhattan in 2016 at the age of eighty-seven.

The speech that follows was given in the East Room of the White House in April 1999 as part of the Millennium Lecture series hosted by President Clinton and First Lady Hillary Clinton. Between the issuing of the invitation to Wiesel and the day of the speech, the United States was part of the intervention in Kosovo in response to the attempted ethnic cleansing of Kosovan Albanians. On the same day that Wiesel was speaking there was an extraordinary meeting of the North Atlantic Council at NATO to agree war aims.

Not long before the invitation to the White House, Elie Wiesel had returned home to Sighet for the first time since the day he was put on the train out. In 1944, just before he was forced to leave, Wiesel had gone into his back yard and buried the watch he had received as a present for his bar mitzvah. In 1997, half a century later, he went home to look for it. He had imagined going home in his novel *La Ville de la Chance* (translated as *The Town beyond the Wall*), but until then he had never done so. Recreating his childlike paces in the yard, he searched for the exact spot he had buried the watch. He dug into the ground with his fingernails and, marvellously, the watch was still there. It was the only thing that was. Family, the friends, the village life, it had all gone. A great deal of time had passed, but whether the times had changed was a different question.

> *Fifty-four years ago to the day, a young Jewish boy from a small town in the Carpathian Mountains woke up, not far from Goethe's beloved Weimar, in a place of eternal infamy called Buchenwald. He was finally free, but there was no joy in his heart. He thought there never would be again. Liberated a day earlier by American soldiers, he remembers their rage at what they saw. And even if he lives to be a very old man, he will always be grateful to them for that rage, and also for their compassion. Though he did not understand their language, their eyes told him what he needed to know — that they, too, would remember, and bear witness ...*

There is so much said in this one opening sentence. The reference to Goethe tells us that culture is no defence when an infection gets into the political bloodstream. Weimar is the republic and the political constitution that fell to the Nazis, as well as the culture that decayed and led to a place of eternal infamy. The fifty-fourth anniversary is not significant particularly and yet there is something deeply touching in this speech taking place on the same day as the liberation. An anniversary is a moment to remember, and there is great poignancy in Wiesel's voice as he says, after a pause, the words 'to the day'. The effect, hard to explain but clear at once on hearing, is to take us back to that day.

The contrast between the delivery and the content is very marked here. Wiesel speaks softly, and his style of argument is forgiving and gentle, but he is reporting rage. The tight compression of this paragraph is possible because the events that Wiesel is relating are well known to the invited dignitaries in the audience. All of them knew his story and everyone understands exactly what was being said. Everyone knows why rage was the appropriate emotion and why the young boy was grateful for the rage of the United States Third Army. Later in the speech Wiesel registers his gratitude to the American nation for its help. Finally, in this condensed opening paragraph Wiesel describes the purpose he gave to his life, which was to bear witness to the terrible events he had been forced to endure. In 1986, in the speech Wiesel gave to accept the Nobel Peace Prize, he recalled asking his father how the world could have remained silent. He then imagined his younger self asking the grown man on the stage: 'Tell me: What have you done with my future? What have you done with your life?' The older Elie replies to the younger: 'I have tried to keep memory alive ... I have tried to fight those who would forget.'

We are on the threshold of a new century, a new millennium. What will the legacy of this vanishing century be? How will it be remembered in the new millennium? Surely it will be judged, and judged severely, in both moral and metaphysical terms. These failures have cast a dark shadow over humanity: two World Wars, countless civil wars, the senseless chain of assassinations – Gandhi, the Kennedys, Martin Luther King, Sadat, Rabin – bloodbaths in Cambodia and Nigeria, India and Pakistan, Ireland and Rwanda, Eritrea and Ethiopia, Sarajevo and Kosovo; the inhumanity in the gulag and the tragedy of Hiroshima. And, on a different level, of course, Auschwitz and Treblinka. So much violence, so much indifference. What is indifference? Etymologically, the word means 'no difference'. A strange and unnatural state in which the lines blur between light and darkness, dusk and dawn, crime and punishment, cruelty and compassion, good and evil. What are its courses and inescapable consequences? Is it a philosophy? Is there a philosophy of indifference conceivable? Can one possibly view indifference as a virtue? Is it necessary at times to practice it simply to keep one's sanity, live normally, enjoy a fine meal and a glass of wine, as the world around us experiences harrowing upheavals? Of course, indifference can be tempting – more than that, seductive. It is so much easier to look away from victims. It is so much easier to avoid such rude interruptions to our work, our dreams, our hopes. It is, after all, awkward, troublesome, to be involved in another person's pain and despair. Yet, for the person who is indifferent, his or her neighbour are of no consequence. And, therefore, their lives are meaningless. Their hidden or even visible anguish is of no interest. Indifference reduces the other to an abstraction.

The title idea of this speech is indifference, a word that appears nineteen times and on which the whole argument pivots. Successive passages deepen the single idea. With one exception, to which we shall come, Wiesel's instances of indifference are cases in which bystanders could have acted but chose not to do so. The indifference of the crowd is the ally of the tyrant who is then permitted to define hated groups – the mentally ill, the infirm, gypsies, homosexuals, Jews – as beneath human dignity. The failure to respect individual dignity is central to the crime committed. The word 'indignation' stresses its origins in the agency of the individual. This is what Wiesel is saying happened in the camps. It is notable that, throughout the speech, he uses the word *human* as an antonym for *indifference*. To be indifferent to the fate of another is therefore to strip them of their humanity. The appalling treatment in the camps is the first humiliation. The indifference of the world is the second.

Though Wiesel is careful to say that Auschwitz and Treblinka are on a different level, his catalogue of contemporary conflicts shows that he thinks indifference is a common human deficiency. The argument has an obvious implication because the actual antonym of indifference is not human. It is intervention. Someone should have intervened, as the Americans belatedly did by liberating Buchenwald. In other speeches and in his published writing Wiesel's hatred of war meant that he was not always a committed advocate for military intervention, but this speech is, in fact, a bold case for action, to stop abuse wherever it occurs. There is one pointed example in his list of conflicts. Rwanda was an instance of ethnic slaughter in which the United States might have chosen to intervene but did not do so. In the question-and-answer session that followed his lecture, Wiesel asked President Clinton directly: 'I know one thing. We could have prevented that massacre. Why didn't we?' There is an important lesson here for the world's conflicts today. Indifference that leads to inaction itself has consequences. Indifference always makes a difference to its victims.

Over there, behind the black gates of Auschwitz, the most tragic of all prisoners were the 'Muselmänner,' as they were called. Wrapped in their torn blankets, they would sit or lie on the ground, staring vacantly into space, unaware of who or where they were, strangers to their surroundings. They no longer felt pain, hunger, thirst. They feared nothing. They felt nothing. They were dead and did not know it. Rooted in our tradition, some of us felt that to be abandoned by humanity then was not the ultimate. We felt that to be abandoned by God was worse than to be punished by Him. Better an unjust God than an indifferent one. For us to be ignored by God was a harsher punishment than to be a victim of His anger. Man can live far from God – not outside God. God is wherever we are. Even in suffering? Even in suffering. In a way, to be indifferent to that suffering is what makes the human being inhuman. Indifference, after all, is more dangerous than anger and hatred. Anger can at times be creative. One writes a great poem, a great symphony, one does something special for the sake of humanity because one is angry at the injustice that one witnesses. But indifference is never creative. Even hatred at times may elicit a response. You fight it. You denounce it. You disarm it. Indifference elicits no response. Indifference is not a response. Indifference is not a beginning, it is an end. And, therefore, indifference is always the friend of the enemy, for it benefits the aggressor – never his victim, whose pain is magnified when he or she feels forgotten. The political prisoner in his cell, the hungry children, the homeless refugees – not to respond to their plight, not to relieve their solitude by offering them a spark of hope is to exile them from human memory. And in denying their humanity we betray our own. Indifference, then, is not only a sin, it is a punishment. And this is one of the most important lessons of this outgoing century's wide-ranging experiments in good and evil.

This is the one story of indifference in the speech that differs from the rest. The 'Muselmänner', the weakest people in the camp at Buchenwald, were not indifferent to the fate of others. They had been so sapped by their treatment that they grew indifferent to their own fate. They became, in effect, nothing, which is Wiesel's point in this section. Indifference does not bring the rage with which he began his speech. It brings emptiness and resignation. This is the weight of the title that Primo Levi gave to his memoir of his time in Auschwitz: *If This Is a Man*. Wiesel himself never submitted to indifference, although his time in the camp did lead him to become feral, which is perhaps the preceding state. In *Night* he described the way his very existence was contingent on his next meal: 'I was nothing but a body. Perhaps even less: a famished stomach. The stomach alone was measuring time.' So obsessed did he become with getting his plate of soup and his crust of bread that he watched helpless, unable to move, as guards beat his father with an iron bar.

The consolation of religion leads Wiesel into a tangle with his idea of indifference which, at times, stretches a little too far. Wiesel had gone into the concentration camps a deeply religious young man. His experience, understandably, jolted his faith severely. He describes the deepest pain of being abandoned by God as 'worse than to be punished by him'. At least a vengeful God cares and treats the sinner as a moral agent. But then Wiesel goes on to describe indifference as a punishment as well as a sin. This has some disturbing implications, the most obvious of which is to ask what it is meant to be a punishment for. What sins of the Wiesel family were being expiated? None, and he cannot really think the punishment merited. The passage thus shows the difficulty of bringing divine justice into a treatise on the inhumanity of men and of the power they wield at the head of brutal states. The real villains here are people charged with religious certainty who worshipped their own power.

In the place that I come from, society was composed of three simple categories: the killers, the victims, and the bystanders. During the darkest of times, inside the ghettoes and death camps ... we felt abandoned, forgotten. All of us did. And our only miserable consolation was that we believed that Auschwitz and Treblinka were closely guarded secrets; that the leaders of the free world did not know what was going on behind those black gates and barbed wire; that they had no knowledge of the war against the Jews that Hitler's armies and their accomplices waged as part of the war against the Allies. If they knew, we thought, surely those leaders would have moved heaven and earth to intervene. They would have spoken out with great outrage and conviction. They would have bombed the railways leading to Birkenau, just the railways, just once. And now we knew, we learned, we discovered that the Pentagon knew, the State Department knew. And the illustrious occupant of the White House then, who was a great leader – and I say it with some anguish and pain, because, today is exactly 54 years marking his death – Franklin Delano Roosevelt died on April the 12th, 1945, so he is very much present to me and to us. No doubt, he was a great leader. He mobilised the American people and the world, going into battle, bringing hundreds and thousands of valiant and brave soldiers in America to fight fascism, to fight dictatorship, to fight Hitler. And so many of the young people fell in battle. And, nevertheless, his image in Jewish history – I must say it – his image in Jewish history is flawed. The depressing tale of the St. Louis *is a case in point. Sixty years ago, its human cargo – maybe 1,000 Jews – was turned back to Nazi Germany. And that happened after the Kristallnacht, after the first state-sponsored pogrom, with hundreds of Jewish shops destroyed, synagogues burned, thousands of people put in concentration camps. And that ship, which was already on the shores of the United States, was sent back. I don't understand. Roosevelt was a good man, with a heart. He understood those who needed help. Why didn't he allow these refugees to disembark? A thousand people – in America, a great country, the greatest democracy, the most generous of all new nations in modern history. What happened? I don't understand. Why the indifference, on the highest level, to the suffering of the victims?*

Here Wiesel borrows categories taken from Raul Hilberg, who defined the scholarship of the Holocaust by classifying actors in the events as perpetrators, victims or bystanders. This is the moment at which the idea of indifference comes into the room in which Wiesel is speaking. Until now it has been a report of events so appalling that they seem distant and impossible. But no, Wiesel is saying, you and people like you were indifferent too. There is something plaintive and therefore harrowing about that final 'I don't understand'. It is stripped of anger and therefore redoubled in pain. The effect is clinched by the pause that Wiesel inserts just before he says it. The incomprehension comes from somewhere very deep, and the silence in the White House has an extraordinary quality to it at this point.

This is a brave passage. It is no small thing, to come to the president's residence, to speak to a select gathering of dignitaries, members of Congress and foreign ambassadors, and to be so candid about a former occupant of the office, especially one so distinguished as Franklin Delano Roosevelt. Wiesel speaks graciously and politely – that 'I must say it' is a gentle touch – but he does not spare anyone. Indifference went all the way to the top. Wiesel adds to the effect in the questions after the speech when he says: 'Can you imagine coming from where I come from and being here in the White House with the President of the United States, when some fifty-odd years ago I couldn't get a visa anywhere, and sixty years ago I belonged to those who were not even considered human beings. But here I am.' President Clinton added that the first Millennium Lecture, the series in which Wiesel was speaking, was given by the historian Bernard Bailyn, who argued that America is still shaped by the ideals of the Founding Fathers. 'They understood', said Clinton, 'that to be indifferent is to be numb.'

Wiesel clarified later, in answer to a question, that he does not believe in collective guilt. He says that he had been moved, on a trip to Germany, by the desire of young Germans to make amends for the crimes of their forefathers, but he is clear he wants to absolve them of blame. He cannot, though, offer the same dispensation to those who stood by at the time. The verdict of indifference is unsparing. This is a highly charged denunciation of the nation that took him in; softly delivered, apologetic and yet devastating.

> But then, there were human beings who were sensitive to our tragedy. Those non-Jews, those Christians, that we called the 'Righteous Gentiles,' whose selfless acts of heroism saved the honour of their faith. Why were they so few? Why was there a greater effort to save SS murderers after the war than to save their

victims during the war? Why did some of America's largest corporations continue to do business with Hitler's Germany until 1942? It has been suggested, and it was documented, that the Wehrmacht could not have conducted its invasion of France without oil obtained from American sources. How is one to explain their indifference? And yet, my friends, good things have also happened in this traumatic century: the defeat of Nazism, the collapse of communism, the rebirth of Israel on its ancestral soil, the demise of apartheid, Israel's peace treaty with Egypt, the peace accord in Ireland. And let us remember the meeting, filled with drama and emotion, between Rabin and Arafat that you, Mr. President, convened in this very place. I was here and I will never forget it. And then, of course, the joint decision of the United States and NATO to intervene in Kosovo and save those victims, those refugees, those who were uprooted by a man who I believe that because of his crimes, should be charged with crimes against humanity. But this time, the world was not silent. This time, we do respond. This time, we intervene.

Has there ever been a more affecting series of rhetorical questions? Could there be? Wiesel was renowned for asking more questions than he supplied answers for, but these questions are not designed to evade an answer. He asks if Americans should have responded differently to the Holocaust and offers no answer. The rhetorical question is a way of dressing a painful statement so as to reduce the offence. It is also a way of communicating the lack of comprehension at how it could have been allowed to happen. There was no answer; there is no answer. That is Wiesel's point. These are questions that are really slightly softened accusations.

Wiesel then changes the tone and the register of the speech rather abruptly. He passes from the specific instance of indifference to the fate of the Jews to a series of more optimistic encounters. The only words that mark the transition are a weak 'And yet ...' This is raising the most significant problem with the speech, which is that Wiesel is unclear as to whether a lesson has, or has not, been learned. The defeat of Nazism and the collapse of communism are events of great historical significance that should either have been ignored — the speech could merely have been about the plight of indifference

– or treated at greater length. Here they are touched *en passant* as if
they hardly matter. But the world has not been, as Wiesel's own list
shows, wholly indifferent to the plight of the suffering. The sense
that this is a manifesto for intervention, for what Kofi Annan was
later to describe as 'the responsibility to protect', is confirmed by
Wiesel's praise for the action in Kosovo. The audience is left a little
unsure about how pessimistic it is meant to feel about the prospect
for regular humanitarian aid. It is the question with which Wiesel
now ends.

> *Does it mean that we have learned from the past? Does it mean that
> society has changed? Has the human being become less indifferent
> and more human? Have we really learned from our experiences?
> Are we less insensitive to the plight of victims of ethnic cleansing
> and other forms of injustices in places near and far? Is today's
> justified intervention in Kosovo, led by you, Mr. President, a lasting
> warning that never again will the deportation, the terrorisation of
> children and their parents be allowed anywhere in the world? Will
> it discourage other dictators in other lands to do the same? What
> about the children? Oh, we see them on television, we read about
> them in the papers, and we do so with a broken heart. Their fate is
> always the most tragic, inevitably. When adults wage war, children
> perish. We see their faces, their eyes. Do we hear their pleas? Do we
> feel their pain, their agony? Every minute one of them dies of
> disease, violence, famine. Some of them – so many of them – could
> be saved. And so, once again, I think of the young Jewish boy from
> the Carpathian Mountains. He has accompanied the old man I
> have become throughout these years of quest and struggle. And
> together we walk towards the new millennium, carried by profound
> fear and extraordinary hope.*

The rhetorical technique of returning at the end to the image
from the beginning gives the speech an organic unity, and because
the young boy from the Carpathian Mountains has, against the odds,
grown to be an old man fifty-four years older, to the day, a moving
conclusion. It is always satisfying when a speech resolves like this,
just as it is with a melody in a minor key. The device of coupling the
Wiesel who is speaking as an old man with the young man who is still

with him is a clever way of saying that this terrible event will never go away. Later Wiesel would say that the scars could never truly heal – the nightmares, the perpetual insecurity, the inability to laugh deeply. 'What about the children?' he asks. One of the children was the seven-year-old Tzipora, to whom *Night* was dedicated.

At the end of the speech, the young boy and the old man join hands to walk towards the new millennium. The emotions they carry are a beautiful expression of what humane politics can do. The spectre of utopia is profound fear; its promise is extraordinary hope. The purpose of politics is to contain the fear so that the hope can thrive. Wiesel's resilience in coming to this conclusion is astonishing. In Buchenwald, the place of eternal infamy, he saw his father yield to dysentery and starvation and could not bear the burden of not being able to try to help him. 'I will never forgive myself,' he wrote. Yet the young boy tattooed indelibly as prisoner A-7713 never gave way to indifference. He found it within himself to hope, and the least we can do is remember.

There is no more affecting passage of rhetoric anywhere than this, from *Night*:

> *Never shall I forget that night, the first night in camp, which has turned my life into one long night, seven times cursed and seven times sealed. Never shall I forget that smoke. Never shall I forget the little faces of the children, whose bodies I saw turned into wreaths of smoke beneath a silent blue sky. Never shall I forget those flames which consumed my faith forever. Never shall I forget the nocturnal silence which deprived me, for all eternity, of the desire to live. Never shall I forget those moments which murdered my God and my soul and turned my dreams to dust. Never shall I forget these things, even if I am condemned to live as long as God himself. Never.*

LET A HUNDRED
FLOWERS BLOOM

No speech has a more forbidding title nor a darker irony in its most compelling phrase. In February 1957, the chairman of the Communist Party of China, Mao Zedong, proclaimed to the Supreme State Conference in Beijing a long disquisition 'On the Correct Handling of the Contradictions among the People'. The speech included a line of Chinese poetry by which it has since become known. 'Let a hundred flowers bloom' is nothing like as benign a phrase as it sounds. It means the opposite of what it says at face value. The licence it promised proved to be lethally counterfeit. 'Let a hundred flowers bloom, let a hundred schools of thought contend' sounds like the reign of free speech; in fact it was the prelude to a crackdown on dissent.

It is notable how often the tyrant borrows the language of democracy to win legitimacy. Liberal democracies permit many voices to be heard, and out of that cacophony improvement proceeds gradually, progressing by trial and error as mistakes are made and slowly rectified. The heroic figure of these societies is the rebel as imagined by Camus: thoughtful, critical, dissenting, reflective and engaged. In Beijing in 1957 Mao appeared to endorse all these attributes, and every word of it he then abused.

Mao had been persuaded by his premier, Zhou Enlai, to be seen to embrace criticism. The year before, Nikita Khrushchev, Stalin's successor, had denounced his predecessor's crimes. What looked like self-criticism was, in fact, the process by which the Soviet Union erased the past. This is the perennial pattern: crime, detection, denunciation, erasure. Mao appeared to be acknowledging fallibility and seeking the wisdom of critical voices. Perhaps, as he said the words, he even meant them. It is not definite that his speech was initially intended as a ruse, designed to flush out dissent. Certainly, Mao's text, taken literally, reads like authentic liberal licence: 'A period of trial is often needed to determine whether something is right or wrong … Often, correct and good things were first regarded not as fragrant flowers but as poisonous weeds.' So far this could be John Stuart Mill talking. Indeed, Mao more or less summarises Mill's view that the truth will emerge as the upshot of spontaneous, free exchange: 'It is only by employing the method of discussion, criticism and reasoning that we can really foster correct ideas and overcome wrong ones.'

There is, though, poison in the last of those flowers in the implication that Mao can arbitrate between 'correct ideas' and 'wrong ones'. The rest of the speech discloses the deceit. The year before Mao's Hundred Flowers speech, the Soviet Union had quelled the Hungarian uprising with brutal efficiency. Mao's section entitled 'Can Bad Things Be Turned into Good Things?' is, apart from the menace, pure *1066 and All That*: 'Everybody knows that the Hungarian incident was not a good thing … Because our Hungarian comrades took proper action in the course of the incident, what was a bad thing has eventually turned into a good one.' The scope for discussion and free speech in Hungary was severely curtailed. The crushing of the rebels was, says Mao, a good thing.

Mao then comes to the core of his speech, which is a study of contradiction. He suggests that error is an objective ideological fact that can be eradicated by conscious reflection. Under the malign influence of Lenin, Mao thought that history obeyed laws and that he knew exactly what they were. He believed he could always spot the difference between a fragrant flower and a poisonous weed: fragrant flowers are those that history allows to flourish. Suddenly sounding as if he is preaching from the revolutionary scriptures, Mao affirms: 'The ceaseless emergence and ceaseless resolution of contradictions constitute the dialectical law of the development of things.' Anyone unversed in the law of the development of things is therefore in the grip of an error. 'The contradiction into which the intellectuals have fallen,' Mao continues, 'is that they have not yet all been remoulded.' For Mao, the theory is true and people have to be made to fit it. It is already clear there is no place in Mao's China for a rebel who speaks freely: 'In the building of a socialist society, everybody needs remoulding.'

It did not take long for the duplicity of this speech to became blatant. Mao had invited citizens to send in their thoughts, but when the complaints duly arrived he declared the criticism had gone too far. Like every dictator who feigns tolerance, Mao had a low threshold for rebels. He launched the Anti-Rightist Campaign in which his thuggish flunkies rounded up hundreds of thousands of critics who were then transported for execution, or for remoulding in labour camps. Mao would later congratulate himself for having 'enticed the snakes out of their lairs'. He had the text of his speech amended *post facto* to take out the references to intellectual freedom. He was erasing his own words no sooner than he had spoken them. If a country has no critical apparatus, a leader can both say and unsay whatever he likes.

In Mao's China the freedom to speak belonged exclusively to the leader, and he could also talk as long as he liked, because listening was not voluntary. Mao, Castro and Hitler could all command the stage for hours at a time. When Stalin spoke, interminably and boringly, nobody wanted to be the first person to stop applauding for fear of the reprisals. Part of the act of authoritarian leadership is the conviction that the voice of the leader and the voice of the people are one and the same. This is why there is no need for free speech. The thoughts of the people are spoken in the leader's rhetoric. The tyrant conducts monologues, as Camus said, above a million solitudes. On this occasion, Mao wasn't even seeking to hide the facts. In the opening to the speech, he bragged that 700,000 counter-revolutionaries had been disposed of. They were rebels in the grip of falsehood. Once they resisted remoulding there was only one fate left for them.

Political murder is a direct and ubiquitous implication of the revolutionary claim to know what cannot be known. Any leader with the zeal to be convinced that they are right at a level too deep for ordinary understanding, and the authority to impose that twisted vision, will do violence to rebels sooner or later. The consequences of Mao's truth claim were predictably calamitous. In 1958 he began an attempt to collectivise labour under the slogan – again displaying the macabre penchant for irony of a man who liked to write poetry – of The Great Leap Forward. Mao confiscated all property and herded people into giant communes where they were coerced into work. The result was a catastrophic grain shortage and, between 1958 and 1962, the death of 45 million people. Mao's arrogant assumption that he understood the laws of history ensured that more people died at his hands in China than were killed in Nazi Germany and Soviet Russia combined.

A democracy would never permit a suspension of the rule of law on that scale. Any leader with a record so bloody could never be allowed to govern, let alone thrive. Mao did lose his grip on power in China, but only temporarily. By 1966 he was back with another crazed idea; the decade-long Great Proletarian Cultural Revolution. This was his campaign to preserve the true communist ideology and purge the infected elements of capitalist and bourgeois thought. Red Guard groups of enthusiastic youths formed around China to carry out Mao's command, under the misleading banner of 'To rebel is justified!' It wasn't, and everybody knew it. The Red Guards set out explicitly to destroy such wisdom as Chinese history contained. They sought to eradicate what they described as 'the four olds' – old ideas, old customs, old habits and old culture. Mao had a new truth to put in their place.

The daily reality of the revolution was dire. Millions of people were persecuted and humiliated in public, subjected to arbitrary imprisonment, torture and hard labour. Intellectuals and party officials deemed to hold treacherous views were murdered or harassed to the point of suicide. Schools and universities were closed and churches, shrines and libraries among the many cultural institutions that were ransacked. When the outcome was a civil war, Mao ordered the People's Army to restore order. 'Let a hundred flowers bloom' had turned out to be a poisonous joke. Mao's revolution had produced a military dictatorship that lasted until 1971. The final death toll of the Cultural Revolution is disputed but it lies somewhere between half a million and two million people. The whole appalling saga came to end only with Mao's death, at the age of eighty-two, in September 1976.

The Foolish Old Man Who Removed the Mountains

What Mao had done, with terrible consequences, was to substitute his own authority for the gradually accumulated wisdom of a liberal society. Like all revolutionaries and tyrants, Mao had no sense that the clash of contending schools of thought was exactly how progress occurs. The speech of the supreme leader is always a protracted essay in complete certainty. In his wise essay *Rationalism in Politics* the conservative philosopher Michael Oakeshott set out the danger of the belief that politics can be written like a rule book. The best cook, Oakeshott pointed out, is not necessarily the one who has memorised the recipe book. Politics is a field of practical wisdom. But Mao believed in the sovereignty of rationalism. He thought all wisdom could be recorded in a book. The book in question, the official manual for the Cultural Revolution, was his *Little Red Book*. The longest entry in it is the credo that Mao had set out in a speech on 11 June 1945, at the Seventh National Congress of the Communist Party of China. The speech was built around a Chinese fable and it is entered in *The Little Red Book* as 'The Foolish Old Man Who Removed the Mountains'.

The context for the speech was what Mao called, with the sinister gift for euphemism that set a rhetorical pattern for his reign, a 'rectification' campaign. This was a purge of rebel elements that he, as chairman of the Secretariat and the Politburo, deemed insufficiently loyal. The speech parades Mao's implausible faith in the innate power of the Chinese peasantry. The hero of the fable around which Mao constructs his rhetorical conceit is an old man who instructs his two sons to begin to dig up the two mountains, Taihang and Wangwu, that block the view from his house. In Mao's clunky retelling of the myth the two mountains represent imperialism and feudalism. A Wise Old Man interrupts the sons' digging to point out that the task is impossible. The Foolish Old Man retorts with the wisdom of the ages. After his sons have finished digging, he says, his grandsons will take over and then their sons will dig after that, and so on, until the mountains disappear.

Apart from Mao's insertion of the twin demons of imperialism and feudalism, this speech is actually a metaphor for the gradualism of a free society. It is a story one might imagine Edmund Burke using to illustrate the connection between the generations and the stock of mute wisdom stored in the institutions of a constitutional democracy. Slowly, gradually, the mountains diminish, but only because every successive generation passes on the task to the next, each continuing the work of its predecessor. Piecemeal progress will not satisfy Mao's vaulting ambition, though. Like every utopian, he wheels on the *deus ex machina*. Mao's story concludes with God being so moved by the old man's conviction that he sends down two angels to carry off the mountains on their backs. The moral of the tale in Mao's telling is therefore quite different: if your conviction is strong enough then it can move mountains.

Mao's speech embodies another crucial difference between the free society and the nation governed by a revolutionary zealot. Politics takes time and democracy calls for patience, but the dictator is always in a tearing hurry. The apparently insuperable position of the tyrant is always more fragile than it seems. Power is a question of court rivalry rather than popular legitimacy, and the man who has arrived, as Mao famously put it, 'at the barrel of a gun' is always fearful that he will depart that way too. The example of Robespierre shows how this breeds impatience, hurried orders and an incapacity to tolerate failure. The great virtue of the democratic leader is that he can make a mistake and, like Peel and Disraeli in nineteenth-century Britain, change course. The dictator, by contrast, always doubles down on an error. When a dictator is in a hole he commands that other people should keep digging. The slogan of the Great Leap Forward – 'the spirit of the Foolish Old Man is the spirit that will transform China' – turned out to be grimly true.

China is no longer the tyranny it was under Mao, though it is a long way yet from a free society. The authoritarian Chinese state lacks Mao's sadistic capacity for violence but it retains his capacity for error on a grand scale. Where dissent is not permitted, authority does not hear the voices saying it might be in the wrong. China has already made a serious error because its leaders chose the wrong side in an old dispute about population. In 1795, in the midst of the revolutionary terror instigated by Robespierre, the Marquis de Condorcet used his enforced period of hiding to write a book called *Sketch for a Historical Picture of the Human Mind*. It is, to this day, one of the great accounts of the idea of human progress. Condorcet argued that social evils were the result of ignorance. He eschewed belief in a utopian end-state, writing that human history was a permanent state of adaptation. The book inspired Thomas Malthus to write *An Essay on the Principle of Population*, which he published in 1798. Malthus infamously argued that the world could not cope with population growth were it not for periodic natural disasters and social catastrophes such as famine. Condorcet thought human societies were flexible enough to adapt; Malthus thought population growth would bring disaster.

In 1979, the Chinese government introduced a centralised family planning programme that limited parents to a single child. The impetus had come from a visit by a senior Chinese official, Song Jian, to Europe in 1979, where he had read *The Limits to Growth*, commissioned by the think-tank the Club of Rome, a pessimistic study of the human capacity for adaptation. Taking his opportunity to commit an error on a vast scale, Song employed Chinese mathematicians to calculate that the optimal population for China, given projected resources, was precisely 700 million people. A plan was duly concocted to reduce China's population of 940 million people to the desired level by 2080.

These calculations inspired the Family Planning Policy of 1979. Enforcement was never total: there were complex provincial exemptions and permissions for a second child if the first was a daughter. But even at the plan's most relaxed, more than a third of the Chinese population was subject to a strict one-child policy. A vast apparatus of registration and inspection was constructed. The invasion of privacy was literal in the case of the Chinese women compelled to have a contraceptive intrauterine device surgically installed after their first child. Those rare women who had a second child were sterilised by tubal ligation. Over 400 million Chinese women have been subject to one or the other of these two procedures. Failure to comply with the regulations could result in a fine, the loss of state employment or the loss of education and health services.

An error of this kind cannot spread so easily in a democracy, although it can easily be made. In India in 1975, Indira Gandhi declared a temporary state of emergency and a suspension of democracy. She placed her son Sanjay in charge of a sterilisation programme.

Some of the tactics used to 'persuade' people to comply were the banning of people with three or more children from government employment unless they had been sterilised, the withholding of irrigation water from the recalcitrant, or the loss of a month's salary or even food rations. There were even reports of the police rounding men up for sterilisation. Between June 1975 and March 1977 there were 11 million sterilisations in India. It was disgraceful and indefensible. It also could not last. There was a flurry of lawsuits for wrongful death after some people contracted infections from unhygienic procedures. There were violent riots in protest. The prime minister called a halt to the state of emergency in March 1977, and the electorate voted her out of office that very month in an election she had called in the expectation that her rule would be vindicated.

In China there was no possibility of lawsuits, protest and popular regulation through the ballot box, so the policy lasted decades. The consequences are now visible. China has too few children to pay the pension liability of their parents. By 2050, one-third of Chinese people will be over sixty years of age, but China's population peaked in 2012. China has too many men, and too many old men in particular. In October 2015, the Communist Party of China declared an end to the one-child policy, but the damage has been done.

The ratio of children and pensioners to those in work is rising in China. The same ratio is falling in India. The fact that India's mean age is twenty-five and China's is thirty-four might offer a clue to the most intriguing rivalry of the twenty-first century. The world is currently conducting a laboratory experiment in which an authoritarian society, China, is pitted against a democracy, India, in a race for economic supremacy. The early indications have all been that the rapid decision-making of China's authoritarian capitalism will prevail over the time and value-consuming conversations of a democracy. Between 1990 and 2014 India grew from 4 per cent of US GDP to 11 per cent. In the same period China leapt from 9 to 60 per cent.

It would be wrong, though, to suppose that this signals the virtue of political command and control. China's superior economic performance is actually owed to the fact that the provisional liberalisation of its economy occurred earlier than India's. In 1958 Mao unwound collective farming in favour of a system of household responsibility and permitted the use of foreign capital, but Chinese growth really took off after the market reforms of Deng Xiaoping twenty years later. India during the same period was weighed down by the business regulation that its Congress Party had inherited from British Fabian socialists. The state-owned airlines, railways, water, electricity, post and telephone services were sclerotic. The Industries Act 1951 required all businesses to get a licence from the government before they could launch, expand or change products. Foreign investment dried up and India came to accept what was known as the 'Hindutva' rate of growth, between 3 and 4 per cent a year. Eventually foreign reserves fell to a crisis level and India accepted help from the International Monetary Fund (IMF) and the World Bank in exchange for necessary liberalisation, which began in 1991 under the finance minister and later prime minister Dr Manmohan Singh. The medicine worked. Adjust the data for the fact that India's liberal reforms began thirteen years after China's and their respective GDP growth rates are close to identical. India's GDP per capita all but doubled between 2007 and 2016, when India overtook China to be the fastest-growing economy in the world.

It may well be the case that India's democratic institutions, so often derided, not least within India itself, as a restraint on growth, are its greatest comparative advantage. Historically, democracy and prosperity have always been companions. The only durable exceptions have been the oil-rich countries, which went straight from poverty to wealth via natural abundance. There are good reasons to suppose that democracies are better hosts for enterprise than autocracies. Prosperity produces a substantial middle class which demands recognition and political rights that the autocracy cannot satisfy. A democracy, in which all have a stake, is better at managing the many conflicting interests generated by capitalism. China today has many such problems and it is not obvious that its political system will be able to manage them. Corporate debt is too high and there are too many inefficient state-owned companies, clustered in yesterday's industries of steel, coal, shipbuilding and heavy machinery. There has been too much poor investment, in the wrong places; exactly the sort of allocation error you would expect in a command economy.

China is seeking to become a rich country in a unique way, without granting any concomitant political freedoms. It is the most potent challenge the world has seen to the argument that the open society is better, because more productive, than all its competitors. But China is yet to exhibit the ingenuity that will be necessary to maintain its progress. The errors of foolish men, thinking they can move mountains on their own, may cost them eventually.

Not that the superiority of India over China relies on victory in the economic race. It is not because of the dry number of GDP per capita that we should prefer India. Even if the fissiparous politics of China do hold during its economic odyssey, freedom has a value of its own. In *Development and Freedom* Amartya Sen argued that any measure of progress must include the degree of liberty that people enjoy. Freedom is, argues Sen, an instrumental cause of growth but it is also a political virtue of the first order and an answer to a human need. On that basis, it would be preferable to live in an India with a lower growth rate than in a China with a higher one. India is a better society because it is a more open society. It is a nation in which argument is encouraged and in which the rebel can exercise the right to free speech. The Chinese government sees the media as tribunes of authority rather than the place for critical voices. In 2016 there were thirty-eight journalists in prison in China. India, by contrast, has 500 television channels and more newspaper readers than any nation on earth.

The Indian novelist Vikram Seth abandoned his doctoral thesis on the demography of China because he wanted to write. His book *Three Chinese Poets* includes a translation of Li Bai's 'The Hard Road': 'Travelling is hard! So many forks in the road. Which one to take?' There was only one road in China. Mao thought he could rid China of contradiction in a rectification programme, but the truth about mistakes is that they cannot be reliably defined in advance, by a supreme leader in a speech. The only way to define an error for sure is to make one and to devise a political system that can cope with the consequences. Good politics has the two virtues to which Mao, in 'Let a Hundred Flowers Bloom' and 'The Foolish Old Man Who Removed the Mountains', made fraudulent claim. It is a cacophony of dissenting voices and it moves mountains gradually. Mao's speech about a hundred flowers blooming ended in repression. His speech about the foolish old man concluded with the angels descending to move the mountain. But there are no angels. There are only, as Abraham Lincoln famously said, the better angels of our nature, and it is only in a democracy that the angels take wing.

The Grand Inquisitor

It is extraordinary that, during the 1960s, it was easy to find Western intellectuals to argue that the cultural revolution taking place in China was an intriguing challenge to the liberal democracies. The tendency for Western intellectuals to pour scorn on the societies in which they exercise their right to a voice is dispiriting. The Mao apologists were the counterparts of those comfortably naive utopians in the 1930s who managed to pass through Stalin's Russia without ever seeing anything untoward. Two notoriously uncritical pilgrims were the British Fabians Beatrice Webb and Sidney Webb, the man who drafted the 1918 constitution of the Labour Party. In 1941 the Webbs published a book, *Soviet Communism: A New Civilisation?*, which was pure Soviet propaganda in effect even if not in intent. In later editions, the question mark, the only accurate thing in the title, was dropped. The same sentiment is now common on the far left of politics where it is always easy to find critics who will decry Western life as, variously, corrupt, shallow, tawdry and materialistic, immorally self-regarding but, above all, capitalist.

There is also a temptation in Western societies, a tendency more usually associated with the political Right, to submit to the authority that poses as a superior wisdom. In their different ways Robespierre, Hitler and Castro promote themselves as the fount of authority. They all claim, as Lenin and Stalin did in Russia and Mao in China, that history is on their side. They disdain freedom and the imperfection of a liberal society in the pursuit and promise of something higher. The tragedy is that the revolution, unless it is done in the name of liberty, is always ultimately a prison cell. It is not by chance that so many of the speakers in this book – Nehru, Mandela, Suu Kyi, La Pasionaria, Pankhurst, Havel and Wiesel – spent time in jail. Words in defence of individual freedom and the virtues of politics are dangerous and the authorities are always wary of them and wish them silenced.

One of the greatest of speeches in fiction is a brilliant essay on this topic, and it takes place in a prison cell. There are some magnificent soliloquies competing for the prize of best fictional address. Shakespeare has a claim to be the greatest speechwriter the world has ever seen. Cassius's speech to Brutus and Mark Antony's funeral oration in *Julius Caesar*, Henry V's address to his troops before the battle of Agincourt and John of Gaunt's description of England in *Richard II* are political speeches of the highest order. Milton gives the devil all the best lines in *Paradise Lost*. Winston Churchill's obscure *Savrola* is a *roman-à-clef* in which the main character is a prime minister who makes some compelling speeches. But no fictional address is more pertinent to the public crimes of the modern era than that scripted by Fyodor Dostoevsky in *The Brothers Karamazov*.

'The Legend of the Grand Inquisitor' is a long speech relayed by Ivan Karamazov to his brother Alyosha, but given by the cardinal of Seville to Christ. It is the story of Christ's return to earth, to Seville at the time of the Inquisition. When Christ performs a series of miracles, to the great acclaim of the people, he is arrested by the Holy Guard of the Grand Inquisitor and sentenced to be burnt to death. On the eve of the *auto-da-fé* the Grand Inquisitor visits Christ in his cell to explain to him the reason why he must be sacrificed. The cardinal delivers a speech devoted to dismissing the notion that freedom can lead to happiness: 'Man is constituted as a mutineer; can mutineers ever be happy?'

Since the departure of Christ, he goes on, man has conquered freedom and has done so in order to win contentment. The Grand Inquisitor claims the credit for the stability and order he has imposed, 'for nothing has ever been more unendurable to man and human society than freedom!' Men will follow those who turn stones into bread, as the devil tried to tempt Christ to do, because the bread of the earthly kind is more important than freedom, the bread of heaven. 'Feed them, and then ask virtue of them!' as the Grand Inquisitor puts it, which is essentially the bargain that China is offering.

The Grand Inquisitor's speech is an encapsulation of the promise of every utopian, every populist and every tyrant. Tyranny begins with a revolution that goes awry, with the arrogant assumption that human satisfaction will be most quickly and fully realised by the concentration of power with an elite who understand the wellsprings of human motivation. The one false step in Orwell's prophetic *Nineteen Eighty-Four* is O'Brien's terrifying speech in which he explains that 'the party seeks power entirely for its own sake. We are not interested in the good of others; we are interested solely in power, pure power'. This is, and Orwell intended it to be, the very depths of human decline. But most politics, even tyrannical politics, is not like that. It is clothed in a justification that there is a greater good disclosed only to the initiated. This is what Robespierre and Hitler promise. It is what Castro really believes he is doing.

The Grand Inquisitor goes to great pains to see off the rebellion promised by Christ. He absolutely thinks he is in the right. 'We corrected your great deed', he says, 'and founded it upon miracle, mystery and authority. And people were glad that they had been brought together into a flock and that at last from their hearts had been removed such a terrible gift.' The veneer always cracks, though. As he closes his long disquisition the Grand Inquisitor is himself tempted to be candid: 'Oh, we shall persuade them that they will only become free when they renounce their freedom for us and submit to us. And what does it matter whether we are right or whether we are telling a lie? They themselves will be persuaded we are right, for they will remember to what horrors of slavery and confusion your freedom has brought them.' The speech of the Grand Inquisitor is a paean to a world without error, a mythical world of total security and complete safety. The trouble is that this always leads to the Committee of Public Safety with a Robespierre at its head. As the Grand Inquisitor puts it, the universal question of all politics is 'before whom should one bow down?' The answer of the rebel, granted the freedom of speech in a democracy, the answer given by Havel and Wiesel, is that one should never bow down.

We need to pay heed to the inspirational figures who refused to bow down. One tragic consolation of twentieth-century tyranny is that it sent three of the finest thinkers to Britain and the United States to teach us the value of what we have. Karl Popper left Vienna in 1937, the year before the Nazi tanks rolled in and forced through the *Anschluss*. He went first to New Zealand, where he wrote one of the great works in defence of liberal freedom, *The Open Society and Its Enemies*. The formative moment in civilisation, says Popper, echoing Pericles, is the moment that a closed society gave way to an open society. Leszek Kołakowski was convinced that Marxism was disgraceful on his first trip to Russia from his native Poland and so began an intellectual journey towards truth that culminated in his monumental *Main Currents of Marxism*, a book of sparkling honesty which is nothing like as dull as its title would suggest and which makes the essential point that the cruelty of Stalinism is not the exception but the rule. Isaiah Berlin witnessed both the February and the October revolutions in 1917 as a young boy in Petrograd. His family fled anti-Semitic abuse to England where, in Oxford, Berlin insisted in *Two Concepts of Liberty* that civilisation rested on a plurality of voices only possible within a polity that respects the liberty of the individual. 'To force people into the neat uniforms demanded by dogmatically believed-in schemes', he wrote, 'is almost always the road to inhumanity.'

They were all three fugitives from the tyrannies of Lenin, Hitler and Stalin. Their work carves out distinctions that are cast-iron, between freedom and unfreedom, between fear and hope. They were not afraid to take sides, largely because they had seen the other side in action. Their combined and collected works are a reminder that the achievement of the open society is not to be taken for granted. Not the least of its virtues is that an open society took them in and housed them for long enough and safely enough for them to be able to write their accounts of why this is the only type of society in which human beings will consent to live for long. They all three lived into old age and died quietly, to be mourned by those around them. It does not take much gruesome imagination to wonder what might have happened had they all stayed at home. The open society would be every bit as desirable, but we would lack the language in which to say so.

To those giants of freedom we can add the name of one more rebel, one more magnificent public speaker. That name is Charles Spencer Chaplin. By 1939 the two best candidates for the title of the most famous man in the world were Adolf Hitler and Charlie Chaplin. They were in direct confrontation. In 1931, on a world publicity tour, Chaplin had been greeted with acclamation in Berlin, a fact that the Nazi hierarchy resented. The visit led to the publication, in 1934, of a book for German children called *The Jews Are Looking at You* in which Chaplin was depicted as a 'disgusting Jewish acrobat'. Chaplin happened not to be Jewish, but he was offended by the book and resolved to retaliate.

It took an intervention from President Roosevelt to ensure that *The Great Dictator*, which Chaplin wrote, directed, produced, starred in and scored in 1940, ever got made. Chaplin was worried that the film would not be shown in England for fear of offending the Germans and that American non-interventionists and pro-Nazi groups would get the film banned in the United States. The president gave a personal guarantee that the film would be released. It is a good thing it was, because *The Great Dictator* ends with one of the great rhetorical expressions of the superiority of liberal democracy over tyranny. Chaplin's first sound production was also inspired by his viewing of Leni Riefenstahl's Nazi propaganda film *Triumph of the Will*, which he found uproariously funny and ripe for satire. Filming began as war loomed in September 1939.

The Great Dictator tells the story of a Jewish barber suffering from amnesia who is mistaken for a dictator he resembles, very clearly Adolf Hitler, known as Adenoid Hynkel in the film. The real Hynkel is mistaken for the barber and arrested, which brings the barber to the stage to make a speech, on which his own life and that of his friends will depend. After a stumbling start the barber finds inspiration and makes a passionate case for brotherhood and good will. 'I don't want to rule or conquer anyone ... The misery that is now upon us is but the passing of greed – the bitterness of men who fear the way of human progress. The hate of men will pass, and dictators die, and the power they took from the people will return to the people. And so long as men die, liberty will never perish ... Dictators free themselves but they enslave the people! Now let us fight to fulfil that promise! ... in the name of democracy, let us all unite!'

Chaplin arranged for the film to be sent to Hitler, though whether or not he ever saw it we cannot be sure. The British government, during the appeasement period, said it would ban the film, though it was seen when the policy changed. *The Great Dictator* was, however, banned in occupied Europe, parts of South America and the Irish Free State. The film was, shamefully, the beginning of the end for Chaplin in America. The great satirist of dictatorship was labelled a communist by the frivolous but dangerous Senator Joseph McCarthy in 1952. When Chaplin tried to return to the United States after going to England for the premiere of *Limelight* he was refused re-entry by the egregious J. Edgar Hoover, who called Chaplin a 'Hollywood parlour Bolshevik'. It was a sorry personal end to the story, for a man who knew which side he was on, to be betrayed by a country he thought would know better.

Liberal democracies need to maintain their confidence. As wildly imperfect as they are, part of the attraction of the open societies is that contentious things can be said without fear. A speech like Chaplin's at the end of *The Great Dictator* would be permitted in all societies except those it satirises. It says more in a few minutes than every interminable hour of Lenin, Stalin, Hitler, Mao, Castro and the rest. The lesson of Chaplin's speech is every bit as important as the lesson of his life, and we should not be tempted to conclude from the latter that Western liberal democracy is therefore a sham.

The Revolution

Every revolution turns full circle. The message of Camus's *The Rebel* is that the revolution begins with a promise of liberation and ends in a tyranny. 'Freedom, "that terrible word inscribed on the chariot of the storm", is the motivating principle of all revolutions,' writes Camus. 'Without it, justice seems inconceivable to the rebel's mind. There comes a time, however, when justice demands the suspension of freedom. Then terror, on a grand or small scale, makes its appearance to consummate the revolution.'

The emergence of modern populism is not the same as egregious tyranny. It is not necessarily the first step on the road to serfdom. But the institutions of liberal democracies are more fragile than we might suppose. President Trump does not appear to understand or respect their norms. Across Europe there are political movements that want to turn back the progress they do not acknowledge. In Africa those democracies that do exist are, as yet, young and vulnerable. The same is true in Asia, where the largest of the nations, China, thinks it is teaching the world a lesson that there is another sustainable path to human happiness. Every generation needs to marshal the arguments for democracy and freedom, because the temptations offered by the Grand Inquisitor are always lurking and they always lead to the wilderness. Silence is not an option, as the example of Elie

Wiesel shows. Indifference is perilous. As Camus puts it: 'To keep quiet is to allow yourself to believe that you have no opinions, that you want nothing, and in certain cases it amounts to really wanting nothing.'

We need to be clear about what it is we want and we need to speak up for it. We want the legitimate popular government defined by Thomas Jefferson. We should be prepared to defend it with all the tenacity and eloquence of Winston Churchill. We want a national community in which we take the same pride as Jawaharlal Nehru took in the midnight's children of Indian independence. We want the recognition of the equal moral worth of all individuals that Martin Luther King expressed so beautifully, and we want, like Elie Wiesel, to live a life in the presence of hope. For all their manifold differences, and the terrible beauty of their rhetoric, the revolutionary cases of Robespierre, Hitler and Castro hold in common the dark truth that no rebel was permitted to speak. There was no licensed dissent and a sense of mission was allowed to replace a sense of history.

This passage from *The Rebel* could have been written directly for Castro, who in the same year was defending himself in court: 'In 1953, excess is always a comfort, and sometimes a career. Moderation, on the one hand, is nothing but pure tension. It smiles, no doubt, and our convulsionists, dedicated to elaborate apocalypses, despise it. But its smile shines brightly at the climax of an interminable effort.' It is a reminder that politics is hard work and that there is no short cut. There is no need, no matter what the injustice on display, to suppose that there is a utopia over the rainbow which would be preferable. The utopia will turn sour, the revolution will go wrong when foolish old men, in the words of Camus, 'forget the present for the future, the fate of humanity for the delusion of power, the misery of the slums for the mirage of the Eternal City, ordinary justice for an empty promised land'.

These temptations can be avoided, but only if we restate, in the finest words that can be uttered on a public podium, the strength and beauty of the political virtues. Camus's manifesto for the rebel is a description of the great service done for politics by all the progressive voices in this book, but it calls to mind, in this context, Havel and Wiesel in particular: 'we all carry within us our places of exile, our crimes, and our ravages. But our task is not to unleash them on the world; it is to fight them in ourselves and in others.' It has been done before, triumphantly and resoundingly, as the rhetoric in this book has shown, and it will need to be done again, and then again. The effort is interminable but it can be done. It must be done.

At the conclusion of the Grand Inquisitor's long speech Christ, who has been silent throughout, kisses him gently on the lips. The Inquisitor then releases Christ into the Seville streets and implores him never to return. The implication at the end of Ivan's long speech is that freedom is still out there somewhere. It need not be entirely smothered by the power of authority. As Elie Wiesel says in his final words, there is, even amidst profound fear, the presence of extraordinary hope. That hope we give the name of politics.

EPILOGUE

WHEN THEY GO LOW,
WE GO HIGH

Barack Obama may be the best male speaker in living memory and the second-best speaker in his own family. At the Democratic Party convention in Philadelphia in 2016, Michelle Obama found a resonant phrase to summarise the responsibility of the liberal democracies in their battle against populism: *When they go low, we go high.*

Obama's speech was a reflection on eight years as First Lady and an endorsement, forlorn as it turned out, of Hillary Clinton as the next president of the United States. It was, at least on the surface, an address of beautiful anxiety about the fame, in the flashbulbs and footlights of public life, that she and her husband the president had imposed on their daughters: 'I will never forget that winter morning as I watched our girls, just seven and ten years old, pile into those black SUVs with all those men with guns. And with all their little faces pressed up against the window, and the only thing I could think was, "What have we done?"'

The argument turned on the public versus the private, a serious question for the American republic, a serious question for any democratic republic. The distinction comes from John Locke, whose *Two Treatises of Government* locates legitimate authority in the consent of the governed. Government gives public security so that people can pursue their private concerns. This distinction is a foundation stone of liberal democracies. Dystopias like Huxley's *Brave New World*, Orwell's *Nineteen Eighty-Four* and Zamyatin's *We* are frightening precisely because they erase the border between public and private.

For Winston Smith there is no privacy. Big Brother is always watching.

Obama's speech is a claim that a voracious popular appetite for publicity is a threat to political life. The reach of social media platforms will produce, if we are not careful to insist on a separation, a panopticon in which everything is visible. The result would not be perfect transparency. It would be an intolerable intrusion in which, as Obama said, Hillary Clinton, a secretary of state and Democratic nominee for president, was subjected to a barrage of criticism about her appearance. Obama emphasised, by relaying her advice to her daughters, that the culture of modern politics has become trivially aggressive: 'How we urged them to ignore those who question their father's citizenship or faith. How we insist that the hateful language they hear from public figures on TV does not represent the true spirit of this country. How we explain that when someone is cruel or acts like a bully, you don't stoop to their level. Our motto is, when they go low, we go high.'

The height to which she was asking people to raise themselves was the summit that is reached by politics. The question at hand, said Obama, is the issue of all republics: 'who will have the power to shape our children for the next four or eight years of their lives'. She spoke of the capacity of politics, pointed in the right direction, to be the champion for every child who needs it: 'kids who take the long way to school to avoid the gangs. Kids who wonder how they will ever afford college. Kids whose parents don't speak a word of English, but dream of a better life'. This is the use of public authority to procure a better life in common. Obama's speech was much more than an endorsement of Hillary Clinton. It was an endorsement of politics: 'The presidency is about one thing and one thing only. It is about leaving something better for our kids.'

The echo of Martin Luther King is audible in Obama's conclusion. Her words call to mind, surely deliberately, King's extraordinary image of the little black boy and the little white boy joining hands, and his moving demand that his children be judged not by the colour of their skin but by the content of their character. It is a historic event that, in the city where segregation in the federal government was introduced, to his shame, by Woodrow Wilson in 1913, the Obama family spent eight years in the White House. Michelle Obama's

WHEN THEY GO LOW, WE GO HIGH

conclusion is the very story of political progress: 'That is the story of this country. The story that has brought me to the stage tonight. The story of generations of people who felt the lash of bondage, the shame of servitude, the sting of segregation, who kept on striving, and hoping, and doing what needed to be done. So that today, I wake up every morning in a house that was built by slaves. And I watch my daughters, two beautiful intelligent black young women, play with the dog on the White House lawn.'

The Shining City on a Hill

This history of rhetoric has many important locations. It starts in Athens and develops in Rome. War is defined and made noble in speeches in London. The story of progress is told in Manchester and infamy of various kinds has been either fashioned or resisted in Berlin. The original American capital of Philadelphia, where Michelle Obama gave her remarkable speech, was where the words that brought America into being were uttered, and not far away, at Gettysburg, was where the popular republic was defined. But the most important city in the story of rhetoric is the one that Obama was speaking of: Washington DC. This was the city where, on 14 April 1865, Abraham Lincoln was one of the five speakers in this book to be assassinated – Cicero, Robespierre, Kennedy and King are the others. More happily, this was where Thomas Jefferson called for equal and exact justice for all men, Woodrow Wilson set out his vision of international cooperation in a League of Nations and John F. Kennedy made his plea for citizens to do what they could for America. It was the place that heard Martin Luther King's dream, Elie Wiesel's warning of the perils of indifference and Barack Obama's expression of hope.

The shining city on a hill has become the staple metaphor of political rhetoric, although the original reference was to a city in the abstract. In 1630, an English lawyer of ardently puritan beliefs called John Winthrop gave a speech with the title 'The Model of Christian Charity'. We cannot be sure whether Winthrop spoke in the dock at Southampton before boarding the *Arbella* to sail to the New World, whether he composed and delivered the speech on board, or whether he waited until his arrival in America, where he was to take up the position of the first governor of the Massachusetts Bay Colony. Wherever the location, the speech's influence has earned Winthrop the title of the forgotten founding father of the American republic. That title is owed to one resonant phrase: 'We shall be as a city upon a hill; the eyes of all people are upon us.'

Winthrop's speech is a scripture of religious devotion. It is a call for brotherly affection and community identification as shared witnesses to the truth of God. There is, though, a secular meaning that can be extended to Winthrop's ambition for his new settlement: 'always having before our eyes ... our community as members of the same body, so shall we keep the unity of the spirit in the bond of peace'. The cost of falling short, he advised, was that 'we shall be made a story and a byword through the world ...' None of this would have won Winthrop's speech a place in the anthology of rhetoric were it not for his borrowing from Christ's Sermon on the Mount, from the gospel of Matthew 5:14, which reads: 'Ye are the light of the world. A city that is set on a hill cannot be hid.'

The phrase entered the modern political lexicon when John F. Kennedy gave a speech of that name to the General Court of Massachusetts on 9 January 1961. 'We must always consider', he declared, 'that we shall be as a city upon a hill – the eyes of all people are upon us.' It was Ronald Reagan, though, who made it a commonplace. Reagan used Winthrop's famous biblical line constantly on the campaign trail. He included it in at least two dozen speeches as president, most notably his address on the eve of the 1980 election, 'A Vision for America', which refers to the city on the hill, aglow with the light of human freedom. Since then it has been a standard metaphor for the speaker seeking to depict the republic as the paragon of democracy. Barack Obama regularly invoked the city, by now almost always shining. In Reagan's farewell address to the nation on 11 January 1989, he said:

> *I've spoken of the shining city all my political life, but I don't know if I ever quite communicated what I saw when I said it. But in my mind it was a tall, proud city built on rocks stronger than oceans, wind-swept, God-blessed, and teeming with people of all kinds living in harmony and peace; a city with free ports that hummed*

*with commerce and creativity. And if there had to be city walls, the
walls had doors and the doors were open to anyone with the will
and the heart to get here. That's how I saw it, and see it still.*

The original city on a hill, where this story of democracy and
rhetoric began, was Athens. The low hill north-west of the Acropolis
is known as the Areopagus. It had been the meeting point for the
earliest council of ancient Athens. In 355 BC Isocrates, one of the
most influential Greek rhetoricians of his day, wrote a speech in
which he argued for the return of power to the Council of Areopagus.
Isocrates never intended to deliver the speech. It was written and
published in rhetorical form, a common practice at the time. In 1644
John Milton borrowed the idea to publish his 'Speech for the Liberty
of Unlicensed Printing', which he addressed to Parliament in defiance of the licensing regime which had been introduced to stop the
spread of anti-royalist propaganda. It is the finest expression of the
importance of free expression in the English language. It is known
as the *Areopagitica*.

Milton's written speech was a broadside against government
censorship of the free flow of ideas. He railed against the need for a
state imprimatur, as government inspectors could never, he argued,
attain the full knowledge required to do a tolerable job. But his main
case was a passionate defence of free expression: 'As good almost kill
a man as kill a good book. Who kills a man kills a reasonable creature,
God's image; but he who destroys a good book, kills reason itself, kills
the image of God, as it were in the eye.' It is through the exchange
of ideas, says Milton, that men acquire character and arrive at the
truth: 'And though all the winds of doctrine were let loose to play
upon the earth, so truth be in the field, we do injuriously by licensing
and prohibiting to misdoubt her strength. Let her and falsehood
grapple; who ever knew truth put to the worse, in a free and open
encounter?'

The shining city on the hill is a dream of how politics might be.
As John Winthrop warned, human beings are liable always to fall
short. There have been plenty of examples in this book of democracies falling short and of the stuttering way they make progress. The
liberal democracies remain, though, the world's most extraordinary
hope. The city on the hill is the place where the hope of utopia is

embodied. It is here in the democratic republic that the political virtues can be protected, where men and women are free to define their political community. Those virtues, as John Milton argued, cannot be commanded by edict. They must derive from liberty, 'the nurse of all wits', and above all from the freedom that, in *Areopagatica*, Milton demanded: 'Give me the liberty to know, to utter, and to argue freely according to conscience, above all liberties.'

The freedom to speak is the value that has been celebrated in this book. The story that has been told in this chronicle of rhetoric is that the politics of the liberal democracies are a great achievement that needs to be defended and argued for anew. The great speakers have all, in their different ways, done this. The idea of popular sovereignty was given poetic life by Marcus Tullius Cicero, Thomas Jefferson, Abraham Lincoln, John F. Kennedy and Barack Obama. The willingness to suspend politics in order to fight for politics was never better expressed than by Pericles, David Lloyd George, Woodrow Wilson, Winston Churchill and Ronald Reagan. A generous idea of national belonging was the rhetorical achievement of Elizabeth I, Benjamin Franklin, Jawaharlal Nehru, Nelson Mandela and Aung San Suu Kyi. The unrivalled capacity of liberal democracies to recognise the equal moral worth of all individuals was argued, with the greatest passion, by William Wilberforce, Emmeline Pankhurst, La Pasionaria, Martin Luther King and Neil Kinnock. The full extent of what is grimly possible if dissent is silenced is there in the chilling words of Maximilien Robespierre and Adolf Hitler. Fidel Castro describes the road to perdition via good intentions. They are answered by the wisdom of Václav Havel and Elie Wiesel, two men who lived under both tyranny and liberal democracy and know which dispensation is to be trusted. With the exceptions of the tyrants, these speakers are among the inhabitants of rhetoric's shining city. Taken as a body of work, their words describe, for the discipline of politics, the best that has been said and done.

Politics, at its best, is about the fulfilment of what Michelle Obama called 'the impossibly big dreams that we all have for our children'. Ernst Bloch, another fugitive from the Nazi tyranny, spent his time in the library at Harvard writing a three-volume book called *The Principle of Hope*. Its subtitle was a phrase that, in Philadelphia,

Michelle Obama used to describe the purpose of democratic politics: *Dreams of a Better Life*.

At the end of his speech at the White House, Elie Wiesel, in response to a question, quoted Camus to the effect that 'where there is no hope, we must invent it'. Wiesel went on to tell a story that precisely locates the source of political wisdom that this book has set out to defend:

> *The story is that once upon a time there was an emperor, and the emperor heard that in his empire there was a man, a wise man with occult powers. He had all the powers in the world. He knew when the wind was blowing what messages it would carry from one country to another. He read the clouds and he realized that the clouds had a design. He knew the meaning of that design. He heard the birds. He understood the language of the birds, the chirping of the birds carried messages. And then he heard there was a man who also knew how to read another person's mind. I want to see him, said the emperor. They found him. They brought him to the emperor. Is it true that you know how to read the clouds? Yes, Majesty. Is it true you know the language of the birds? Yes, Majesty. What about the wind? Yes, I know. Okay, says the emperor. I have in my hands behind my back a bird. Tell me, is it alive or not? And the wise man was so afraid that whatever he would say would be a tragedy, that if he were to say that the bird is alive, the emperor, in spite, would kill it. So he looked at the emperor for a long time, smiled, and said, Majesty, the answer is in your hands. It's always in our hands.*

BIBLIOGRAPHY

Anthologies

Burnet, Andrew (ed.), *Chambers Book of Great Speeches*, Chambers Harrap, 2013

Carey, John (ed.), *The Faber Book of Utopias*, Faber and Faber, 1999

Glover, Dennis, *The Art of Great Speeches and Why We Remember Them*, Cambridge University Press, 2011

MacArthur, Brian (ed.), *The Penguin Book of Historic Speeches*, Viking, 1995

MacArthur, Brian (ed.), *The Penguin Book of Twentieth-Century Speeches*, Viking, 1999

Safire, William, *Lend Me Your Ears*, W. W. Norton, 2004

Sebag Montefiore, Simon, *Speeches That Changed the World*, Quercus, 2007

Prologue

Aristotle, *The Art of Rhetoric*, Penguin, 1991

Cicero, Marcus Tullius, *De oratore*, Oxford University Press, 2001

Cicero, Marcus Tullius, *The Republic and the Laws*, Oxford University Press, 1998

Chapter One: Democracy

Barton, William E., *Lincoln at Gettysburg*, New York, 1950

Blair, Tony, *A Journey*, Penguin, 2010

Claeys, Gregory, *Searching for Utopia*, Thames and Hudson, 2011

Crick, Bernard, *In Defence of Politics*, Penguin, 1984

Fukuyama, Francis, *The End of History and the Last Man*, Penguin, 1992

Hume, David, 'Idea of a Perfect Commonwealth' in *Philosophical Works Volume III*, Edinburgh, 1984

Huxley, Aldous, *Brave New World*, Vintage, 2007

Kant, Immanuel, *Perpetual Peace*, London, 1795

Kateb, George, *Utopia and Its Enemies*, Macmillan, 1963

Kumar, Krishan, *Utopia and Anti-Utopia in Modern Times*, Basil
  Blackwell, 1987

Mill, John Stuart, *On Liberty*, Cosimo, 2005

More, Thomas, *Utopia*, Penguin, 1965

Morris, William, *News From Nowhere*, Penguin, 1993

Nozick, Robert, *Anarchy, State and Utopia*, Basil Blackwell, 1974

Orwell, George, *Nineteen Eighty-Four*, Penguin, 1949

Plato, *The Republic*, Penguin, 1955

Rorty, Richard, *Contingency, Irony and Solidarity*, Cambridge University
  Press, 1989

Runciman, David, *The Confidence Trap*, Princeton, 2013

Schlesinger, Robert, *White House Ghosts*, Simon and Schuster, 2008

Schurz, Carl, Preface, in Tom Griffith (ed.), *Abraham Lincoln: Life,
  Speeches, and Letters*, Wordsworth Editions Ltd, 2009

Shklar, Judith, *After Utopia: The Decline of Political Faith*, Princeton,
  1957

Skinner, Quentin, *The Foundations of Modern Political Thought*,
  Cambridge University Press, 1978

Tocqueville, Alexis de, *Democracy in America Volumes I and II*,
  HarperCollins, 1969

Wills, Garry, *Lincoln at Gettysburg*, Simon and Schuster, 1992

Zamyatin, Yevgeny, *We*, Penguin, 1993

Chapter Two: War

Angell, Norman, *The Great Illusion*, Cosimo, 2007

Aquinas, Thomas, *Summa theologicae*, New York, 1948

Cannadine, David, Introduction to *The Speeches of Winston Churchill*,
  Penguin, 1990

Fraser, Antonia, Introduction, in Neville Williams, *Elizabeth I*, Sphere
  Books Ltd, 1975

Frye, Susan, 'The Myth of Elizabeth at Tilbury', *The Sixteenth Century
  Journal*, Vol. 23, No. 1, Spring, 1992, pp. 95–114

Gilbert, Martin, *Winston S. Churchill, Volume VI: Finest Hour 1939–1941*,
  Heinemann, 1983

Grotius, Hugo, *De jure belli ac pacis (On the Law of War and Peace)*,
  Cambridge University Press, 2012

Keynes, John Maynard, *The Economic Consequences of the Peace*,
  Penguin, 2017

Larkin, Philip, *Collected Poems*, Faber and Faber, 1988

McLean, Iain, *Rational Choice: An Analysis of Rhetoric and Manipulation from Peel to Blair*, Oxford University Press, 2001

Robinson, Peter, '"Tear Down This Wall": How Top Advisers Opposed Reagan's Challenge to Gorbachev – But Lost', Archives.gov website, https://www.archives.gov/publications/prologue/2007/summer/berlin.html

Russett, Bruce, and John Oneal, *Triangulating Peace*, Norton, 2001

Stevenson, Frances, *Lloyd George: A Diary*, edited by A. J. P. Taylor, Hutchinson & Co, 1971

Thucydides, *History of the Peloponnesian War*, Penguin, 2000

Toye, Richard, 'Lloyd George's War Rhetoric', *Journal of Liberal History* 77, Winter 2012–13, pp. 24–9

Toye, Richard, *The Roar of the Lion: The Untold Story of Churchill's World War II Speeches*, Oxford University Press, 2013

Walzer, Michael, *Just and Unjust Wars*, Basic Books, 2015

Wilson, Woodrow, *History of the American People*, Wise and Co., 1930

Chapter Three: Nation

Anderson, Benedict, *Imagined Communities*, Verso, 1983

Brown, Judith M., *Nehru: A Political Life*, Yale University Press, 2003

Colley, Linda, *Britons: Forging the Nation 1707–1837*, Yale University Press, 1994

Franklin, Benjamin, *Autobiography*, Dover Thrift, 2015

Gellner, Ernest, *Nations and Nationalism*, Cornell University Press, 1983

Havel, Václav, Foreword, in Aung San Suu Kyi, *Freedom from Fear and Other Writings*, edited by Michael Aris, Viking, 1991

Hobsbawm, Eric, and Terence Ranger, *The Invention of Tradition*, Cambridge, 1983

Ignatieff, Michael, *Fire and Ashes: Success and Failure in Politics*, Harvard, 2013

Kertzer, David, *Ritual, Politics and Power*, Yale, 1988

Madison, James, Alexander Hamilton and John Jay, *The Federalist Papers*, Soho Books, 2011

Mandela, Nelson, *Long Walk to Freedom*, Little, Brown, 1994

Nairn, Tom, *The Enchanted Glass: Britain and Its Monarchy*, Picador, 1988

Plato, *The Last Days of Socrates*, Penguin, 1957

Renan, Ernst, *What Is a Nation?*, conference at the Sorbonne, Paris, 11 March 1882

Rushdie, Salman, *Midnight's Children*, Picador, 1981

Rushdie, Salman, *Shame*, Vintage, 1995

Chapter Four: Progress

Disraeli, Benjamin, *Coningsby*, Nabu Press, 2010

Engels, Friedrich, *The Condition of the Working Class in England*, Penguin, 2009

Gómez, Isidora Dolores Ibárruri, *El Unico Camino*, Castalia, 1962

Hague, William, *William Wilberforce: The Life of the Great Anti-Slave Trade Campaigner*, Harper Perennial, 2008

Hemingway, Ernest, *For Whom the Bell Tolls*, Arrow, 1994

Hobbes, Thomas, *Leviathan*, Pelican, 1968

Jones, Clarence B., *Behind the Dream*, St Martin's Griffin, 2012

Marx, Karl, and Friedrich Engels, *The Communist Manifesto*, Penguin, 2015

Orwell, George, *Homage to Catalonia*, Penguin, 2000

Pankhurst, Christabel, *Unshackled: The Story of How We Won the Vote*, Ebury, 1987

Pankhurst, Emmeline, *The Importance of the Vote*, Women's Press, 1913

Pankhurst, Emmeline, *My Own Story*, Wembley Press, 2015

Pankhurst, Sylvia, *The Suffragette Movement*, Wharton Press, 2010

Purvis, June, *Emmeline Pankhurst: A Biography*, Routledge, 2002

Roth, Philip, *The Plot Against America*, Vintage, 2005

Shelley, Percy Bysshe, *The Mask of Anarchy*, Templar Poetry, 2016

Young, Michael, *The Rise of the Meritocracy*, Transaction, 1994

Chapter Five: Revolution

Aron, Raymond, *The Opium of the Intellectuals*, Transaction, 2001

Berlin, Isaiah, *Four Essays on Liberty*, Oxford University Press, 1969

Berlin, Isaiah, *The Crooked Timber of Humanity*, John Murray, 1990

Bracher, Karl-Dietrich, *The German Dictatorship*, Penguin, 1970

Burke, Edmund, *Reflections on the Revolution in France*, Penguin, 1968

Caistor, Nick, *Fidel Castro*, Reaktion Books, 2013

Camus, Albert, *The Rebel*, Penguin, 1971

Camus, Albert, *The Stranger*, Hamish Hamilton, 1982

Camus, Albert, *The Plague*, Penguin, 1986

Chang, Jung, *Wild Swans*, William Collins, 2012

Condorcet, *Sketch for a Historical Picture of the Human Mind*, Bibiolife, 2009

Dostoevsky, Fyodor, *The Brothers Karamazov*, Penguin, 2003

Goebbels, Joseph, 'Der Führer als Redner', *Adolf Hitler. Bilder aus dem Leben des Führers*, Hamburg, 1936

Havel, Václav, *The Power of the Powerless*, Routledge, 1985

Havel, Václav, *To the Castle and Back*, Portobello Books, 2008

Haydon, Colin and William Doyle (eds), *Robespierre*, Cambridge
University Press, 1999

Hillberg, Raul, *Perpetrators, Victims, Bystanders: The Jewish Catastrophe,
1933–1945*, New York, 1992

Hitler, Adolf, *Mein Kampf*, Jairo, 2007

James, Clive, *Cultural Amnesia*, Picador, 2007

Koestler, Arthur, *Darkness at Noon*, Vintage, 1994

Kołakowski, Leszek, *Main Currents of Marxism*, W. W. Norton, 2008

Lasky, Melvin, *Utopia and Revolution*, Chicago, 1976

Levi, Primo, *If This Is a Man*, Abacus, 1991

Malthus, Thomas, *An Essay on the Principle of Population*, Oxford
University Press, 2008

Mao, *The Little Red Book*, Hinky, 1972

Montesquieu, Charles, *The Spirit of the Laws*, Cosimo, 2011

Oakeshott, Michael, *Rationalism in Politics*, Methuen, 1962

Popper, Karl, *The Open Society and Its Enemies*, Routledge and Kegan
Paul, 1991

Revuelta, Alina Fernández, *Castro's Daughter*, St Martin's Press, 1999

Rousseau, Jean-Jacques, *The Social Contract*, Wordsworth Editions, 1998

Sartre, Jean-Paul, *The Communists and Peace*, Hamish Hamilton, 1969

Sartre, Jean-Paul, *The Wall*, New Directions, 1969

Sen, Amartya, *Development and Freedom*, Oxford University Press, 1999

Seth, Vikram, *Three Chinese Poets*, Faber and Faber, 1992

Scurr, Ruth, *Fatal Purity: Robespierre and the French Revolution*, Chatto
and Windus, 2006

Short, Philip, *Mao: A Life*, I. B. Tauris and Co. Ltd, 1999

Webb, Sidney and Beatrice, *Soviet Communism: A New Civilisation?*, New
York, 1936

Wiesel, Elie, *Night*, Penguin, 2008

Zantovsky, Michael, *Havel: A Life*, Atlantic Books, 2014

Epilogue

Bloch, Ernst, *The Principle of Hope*, Basil Blackwell, 1986

Bremer, Francis J., *John Winthrop: America's Forgotten Founding Father*,
Oxford University Press, 2003

Locke, John, *Two Treatises of Government*, Cambridge University Press,
1988

Milton, John, *Areopagitica*, New York, 1951

INDEX

INDEX

Hemings, Sally, 32
Hemingway, Ernest, 9, 258
Hesiod, 79
Hilberg, Raul, 377
Hitler, Adolf, 164, 317, 331–4, 395–6;
 Mein Kampf, 331, 332, 342;
 Nuremberg rally (September 1938),
 335, 337, 339, 341; rhetorical skill,
 331, 332, 335, 339, 341–2; speech in
 Sportpalast, Berlin (September 1938),
 334–8, 339–40
Hobbes, Thomas, 290
Hofstadter, Richard, 77
Holocaust, 12, 333, 370–81
Homer, *Iliad*, 149
Hoover, Herbert, 6, 69
Hoover, J. Edgar, 397
hope, 4, 5, 82–3, 118–19, 277, 323, 358;
 Ernst Bloch on, 83–4, 408–9;
 foundation of good politics, 17, 18–19,
 407–8; and Kennedy, 46, 47–8, 57; La
 Pasionaria as symbol of, 257–8, 262;
 Obama's, 18, 37, 57–67, 405; and Elie
 Wiesel, 380, 381, 398, 399, 409
House, Edward M., 117
Howe, Geoffrey, 221, 223–4
Hudson, Hugh, 281–2
Hughes, Emmet J., 7
Hume, David, 174
Hungary, 74, 81, 370, 372, 383
Hunt, Henry, 295, 296, 297, 298, 304
Huxley, Aldous, *Brave New World*, 80,
 403–4

Ibárruri, Dolores (La Pasionaria), 231,
 256–66, 302
Ignatieff, Michael, 204–5
India, 124, 165, 181, 182–9, 211, 388–91
International Criminal Court, 149
International Monetary Fund, 73
internet, 9, 180
Iraq War (from 2003), 73, 150, 151, 152
Irish potato famine (from 1845), 300–1
Islam, 74, 75
Isocrates, 407

Jackson, Mahalia, 275

Jay, John, 177
Jefferson, Thomas, 6, 18, 28, 29–30, 32,
 94, 174, 328, 398; First Inaugural
 Address, Washington DC (1801),
 30–7, 77, 81, 83
Jenkins, Roy, 253
Johnson, Lyndon B., 46, 70
Jones, Clarence B., 274–5
Judt, Tony, 317
Juncker, Jean-Claude, 215
Juvenal, *Tenth Satire*, 27

Kaczyński, Jarosław, 80, 81
Kant, Immanuel, 157, 173
Kaufman, Gerald, 280
Kennedy, Joe, 46
Kennedy, John F., 18, 45–56, 68, 270–1,
 345, 406; assassination of (22
 November 1963), 45, 47, 69; 'Ich bin
 ein Berliner' speech (26 June 1963),
 138, 139, 155–6, 157; inaugural
 address (1961), 48, 49–51, 53–6, 62,
 77, 83, 364; and Sorensen, 7, 48, 51,
 52, 53, 55, 156; voice of, 4, 237
Kenney, Annie, 306
Kerensky, Alexander, 119
Keynes, J.M., *The Economic
 Consequences of the Peace*, 150
Khin Kyi, 202, 205, 211
Khrushchev, Nikita, 46, 53, 157, 345, 382
King, Martin Luther, 60, 66, 267–79,
 309, 398; 'I Have a dream' speech
 (1963), 232–3, 269–70, 271–9, 404;
 Letter from a Birmingham Jail, 70,
 268
Kinnock, Neil, 231, 280–93, 308
Kołakowski, Leszek, 394–5
Komensk, Jan Amos, 368, 369
Korean War, 154
Kosovo, 148–9, 151, 158, 371–2, 379, 380
Kundera, Milan, 362–3, 369

La Rochefoucauld, François de, 18, 118
Labour Party, 63, 88, 124, 146, 215,
 218–20, 229–31, 254, 280–93, 306,
 392
Lafayette, Marquis de, 328

419

INDEX

Larkin, Philip, 111, 175, 364
Le Pen, Marine, 74
Leadsom, Andrea, 98
League of Nations, 112, 119, 122, 164, 216–17
left wing politics, 10–11, 76, 77, 157, 231, 285, 352; attitudes to USA, 73, 316, 345–6, 349; critics of capitalism, 142, 263–4, 266, 392; see also communism; Labour Party
Levi, Primo, If This Is a Man, 376
Liberal Party, 100–1, 254, 301, 305–6
Lincoln, Abraham, 6, 18, 28, 38–9, 41, 62, 391; assassination of (14 April 1865), 38, 69; Gettysburg Address, 4, 8, 38–44, 48, 66, 68–9, 77, 81, 83, 88; voice of, 4, 237
Liverpool, Lord, 295–6, 297
Lloyd George, David, 88, 100–1, 124–5, 152, 230; Queen's Hall speech (September 1914), 101–10, 157, 158, 159
Locke, John, 81, 403
London, 45, 100, 103, 173, 182, 231, 235, 241, 251, 405
Louis XIV, King of France, 164
Louis XVI, King of France, 319, 324
Lusitania, sinking of (1915), 116
Luther, Martin, 122

Macmillan, Harold, 217, 218, 219
Madison, James, 6, 177
Madrid, siege of (1936), 258
Major, John, 224, 281, 293
Malthus, Thomas, 388
Manchester, 294–8, 301–2, 307–8, 309, 405; Free Trade Hall, 231, 295, 299, 300, 302–3, 304–6, 307, 309–10
Manchester Guardian, 297
Manchester School, 298–300, 301, 304–5, 309
Mandela, Nelson, 165, 190–2, 200–1, 247; Supreme Court trial defence speech (April 1964), 192–200, 201
Mandelson, Peter, 282
Mao Zedong, 382–7, 389, 391
Marcus, Greil, 279

Marie Antoinette, 319, 321
Mark Antony, 21–8
Martí, José, 349, 355
Marvell, Andrew, 131
Marx, Karl, 301–2, 306
Mauriac, François, 371
May, Theresa, 215, 225, 255, 292
Mbeki, Thabo, 192
McCarthy, Senator Joseph, 76, 396
McHenry, James, 175
Meinecke, Friedrich, 335
Mengele, Dr Joseph, 370
meritocracy, 308–9
migration, 5, 79, 80, 188
Miliband, David, 215
Mill, John Stuart, 383
Millar, Ronald, 7
Milton, John, 393, 407, 408
minority rights, 10, 31, 32, 36, 80, 83, 323
Mitford, Diana, 308
Monroe, James, 32, 122
Montesquieu, 81
More, Thomas, Utopia, 17–19, 78
Morgan, Kenneth, 106
Morris, William, News From Nowhere, 76
Mosley, Sir Oswald, 306–8
Mountbatten, Louis, 182, 184
Munich Agreement (29 September 1938), 340–1

nation states: Elizabeth I's Tilbury speech, 168–72; Hitler's conception of, 338–9; idea of Britain as a nation, 215–16, 226; Indian independence, 182–9; as invented/imagined, 163–6, 169, 225, 226; narrow populist view of, 79–80, 225–6; Quincy Adams on, 163; Ernst Renan on, 184; Thatcher's view of, 223
National Union of Mineworkers, 280–1
National Union of Women's Suffrage Societies (NUWSS), 251–2
Nazi Germany, 125–6, 164, 332–4; appeasement of, 124, 152, 333, 340–1, 396; see also Hitler, Adolf